The UNITED STATES
Department of Homeland Security

AN OVERVIEW

by CW Productions Ltd.

Edited by Richard White and Kevin Collins

PEARSON

Custom
Publishing

PEARSON CUSTOM PUBLISHING
75 Arlington Street, Suite 300, Boston, MA 02116
A Pearson Education Company

Preface

On November 25th, 2002, President George W. Bush signed into law the Homeland Security Act undertaking the largest government re-organization since the creation of the Department of Defense (DoD) in 1947. Like its counterpart, the resulting Department of Homeland Security (DHS) rose in the wake of a treacherous surprise attack wreaking unthinkable mass destruction on the United States; and like the DoD, DHS was established to prevent such an attack from happening again. But if the nation already has a Department of Defense, why does it need a separate Department of Homeland Security? What is the difference between their two missions? What is "homeland security", and why after thousands of years is terrorism suddenly deemed a significant threat? These questions prompted a close look at the new Department. This book attempts to sort through the confusion and answer the most critical questions by examining DHS' origins, mission, organization, and initiatives. It was compiled from the collective works of authoritative sources in the field, and edited to eliminate most of the contradictory and misleading data to create a concise, meaningful, and informative compendium addressing the fundamental issue: "What is the Department of Homeland Security and how does it protect America?"

About the Authors

Richard White

Richard White is CEO of CW Productions LLC. Rick holds a Bachelor of Science in History from Southern Illinois University and a Master of Science in Computer Science from Old Dominion University. He retired from the Air Force after 20 years of service.

He began his Air Force career as a program analyst maintaining software for the joint cruise missile program. He was instrumental in deploying computers and equipment critical to building and distributing the Air Tasking Order during the Gulf War. In addition, he commanded a remote detachment representing American interests in a Luftwaffe unit providing command and control to allied air forces in Central Europe and was deployed as the Director of Communications for Operation PROVIDE COMFORT (northern Iraq). After PROVIDE COMFORT, Rick took control of the Network Control Flight, 786th Communications Squadron at Ramstein Air Base in Germany.

Leaving Germany, Rick transferred to Colorado Springs, CO where he served as the Flight Systems Control Commander and also as the Deputy Commander for the Communications Squadron at NORAD. After his tour at NORAD, he moved over to the academic side of the military, the U.S. Air Force Academy.

At the Academy, Rick directed the activities of the Center for Educational Multimedia, the Planetarium and the cadet War-Game Laboratories. Rick concluded his military career as an assistant professor and Chief, Space Warfare Division at the United States Air Force Academy in the Department of Military Strategic Studies.

Kevin Collins

Kevin Collins is President of CW Productions LLC.

Before starting CW Productions with Rick White, Mr. Collins worked for Spectrum, where he oversaw Spectrum's work in national security programs, Department of Defense (DoD), the intelligence community, and other federal agencies as well as security programs for Spectrum's commercial customers for information assurance (IA). His work for government and commercial clients included: strategic and program policy planning, risk and vulnerability assessments, continuity and disaster recovery planning, computer security incident response handling, intrusion detection, and security engineering.

Before joining Spectrum, Mr. Collins served in several different security roles across industry (Cisco Systems), Government (FAA) and academia (Indiana University) as well has a long history of Information Technology and security work with the United States Air Force.

Mr. Collins is active in several industry associations: Hampton Roads Information Systems Security Association, the ISSA national chapter, and was instrumental in helping the FAA build a Computer Security Incident Response Center through PDD-63. He is a member of York County's grievance committee, Regional Issues Committee and is an Adjunct Professor of Computer Science at Saint Leo University, teaching On-line/Distance Learning Classes as well as in class studies.

Contents

Contents

Part I: Mission Requirement

## Chapter 1

9-11 Survivors

Objectives

- Describe the ordeal of victims caught in the Twin Towers on September 11th.
- Identify successful survival tactics.
- Propose improved methods for surviving a similar disaster.
- Consider your chances of surviving such a catastrophe.

Introduction

The World Trade Center in New York City was a complex of seven buildings built around a central plaza, near the south end of Manhattan in the downtown financial district. The World Trade Center was best known for its iconic 110-story Twin Towers. When the towers were completed in 1972 and 1973, respectively, they were the tallest buildings on Earth. Their stature and symbolism made them the target of a failed terrorist attack in February 1993. On the morning of Tuesday, September 11, 2001, the World Trade Center was again targeted by terrorists.

North Tower, World Trade Center

Greg Trevor worked in the Public Affairs department for the New York Port Authority. His offices were on the 68th floor of the World Trade Center. He had just finished a phone call to a colleague and stood to stretch his legs. Greg was looking out the window at the Statue of Liberty when he was nearly knocked to the floor by the force of a sudden impact. American Airlines Flight 11 had just slammed into the north side of the North Tower of the World Trade Center between the 94th and 98th floors.[1] *"I heard a loud thud, followed by an explosion. The building felt like it swayed ten feet to the south. It shuddered back to the north, and shimmied back and forth. Out the window I saw a parabola of flame fall toward the street, followed by a blizzard of paper and glass. Then I heard two sounds: emergency sirens on the street, and phones ringing across the 68th floor—calls from reporters wondering what had happened."*[2]

Adam Mayblum's offices were on the 87th floor of the World Trade Center. Adam had arrived shortly before 8:00 a.m., and was just getting set for the day when Flight 11 crashed into the building. *"The building lurched violently and shook as if it were an earthquake. People screamed. I watched out my window as the building seemed to move 10 to 20 feet in each direction."* Adam grabbed a co-worker and ran for cover. *"Light fixtures and parts of the ceiling collapsed. The kitchen was destroyed. We were certain it was a bomb. We looked out the windows. Reams of paper were flying everywhere, like a ticker tape parade. I looked down at the street. I could see people in Battery Park City looking up. Smoke started billowing in through the holes in the ceiling."*[3]

Carmen and Arturo Griffith were elevator operators in the North Tower of the World Trade Center. Arturo was running 50A, a big freight elevator, and was going from the second-level basement to the 49th floor when American Airlines Flight 11 struck at 8:46 a.m... Arturo heard a sudden whistling sound and the impact. Cables were severed and Arturo's car plunged into free fall. *"The only thing I remember was saying 'Oh God, Oh, God, I'm going to die'."* The emergency brakes caught after 15 or 16 floors, but the elevator door imploded, crushing Arturo's right knee and breaking his tibia. All that morning, Carmen had been carrying hundreds of passengers from the 78th-floor sky lobby to the bond-trading offices of Cantor Fitzgerald on the 101st and 105th floors and the Windows on the World restaurant above that. A full elevator had just left the 78th floor, and Carmen was about to carry up six or seven stragglers. The plane struck as the doors of her elevator closed. They could hear debris smash into the top of the car; then the elevator cracked open, and flames poured in. Carmen jammed her fingers between the closed doors, pulled them partly open and held them as passengers clambered over and under her 5-foot-6 frame to escape.[4]

South Tower, World Trade Center

Cara LaTorre worked in the South Tower of the World Trade Center. She had just arrived at her 100th floor office and was walking over to wish her friends good morning. *"Oh my god, the building shakes, the lights flicker, and then I hear an explosion. I look out the window behind my best friend and I see fire, paper and bodies flying out the window. My best friend yells out, 'Cara, Paulie works there! Paulie works there!'"[5]*

Jaede Barg worked in the same office with Cara LaTorre. He was preparing for a visit from a potential business partner when he heard a co-worker scream. *"As we quickly looked toward the windows, we all saw what was clearly a fireball hitting the [North Tower] head-on, the force and heat clearly felt upon my face. The force was so powerful that the wind from the strike picked up papers from the cubicle desks in between my office and the outer offices, and I felt the heat, along with an undeniable smell of fuel. The force of the fireball slamming into our tower made the building shake violently at first, and then sway. Amazingly, the windows did not break, as I ran to them in disbelief that they were still intact, and also to ascertain if the explosion was within our building or elsewhere."[6]*

Phyllis Borgo was checking meeting arrangements at the Millennium Hilton across the street from the World Trade Center. She was on her way back to her 102nd floor office in the South Tower, stepping from the hotel elevator when she noticed large pieces of debris flying in the air outside, and a gray cloud. Several people were standing at the lobby windows on their cell phones. When she asked what happened, they told her there was a "blast" at the World Trade Center across the street. *"I ran to the window, looked up and saw the most horrifying scene of my life. The North Tower was in ablaze from about floor 90! I immediately got on the phone to call home and let [my husband] know I was not in the building and was currently okay."[7]*

Ladder Company 6

Billy Butler and Sal D'Agostino were members of the Fire Department of New York Ladder Company 6. *"I was still asleep at 8:48 when the first plane hit,"* said D'Agostino. *"I had been up late working the night before and was getting every moment of sleep I could before the roll call at 9. When I heard that a plane had hit the North Tower, I thought it was a joke,"* he continued, explaining that false alarms are sometimes sounded to wake up the rookies in the department and get them to suit up. *"I also thought it was a bad joke until I saw our captain [John Jonas] suiting up, and he never was in on the rookie jokes,"* said Butler. *"Once we got outside we knew that this was really bad."[8]*

* * *

Back in the North Tower, Greg Trevor ran to alert his director who was already on the phone to the Port Authority's Chief Operating Officer, Ernesto Butcher. Greg picked up another line and contacted the Port Authority Police Department in Jersey City. He and his boss then forwarded the phones and prepared to evacuate when a staff member said two media calls were holding. Gregg picked up and answered one of them. *"Hi, I'm with NBC national news. If you could hold on for about 5 minutes, we're going to put you on a live phone interview."* Gregg answered that they were evacuating the building. *"But this will only take a minute."* Gregg repeated that they were leaving the building immediately. The caller seemed stunned. *"But, but this is NBC NATIONAL news".* Gregg said he was sorry and hung up.[9]

On the 87th floor, Adam Mayblum and his colleagues thought the worst was over. The building was standing, and though they were shaken, they were alive. They checked the halls. *"The smoke was thick and white and did not smell like I imagined smoke should smell. Not like your BBQ or your fireplace or even a bonfire."* Adam called home and left a message for his wife that he was okay and on his way out. He grabbed his laptop from his office. Then he removed his tee shirt, tore it into three pieces, gave two to his friends, soaked it in water, and tied it around his face to act as an air filter. Everybody started moving to the staircase.[10]

Shortly after starting down the stairwell, Adam Mayblum and an associate returned to their office to drag out a partner who stayed behind. There was no air, only white smoke. They called his name as they searched. No response. They figured he succumbed to the smoke and made their way back to the stairwell. They proceeded to the 78th floor where they had to change over to a different stairwell. *"I expected to see more people. There were some 50 to 60 more. Not enough. Wires and fires all over the place. Smoke too. A brave man was fighting a fire with the emergency hose. I stopped with two friends to make sure that everyone from our office was accounted for. We ushered them and confused people into the stairwell."*[11]

For more than an hour, Greg Trevor joined the thousands of fellow World Trade Center workers who patiently descended the emergency stairwells. *"I wasn't scared at first. My initial feelings were disorientation and disbelief."*[12]

Before finally throwing herself onto the lobby floor, Carmen Griffith glanced back to be sure her elevator was empty. That was when fire scorched her face with second- and third-degree burns, and literally welded her hooped right earring to her neck. Her hands were badly burned. Carmen was helped down the 78 floors to an ambulance just as her husband was carried out of the basement on a piece of plywood, each certain that the other was dead.[13]

At the Millennium Hilton, Phyllis Borgo's husband called back telling her to return home immediately. As Phyllis started to lose the call, she stepped outside to gain better reception. Standing on Church Street, Phyllis stared up and looked in disbelief at the burning North Tower. As she looked, she saw a man in a business suit jump from about the 60th floor. *"Oh my God, Oh my God, Oh my God!"* Phyllis became hysterical. She was rushed back inside the hotel and told to sit down and not look outside.[14]

* * *

Across the street, on the 100th floor of the South Tower, Cara LaTorre started screaming, *"We have to get out of here, we have to get the f*** out of here!"* Jaede Barg began to evacuate his office. Recalling his training as a fire marshal assistant, he told people not to use the elevators. Cara quickly grabbed her purse and started running down the stairs. *"After around 10 stories my shoes start to hurt so I take them off and start running barefoot."* Jaede held the stairwell door open for others to escape. Then he went back and checked the floor for stragglers before entering the stairwell himself.[15]

At the 87th floor of the South Tower, Jaede Barg paused to take a rest. He had just retrieved a Diet Coke from a vending machine when he heard several men scream. He ran over to the window and found himself staring almost eye level at the fire-engulfed hole in the North Tower. *"I saw the unthinkable: people jumping out of the building to escape the flames all around them. I painfully remember the same panic-stricken guy crying out '...they're holding hands' as a man and woman jumped out together toward their end. I did not view their leap, as I had to look away after the first two jumps I witnessed—there were so many people jumping."*[16]

On the way to the towers, the men of Ladder Company 6 could see the gaping hole in the upper floors of the North Tower. The streets were lined with thousands of people just staring at the tower, many with camcorders and cameras in their hands, said Butler. Debris was falling from the tower and large sections of the airplane were strewn across the ground directly beneath. *"We parked and immediately began to grab our gear, but we had to constantly watch out for falling debris. Computers were falling from 100 stories high and we had to make sure that no one in our unit got hit,"* said D'Agostino. When the men entered the building, they were met by the sight of buckled floors, smashed elevators, and a frenzy of people not knowing exactly where to go. *"We saved lives that day not by carrying people out on our backs, but by giving them direction,"* said Butler.[17]

* * *

High in the emergency stairwell, Greg Trevor and Adam Mayblum continued to make an orderly escape from the North Tower. *"We checked our cell phones. Surprisingly, there was a very good signal"*, said Mayblum. Greg Trevor called a colleague to let his wife know he was safe. *"I knew I could not reach my wife"* said Mayblum, *"so I called my parents. I told them what happened and that we were all okay and on the way down. Soon, my sister-in-law reached me. I told her we were fine and moving down. I believe that was about the 65th floor. We were bored and nervous. I called my friend Angel in San Francisco. I knew he would be watching. He was amazed I was on the phone. He told me to get out, that there was another plane on its way."*[18]

* * *

Jaede Barg had resumed his descent down the emergency stairwell in the South Tower when the fire department made an announcement over the public address system. They said the South Tower was secure, that a plane hit the North Tower. They offered that people could evacuate if they wished, but again asserted that the South Tower was secure. Jaede continued down the stairwell without hesitation. He did not go too far before he heard a roaring noise. *"The five of us were launched off our feet by the strike, into the wall, and back on our feet in an instant—remarkably, no one hurt. I remember my brief-case flying through the air up the stairs, and me automatically going after it. The incredible noise of the crash seemed like an explosion very close."*[19]

As the firemen from Ladder Company 6 raced toward the North Tower, they were stopped by the roar of jet engines. They saw the shadow of a plane on the ground, and finally a fireball resulting from the second plane hitting the South Tower.[20]

At 9:02 a.m., United Airlines Flight 175 impacted the south side of the South Tower of the World Trade Center between the 78th and 84th floors at a speed of over 500 miles per hour. Parts of the plane including an engine exited the building from its north side, and were found on the ground up to six blocks away.[21]

Cara LaTorre was descending the stairwell somewhere in the high 60's of the South Tower when she heard an explosion. *"The building shakes, the walls begin to crumble and a piece of metal comes flying between us. Oh my god, they bombed our building now! We don't know what to do. The only thing in my mind is that I have to call my husband, Frank, who works nearby to tell him that I am okay. The heat, we could feel the heat. We haven't started to cry yet because we are in shock."*[22]

Phyllis Borgo recalled, *"It all seemed to happen so fast, but there was more to come: the South Tower was hit—my building—my friends—everyone from the street began to run into the lobby of the Millennium and at that point I became panicky—we were being pushed to the back of a wall and elevator banks, and I thought we might be crushed. Luckily, the hotel personnel took charge and pro-ceeded to lead all of us out the side door and out onto Fulton Street, telling us to get as far away from the Towers as possible."*[23]

Jaede Barg remembered the lights going out. *"There were cracks in the stair-well walls with exposed pipes breaking through the plaster. The building was forcefully swaying, enough to require significant balancing. I recall the incredi-ble sound of twisting metal with each sway of the building. Smoke almost im-mediately started rising up from the lower floors, yet we all moved down the stairwell knowing this was the only way out."*[24]

Cara LaTorre also continued down the stairs with her companions. *"My legs are getting weaker and weaker I can hardly walk. Joanie wants to quit but Marci and I pump her up, then at times I feel like I can not run any more but they pump me up. Marci keeps us strong. I am having trouble breathing. A man hands me an energy water pack. My shirt become unbuttoned and I actu-ally stop to button it up again."*[25]

* * *

Over at the North Tower, Ladder Company 6 started making their way up the stairwell. As they did, they continued to tell people where to go once they reached the lobby, and, in return, people kept giving them positive reinforce-ment. *"People were giving us water and saying 'God bless you' as we passed them in the stairwell,"* said Butler, explaining that the firefighters gave most of that water back to exhausted civilians walking down from their offices high atop the trade center.[26] Above them, Greg Trevor and Adam Mayblum continued to work their way downstairs.

Greg recalled, *"Every few floors, we would stop, move to the right of the stairwell and make room for injured people walking down—and firefighters and Port Authority Police officers running up".*[27]

On the 53rd floor, Adam came across a heavyset man sitting on the stairs. The man needed help. Adam knew he couldn't carry him, so he offered to tell the rescue workers his location. The man said okay. On the 44th floor Adam's cell phone rang. It was his parents. They were hysterical. They said a third plane was coming. Adam tried to calm his parents as he noticed rescue workers coming up the stairs. He stopped a number of them and told them about the man on the 53rd floor, and his partner he couldn't find back in the office on the 87th. "I later felt terrible about this. They headed up to find those people and met death instead."[28]

Outside, Phyllis Borgo ran up Fulton St. toward Broadway. She noticed many people injured and bleeding from the debris. One man was down on the pavement, blood pouring from his head as if a bucket had emptied. Two people were watching over him and paramedics were nearby. *"I prayed for him as I passed and looked away as to not get more upset."* Phyllis continued to walk uptown, trying to make her way home with the rest of the city. At Lafayette Street she noticed people milling about outside a Holiday Inn talking about the latest news. *"They told us the Pentagon had just been hit by another plane."*[29]

* * *

At 9:37 a.m., American Airlines Flight 77 was lost from radar screens and impacted the western side of the Pentagon.[30] Terry Morin, a Marine Corps aviator, witnessed the event.

"I can't remember exactly what I was thinking about at that moment, but I started to hear an increasingly loud rumbling behind me and to my left. As I turned to my left, I immediately realized the noise was bouncing off the 4-story structure that was Wing 5 [of Federal Office Building #2 across from the Pentagon]. One or two seconds later the airliner came into my field of view. By that time the noise was absolutely deafening. I instantly had a very bad feeling about this but things were happening very quickly. The aircraft was essentially right over the top of me and the outer portion of the FOB. Everything was shaking and vibrating, including the ground. I estimate that the aircraft was no more than 100 feet above me in a slight nose down attitude. The plane had a silver body with red and blue stripes down the fuselage. I believed at the time that it belonged to American Airlines, but I couldn't be sure."

Terry watched as the aircraft headed towards the Pentagon. *"I estimated the aircraft speed at between 350 and 400 knots. The flight path appeared to be deliberate, smooth, and controlled. As the aircraft approached the Pentagon, I saw a minor flash (later found out that the aircraft had sheared off a portion of a highway light pole down on Hwy 110). As the aircraft flew ever lower I started to lose sight of the actual airframe as a row of trees to the Northeast of the FOB blocked my view. I could now only see the tail of the aircraft. I believe I saw the tail dip slightly to the right indicating a minor turn in that direction. The tail was barely visible when I saw the flash and subsequent fireball rise approximately 200 feet above the Pentagon. There was a large explosion noise and the low frequency sound echo that comes with this type of sound. Associated with that was the increase in air pressure, momentarily, like a small gust of wind. For those formerly in the military, it sounded like a 2000 lb. bomb going off roughly ½ mile in front of you. At once there was a huge cloud of black smoke that rose several hundred feet up."[31]*

* * *

Back at the South Tower, Cara LaTorre managed to make it down from her 100th floor office. *"We finally get to the first floor and the lights are all out. There are guards directing us through the mall level, which leads us to an escalator near the Borders bookstore. I did not want to walk up the escalator but Marci pumped me up and Joanie said we are almost on the street. We finally get out of the building and I still don't have any shoes on. We slow down in the middle of the street to use our cell phones when a female cop starts to yell in our faces. She is telling us to run, it is not safe here. I will always remember the woman's face."[32]*

Still trying to manage his own escape from the South Tower, Jaede Barg ran into an impasse on the 77th floor. *"The stairwell was no longer passable and ended. The floor was filled with smoke, plaster, dust, and fire was all along the outside of the floor. There was destruction all over, with beams caved in from the above floor and rubble everywhere. It was very difficult to see, and as I wear glasses (thankfully so), but I could hear murmurs emanating from the perimeter of the floor. We were in the interior of the floor, and here we found two women who were apparently on the floor when the plane hit. I met the first lady, who was a very scared 30-year-old woman named Florence. We were together for the rest of our escape."[33]*

Jaede and Florence began frantically looking for an exit. They were breathing smoke and gasping for air. Everybody was coughing. They couldn't see each other. It was clear the fire was moving closer. *"We could not go back the way we came, as that was certain death. Three of us found another stairwell entrance door, but it would not open, no matter how hard we pushed and pulled."* Jaede despaired. *"This was the one point that day I began to lose faith in our escape."[34]*

"As if in a dream, the three of us banging on the stairway door, [we] heard a voice calling out to us from a place we thought was rubble. I do not really remember the guy, but he was the reason we made it off the burning floor." Jaede, along with a small group of people—including Florence—followed the man's voice until it brought them to an open stairwell. From there, the people slowly descended out of the South Tower. They escaped the building about 12 to 15 minutes before it collapsed.[35]

* * *

At 9:59 a.m., the South Tower of the World Trade Center suddenly collapsed, plummeting into the streets below. A massive cloud of dust and debris quickly filled lower Manhattan.[36]

When the men of Ladder Company 6 hit the 27th floor of the North Tower, they stopped to regroup and stood motionless as they heard the roar of the South Tower collapsing. Knowing that the fire was now the least of their concerns, the men turned and gave the order to evacuate. *"We were now walking briskly down the stairs hoping to make it out of the building before it collapsed"*, said D'Agostino.[37]

Up on Lafayette Street at the Holiday Inn, Phyllis Borgo paused to watch the news unfolding on TV. *"As we watched in horror, the South Tower began to collapse to the ground in a matter of seconds. I put my hands in my face and began to cry... all I could think about were the firemen, EMS workers and police that were probably in the building trying to save lives and my fellow co-workers and friends that didn't make it out in time."*[38]

* * *

Greg Trevor had reached the 5th floor of the North Tower when he heard a loud rumble. *"The building shook violently. I was thrown from one side of the stairwell to the other. We didn't know it at the time, but the South Tower had just collapsed. Our stairwell filled with smoke and concrete dust. Breathing became difficult. The lights died. A steady stream of water, about 4 inches deep, began running down the stairs. It felt like we were wading through a dark, dirty, rapid river—at night in the middle of a forest fire. The smartest decision I made that day was to wear a knit tie to work. I put the blue tie over my nose and mouth to block the smoke and dust. To keep from hyperventilating, I remembered the breathing exercises my wife and I learned in our Lamaze classes. Someone yelled that we should put our right hand on the shoulder of the person in front of us and keep walking down. We descended one more flight, to the fourth floor, when I heard someone say: 'Oh shit, the door's blocked.' The force from the collapse of the South Tower had apparently jammed the emergency exit. We were ordered to turn around and head back up the stairs, to see if we could transfer to another stairwell."*[39]

Minutes later, emergency workers cleared the fourth floor exit. Greg Trevor and the other survivors turned and darted down the stairs when they heard Port Authority Police Officer David Lim shout *"Down is good! Down is good!"* The emergency exit led to the mezzanine level of the North Tower. *"The mezzanine was filled with dull-beige concrete dust—on the floor, in the air, caked against the floor-to-ceiling windows. It felt like we were walking through a huge, dirty snow globe that had just been shaken. It was even worse when we walked outside, near Six World Trade Center. The plaza was a minefield of twisted metal, covered by a layer of concrete dust several inches thick. I am grateful for that dust, because it means I didn't see any bodies."* Greg exited the plaza and turned up Church Street and headed north. *"I looked back at the Trade Center. The upper third of the North Tower was on fire. There was so much smoke and dust, I couldn't tell that the South Tower had collapsed."*[40]

Adam Mayblum was on the 3rd floor when he heard the South Tower collapse next door. The lights went out. Adam recommended that everyone place a hand on the shoulder of the person in front of them and call out if they hit an obstacle so others would know to avoid it. As they reached another stairwell a female officer emerged soaking wet and covered in soot. She said they couldn't go that way, it was blocked. She told them to go up and use the 4th floor exit. Just as they turned she called back that it was okay to go down instead. Adam and his party emerged into an enormous room. *"It was light but filled with smoke. I commented to a friend that it must be under construction. Then we realized where we were. It was the second floor. The one that overlooks the lobby. We were ushered out into the courtyard, the one where the fountain used to be. My first thought was of a TV movie I saw once about nuclear winter and fallout. I could not understand where all this debris came from. There was at least five inches of this gray pasty dusty drywall soot on the ground as well as a thickness of it in the air."* Adam made it out and began walking towards Houston Street.[41]

* * *

Adam and his friend Kern walked several blocks until they came to a post office. Both stopped and looked up. *"Our building, exactly where our office is (was), was engulfed in flame and smoke. A postal worker said that the South Tower had fallen down. I looked again and sure enough it was gone."* Adam tried calling his wife, but couldn't get through. He called his parents to let them know he was fine, and they relayed the message to his wife. Adam and Kern sat down to rest. *"A girl on a bike offered us some water. Just as she took the cap off her bottle we heard a rumble. We looked up and our building, the North Tower collapsed."* Adam had escaped by less than 15 minutes.[42]

The crew of Ladder Company 6 was not so lucky. *"On the 18th floor we ran into Josephine Harris who was slowly walking down the stairs. We immediately helped her but the going was slow—one step at a time—and she kept insisting that we go on without her,"* said Butler. When the company reached the fourth floor, Harris stopped and said that she was going no further. As soon as she finished speaking, the men heard the dreaded and unmistakable rumble of the building above them. *"We could hear the floors above smashing together one by one and it became faster and louder,"* said D'Agostino. *"I was thrown down to the next landing and immediately the dust blacked out my vision. When the noise subsided, I thanked God I was alive and then started to move some of the debris out of my way. As I did so, Josephine popped out unhurt,"* said Butler.[43]

As the dust settled, the company took roll and found that all its members had survived and none were seriously injured. For the next four hours and 40 minutes, the men attempted to survive using their oxygen sparingly and trying to get through to the firefighters outside the building via a radio. *"The place was a mess,"* said D'Agostino. *"We knew where we were in the building, but the collapse of the two towers had made it hard for the firefighters on the outside to see anything or even recognize the former World Trade Center."*[44]

"A Port Authority officer who was trapped with us had two cell phones... I was able to get a hold of my wife... I told her to call the fire department and tell them that we are alive but trapped in the North Tower," said Butler.[45]

Eventually the men were found, and after walking across narrow I-beams and avoiding numerous fires, the entire company walked out of the North Tower after leaving Mrs. Harris with members of Ladder Company 43.[46]

Conclusion

Greg Trevor, Adam Mayblum, Jaede Barg, Phyllis Borgo, Cara LaTorre, Carmen Griffith, Arturo Griffith, and the men of Ladder Company Six survived the attacks of September 11th. Carmen and Arturo Griffith were taken to separate New York hospitals and later reunited.[47] An estimated 3,000 people were killed in the attacks, including 184 at the Pentagon, and 40 aboard United Airlines Flight 93 which crashed near Shanksville Pennsylvania.[48] Altogether is was the single worst loss of life on American soil since the Civil War, and the first attack against American territory since World War Two.

Questions

1. How do you escape a burning high rise?

2. What decisions proved fateful to survivors who escaped the Twin Towers on September 11th?

3. How could they have prepared better for this disaster?

4. Are you prepared to survive a similar catastrophe?

Chapter 2

9-11 Attacks

Objectives

- Understand the events of September 11th.
- Explain how the terrorists were able to conduct a successful attack.
- Identify weaknesses with the security measures of the day.
- Analyze the method and timing of the attacks.

Introduction

Tuesday, September 11, 2001, dawned temperate and nearly cloudless in the eastern United States. Millions of men and women readied themselves for work. Some made their way to the Twin Towers, the signature structures of the World Trade Center complex in New York City. Others went to Arlington, Virginia, to the Pentagon. Across the Potomac River, the United States Congress was back in session. At the other end of Pennsylvania Avenue, people began to line up for a White House tour. In Sarasota, Florida, President George W. Bush went for an early morning run.

For those heading to an airport, weather conditions could not have been better for a safe and pleasant journey. Among the travelers were Mohamed Atta and Abdul Aziz al Omari, who arrived at the airport in Portland Maine.

Boston: American 11 and United 175

On Tuesday, September 11, 2001, Mohammed Atta and Abul Aziz al Omari arrived at the airport in Portland Maine to catch a 6:00 a.m. flight to Boston's Logan International Airport.

When he checked in for his flight to Boston, Atta was selected by a computerized prescreening system known as CAPPS (Computer Assisted Passenger Prescreening System), created to identify passengers who should be subject to special security measures. Under security rules in place at the time, the only consequence of Atta's selection by CAPPS was that his checked bags were held off the plane until it was confirmed that he had boarded the aircraft.

At 6:45 a.m., Atta and Omari arrived in Boston. Between 6:45 and 7:40, Atta and Omari, along with Satam al Suqami, Wail al Shehri, and Waleed al Shehri, checked in and boarded American Airlines Flight 11, bound for Los Angeles. The flight was scheduled to depart at 7:45.

Elsewhere at Logan Airport, Marwan al Shehhi, Fayez Banihammad, Mohand al Shehri, Ahmed al Ghamdi, and Hamza al Ghamdi checked in for United Airlines Flight 175, also bound for Los Angeles. Their flight was scheduled to depart at 08:00.

As Atta's team passed through passenger screening, three members—Suqami, Wail al Shehri, and Waleed al Shehri—were selected by CAPPS. Their selection affected only the handling of their checked bags, not their screening at the checkpoint. All five men cleared the checkpoint and made their way to the gate for American 11. Atta, Omari, and Suqami took their seats in business class. The Shehri brothers had adjacent seats in row 2 in the first-class cabin. They boarded American 11 between 7:31 and 7:40. The aircraft pushed back from the gate at 7:40.

Shehhi and his team, none of whom had been selected by CAPPS, boarded United 175 between 7:23 and 7:28. Their aircraft pushed back from the gate just before 8:00.

Washington Dulles: American 77

At 7:15 a.m., Khalid al Mihdhar and Majed Moqed checked in with the American Airlines ticket counter at Dulles International Airport in Virginia. Both were ticketed for Flight 77 bound for Los Angeles. Within 20 minutes, three other members of the team checked in including Hani Hanjour, Nawaf al Hazmi, and Salem al Hazmi. Hani Hanjour, Khalid al Mihdhar, and Majed Moqed were flagged by CAPPS. The Hazmi brothers were also selected for extra security by the airline's customer service representative at the check-in counter. He did so because one of the brothers did not have photo identification nor could he understand English, and because the agent found both passengers to be suspicious. The only consequence of their selection was that their checked bags were held off the plane until it was confirmed that they had boarded the aircraft.

The five hijackers proceeded to the Main Terminal's west security screening point. The checkpoint featured closed-circuit television that recorded all passengers, including the hijackers as they were screened. Both Mihdhar and Moqed set off the metal detector and were directed to a second metal detector. Mihdhar did not trigger the alarm and was permitted through the checkpoint. Moqed set it off, a screener wanded him with a hand-held magnetic detector. He passed this inspection. About 20 minutes later, Hani Hanjour, Nawaf al Hazmi, and Salem al Hazmi entered the screening area. Nawaf al Hazmi set off both the first and second metal detectors and was then hand-wanded before being passed. In addition, his over-the-shoulder carry-on bag was swiped by an explosive trace detector and then passed.

At 7:50 a.m., Majed Moqed and Khalid al Mihdhar boarded American 77 and were seated in 12A and 12B in coach. Hani Hanjour, assigned to seat 1B in first class, soon followed. The Hazmi brothers, sitting in 5E and 5F, joined Hanjour in the first-class cabin.

Newark: United 93

At Newark Airport in New Jersey, another hijacking team assembled. Between 7:03 and 7:39, Saeed al Ghamdi, Ahmed al Nami, Ahad al Haznawi, and Ziad Jarrah checked in at the United Airlines Ticket counter for Flight 93, going to Los Angeles. Haznawi was selected by CAPPS. His checked bag was screened for explosives and then loaded on the plane.

The four men passed though the security checkpoint and boarded their plane between 7:39 and 7:48. All four had seats in the first-class cabin. Jarrah was in seat 1B, closest to the cockpit; Nami was in 3C, Ghamdi in 3D, and Haznawi in 6B.

The 19 men were aboard four transcontinental flights. They were planning to hijack these planes and turn them into large guided missiles, loaded with up to 11,400 gallons of jet fuel. By 8:00 a.m. on the morning of Tuesday, September 11, 2001, they had defeated all the security layers that America's civil aviation security system then had in place to prevent hijacking.

The 19 men were aboard four transcontinental flights. They were planning to hijack these planes and turn them into large guided missiles, loaded with up to 11,400 gallons of jet fuel. By 8:00 a.m. on the morning of Tuesday, September 11, 2001, [the terrorists] had defeated all the security layers that America's civil aviation security system then had in place to prevent hijacking.

The Hijacking of American 11

American Airlines Flight 11 provided nonstop service from Boston to Los Angeles. On September 11, Captain John Ogonowski and First Officer Thomas McGuinness piloted the Boeing 767. It carried its full capacity of nine flight attendants. Eighty-one passengers boarded the flight with them, including the five terrorists.

American Flight 11 took off at 7:59. Just before 8:14, it had climbed to 26,000 feet, not quite its initial assigned cruising altitude of 29,000 feet. All communications and flight profile data were normal. About this time, the "Fasten Seatbelt" sign would usually have been turned off and the flight attendants would have begun preparing for cabin service.

At this time, American 11 had its last routine communication with the ground when it acknowledged navigational instructions from the FAA's air traffic control (ATC) center in Boston. Sixteen seconds after that transmission, ATC instructed the aircraft's pilots to climb to 35,000 feet. That message and all subsequent attempts to contact the flight were not acknowledged. From this and other evidence, it is believed the hijacking began at 8:14 or shortly thereafter.

Reports from two flight attendants in the coach cabin, Betty Ong and Madeline "Amy" Sweeney, tell us most of what we know about how the hijacking happened. As it began, some of the hijackers—most likely Wail al Shehri and Waleed al Shehri, who were seated in row 2 in first class—stabbed the two unarmed flight attendants who would have been preparing for cabin service.

It's not known exactly how the hijackers gained access to the cockpit; FAA rules required that the doors remain closed and locked during flight. Ong speculated that they had "jammed their way" in. Perhaps the terrorists stabbed the flight attendants to get a cockpit key, to force one of them to open the cockpit door, or to lure the captain or first officer out of the cockpit.

At the same time or shortly thereafter, Atta—the only terrorist on board trained to fly a jet—would have moved to the cockpit from his business-class seat, possibly accompanied by Omari. As this was happening, passenger Daniel Lewin, who was seated in the row just behind Atta and Omari, was stabbed by one of the hijackers—probably Satam al Suqami, who was seated directly behind Lewin. Lewin had served four years as an officer in the Israeli military. He may have made an attempt to stop the hijackers in front of him, not realizing that another was sitting behind him.

The hijackers quickly gained control and sprayed Mace, pepper spray, or some other irritant in the first-class cabin, in order to force the passengers and flight attendants toward the rear of the plane. They claimed they had a bomb.

About five minutes after the hijacking began, Betty Ong contacted the American Airlines Southeastern Reservations Office in Cary, North Carolina, via an AT&T airphone to report an emergency aboard the flight. The emergency call lasted approximately 25 minutes, as Ong calmly and professionally relayed information about events taking place aboard the airplane to authorities on the ground.

At 8:19, Ong reported: *"The cockpit is not answering, somebody's stabbed in business class—and I think there's Mace—that we can't breathe—I don't know, I think we're getting hijacked."* She then told of the stabbings of the two flight attendants.

American's Southeastern Reservations Office quickly contacted the American Airlines operations center in Fort Worth, Texas, who soon contacted the FAA's Boston Air Traffic Control Center. Boston Center knew of a problem on the flight in part because just before 8:25 the hijackers had attempted to communicate with the passengers. The microphone was keyed, and immediately one of the hijackers said, "*Nobody move. Everything will be okay. If you try to make any moves, you'll endanger yourself and the airplane. Just stay quiet.*" Air traffic controllers heard the transmission; Ong did not. The hijackers probably did not know how to operate the cockpit radio communication system correctly, and thus inadvertently broadcast their message over the air traffic control channel instead of the cabin public-address channel. Also at 8:25, and again at 8:29, Amy Sweeney got through to the American Flight Services Office in Boston but was cut off after she reported someone was hurt aboard the flight. Three minutes later, Sweeney was reconnected to the office and began relaying updates to her manager.

At 8:26, Ong reported that the plane was "flying erratically." A minute later, Flight 11 turned south. American also began getting identifications of the hijackers, as Ong and then Sweeney passed on some of the seat numbers of those who had gained unauthorized access to the cockpit.

At 8:41 Sweeney reported that passengers in coach were under the impression there was a routine medical emergency in first class. Other flight attendants were busy at duties such as getting medical supplies while Ong and Sweeney were reporting events.

At 8:41, American's operations center learned that air traffic controllers had declared Flight 11 a hijacking, and thought it was headed toward Kennedy airport in New York City. Air traffic control was busy moving other flights out of the way as they tracked Flight 11 on primary radar, which seemed to show the aircraft descending.

At 8:44 contact was lost with Betty Ong. About this time Sweeney reported *"Something is wrong. We are in a rapid descent... we are all over the place."* When asked to look out the window, Sweeney reported *"We are flying low. We are flying very, very low. We are flying way too low."* Seconds later she said, *"Oh my God we are way too low."* The phone call ended.

At 8:46:40, American 11 crashed into the North Tower of the World Trade Center in New York City. All on board, along with an unknown number of people in the tower, were killed instantly.

The Hijacking of United 175

United Airlines Flight 175 was scheduled to depart for Los Angeles at 8:00. Captain Victor Saracini and First Officer Michael Horrocks piloted the Boeing 767, which had seven flight attendants. Fifty-six passengers boarded the flight.

United 175 pushed back from its gate at 7:58 and departed Logan Airport at 8:14. By 8:33, it had reached its assigned cruising altitude of 31,000 feet. The flight attendants would have begun their cabin service.

The hijackers attacked sometime between 8:42 and 8:46. They used knives, Mace, and the threat of a bomb. They stabbed members of the flight crew. Both pilots had been killed. The eyewitness accounts came from calls made from the rear of the plane, from passengers originally seated further forward in the cabin, a sign that passengers and perhaps crew had been moved to the back of the aircraft.

The first operational evidence that something was abnormal on United 175 came at 8:47 when the aircraft changed beacon codes twice within a minute. At 8:51, the flight deviated from its assigned altitude, and a minute later New York air traffic controllers began repeatedly and unsuccessfully trying to contact it.

At 8:52, in Easton, Connecticut, a man named Lee Hanson received a phone call from his son Peter, a passenger on United 175. His son told him: *"I think they've taken over the cockpit—an attendant has been stabbed—and someone else up front may have been killed. The plane is making strange moves. Call United Airlines—Tell them it's Flight 175, Boston to LA."* Lee Hansen then called the Easton Police Department and relayed what he had heard.

Also at 8:52, a male flight attendant called a United office in San Francisco. The flight attendant reported that the flight had been hijacked, both pilots killed, a flight attendant stabbed, and the hijackers were probably flying the plane. The call lasted about two minutes.

At 8:58, the flight took a heading toward New York City. At 8:59, Flight 175 passenger Brian David Sweeney tried to call his wife, Julie. He left a message on their home answering machine that the plane had been hijacked. He then called his mother, Luise Sweeney, told her the flight had been hijacked, and added that the passengers were thinking about storming the cockpit to take control of the plane away from the hijackers.

At 9:00, Lee Hanson received a second call from his son Peter: *"It's getting bad, Dad—A stewardess was stabbed—They seem to have knives and Mace—They said they have a bomb—It's getting very bad on the plane—Passengers are throwing up and getting sick—The plane is making jerky movements—I don't think the pilot is flying the plane—I think we are going down—I think they intend to go to Chicago or someplace and fly into a building—Don't worry Dad—If it happens, it'll be very fast—My God, my God."*

The call ended abruptly. Lee Hanson had heard a woman scream just before it cut off. He turned on a television, and in her home so did Luise Sweeney. Both then saw the second aircraft hit the World Trade Center.

At 9:03:11, United Airlines Flight 175 struck the South Tower of the World Trade Center. All on board, along with an unknown number of people in the tower, were killed instantly.

The Hijacking of American 77

American Airlines Flight 77 was scheduled to depart from Washington Dulles for Los Angeles at 8:10. The aircraft was a Boeing 757 piloted by Captain Charles F. Burlingame and First Officer David Charlebois. There were four flight attendants. On September 11, the flight carried 58 passengers.

American 77 pushed back from its gate at 8:09 and took off at 8:20. At 8:46, the flight reached its assigned cruising altitude of 35,000 feet. Cabin service would have begun. At 8:51, American 77 transmitted its last routine radio communication. The hijacking began between 8:51 and 8:54. As on American 11 and United 175, the hijackers used knives and moved all the passengers to the rear of the aircraft. Unlike the earlier flights, the Flight 77 hijackers were reported by a passenger to have box cutters. Finally, a passenger reported that an announcement had been made by the "pilot" that the plane had been hijacked. Neither of the firsthand accounts mentioned any stabbings or the threat or use of either a bomb or Mace, though both witnesses began the flight in the first-class cabin.

At 8:54, the aircraft deviated from its assigned course, turning south. Two minutes later the transponder was turned off and even primary radar contact with the aircraft was lost. The Indianapolis Air Traffic Control Center repeatedly tried and failed to contact the aircraft. American Airlines dispatchers also tried, without success.

At 9:00, American Airlines Executive Vice President Gerard Arpey learned that communications had been lost with American 77. This was now the second American aircraft in trouble. He ordered all American Airlines flights in the Northeast that had not taken off to remain on the ground. After learning that United Airlines was missing a plane, American Airlines headquarters extended the ground stop nationwide.

At 9:12, Renee May called her mother, Nancy May, in Las Vegas. She said her flight was being hijacked by six individuals who had moved them to the rear of the plane. She asked her mother to alert American Airlines. Nancy May and her husband promptly did so.

At some point between 9:16 and 9:26, Barbara Olson called her husband, Ted Olson, the solicitor general of the United States. She reported that the flight had been hijacked, and the hijackers had knives and box cutters. She further indicated that the hijackers were not aware of her phone call, and that they had put all the passengers in the back of the plane. About a minute into the conversation the call was cut off.

Shortly after the first call, Barbara Olson reached her husband again. She reported that the pilot had announced that the flight had been hijacked, and she asked her husband what she should tell the captain to do. Ted Olson asked for her location and she replied that the aircraft was then flying over houses. Another passenger told her they were traveling northeast. The Solicitor General then informed his wife of the two previous hijackings and crashes. She did not display signs of panic and did not indicate any awareness of an impending crash. At that point the second call was cut off.

At 9:20, the autopilot on American 77 was disengaged; the aircraft was at 7,000 feet and approximately 38 miles west of the Pentagon. At 9:32, controllers at the Dulles Terminal Radar Approach Control *"observed a primary radar target tracking eastbound at a high rate of speed."* This was later determined to have been Flight 77.

At 9:34, Ronald Reagan Washington National Airport advised the Secret Service of an unknown aircraft heading in the direction of the White House. American 77 was then 5 miles west-southwest of the Pentagon and began a 330 degree turn. At the end of the turn, it was descending through 2,200 feet, pointed toward the Pentagon and downtown Washington. The hijacker pilot then advanced the throttles to maximum power an dove toward the Pentagon.

At 9:37:46, American Airlines Flight 77 crashed into the Pentagon, traveling at approximately 530 miles per hour. All on board, as well as many civilian and military personnel in the building, were killed.

The Battle for United 93

At 8:42, United Airlines Flight 93 took off from Newark (New Jersey) Liberty International Airport bound for San Francisco. The aircraft was piloted by Captain Jason Dahl and First Officer Leroy Homer, and there were five flight attendants. Thirty-seven passengers, including the hijackers, boarded the plane. Scheduled to depart the gate at 8:00, the Boeing 757's takeoff was delayed because of the airport's typically heavy morning traffic.

As United 93 left Newark, the flight's crew members were unaware of the hijacking of American 11. Around 9:00, the FAA, American, and United were facing the staggering realization of apparent multiple hijackings. At 9:03, they would see another aircraft strike the World Trade Center. Crisis managers at the FAA and the airlines did not yet act to warn other aircraft. At the same time, Boston Center realized that a message transmitted just before 8:25 by the hijacker pilot of American 11 included the phrase, *"We have some planes."*

The hijackers attacked at 9:28. While traveling 35,000 feet above eastern Ohio, United 93 suddenly dropped 700 feet. Eleven seconds into the descent, the FAA's air traffic control center in Cleveland received the first of two radio transmissions from the aircraft. During the first broadcast, the captain or first officer could be heard declaring *"Mayday"* amid the sounds of a physical struggle in the cockpit. The second radio transmission, 35 seconds later, indicated that the fight was continuing. The captain or first officer could be heard shouting: *"Hey get out of here—get out of here—get out of here."*

At 9:32, a hijacker, probably Jarrah, made or attempted to make the following announcement to the passengers of Flight 93: *"Ladies and Gentlemen: Here the captain, please sit down keep remaining sitting. We have a bomb on board. So, sit."* The flight data recorder (also recovered) indicates that Jarrah then instructed the plane's autopilot to turn the aircraft around and head east.

The cockpit voice recorder data indicate that a woman, most likely a flight attendant, was being held captive in the cockpit. She struggled with one of the

Crisis managers at the FAA and the airlines did not yet act to warn other aircraft. At the same time, Boston Center realized that a message transmitted just before 8:25 by the hijacker pilot of American 11 included the phrase, "We have some planes."

hijackers who killed or otherwise silenced her.

Shortly thereafter, the passengers and flight crew began a series of calls from GTE airphones and cellular phones. The calls between family, friends, and colleagues took place until the end of the flight and provided those on the ground with firsthand accounts. They enabled the passengers to gain critical information, including the news that two aircraft had slammed into the World Trade Center.

Five calls described the intent of passengers and surviving crew members to revolt against the hijackers. According to one call, they voted on whether to rush the terrorists in an attempt to retake the plane. They decided, and acted.

At 9:57, the passenger assault began. Several passengers had terminated phone calls with loved ones in order to join the revolt. One of the callers ended her message as follows: *"Everyone's running up to first class. I've got to go. Bye."*

The cockpit voice recorder captured the sounds of the passenger assault muffled by the intervening cockpit door. Some family members who listened to the recording report that they can hear the voice of a loved one among the din. We cannot identify whose voices can be heard. But the assault was sustained.

In response, Jarrah immediately began to roll the airplane to the left and right, attempting to knock the passengers off balance. At 9:58:57, Jarrah told another hijacker in the cockpit to block the door. Jarrah continued to roll the airplane sharply left and right, but the assault continued. At 9:59:52, Jarrah changed tactics and pitched the nose of the airplane up and down to disrupt the assault. The recorder captured the sounds of loud thumps, crashes, shouts, and breaking glasses and plates. At 10:00:03, Jarrah stabilized the airplane.

Five seconds later, Jarrah asked, *"Is that it? Shall we finish it off?"* A hijacker responded, *"No. Not yet. When they all come, we finish it off."* The sounds of fighting continued outside the cockpit. Again, Jarrah pitched the nose of the aircraft up and down. At 10:00:26, a passenger in the background said, *"In the cockpit. If we don't we'll die!"* Sixteen seconds later, a passenger yelled, *"Roll it!"* Jarrah stopped the violent maneuvers about 10:01:00 and said, *"Allah is the greatest! Allah is the greatest!"* He then asked another hijacker in the cockpit. *"Is that it? I mean, shall we put it down?"* To which the other replied, *"Yes, put it in it, and pull it down."*

The passengers continued their assault and at 10:02:23, a hijacker said, *"Pull it down! Pull it down!"* The hijackers remained at the controls but must have judged that the passengers were only seconds from overcoming them. The airplane headed down; the control wheel was turned hard to the right. The airplane rolled onto its back, and one of the hijackers began shouting *"Allah is the greatest. Allah is the greatest."* With the sounds of the passenger counterattack continuing, the aircraft plowed into an empty field in Shanksville, Pennsylvania, at 580 miles per hour, about 20 minutes flying time from Washington, D.C.

Jarrah's objective was to crash his airliner into symbols of the American Republic, the Capitol or the White House. He was defeated by the alerted, unarmed passengers of United 93.[1]

Conclusion

More than 2,600 people died at the World Trade Center; 125 died at the Pentagon; 256 died on the four planes. The death toll surpassed that at Pearl Harbor in December 1941. This immeasurable pain was inflicted by 19 young Arabs acting at the behest of Islamist extremists headquartered in distant Afghanistan. Some had been in the United States for more than a year, mixing with the rest of the population. Though four had training as pilots, most were not well-educated. Most spoke English poorly, some hardly at all. In groups of four or five, carrying with them only small knives, box cutters, and cans of Mace or pepper spray, they had hijacked the four planes and turned them into deadly guided missiles.[2]

Questions

1. How were the highjackers able to overcome security measures?

2. What was the purpose of highjacking trans-continental flights?

3. How did the FAA respond to the highjackings?

4. Would similar highjackings succeed today?

## Chapter 3

9-11 Analysis

Objectives

- Explain how the events of 9-11 should have been anticipated.

- Understand the roles and responsibilities of the different agencies protecting America on 9-11.

- Describe how the various agencies failed to prevent the attacks of 9-11.

- Identify policies that unwittingly supported the terrorist efforts.

- Discuss the difficulties encountered by emergency personnel responding to 9-11.

Introduction

On November 27, 2002, Congress and the President created the National Commission on Terrorist Attacks Upon the United States (Public Law 107-306) to investigate the "facts and circumstances relating to the terrorist attacks of September 11, 2001." Later known as the "9-11 Commission", the bi-partisan panel released its 585-page report July 22, 2004. The following analysis is excerpted from the "9/11 Report".

A Nation Transformed

At 8:46 on the morning of September 11, 2001, the United States became a nation transformed.

An airliner traveling at hundreds of miles per hour and carrying some 10,000 gallons of jet fuel plowed into the North Tower of the World Trade Center in Lower Manhattan. At 9:03, a second airliner hit the South Tower. Fire and smoke billowed upward. Steel, glass, ash, and bodies fell below. The Twin Towers, where up to 50,000 people worked each day, both collapsed less than 90 minutes later.

At 9:37 that same morning, a third airliner slammed into the western face of the Pentagon. At 10:03, a fourth airliner crashed in a field in southern Pennsylvania.

More than 2,600 people died at the World Trade Center; 125 died at the Pentagon; 256 died on the four planes.

This immeasurable pain was inflicted by 19 young Arabs acting at the behest of Islamist extremists headquartered in distant Afghanistan. Some had been in the United States for more than a year, mixing with the rest of the population. Though four had training as pilots, most were not well-educated. Most spoke English poorly, some hardly at all. In groups of four or five, carrying with them only small knives, box cutters, and cans of Mace or pepper spray, they had hijacked the four planes and turned them into deadly guided missiles.

The 9/11 attacks were a shock, but they should not have come as a surprise. Islamist extremists had given plenty of warning that they meant to kill Americans indiscriminately and in large numbers.

A Shock, Not a Surprise

The 9/11 attacks were a shock, but they should not have come as a surprise. Islamist extremists had given plenty of warning that they meant to kill Americans indiscriminately and in large numbers. Although Usama Bin Ladin himself would not emerge as a signal threat until the late 1990s, the threat of Islamist terrorism grew over the decade.

In February 1993, a group led by Ramzi Yousef tried to bring down the World Trade Center with a truck bomb. They killed six and wounded a thousand. Plans by Omar Abdel Rahman and others to blow up the Holland and Lincoln tunnels and other New York City landmarks were frustrated when the plotters were arrested. In October 1993, Somali tribesmen shot down U.S. helicopters, killing 18 and wounding 73 in an incident that came to be known as

"Black Hawk down." Years later it would be learned that those Somali tribesmen had received help from al Qaeda.

In early 1995, police in Manila uncovered a plot by Ramzi Yousef to blow up a dozen U.S. airliners while they were flying over the Pacific. In November 1995, a car bomb exploded outside the office of the U.S. program manager for the Saudi National Guard in Riyadh, killing five Americans and two others. In June 1996, a truck bomb demolished the Khobar Towers apartment complex in Dhahran, Saudi Arabia, killing 19 U.S. servicemen and wounding hundreds. The attack was carried out primarily by Saudi Hezbollah, an organization that had received help from the government of Iran.

Until 1997, the U.S. intelligence community viewed Bin Ladin as a financier of terrorism, not as a terrorist leader. In February 1998, Usama Bin Ladin and four others issued a self-styled fatwa, publicly declaring that it was God's decree that every Muslim should try his utmost to kill any American, military or civilian, anywhere in the world, because of American "occupation" of Islam's holy places and aggression against Muslims.

In August 1998, Bin Ladin's group, al Qaeda, carried out near-simultaneous truck bomb attacks on the U.S. embassies in Nairobi, Kenya, and Dar es Salaam, Tanzania. The attacks killed 224 people, including 12 Americans, and wounded thousands more.

In December 1999, Jordanian police foiled a plot to bomb hotels and other sites frequented by American tourists, and a U.S. Customs agent arrested Ahmed Ressam at the U.S. Canadian border as he was smuggling in explosives intended for an attack on Los Angeles International Airport.

In October 2000, an al Qaeda team in Aden, Yemen, used a motorboat filled with explosives to blow a hole in the side of a destroyer, the USS Cole, almost sinking the vessel and killing 17 American sailors.

The 9/11 attacks on the World Trade Center and the Pentagon were far more elaborate, precise, and destructive than any of these earlier assaults. But by September 2001, the executive branch of the U.S. government, the Congress, the news media, and the American public had received clear warning that Islamist terrorists meant to kill Americans in high numbers.

The August 1998 bombings of U.S. embassies in Kenya and Tanzania established al Qaeda as a potent adversary of the United States.

1998 to September 11, 2001

The August 1998 bombings of U.S. embassies in Kenya and Tanzania established al Qaeda as a potent adversary of the United States.

After launching cruise missile strikes against al Qaeda targets in Afghanistan and Sudan in retaliation for the embassy bombings, the Clinton administration applied diplomatic pressure to try to persuade the Taliban regime in Afghanistan to expel Bin Ladin. The administration also devised covert operations to use CIA-paid foreign agents to capture or kill Bin Ladin and his chief lieutenants. These actions did not stop Bin Ladin or dislodge al Qaeda from its sanctuary.

By late 1998 or early 1999, Bin Ladin and his advisers had agreed on an idea brought to them by Khalid Sheikh Mohammed (KSM) called the "planes operation." It would eventually culminate in the 9/11 attacks. Bin Ladin and his chief of operations, Mohammed Atef, occupied undisputed leadership positions atop al Qaeda. Within al Qaeda, they relied heavily on the ideas and enterprise of strong-willed field commanders, such as KSM, to carry out worldwide terrorist operations.

KSM claims that his original plot was even grander than those carried out on 9/11—ten planes would attack targets on both the East and West coasts of the United States. This plan was modified by Bin Ladin, KSM said, owing to its scale and complexity. Bin Ladin provided KSM with four initial operatives for suicide plane attacks within the United States, and in the fall of 1999 training for the attacks began. New recruits included four from a cell of expatriate Muslim extremists who had clustered together in Hamburg, Germany. One became the tactical commander of the operation in the United States: Mohamed Atta.

U.S. intelligence frequently picked up reports of attacks planned by al Qaeda. Working with foreign security services, the CIA broke up some al Qaeda cells. The core of Bin Ladin's organization nevertheless remained intact. In December 1999, news about the arrests of the terrorist cell in Jordan and the arrest of a terrorist at the U.S.-Canadian border became part of a "millennium alert." The government was galvanized, and the public was on alert for any possible attack.

U.S. intelligence frequently picked up reports of attacks planned by al Qaeda. Working with foreign security services, the CIA broke up some al Qaeda cells. The core of Bin Ladin's organization nevertheless remained intact.

In January 2000, the intense intelligence effort glimpsed and then lost sight of two operatives destined for the "planes operation." Spotted in Kuala Lumpur, the pair were lost passing through Bangkok. On January 15, 2000, they arrived in Los Angeles.

After arriving in California, the two al Qaeda operatives sought out and found a group of ideologically like-minded Muslims with roots in Yemen and Saudi Arabia, individuals mainly associated with a young Yemeni and others who attended a mosque in San Diego. After a brief stay in Los Angeles, the al Qaeda operatives lived openly in San Diego under their true names. They managed to avoid attracting much attention.

By the summer of 2000, three of the four Hamburg cell members had arrived on the East Coast of the United States and had begun pilot training. In early 2001, a fourth future hijacker pilot, Hani Hanjour, journeyed to Arizona with another operative, Nawaf al Hazmi, and conducted his refresher pilot training there. A number of al Qaeda operatives had spent time in Arizona during the 1980s and early 1990s.

During 2000, President Bill Clinton and his advisers renewed diplomatic efforts to get Bin Ladin expelled from Afghanistan. They also renewed secret efforts with some of the Taliban's opponents—the Northern Alliance—to get enough intelligence to attack Bin Ladin directly. Diplomatic efforts centered on the new military government in Pakistan, and they did not succeed. The efforts with the Northern Alliance revived an inconclusive and secret debate about whether the United States should take sides in Afghanistan's civil war and support the Taliban's enemies. The CIA also produced a plan to improve intelligence collection on al Qaeda, including the use of a small, unmanned airplane with a video camera, known as the Predator.

After the October 2000 attack on the USS Cole, evidence accumulated that it had been launched by al Qaeda operatives, but without confirmation that Bin Ladin had given the order. The Taliban had earlier been warned that it would be held responsible for another Bin Ladin attack on the United States. The CIA described its findings as a "preliminary judgment"; President Clinton and his chief advisers were waiting for a conclusion before deciding whether to take military action. The military alternatives remained unappealing to them.

The transition to the new Bush administration in late 2000 and early 2001 took place with the Cole issue still pending. President George W. Bush and his chief advisers accepted that al Qaeda was responsible for the attack on the Cole, but did not like the options available for a response.

The Bush administration began developing a new strategy with the stated goal of eliminating the al Qaeda threat within three to five years. During the spring and summer of 2001, U.S. intelligence agencies received a stream of warnings that al Qaeda planned, as one report put it, "something very, very, very big." Director of Central Intelligence George Tenet stated, " The system was blinking red."

Although Bin Ladin was determined to strike in the United States, as President Clinton had been told and President Bush was reminded in a Presidential Daily Brief article briefed to him in August 2001, the specific threat information pointed overseas. Numerous precautions were taken overseas. Domestic agencies were not effectively mobilized. The threat did not receive national media attention comparable to the millennium alert.

While the United States continued disruption efforts around the world, its emerging strategy to eliminate the al Qaeda threat was to include an enlarged covert action program in Afghanistan, as well as diplomatic strategies for Afghanistan and Pakistan. The process culminated during the summer of 2001 in a draft presidential directive and arguments about the Predator aircraft, which was soon to be deployed with a missile of its own, so that it might be used to attempt to kill Bin Ladin or his chief lieutenants. At a September 4 meeting, President Bush's chief advisers approved the draft directive of the strategy and endorsed the concept of arming the Predator. This directive on the al Qaeda strategy was awaiting President Bush's signature on September 11, 2001.

Though the "planes operation" was progressing, the plotters had problems of their own in 2001. Several possible participants dropped out; others could not gain entry into the United States (including one denial at a port of entry and visa denials not related to terrorism). One of the eventual pilots may have considered abandoning the planes operation. Zacarias Moussaoui, who showed up at a flight training school in Minnesota, may have been a candidate to replace him.

Some of the vulnerabilities of the plotters become clear in retrospect. Moussaoui aroused suspicion for seeking fast-track training on how to pilot large jet airliners. He was arrested on August 16, 2001, for violations of immigration

Some of the vulnerabilities of the plotters become clear in retrospect. Moussaoui aroused suspicion for seeking fast-track training on how to pilot large jet airliners.

regulations. In late August, officials in the intelligence community realized that the terrorists spotted in Southeast Asia in January 2000 had arrived in the United States.

These cases did not prompt urgent action. No one working on these late leads in the summer of 2001 connected them to the high level of threat reporting. In the words of one official, no analytic work foresaw the lightning that could connect the thundercloud to the ground.

As final preparations were under way during the summer of 2001, dissent emerged among al Qaeda leaders in Afghanistan over whether to proceed. The Taliban's chief, Mullah Omar, opposed attacking the United States. Although facing opposition from many of his senior lieutenants, Bin Ladin effectively overruled their objections, and the attacks went forward.

September 11, 2001

The day began with the 19 hijackers getting through a security checkpoint system that they had evidently analyzed and knew how to defeat. They took over the four flights, taking advantage of air crews and cockpits that were not prepared for the contingency of a suicide hijacking.

On 9/11, the defense of the U.S. airspace depended on close interaction between two federal agencies: the Federal Aviation Administration (FAA) and North American Aerospace Defense Command (NORAD).

On 9/11, the defense of the U.S. airspace depended on close interaction between two federal agencies: the Federal Aviation Administration (FAA) and North American Aerospace Defense Command (NORAD). Existing protocols on 9/11 were unsuited in every respect for an attack in which hijacked planes were used as weapons.

What ensued, was a hurried attempt to improvise a defense by civilians who had never handled a hijacked aircraft that attempted to disappear, and by a military unprepared for the transformation of commercial aircraft into weapons of mass destruction.

A shootdown authorization was not communicated to the NORAD air defense sector until 28 minutes after United 93 had crashed in Pennsylvania. Planes were scrambled, but ineffectively, as they did not know where to go or what target they were to intercept. And once the shootdown order was given, it was not communicated to the pilots. In short, while leaders in Washington believed that the fighters circling above them had been instructed to "take out" hostile aircraft, the only orders actually conveyed to the pilots were to "ID type and tail."

Like the national defense, the emergency response on 9/11 was necessarily improvised.

In New York City, the Fire Department of New York, the New York Police Department, and the Port Authority of New York and New Jersey, the building employees, and the occupants of the buildings did their best to cope with the effects of almost unimaginable events—unfolding furiously over 102 minutes. Casualties were nearly 100 percent at and above the impact zones and were very high among first responders who stayed in danger as they tried to save lives. Despite weaknesses in preparations for disaster, failure to achieve unified incident command, and inadequate communications among responding agencies, all but approximately one hundred of the thousands of civilians who worked below the impact zone escaped, often with help from the emergency responders.

At the Pentagon, while there were also problems of command and control, the emergency response was generally effective. The Incident Command System, a formalized management structure for emergency response in place in the National Capital Region, overcame the inherent complications of a response across local, state, and federal jurisdictions.

General Findings

Since the plotters were flexible and resourceful, it cannot be known whether any single step or series of steps would have defeated them. What can be said with confidence is that none of the measures adopted by the U.S. government from 1998 to 2001 disturbed or even delayed the progress of the al Qaeda plot. Across the government, there were failures of imagination, policy, capabilities, and management.

Imagination

The most important failure was one of imagination. We do not believe leaders understood the gravity of the threat. The terrorist danger from Bin Ladin and al Qaeda was not a major topic for policy debate among the public, the media, or in the Congress. Indeed, it barely came up during the 2000 presidential campaign.

Across the government, there were failures of imagination, policy, capabilities, and management.

Al Qaeda's new brand of terrorism presented challenges to U.S. governmental institutions that they were not well-designed to meet. Though top officials all said that they understood the danger, there was uncertainty among them as to whether this was just a new and especially venomous version of the ordinary terrorist threat the United States had lived with for decades, or it was indeed radically new, posing a threat beyond any yet experienced.

As late as September 4, 2001, Richard Clarke, the White House staffer long responsible for counterterrorism policy coordination, asserted that the government had not yet made up its mind how to answer the question: "Is al Qida [sic] a big deal?" A week later came the answer.

Policy

Terrorism was not the overriding national security concern for the U.S. government under either the Clinton or the pre-9/11 Bush administration.

The policy challenges were linked to this failure of imagination. Officials in both the Clinton and Bush administrations regarded a full U.S. invasion of Afghanistan as practically inconceivable before 9/11.

Capabilities

Before 9/11, the United States tried to solve the al Qaeda problem with the capabilities it had used in the last stages of the Cold War and its immediate aftermath. The capabilities were insufficient. Little was done to expand or reform them.

The CIA had minimal capacity to conduct paramilitary operations with its own personnel, and it did not seek a large-scale expansion of these capabilities before 9/11. The CIA also needed to improve its capability to collect intelligence from human agents.

At no point before 9/11 was the Department of Defense fully engaged in the mission of countering al Qaeda, even though this was perhaps the most dangerous foreign enemy threatening the United States.

America's homeland defenders faced outward. NORAD itself was barely able to retain any alert bases at all. Its planning scenarios occasionally considered the danger of hijacked aircraft being guided to American targets, but only aircraft that were coming from overseas.

The most serious weakness in agency capabilities were in the domestic arena. The FBI did not have the capability to link the collective knowledge of agents in the field to national priorities. Other domestic agencies deferred to the FBI.

FAA capabilities were weak. Any serious examination of the possibility of a suicide hijacking could have suggested changes to fix glaring vulnerabilities— expanding no-fly lists, searching passengers identified by the CAPPS screening system, deploying federal air marshals domestically, hardening cockpit doors, alerting air crews to a different kind of hijacking possibility than they had been trained to expect. Yet the FAA did not adjust either its own training or training with NORAD to take account of threats other than those experienced in the past.

The CIA had minimal capacity to conduct paramilitary operations with its own personnel, and it did not seek a large-scale expansion of these capabilities before 9/11. The CIA also needed to improve its capability to collect intelligence from human agents.

Management

The missed opportunities to thwart the 9/11 plot were also symptoms of a broader inability to adapt the way government manages problems to the new challenges of the twenty-first century. Action officers should have been able to draw on all available knowledge about al Qaeda in the government. Management should have ensured that information was shared and duties were clearly assigned across agencies, and across the foreign-domestic divide.

There were also broader management issues with respect to how top leaders set priorities and allocated resources. For instance, on December 4, 1998, DCI Tenet issued a directive to several CIA officials and the Deputy Director of Central Intelligence (DDCI) for Community Management, stating: *"We are at war. I want no resources or people spared in this effort, either inside CIA or the Community."* The memorandum had little overall effect on mobilizing the CIA or the intelligence community. This episode indicates the limitations of the DCI's authority over the direction of the intelligence community, including agencies within the Department of Defense.

The U.S. government did not find a way of pooling intelligence and using it to guide the planning and assignment of responsibilities for joint operations involving entities as disparate as the CIA, the FBI, the State Department, the military, and the agencies involved in homeland security.

Specific Findings

Unsuccessful Diplomacy

Beginning in February 1997, and through September 11, 2001, the U.S. government tried to use diplomatic pressure to persuade the Taliban regime in Afghanistan to stop being a sanctuary for al Qaeda, and to expel Bin Ladin to a country where he could face justice. These efforts included warnings and sanctions, but they all failed.

The U.S. government also pressed two successive Pakistani governments to demand that the Taliban cease providing a sanctuary for Bin Ladin and his organization and, failing that, to cut off their support for the Taliban. Before 9/11, the United States could not find a mix of incentives and pressure that would persuade Pakistan to reconsider its fundamental relationship with the Taliban.

From 1999 through early 2001, the United States pressed the United Arab Emirates, one of the Taliban's only travel and financial outlets to the outside world, to break off ties and enforce sanctions, especially those related to air travel to Afghanistan. These efforts achieved little before 9/11.

Saudi Arabia has been a problematic ally in combating Islamic extremism. Before 9/11, the Saudi and U.S. governments did not fully share intelligence information or develop an adequate joint effort to track and disrupt the finances of the al Qaeda organization. On the other hand, government officials of Saudi Arabia at the highest levels worked closely with top U.S. officials in major initiatives to solve the Bin Ladin problem with diplomacy.

[Senior military officials] did not want to risk significant collateral damage, and they did not want to miss Bin Ladin and thus make the United States look weak while making Bin Ladin look strong.

Lack of Military Options

In response to the request of policymakers, the military prepared an array of limited strike options for attacking Bin Ladin and his organization from May 1998 onward. When they briefed policymakers, the military presented both the pros and cons of those strike options and the associated risks. Policymakers expressed frustration with the range of options presented.

Following the August 20, 1998, missile strikes on al Qaeda targets in Afghanistan and Sudan, both senior military officials and policymakers placed great emphasis on actionable intelligence as the key factor in recommending or deciding to launch military action against Bin Ladin and his organization. They did not want to risk significant collateral damage, and they did not want to miss Bin Ladin and thus make the United States look weak while making Bin Ladin look strong. On three specific occasions in 1998–1999, intelligence was deemed credible enough to warrant planning for possible strikes to kill Bin

Ladin. But in each case the strikes did not go forward, because senior policymakers did not regard the intelligence as sufficiently actionable to offset their assessment of the risks.

The Director of Central Intelligence, policymakers, and military officials expressed frustration with the lack of actionable intelligence. Some officials inside the Pentagon, including those in the special forces and the counterterrorism policy office, also expressed frustration with the lack of military action. The Bush administration began to develop new policies toward al Qaeda in 2001, but military plans did not change until after 9/11.

Problems with the Intelligence Community

The intelligence community struggled throughout the 1990s and up to 9/11 to collect intelligence on and analyze the phenomenon of transnational terrorism. The combination of an overwhelming number of priorities, flat budgets, an outmoded structure, and bureaucratic rivalries resulted in an insufficient response to this new challenge.

Many dedicated officers worked day and night for years to piece together the growing body of evidence on al Qaeda and to understand the threats. Yet while there were many reports on Bin Laden and his growing al Qaeda organization, there was no comprehensive review of what the intelligence community knew and what it did not know, and what that meant. There was no National Intelligence Estimate on terrorism between 1995 and 9/11.

Before 9/11, no agency did more to attack al Qaeda than the CIA. But there were limits to what the CIA was able to achieve by disrupting terrorist activities abroad and by using proxies to try to capture Bin Ladin and his lieutenants in Afghanistan. CIA officers were aware of those limitations.

The FBI's approach to investigations was case specific, decentralized, and geared towards prosecution.

Problems with the FBI

From the time of the first World Trade Center attack in 1993, FBI and Department of Justice leadership in Washington and New York became increasingly concerned about the terrorist threat from Islamist extremists to U.S. interests, both at home and abroad. Throughout the 1990s, the FBI's counterterrorism efforts against international terrorist organizations included both intelligence and criminal investigations. The FBI's approach to investigations was case specific, decentralized, and geared towards prosecution. Significant FBI resources were devoted to after-the-fact investigations of major terrorist attacks, resulting in several prosecutions.

The FBI attempted several reform efforts aimed at strengthening its ability to prevent such attacks, but these reform efforts failed to implement organization-wide institutional change. On September 11, 2001, the FBI was limited in several areas critical to an effective preventive counterterrorism strategy. Those working counterterrorism matters did so despite limited intelligence collection and strategic analysis capabilities, limited capacity to share information both internally and externally, insufficient training, perceived legal barriers to sharing information, and inadequate resources.

Permeable Borders and Immigration Controls

There were opportunities for intelligence and law enforcement to exploit al Qaeda's travel vulnerabilities. Considered collectively, the 9/11 hijackers:

- included known al Qaeda operatives who could have been watchlisted;

- presented passports manipulated in a fraudulent manner;

- presented passports with suspicious indicators of extremism;

- made detectable false statements on visa applications;

- made false statements to border officials to gain entry into the United States; and

- violated immigration laws while in the United States.

Neither the State Department's consular officers nor the Immigration and Naturalization Service's inspectors and agents were ever considered full partners in a national counterterrorism effort. Protecting borders was not a national security issue before 9/11.

Permeable Aviation Security

Hijackers studied publicly available materials on the aviation security system and used items that had less metal content than a handgun and were most likely permissible. Though two of the hijackers were on the U.S. TIPOFF terrorist watchlist, the FAA did not use TIPOFF data. The hijackers had to beat only one layer of security—the security checkpoint process. Even though several hijackers were selected for extra screening by the CAPPS system, this led only to greater scrutiny of their checked baggage. Once on board, the hijackers were faced with aircraft personnel who were trained to be nonconfrontational in the event of a hijacking.

Protecting borders was not a national security issue before 9/11.

Financing

The 9/11 attacks cost somewhere between $400,000 and $500,000 to execute. The operatives spent more than $270,000 in the United States. Additional expenses included travel to obtain passports and visas, travel to the United States, expenses incurred by the plot leader and facilitators outside the United States, and expenses incurred by the people selected to be hijackers who ultimately did not participate.

The conspiracy made extensive use of banks in the United States. The hijackers opened accounts in their own names, using passports and other identification documents. Their transactions were unremarkable and essentially invisible amid the billions of dollars flowing around the world every day.

To date, the origin of the money used for the 9/11 attacks has not been determined. Al Qaeda had many sources of funding and a pre-9/11 annual budget estimated at $30 million. If a particular source of funds had dried up, al Qaeda could easily have found enough money elsewhere to fund the attack.

An Improvised Homeland Defense

The civilian and military defenders of the nation's airspace—FAA and NORAD—were unprepared for the attacks launched against them. Given that lack of preparedness, they attempted and failed to improvise an effective homeland defense against an unprecedented challenge.

The events of that morning do not reflect discredit on operational personnel. NORAD's Northeast Air Defense Sector personnel reached out for information and made the best judgments they could based on information they received. Individual FAA controllers, facility managers, and command center managers were creative and agile in recommending a nationwide alert, ground-stopping local traffic, ordering all aircraft nationwide to land, and executing that unprecedented order flawlessly.

At more senior levels, communication was poor. Senior military and FAA leaders had no effective communication with each other. The chain of command did not function well. The President could not reach some senior officials. The Secretary of Defense did not enter the chain of command until the morning's key events were over. Air National Guard units with different rules of engagement were scrambled without the knowledge of the President, NORAD, or the National Military Command Center.

Effective decision making in New York was hampered by problems in command and control and in internal communications.

Emergency Response

The civilians, firefighters, police officers, emergency medical technicians, and emergency management professionals exhibited steady determination and resolve under horrifying, overwhelming conditions on 9/11. Their actions saved lives and inspired a nation.

Effective decision making in New York was hampered by problems in command and control and in internal communications. Within the Fire Department of New York, this was true for several reasons: the magnitude of the incident was unforeseen; commanders had difficulty communicating with their units; more units were actually dispatched than were ordered by the chiefs; some units self-dispatched; and once units arrived at the World Trade Center, they were neither comprehensively accounted for nor coordinated. The Port Authority's response was hampered by the lack both of standard operating procedures and of radios capable of enabling multiple commands to respond to an incident in unified fashion. The New York Police Department, because of its history of mobilizing thousands of officers for major events requiring crowd control, had a technical capability and protocols more easily adapted to an incident of the magnitude of 9/11.

Congress

The Congress, like the executive branch, responded slowly to the rise of transnational terrorism as a threat to national security. The legislative branch adjusted little and did not restructure itself to address changing threats. Its attention to terrorism was episodic and splintered across several committees. The Congress gave little guidance to executive branch agencies on terrorism, did not reform them in any significant way to meet the threat, and did not systematically perform robust oversight to identify, address, and attempt to resolve the many problems in national security and domestic agencies that became apparent in the aftermath of 9/11.[1]

Conclusion

In pursuing its mandate, the 9/11 Commission reviewed more than 2.5 million pages of documents and interviewed more than 1,200 individuals in ten countries, including nearly every senior official from the Bush and Clinton administrations. Their aim was not to assign individual blame, but to provide the fullest possible account of the events surrounding 9/11 and to identify lessons learned.

The Commission learned about an enemy who is sophisticated, patient, disciplined, and lethal. The enemy rallies broad support in the Arab and Muslim world demanding redress of political grievances, but its hostility toward the United States and American values is limitless. Its purpose is to rid the world of religious and political pluralism, the plebiscite, and equal rights for women. It makes no distinction between military and civilian targets. Collateral damage is not in its lexicon.

The Commission learned that the institutions charged with protecting the nation's borders, civil aviation, and national security did not understand how grave this threat could be, and did not adjust their policies, plans, and practices to deter or defeat it. The Commission learned about fault lines within our government – between foreign and domestic intelligence, and between and within agencies. It learned of the pervasive problems of managing and sharing information across a large and unwieldy government that had been built in a different era to confront different dangers.

In chronicling the terrible losses in its report, the Commission strove to create something positive – an America that is safer, stronger, and wiser.[2]

Questions

1. Why should the events of 9-11 have been anticipated?

2. Why didn't the DoD and CIA stop Bin Ladin in Afghanistan?

3. How was al Qaeda able to elude the FBI, NORAD, and CIA?

4. List some of the failures of the FAA on 9-11.

5. How were fire and rescue operations hindered on 9-11?

Chapter 4

Terrorist Threat

Objectives

- Describe the history of terrorism.

- Know the definition of terrorism according to the National Strategy for Homeland Security.

- Discuss changing terrorist tactics that made terrorism a significant threat.

- Understand the motives and objectives of terrorists.

- Summarize the al Qaeda threat.

- Explain the ultimate threat posed by terrorism today.

Introduction

September 11th 2001 was a wakeup call to the American public that the United States isn't immune to the effects of international terrorism. The American government, aware of the threat, was nonetheless unprepared for what happened. To prevent it from happening again, the president signed the Homeland Security Act establishing the Department of Homeland Security, November 25th 2002.[1]

Historical Perspective

Terrorism has been practiced throughout history and throughout the world. The ancient Greek historian Xenophon (c. 431 - c. 350 BC) wrote of the effectiveness of psychological warfare against enemy populations. Roman emperors such as Tiberius (reigned AD 14 - 37) and Caligula (reigned AD 37 - 41) used banishment, expropriation of property, and execution as means to discourage opposition to their rule.[2]

The word 'terrorism' entered into European languages in the wake of the French revolution of 1789. In the early revolutionary years, it was largely by violence that governments in Paris tried to impose their radical new order on reluctant citizenry. As a result, the first meaning of the word 'terrorism', as recorded by the Academie Francaise in 1798, was 'system or rule of terror'.[3]

Today, there's no single, universally accepted, definition of terrorism.[4] The National Strategy for Homeland Security characterizes terrorism as:

> *"Any premeditated, unlawful act dangerous to human life or public welfare that is intended to intimidate or coerce civilian populations or governments."*
>
> *– National Strategy for Homeland Security, July 2002*

"Terrorism: Any premeditated, unlawful act dangerous to human life or public welfare that is intended to intimidate or coerce civilian populations or governments."

– National Strategy for Homeland Security, July 2002

During the 19th century, terrorism underwent a fateful transformation, coming to be associated, as it still is today, with non-governmental groups. One such group—the small band of Russian revolutionaries of 'Narodnaya Volya' (the people's will) in 1878-81—developed certain ideas that were to become the hallmark of subsequent terrorism in many countries. They believed in the targeted killing of the 'leaders of oppression'; they were convinced that the developing technologies of the age—symbolized by bombs and bullets—enabled them to strike directly and discriminately. Above all, they believed that the Tsarist system against which they were fighting was fundamentally rotten. They propagated what has remained the common terrorist delusion that violent acts would spark off revolution. Their efforts led to the assassination of Tsar Alexander II on 13 March 1881—but that event failed completely to have the revolutionary effects of which the terrorists had dreamed.

Terrorism continued for many decades to be associated primarily with the assassination of political leaders and heads of state. In general, the extensive practice of assassination in the 20th century seldom had the particular effects for which the terrorists hoped.

In the half-century after World War Two, terrorism broadened well beyond assassination of political leaders and heads of state. In certain European colonies, terrorist movements developed, often with two distinct purposes. The first was obvious: to put pressure on the colonial powers (such as Britain, France, and the Netherlands) to hasten their withdrawal. The second was more subtle: to intimidate the indigenous population into supporting a particular group's claims to leadership of the emerging post-colonial state. Sometimes these strategies had some success, but not always. India's achievement of independence in 1947 was mainly the result, not of terrorism, but of the movement of non-violent civil disobedience led by Gandhi. In Malaya, communist terrorists launched a major campaign in 1948 but they failed due to a mixture of determined British military opposition and a program of political reform leading to independence.

Terrorism did not disappear as European nations relinquished their colonial holdings in the 1950s and 1960s. It continued in many regions in response to many circumstances. In South-East Asia, the Middle East and Latin America there were killings of policemen and local officials, hostage-takings, hijackings of aircraft, and bombings of buildings. In many actions, civilians became targets. In some cases governments became involved in supporting terrorism, almost invariably at arm's length so as to be deniable. The causes espoused by terrorists encompassed not just revolutionary socialism and nationalism, but also in a few cases religious doctrines. Law, even the modest body of rules setting some limits in armed conflict between states, could be ignored in a higher cause.

Change in Tactics

How did certain terrorist movements come to be associated with indiscriminate killings? When in September 1970 Palestinian terrorists hijacked several large aircraft and blew them up on the ground in Jordan but let the passengers free, these acts were viewed by many with as much fascination as horror. Then in September 1972, eleven Israelis were murdered in a Palestinian attack on Israeli athletes at the Olympic Games at Munich. This event showed a determination to kill: the revulsion felt in many countries was stronger than two years earlier.[5]

The terrorist attacks of the 1970s and 1980s had clear political objectives. These attacks resulted in just enough bloodshed and loss of life to gain attention to the terrorists' cause yet not enough to alienate them from the public support they sought. Bombings, kidnappings, and aircraft hijacking were accomplished by declared, identifiable groups with specific political goals in mind.

In contrast, the decade of the 1990s produced a different type of terrorism—terrorism designed to produce massive casualties with little regard for distinct political goals and often no claims of responsibility.[6] The change in tactics was noted with great concern by William Studeman, acting director of the Central Intelligence Agency, in 1995 testimony before Congress:

> "Mr. Chairman, we have seen a most disturbing change in the nature of the terrorist threat over the recent past, and this change will make

In contrast, the decade of the 1990s produced a different type of terrorism—terrorism designed to produce massive casualties with little regard for distinct political goals and often no claims of responsibility.

the world an increasingly dangerous place for Americans. In general, international terrorists today are focusing less on hostage-taking and hijackings and more on the indiscriminate slaughter of innocent men, women, and children. Although the number of international terrorist incidents has decreased over the past 10 years, the trend is toward a higher number of civilian casualties, more extensive property damage, and increasingly devastating effects on economies."

—Testimony of Acting DCI William O. Studeman, Omnibus Counter-terrorism Act of 1995, April 6, 1995

As evidence of the new trend, Mr. Studeman cited the 1993 bombing of the World Trade center that resulted in six deaths and over 1,000 injuries, the 1994 bombing of a Jewish cultural center in Buenos Aires that left nearly 100 dead and over 250 wounded, and the 1995 gassing in the Tokyo subway that killed 10 people and injured 5,500 more.[7]

In 1996, Saudi dissidents killed 19 U.S. airmen and wounded 240 others in attacks against the Khobar Towers barracks in Dahran Saudi Arabia. In 1998, simultaneous attacks against U.S. embassies in Nairobi, Kenya, and Dar es Salaam, Tanzania, killed 224 and wounded 4,500 more.[8]

Mass Casualties

Alarmed by the growing ferocity of terrorist attacks, Congress in 1998 established the National Commission on Terrorism. In a report issued June 5th 2000, the NTC attributed the trend toward higher casualties, in part on the changing motivation of terrorists:

> *"Religiously motivated terrorist groups, such as Usama bin Ladin's group, al-Qaida, which is believed to have bombed the U.S. Embassies in Africa, represent a growing trend toward hatred of the United States. Other terrorists groups are driven by visions of a post apocalyptic future or by ethnic hatred. Such groups may lack a concrete political goal other than to punish enemies by killing as many of them as possible, seemingly without concern about alienating sympathizers. Increasingly, attacks are less likely to be followed by claims of responsibility or lists of political demands."*
>
> *—Countering the Changing Threat of International Terrorism, Report of the National Commission on Terrorism, June 5, 2000*

While the NTC highlighted the growing threat represented by extremist Islamic groups, it also noted not all terrorist acts are religiously motivated nor perpetrated by foreign nationals. In April 1995 the Alfred P. Murrah Federal Building in Oklahoma City was destroyed by a car bomb killing 168 innocent civilians. Timothy McVeigh, a Gulf War veteran, was arrested by an Oklahoma Highway Patrolman within an hour of the explosion. At his trial, the United States Government asserted that the motivation for the attack was to avenge the deaths of Branch Davidians at Waco, Texas, whom McVeigh believed had been murdered by agents of the federal government.[9]

Classifying Terrorism

The Federal Bureau of Investigation distinguishes between domestic and international terrorism, depending on the origin, base, and objectives of the terrorist organization:

> *"Domestic terrorism is the unlawful use, or threatened use, of force or violence by a group or individual based and operating entirely within the United States or Puerto Rico without foreign direction, committed against persons or property to intimidate or coerce a government, the civilian population, or any segment thereof in furtherance of political or social objectives.*
>
> *International terrorism involves violent acts or acts dangerous to human life that are a violation of the criminal laws of the United States or any state, or that would be a criminal violation if committed within the jurisdiction of the United States or any state. These acts appear to be intended to intimidate or coerce a civilian population, influence the policy of a government by intimidation or coercion, or affect the conduct of a government by assassination or kidnapping. International terrorist acts occur outside the United States, or transcend national boundaries in terms of the means by which they are accomplished, the persons they appear intended to coerce, or the locale in which their perpetrators operate or seek asylum."*
>
> —Federal Bureau of Investigation, Terrorism in the United States, 1998

Although terrorism is defined in different ways by various U.S. government agencies, it is generally accepted that terrorism is a crime designed to coerce others into actions they would not otherwise take or into refraining from actions that they desire to take. Today's terrorists, like their predecessors, seek to instill fear, undermine government authority, and possibly goad the government into overreacting to the incident or threat. What has changed in the past decade is the willingness of the terrorist to inflict indiscriminate casualties. The possible inclusion of weapons of mass destruction in the terrorists' arsenal now makes this an even more dangerous proposition.[10]

al Qaeda

The attacks of September 11th 2001 were perpetrated by international terrorists and members of an extreme Islamic group known as al Qaeda founded by Saudi dissident Osama bin Laden.

In the 1980s, young Muslims from around the world went to Afghanistan to join as volunteers in a jihad (or holy struggle) against the Soviet Union. A wealthy Saudi, Osama bin Laden, was one of them. Following the defeat of the Soviets in the late 1980s, bin Laden and others formed al Qaeda ("the base") to mobilize jihads elsewhere.

The history, culture, and body of beliefs from which bin Laden shapes and spreads his message are largely unknown to many Americans. Seizing on symbols of Islam's past greatness, he promises to restore pride to people who consider themselves the victims of successive foreign masters. He uses cultural and religious allusions to the holy Qur'an and some of its interpreters. He appeals to people disoriented by cyclonic changes as they confront modernity and globalization. His rhetoric selectively draws from multiple sources— Islam, history, and the region's political and economic malaise.

Bin Laden also stresses grievances against the United States widely shared in the Muslim world. He inveighed against the presence of U.S. troops in Saudi Arabia, which is the home of Islam's holiest sites, and against other U.S. policies in the Middle East.

Upon this political and ideological foundation, Bin Laden built over the course of a decade a dynamic and lethal organization. He built an infrastructure and organization in Afghanistan that could attract, train, and use recruits against ever more ambitious targets. He rallied new zealots and new money with each demonstration of al Qaeda's capability. He forged a close alliance with the Taliban, a regime providing sanctuary for al Qaeda.

Since 9/11, the United States and its allies have killed or captured a majority of al Qaeda's leadership, toppled the Taliban, which gave al Qaeda sanctuary in Afghanistan; and severely damaged the organization. Yet terrorist attacks continue. Even as we have thwarted attacks, nearly everyone expects they will come. How can this be?

Killing or capturing [Bin Laden], while extremely important, would not end terror. His message of inspiration to a new generation of terrorists would continue.

The problem is that al Qaeda represents an ideological movement, not a finite group of people. It initiates and inspires, even if it no longer directs. In this way it has transformed itself into a decentralized force. Bin Laden may be limited in his ability to organize major attacks from his hideouts. Yet killing or capturing him, while extremely important, would not end terror. His message of inspiration to a new generation of terrorists would continue.[11]

The Terrorist Threat

Although many analysts agree that terrorists are most likely to use conventional explosives, their use of a WMD in the U.S. is now seen as a possibility.[12]

Writing before September 11th, 2001, the United States Commission on National Security/21st Century stated:

> *"The combination of unconventional weapons proliferation with the persistence of international terrorism will end the relative invulnerability of the U.S. homeland to catastrophic attack. A direct attack against American citizens on American soil is likely over the next quarter century."*
>
> —*U.S. Commission on National Security/21st Century, February 15, 2001*

Until recently, terrorism to many Americans was a remote, if frightening possibility that affected only individuals or groups outside the territorial boundaries of the United States. Events of the past decade indicate that the terrorist threat has changed significantly in ways that make it more dangerous and more difficult to counter. Although terrorists have long intended to harm the public, now they may posses much greater capabilities to do so.[13]

In December 2000, the Central Intelligence Agency and the National Intelligence Council forecast the following trends that may affect the future of the United States:

> *"Asymmetric threats in which state and non-state adversaries avoid direct engagements with the US military but devise strategies, tactics, and weapons—some improved by "sidewise" technology—to minimize US strengths and exploit perceived weaknesses.*
>
> *Internal conflicts stemming from religious, ethnic or political disputes will remain at current numbers or even increase in number.*
>
> *Prospects will grow that more sophisticated weaponry, including weapons of mass destruction—indigenously produced or externally acquired—will get into the hands of state and non-state belligerents, some hostile to the United States. The likelihood will increase over this period that WMD will be used either against the United States or its forces, facilities, and interests overseas.*
>
> *Chemical and biological threats to the United States will become more widespread; such capabilities are easier to develop, hide, and deploy than nuclear weapons. Some terrorists or insurgents will attempt to use such weapons against US interests—against the United States itself, its forces or facilities overseas, or its allies."*
>
> —Central Intelligence Agency, *Global Trends 2015,* December 2000

Conclusion

The consequences of failing to deter, detect, or preempt terrorist attacks, some possibly with WMD, would be devastating. In addition to the tragedy of hundreds of thousands of dead and injured citizens, the long and lasting serious economic and psychological damage to American society could well prove to be the terrorists' greatest victory.[14]

Questions

1. How long has terrorism existed?

2. How was the term "terrorism" originally applied?

3. How did terrorism evolve over time?

4. List some of the motives of modern terrorists.

5. How have terrorist objectives changed since 1995?

6. Would terrorism end if Bin Laden was captured?

7. What is the ultimate threat posed by terrorism today?

Chapter 5

Islamic Extremism

Objectives

- Discuss the history of Islam.

- Know the two major sects of Islam.

- Describe the political evolution of Islamic states.

- Understand the minority views of fundamental Islamists.

- Discuss the appeal of al Qaeda in the Muslim world.

- Explain Bin Ladin's objective.

Introduction

Islam is not the enemy. It is not synonymous with terror. Nor does Islam teach terror. Lives guided by religious faith, including literal beliefs in holy scriptures, are common to every religion, and represent no threat. The following dissertation excerpted from the "9/11 Report" examines Islamic extremism representing a minority of "violent zealots" following what the 9/11 Commission calls a "perversion of Islam".

A Declaration of War

In February 1998, the 40-year-old Saudi exile Usama Bin Ladin and a fugitive Egyptian physician, Ayman al Zawahiri, arranged from their Afghan headquarters for an Arabic newspaper in London to publish what they termed a fatwa issued in the name of a "World Islamic Front." A fatwa is normally an interpretation of Islamic law by a respected Islamic authority, but neither Bin Ladin, Zawahiri, nor the three others who signed this statement were scholars of Islamic law. Claiming that America had declared war against God and his messenger, they called for the murder of any American, anywhere on earth, as the "individual duty for every Muslim who can do it in any country in which it is possible to do it."

Islam is not the enemy. It is not synonymous with terror. Nor does Islam teach terror.

Three months later, when interviewed in Afghanistan by ABC-TV, Bin Ladin enlarged on these themes. He claimed it was more important for Muslims to kill Americans than to kill other infidels. *"It is far better for anyone to kill a single American soldier than to squander his efforts on other activities,"* he said. Asked whether he approved of terrorism and of attacks on civilians, he replied: *"We believe that the worst thieves in the world today and the worst terrorists are the Americans. Nothing can stop you except perhaps retaliation in kind. We do not have to differentiate between military or civilians. As far as we are concerned, they are all targets."*

Though novel for its open endorsement of indiscriminate killing, Bin Ladin's 1998 declaration was only the latest in the long series of his public and private calls since 1992 that singled out the United States for attack.

In August 1996, Bin Ladin had issued his own self-styled fatwa calling on Muslims to drive American soldiers out of Saudi Arabia. The long, disjointed document condemned the Saudi monarchy for allowing the presence of an army of infidels in a land with the sites most sacred to Islam, and celebrated recent suicide bombings of American military facilities in the Kingdom. It praised the 1983 suicide bombing in Beirut that killed 241 U.S. Marines, the 1992 bombing in Aden, and especially the 1993 firefight in Somalia after which the United States "left the area carrying disappointment, humiliation, defeat and your dead with you."

Bin Ladin said in his ABC interview that he and his followers had been preparing in Somalia for another long struggle, like that against the Soviets in Afghanistan, but *"the United States rushed out of Somalia in shame and disgrace."* Citing the Soviet army's withdrawal from Afghanistan as proof that a ragged army of dedicated Muslims could overcome a superpower, he told the interviewer: *"We are certain that we shall—with the grace of Allah—prevail over the Americans."* He went on to warn that *"If the present injustice continues..., it will inevitably move the battle to American soil."*

Plans to attack the United States were developed with unwavering singlemindedness throughout the 1990s. Bin Ladin saw himself as called "to follow in the footsteps of the Messenger and to communicate his message to all nations," and to serve as the rallying point and organizer of a new kind of war to destroy America and bring the world to Islam.

Bin Ladin's Appeal in the Islamic World

It is the story of eccentric and violent ideas sprouting in the fertile ground of political and social turmoil. It is the story of an organization poised to seize its historical moment. How did Bin Ladin—with his call for the indiscriminate killing of Americans—win thousands of followers and some degree of approval from millions more?

The history, culture, and body of beliefs from which Bin Ladin has shaped and spread his message are largely unknown to many Americans. Seizing on symbols of Islam's past greatness, he promises to restore pride to people who consider themselves the victims of successive foreign masters. He uses cultural and religious allusions to the holy Qur'an and some of its interpreters. He appeals to people disoriented by cyclonic change as they confront modernity and globalization. His rhetoric selectively draws from multiple sources—Islam, history, and the region's political and economic malaise. He also stresses grievances against the Untied States widely shared in the Muslim world. He inveighed against the presence of U.S. troops in Saudi Arabia, the home of Islam's holiest sites. He spoke of the suffering of the Iraqi people as a result of sanctions imposed after the Gulf War, and he protested U.S. support for Israel.

Islam is divided into two main branches, Sunni and Shia. Shia hold that any leader of the Ummah must be a direct descendant of the Prophet; Sunni argue that lineal descent is not required if the candidate meets other standards of faith and knowledge.

Islam

Islam (a word that literally means "surrender to the will of God") arose in Arabia with what Muslims believe are a series of revelations to the Prophet Mohammed from the one and only God, the God of Abraham and of Jesus. These revelations, conveyed by the angel Gabriel, are recorded in the Qur'an. Muslims believe that these revelations, given to the greatest and last of a chain of prophets stretching from Abraham through Jesus, complete God's message to humanity. The Hadith, which recount Mohammed's sayings and deeds as recorded by his contemporaries, are another fundamental source. A third key element is the Sharia, the code of law derived from the Qur'an and the Hadith.

Islam is divided into two main branches, Sunni and Shia. Soon after the Prophet's death, the question of choosing a new leader, or caliph, for the Muslim community, or "Ummah", arose. Initially, his successors could be drawn from the Prophet's contemporaries, but with time, this was no longer possible. Those who became the Shia held that any leader of the Ummah must be a direct descendant of the Prophet; those who became the Sunni argued that lineal descent was not required if the candidate met other standards of faith and knowledge. After bloody struggles, the Sunni became (and remain) the majority sect. (The Shia are dominant in Iran.) The Caliphate—the institutionalized leadership of the Ummah—thus was a Sunni institution that continued until 1924, first under Arab and eventually under Ottoman Turkish control.

Many Muslims look back at the century after the revelations to the Prophet Mohammed as a golden age. Its memory is strongest among the Arabs. What happened then—the spread of Islam from the Arabian Peninsula throughout the Middle East, North Africa, and even into Europe within less than a century—seemed, and seems, miraculous. Nostalgia for Islam's past glory remains a powerful force.

Islam is both a faith and a code of conduct for all aspects of life. For many Muslims, a good government would be one guided by the moral principles of their faith. This does not necessarily translate into a desire for clerical rule and the abolition of a secular state. It does mean that some Muslims tend to be uncomfortable with distinctions between religion and state, though Muslim rulers throughout history have readily separated the two.

To extremists, however, such divisions, as well as the existence of parliaments and legislation, only prove these rulers to be false Muslims usurping God's authority over all aspects of life. Periodically, the Islamic world has seen surges of what, for want of a better term, is often labeled "fundamentalism." Denouncing waywardness among the faithful, some clerics have appealed for a return to observance of the literal teachings of the Qur'an and Hadith. One scholar from the fourteenth century from who Bin Ladin selectively quotes, Ibn Taimiyyah, condemned both corrupt rulers and clerics who failed to criticize them. He urged Muslims to read the Qur'an and the Hadith for themselves, not to depend solely on learned interpreters like himself but to hold one another to account for the quality of their observance.

The extreme Islamist version of history blames the decline from Islam's golden age on the rulers and people who turned away from the true path of their religion, thereby leaving Islam vulnerable to encroaching foreign powers eager to steal their land, wealth, and even their souls.

Bin Ladin's Worldview

Despite his claims to universal leadership, Bin Ladin offers an extreme view of Islamic history designed to appeal mainly to Arabs and Sunnis. He draws on fundamentalists who blame the eventual destruction of the Caliphate on leaders who abandoned the pure path of religious devotion. He repeatedly calls on his followers to embrace martyrdom since "the walls of oppression and humiliation cannot be demolished except in a rain of bullets." For those yearning for a lost sense of order in an older, more tranquil world, he offers his "Caliphate" as an imagined alternative to today's uncertainty. For others, he offers simplistic conspiracies to explain their world.

Bin Ladin also relies heavily on the Egyptian writer Sayyid Qutb. A member of the Muslim Brotherhood executed in 1966, Qutb mixed Islamic scholarship with a very superficial acquaintance with Western history and thought. Sent

Despite his claims to universal leadership, Bin Ladin offers an extreme view of Islamic history designed to appeal mainly to Arabs and Sunnis. He draws on fundamentalists who blame the eventual destruction of the Caliphate on leaders who abandoned the pure path of religious devotion.

by the Egyptian government to study in the United States in the late 1940s, Qutb returned with an enormous loathing of Western society and history. He dismissed Western achievements as entirely material, arguing that Western society possesses "nothing that will satisfy its own conscience and justify its existence."

Three basic themes emerge from Qutb's writings. First, he claimed that the world was beset with barbarism, licentiousness, and unbelief (a condition he called "jahiliyya", the religious term for the period of ignorance prior to the revelations given to the Prophet Mohammed). Qutb argued that humans can choose only between Islam and jahiliyya. Second, he warned that more people, including Muslims, were attracted to jahilyya and its material comforts that to his view of Islam; jahiliyya could therefore triumph over Islam. Third, no middle ground exists in what Qutb conceived as a struggle between God and Satan. All Muslims—as he defined them—therefore must take up arms in this fight. Any Muslim who rejects his ideas is just one more nonbeliever worthy of destruction.

Bin Ladin shares Qutb's view, permitting him and his followers to rationalize even unprovoked mass murder as righteous defense of an embattled faith. Many Americans have wondered, "Why do 'they' hate us?" Some also ask, "What can we do to stop these attacks?"

Bin Ladin and al Qaeda have given answers to both these questions. To the first, they say that America had attacked Islam; America is responsible for all conflicts involving Muslims. Thus Americans are blamed when Israelis fight with Palestinians, when Russians fight with Chechens, when Indians fight with Kashmiri Muslims, and when the Philippine government fights ethnic Muslims in its southern islands. America is also held responsible for the governments of Muslim countries, derided by al Qaeda as "your agents." Bin Ladin has stated flatly, *Our fight against these governments is not separate from our fight against you."* These charges found a ready audience among millions of Arabs and Muslims angry at the United States because of issues ranging from Iraq to Palestine to America's support for their countries' repressive rulers.

Bin Ladin's grievance with the United States may have started in reaction to specific U.S. policies but it quickly became far deeper. To the second question, what America could do, al Qaeda's answer was that America should abandon the Middle East, convert to Islam, and end the immorality and godlessness of its society and culture: *"It is saddening to tell you that you are the worst civilization witnessed by the history of mankind."* If the United States did not comply, it would be at war with the Islamic nation, a nation that al Qaeda's leaders said "desires death more than you desire life."

Some ask "What can we do to stop these attacks?" Al Qaeda answers that America should abandon the Middle East, convert to Islam, and end the immorality and godlessness of its society and culture

History and Political Context

Few fundamentalist movements in the Islamic world gained lasting political power. In the nineteenth and twentieth centuries, fundamentalists helped articulate anticolonial grievances but played little role in the overwhelmingly secular struggles for independence after World War I. Western-educated lawyers, soldiers, and officials led most independence movements, and clerical influence and traditional culture were seen as obstacles to national progress.

After gaining independence from Western powers following World War II, the Arab Middle East followed an arc from initial pride and optimism to today's mix of indifference, cynicism, and despair. In several countries, a dynastic state already existed or was quickly established under a paramount tribal family. Monarchies in countries such as Saudi Arabia, Morocco, and Jordan still survive today. Those in Egypt, Libya, Iraq, and Yemen were eventually overthrown by secular nationalist revolutionaries.

The secular regimes promised a glowing future, often tied to sweeping ideologies (such as those promoted by Egyptian President Gamal Abdel Nasser's Arab Socialism or the Ba'ath Party of Syria and Iraq) that called for a single, secular Arab state. However, what emerged were almost invariably autocratic regimes that were usually unwilling to tolerate any opposition—even in countries, such as Egypt, that had a parliamentary tradition. Over time, their policies—repression, rewards, emigration, and the displacement of popular anger onto scapegoats (generally foreign—were shaped by the desire to cling to power.

The bankruptcy of secular, autocratic nationalism was evident across the Muslim world by the late 1970s. At the same time, these regimes had closed off nearly all paths for peaceful opposition, forcing their critics to choose silence, exile, or violent opposition. Iran's 1979 revolution swept a Shia theocracy into power. Its success encouraged Sunni fundamentalists elsewhere.

In the 1980s, awash in sudden oil wealth, Saudi Arabia competed with Shia Iran to promote its Sunni fundamentalist interpretation of Islam, Wahhabism. The Saudi government, always conscious of its duties as the custodian of Islam's holiest places, joined with wealthy Arabs from the Kingdom and other states bordering the Persian Gulf in donating money to build mosques and religious schools that could preach and teach their interpretation of Islamic doctrine.

In this competition for legitimacy, secular regimes had no alternative to offer. Instead, in a number of cases their rulers sought to buy off local Islamist movements by ceding control of many social and educational issues. Emboldened rather than satisfied, the Islamists continued to push for power—a trend especially clear in Egypt. Confronted with a violent Islamist movement that killed President Anwar Sadat in 1981, the Egyptian government combined harsh repression of Islamic militants with harassment of moderate Islamic scholars and authors, driving many into exile. In Pakistan, a military regime sought to justify its seizure of power by a pious public stance and an embrace of unprecedented Islamist influence on education and society.

These experiments in political Islam faltered during the 1990s: the Iranian revolution lost momentum, prestige, and public support, and Pakistan's rulers found that most of its population had little enthusiasm for fundamentalist Islam. Islamist revival movements gained followers across the Muslim world, but failed to secure political power except in Iran and Sudan. In Algeria, where in 1991 Islamists seemed almost certain to win power through the ballot box, the military preempted their victory, triggering a brutal civil war that continues today. Opponents of today's rulers have few, if any, ways to participate in the existing political system. They are thus a ready audience for calls to Muslims to purify their society, reject unwelcome modernization, and adhere strictly to Sharia.

Social and Economic Malaise

In the 1970s and 1980s, an unprecedented flood of wealth led the then largely unmodernized oil states to attempt to shortcut decades of development. They funded huge infrastructure projects, vastly expanded education, and created subsidized social welfare programs. These programs established a widespread feeling of entitlement without a corresponding sense of social obligations. By the late 1980s, diminishing oil revenues, the economic drain from many unprofitable development projects, and population growth made these entitlement programs unsustainable. The resulting cutbacks created enormous resentment among recipients who had come to see government largesse as their right. This resentment was further stoked by public understanding of how much oil income had gone straight into the pockets of the rulers, their friends, and their helpers.

Unlike the oil states (or Afghanistan, where real economic development has barely begun), the other Arab nations and Pakistan once had seemed headed toward balanced modernization. The established commercial, financial, and industrial sectors in these states, supported by entrepreneurial spirit and widespread understanding of free enterprise, augured well. But unprofitable heavy industry, state monopolies, and opaque bureaucracies slowly stifled growth. More importantly, these state-centered regimes placed their highest priority on preserving the elite's grip on national wealth. Unwilling to foster dynamic economies that could create jobs attractive to educated young men, the countries became economically stagnant and reliant on the safety valve of worker emigration either to the Arab oil states or to the West. Furthermore, the repression and isolation of women in many Muslim countries has not only seriously limited individual opportunity but also crippled overall economic productivity.

By the 1990s, high birthrates and declining rates of infant mortality had produced a common problem throughout the Muslim world: a large, steadily increasing population of young men without any reasonable expectation of suitable or steady employment—a sure prescription for social turbulence. Many of these young men, such as the enormous number trained only in religious schools, lacked the skills needed by their societies. Far more acquired valuable skills but lived in stagnant economies that could not generate satisfying jobs.

Millions, pursuing secular as well as religious studies, were products of educational systems that generally devoted little if any attention to the rest of the world's thought, history, and culture. The secular education reflected a strong cultural preference for technical fields over the humanities and social sciences. Many of these young men, even if able to study abroad, lacked the perspective and skills needed to understand a different culture.

By the 1990s, high birthrates and declining rates of infant mortality had produced a common problem throughout the Muslim world: a large, steadily increasing population of young men without any reasonable expectation of suitable or steady employment—a sure prescription for social turbulence.

Frustrated in their search for a decent living, unable to benefit from an education often obtained at the cost of great family sacrifice, and blocked from starting families of their own, some of these young men were easy targets for radicalization.

Bin Ladin's Historical Opportunity

Most Muslims prefer a peaceful and inclusive vision of their faith, not the violent sectarianism of Bin Ladin. Among Arabs, Bin Ladin's followers are commonly nicknamed *takfiri, or* "those who define other Muslims as unbelievers," because of their readiness to demonize and murder those with whom they disagree. Beyond the theology lies the simple human fact that most Muslims, like most other human beings, are repelled by mass murder and barbarism whatever their justification.

"All Americans must recognize that the face of terror is not the true face of Islam," President Bush observed. *"Islam is a faith that brings comfort to a billion people around the world. It's a faith that has made brothers and sisters of every race. It's a faith based upon love, not hate."* Yet as political, social, and economic problems created flammable societies, Bin Ladin used Islam's most extreme, fundamentalist traditions as his match. All these elements—including religion—combined in an explosive compound.

Conclusion

Other extremists had, and have, followings of their own. But in appealing to societies full of discontent, Bin Ladin remained credible as other leaders and symbols faded. He could stand as a symbol of resistance—above all, resistance to the West and to America. He could present himself and his allies as victorious warriors in the one great successful experience for Islamic militancy in the 1980s: the Afghan jihad against the Soviet occupation. By 1998, Bin Ladin had a distinctive appeal, as he focused on attacking America. He argued that other extremists, who aimed at local rulers or Israel, did not go far enough. They had not taken on what he called "the head of the snake."

Finally, Bin Ladin had another advantage: a substantial, worldwide organization. By the time he issued his February 1998 declaration of war, Bin Ladin had nurtured that organization for nearly ten years. He could attract, train, and use recruits for ever more ambitious attacks, rallying new adherents with each demonstration that his was the movement of the future.

Questions

1. What is the birthplace of Islam?

2. Identify the two major sects of Islam and explain how they differ.

3. How did political failures of the 20th century give rise to fundamentalist views in the 21st century?

4. How is al Qaeda able to attract fundamentalist support?

5. What is Bin Ladin's goal?

Chapter 6

CBRNE

Objectives

- Understand the definition of WMD according to Title 50, US Code.

- . Describe the different classes of WMD.

- Discuss why terrorists might resort to using WMD.

- Compare and contrast the various capabilities of different classes of WMD.

Introduction

The growing proclivity toward violence appears to be evidence of a portentous shift in terrorism, away from its traditional emphasis on discrete, selective attacks toward a mode of violence that is now aimed at inflicting indiscriminate and wanton slaughter. The implication, therefore, is that terrorism is now on an escalation spiral of lethality that may well culminate in the indiscriminate use of CBRN weapons.[1]

Weapons of Mass Destruction

"CBRN" refers to Chemical, Biological, Radiological, and Nuclear weapons which are generally classed as weapons of mass destruction. Just as there is no single definition for "terrorism", there are multiple interpretations of WMD. Title 50 of the U.S. Code, "War and National Defense", defines WMD:

> *"Any weapon or device that is intended, or has the capability, to cause death or serious bodily injury to a significant number of people through the release, dissemination, or impact of—(A) toxic or poisonous chemicals or their precursors; (B) a disease organism; or (C) radiation or radioactivity."*
>
> —*Title 50, United States Code, Chapter 40, Section 2302*

The term "WMD" was first applied in 1937 to describe the effects of aerial bombardment on civilian populations. Most definitions agree that WMD are "weapons designed to kill large numbers of people."[2] Consequently, more recent U.S. laws, official statements, and documents define WMD as including additional types of weapons.[3] Both the terrorist attacks of September 11th 2001, and the Oklahoma City bombing, April 19th 1995 used conventional explosives to inflict mass casualties. As a result, the definition of WMD has been expanded to include any form of high explosives, thus CBRNE.

Motives and Rationales

If, in fact, we are approaching a new era of "super" CBRNE terrorism, why would groups seek to escalate to this level? One can identify five possible motivating rationales.

First, and at the most basic level, may be simply the desire to kill as many people as possible. CBRNE weapons could give a terrorist group the potential ability to wipe out thousands, possibly even hundreds of thousands, in a single strike. The following statement of a former FEMA director gives an indication of the potential killing power of these agents compared to conventional high explosives (HE): "To produce about the same number of deaths within a square mile, it would take 32 million grams of fragmentation cluster bomb material; 3.2 million grams of mustard gas; 800,000 grams of nerve gas; 5,000 grams of material in a crude fission weapon; 80 grams of botulinal toxin type A; or only 8 grams of anthrax spores." Such weapons would provide terrorist with the perfect means to seek revenge against, even to annihilate, their enemies, however defined, categorized, or otherwise determined.

WMD: "Any weapon or device that is intended, or has the capability, to cause death or serious bodily injury to a significant number of people through the release, dissemination, or impact of—(A) toxic or poisonous chemicals or their precursors; (B) a disease organism; or (C) radiation or radioactivity."
—Title 50, US Code

A second reason for groups to seek to escalate to the CBRNE level could be to exploit the classic weapon of the terrorist—fear. Terrorism, in essence, is a form of psychological warfare. The ultimate objective is to destroy the structural supports that give society its strength by showing that the government is unable to fulfill its primary security function and, thereby, eliminating the solidarity, cooperation, and interdependence on which social cohesion and functioning depend. Viewed in this context, even a "limited" terrorist attack involving CBRNE agents would have disproportionately large psychological consequences, generating unprecedented fear and alarm throughout society. The 1995 Aum sarin nerve gas attack, for instance, which resulted in 12 deaths, not only galvanized mass panic in Tokyo, it also shattered the popular perception among the Japanese people, who, hitherto, had considered their country to be among the safest in the world. Moreover, it served to galvanize American attention to CBRNE terrorism, despite taking place overseas.

A third possible rationale for resorting to CBRNE weapons could be the desire to negotiate from a position of unsurpassed strength. A credible threat to use a chemical, biological, or nuclear weapon would be unlikely to go unanswered by a government and could therefore, provide an organization with a tool of political blackmail of the highest order.

A fourth reason, with specific reference to biological agents, could derive from certain logistical and psychological advantages that such weapons might offer terrorists. A biological attack, unlike a conventional bombing, would not likely attract immediate attention, and could initially go unnoticed, only manifesting itself days or even weeks after the event. This would be well suited to groups that wish to remain anonymous, either to minimize the prospect of personal retribution or to foment greater insecurity in their target audience by appearing as enigmatic, unseen, and unknown assailants.

Fifth, a group may wish to use CBRNE weapons, and more specifically biological agents, to cause economic and social damage by targeting a state's or region's agricultural sector. On several previous occasions in other parts of the world, terrorists have contaminated agricultural produce or threatened to do so. Between 1977 and 1979, more than 40 percent of the Israeli European citrus market was curtailed by a Palestinian plot to inject Jaffa oranges with mercury. In 1989, a Chilean left-wing group that was part of an anti-Pinochet movement claimed that it had lanced grapes bound for U.S. markets with sodium cyanide, causing suspensions of Chilean fruit imports by the Untied States, Canada, Denmark, Germany, and Hong Kong. In the early 1980s, Tamil separatists in Sri Lanka threatened to infect Sri Lankan rubber and tea plantations with nonindigenous diseases as part of a total biological war strategy designed to cripple the Sinhalese-dominated government.[4]

Among weapons of mass destruction, biological weapons are more destructive than chemical weapons, including nerve gas. In certain circumstances, biological weapons can be as devastating as nuclear ones—a few kilograms of anthrax can kill as many people as a Hiroshima-size nuclear weapon.

Biological Attack

Among weapons of mass destruction, biological weapons are more destructive than chemical weapons, including nerve gas. In certain circumstances, biological weapons can be as devastating as nuclear ones—a few kilograms of anthrax can kill as many people as a Hiroshima-size nuclear weapon.[5]

Terrorism involving biological weapons—referred to along with chemical weapons as "the poor man's nuclear weapon"—can range from putting deadly substances in the nation's food supply to the aerosolized release of a contagious virus over a city the size of New York or San Francisco.

The Biological Weapons Convention, signed in 1972, prohibits the manufacture, stockpiling and use of biological weapons. But there are several countries that continue to make and study them. Former President Nixon banned the production and use of biological warfare agents in 1969, ending the U.S. biowarfare program. The Soviet Union's biowarfare program, Biopreparat, lasted until the 1990s.

Anthrax, botulinum toxin, plague, ricin, smallpox, tularemia and viral hemorrhagic fevers are on the top of the Centers for Disease Control and Prevention's list of biological weapons, considered "Category A" weapons most likely to be used in an attack.

"Category B" weapons are second-highest priority to the CDC, because they are fairly easy to disseminate, cause moderate amounts of disease and low fatality rates. But these weapons require specific public-health action such as improved diagnostic and detection systems. These agents include: Q fever, brucellosis, glanders, ricin, Enterotoxin B, viral encephalitis, food safety threats, water safety threats, meliodosis, psittacosis and typhus fever.

"Category C" weapons, described by the CDC as "emerging infectious disease threats," are fairly easy to obtain, produce and disseminate and can produce high rates of disease and mortality. These include the Nipah virus and Hantavirus.

Other agents some nations may use as weapons include: aflatoxin, trichothecene mycotoxins, multi-drug tuberculosis, bacteria such as trench fever and scrub typhus, viruses such as influenza and various forms of hemorrhagic fever, fungi and protozoa.

Agricultural bioterrorism could produce famine or widespread malnutrition. These include foot-and-mouth disease, mad cow disease, swine fever and karnal bunt of wheat.[6]

The United States is unprepared to deal with a biological attack. Over the past several years, preparedness strides have been made, especially in the largest cities. However, much of the needed equipment is not available. Pathogen sensors are not in place to detect that a biological attack has taken place. New medicines are needed. In combating terrorist attacks, treatment is a more practical approach than prevention, yet many biological agents are extremely difficult to treat with existing medicines once the symptoms appear. In addition, many of the most important prophylactic drugs have limited shelf lives and cannot be stockpiled. Moreover, their effectiveness could be compromised by a sophisticated attacker.

Biological weapons can range in lethality from salmonella used to temporarily incapacitate to super bubonic plague engineered for mass casualties. Biological weapons include ricin, which an extremist may use to assassinate a single local official, as well as pathogens with high transmissibility and broad potential impact. Biological agents may be used to kill or disable humans or to attack plants or animals to harm a nation's economy Given that broad scope, biological attacks have already taken place and continue to be a distinct probability for the foreseeable future. However, of greatest concern is the capability to deliver a sizable lethal attack against a population center.

Making biological weapons requires art as well as science. Such weapons are not readily adaptable to "cookbook" type recipes that can be implemented by novices. Nevertheless, technical expertise and sophistication about biological processes have become much more widespread. Moreover, even though technical expertise is required to produce high-quality, military-grade biological weapons and reliable means of dissemination, terrorist applications are less demanding.

Making biological weapons requires sample cultures; the means to grow, purify, and stabilize them; and the means to reliably disseminate them. All these tasks pose substantial but not insurmountable challenges. More than 1,500 biological culture libraries worldwide, as well as numerous research institutions and natural sources, maintain cultures. Growth media and fermenters to multiply the sample cultures are widely available. Purifying, concentrating, and stabilizing agents is demanding and dangerous but not a great technical challenge. Freeze-drying the product and milling it into particles of uniform desirable size requires even more technical capabilities. A state sponsor may be needed to do it, although companies and institutes regularly spray dry and mill commercial microbes. Moreover, a respirable aerosol of germs can be achieved through other high-pressure devices.

Biological production and weapon-producing facilities can be small, inexpensive, and inconspicuous. Equipment to develop biological arms may have legitimate commercial and research purposes, as well as nefarious ones. Unlike nuclear weapons, biological weapons do not require unique ingredients that are ready objects of arms control.[7]

Chemical Attack

Chemical warfare is the use of non-explosive chemical agents (that are not themselves living organisms) to cause injury or death.[8]

The first major use of chemical weapons in modern times came when Germany launched a large-scale poison gas attack against French troops on the battlefield of Ypres in 1915. Allies responded with their own chemical weapons. By the end of the war, chemical warfare had inflicted over 1 million casualties, of which around 90,000 were fatal.

The 1925 Geneva Protocol prohibits "the use in war of asphyxiating, poisonous or other gases, and of bacteriological methods of warfare." But it didn't prohibit the manufacturing and stockpiling of these weapons.

A UN working group began work on chemical disarmament in 1980. On April 4, 1984, U.S. President Ronald Reagan called for an international ban on chemical weapons. U.S. President George H. W. Bush and Soviet Union leader Mikhail Gorbachev signed a bilateral treaty on June 1, 1990 to end chemical weapon production and start destroying each of their nation's stockpiles. The multilateral Chemical Weapons Convention (CWC) was signed in 1993 and came into effect in 1997. The Organization for the Prohibition of Chemical Weapons declared that at the end of 2003, 8000 metric tons of chemical agent had been destroyed worldwide from a declared stockpile of 70,000 metric tons. For its part, by 2003, the United States had destroyed 23% of its total chemical arsenal, although doubts existed whether it could reach total elimination by the treaty deadline of 2012 due to technical difficulties and environmental regulations.

Chemical agents are classified according to the symptoms they cause, such as blistering and nerve agents. Mustard gas, sarin (GB), VX, soman (GD) and tabun are blistering and nerve agents that were weaponized for military purposes. Other forms of chemical agents include: blood agents, including cyanide, arsine, cyanogens chloride and hydrogen chloride; choking agents, including chlorine, phosphane and phosgene; other nerve agents; and vesicants such as distilled mustard, ethyldichlorarsine, mustard-lewsite mixture and forms of nitrogen mustard.[9]

Chemical weapons are made from readily available material used in various industrial operations. The most common types of hazardous materials used in toxic weapons are irritants, choking agents, flammable industrial gas, water supply contaminants, oxidizers, chemical asphyxiates, incendiary gases and liquids, industrial compounds and organophosphate pesticides.[10]

On March 20, 1995, members of Aum Shinkrikyo released sarin gas on several lines of the Tokyo Subway, killing 12 people and injuring some 6000 more. The attack was initiated at the peak of Monday morning rush hour on one of the world's busiest commuter transport systems. Five teams of two-men were issued plastic bags containing approximately one liter of liquid sarin each. A single drop of sarin the size of the head of a pin can kill an adult.

Sarin is classified as a nerve agent. It was discovered in 1938 by two German scientists while attempting to create stronger pesticides. At room temperature, sarin is both odorless and colorless. Its relatively high vapor pressure means that it evaporates quickly. Its vapor is also odorless and colorless. Sarin attacks the nervous system of the human body. Initial symptoms following exposure are a runny nose, tightness in the chest and dilation of the pupils. The victim will begin to lose control of bodily functions and eventually become comatose and suffocate as a consequence of convulsive spasms.

Carrying their packets of sarin and umbrellas with sharpened tips, the perpetrators boarded their appointed trains; at prearranged stations, each perpetrator dropped his package and punctured it several times with the sharpened tip of his umbrella before escaping to his accomplice's waiting get-away car.

Passengers began to be affected immediately. Those nearest the release were overcome by symptoms and began to drop causing others to panic and press the emergency stop buttons. Witnesses have said that subway entrances resembled battlefields. In many cases, the injured simply lay on the ground, many unable to breathe. Incredibly, several of those affected by sarin went to work in spite of their symptoms. Most of these left and sought medical treatment as the symptoms worsened. Several of those affected were exposed to sarin only by helping passengers from the trains (these include passengers on

Chemical weapons are made from readily available material used in various industrial operations. The most common types of hazardous materials used in toxic weapons are irritants, choking agents, flammable industrial gas, water supply contaminants, oxidizers, chemical asphyxiates, incendiary gases and liquids, industrial compounds and organophosphate pesticides.

other trains, subway workers and health care workers).

The sarin gas attack was the most serious terrorist attack in Japan's modern history. It caused massive disruption and widespread fear in a society that had been considered virtually free of crime.

Shortly after the attack, Aum lost its status as a religious organization, and many of its assets were seized. However, the Diet of Japan rejected a request from government officials to outlaw the sect altogether because the officials could not prove that the Aum posed a 'threat to society'.

About twenty of Aum's followers, including its leader, Shoko Asahara, are either standing trial or have already been convicted for crimes related to the attack. As of July 2004, eight Aum members have received death sentences for their roles in the attack.[11]

Nuclear Attack

Nuclear weapons produce devastating and long-term effects on human and animal life, as well as the environments in which they live. These are the hardest of all types of weapons to make because the critical nuclear elements—plutonium and/or highly enriched uranium—are hard to come by, and are very expensive.

The United States dropped one atomic bomb on Hiroshima and Nagasaki in 1945, bringing an end to World War II. The Soviet Union became the next country to develop atomic weapons, igniting an arms race and a global interest in nuclear fission devices.

Decades of arms control have greatly reduced the number of nuclear weapons around the world. Since 1991, the U.S. Nunn-Lugar Cooperative Threat Reduction program has deactivated 6,032 nuclear warheads and has destroyed 491 ballistic missiles, 438 ballistic missile silos, 101 bombers, 365 submarine-launched missiles, 408 submarine missile launchers, and 25 strategic missile submarines. It has sealed 194 nuclear test tunnels.[12]

The key question is whether or not terrorists could build a nuclear explosive device. Weapons experts at the Nuclear Control Institute say the answer is "yes." They conjecture that a crude nuclear device could be constructed by a group not previously engaged in designing or building nuclear weapons. Successful execution would require efforts of a team having knowledge and skills additional to those usually associated with terrorist groups, but could be accomplished relatively quick with careful preparations and the right materials. The completed device would probably weigh more than a ton, but still be small enough to fit within the back of a truck. According to the experts, an implosion device could be constructed with reactor-grade plutonium or highly enriched uranium providing a nominal yield of 10 kilotons, equivalent to the atomic bombs used over Hiroshima and Nagasaki in World War II.[13]

Limited access to fissile materials—the essential ingredients of nuclear weapons—is the principal technical barrier to nuclear proliferation in the world today. Global stockpiles of such material are large and widespread. A decade after the end of the Cold War, there are still some 30,000 nuclear weapons in

Limited access to fissile materials—the essential ingredients of nuclear weapons—is the principal technical barrier to nuclear proliferation in the world today.

the world (more than 95% of them in the U.S. and Russian arsenals). The world's stockpiles of separated plutonium and highly enriched uranium (HEU), the essential ingredients of nuclear weapons, are estimated to include some 450 tons of military and civilian separated plutonium, and over 1700 tons of HEU. These stockpiles, both military and civilian, are overwhelmingly concentrated in the five nuclear weapon states acknowledged by the Nonproliferation Treaty, but enough plutonium for many nuclear weapons also exists in India, Israel, Belgium, Germany, Japan, and Switzerland. In addition, as of estimates made in 2000, a total of more than 2,772 kilograms of civilian HEU existed in research reactors in 43 countries, sometimes in quantities large enough to make a bomb.

Most of these weapons and materials are reasonably well secured and accounted for. But this is by no means universally the case. Levels of security and accounting for both the military and civilian material vary widely, with no binding international standards in place. Some weapons-usable material is dangerously insecure and so poorly accounted for that if it were stolen, no one might ever know.

Today, the problem is most acute in the former Soviet Union, where the collapse of the Soviet state left a security system designed for a closed society with closed borders, well-paid nuclear workers, and everyone under close surveillance by the KGB facing a new world it was never designed to address. Nuclear weapons, which are large and readily accountable objects, remain under high levels of security—though even there, scarce resources for maintaining security systems and paying nuclear guards raise grounds for concern. For nuclear material, the problem is more urgent. Many nuclear facilities in Russia have no detector at the door that would set off an alarm if someone were carrying plutonium in a briefcase, and no security cameras where the plutonium is stored. Nuclear workers and guards protecting material worth millions of dollars are paid $200 a month. As a result, there have been a number of confirmed cases of theft of kilogram quantities of weapons-usable material in the former Soviet Union. Russian officials have confirmed as recently as 1998, there was an insider conspiracy at one of Russia's largest nuclear weapons facilities to steal 18.5 kilograms of HEU—one that was stopped before the material actually left the gates. These are conditions that led a distinguished U.S. bipartisan panel to warn in 2001, that "the most urgent unmet national security threat to the United States today is the danger that weapons of mass destruction or weapons-usable material in Russia could be stolen and sold to terrorists or hostile nation states."

The problem of insecure nuclear material, however, is by no means limited to the former Soviet Union. Many analysts have expressed concern that the current anti-terrorist campaign could create instabilities in South Asia that could put nuclear stockpiles and facilities at risk. In the United States itself, which has among the toughest physical protection regulations in the world, there have been repeated scandals going back decades over inadequate security for weapons-usable nuclear material. In countries around the world, there are research facilities with fresh HEU fuel that simply do not have the resources to sustain effective security for this material over the long haul. The problem was highlighted by the 19.9% enriched uranium seized in 1998 from criminals trying to sell it in Italy, which appears to have been stolen from a research reactor in the Congo. Theft of insecure HEU and plutonium, in short, is not a hypothetical worry: it is an ongoing reality, not only from the former Soviet Union but from other states as well.

At the same time, tens of thousands of people worldwide have critical knowledge related to the manufacture of nuclear weapons and their essential ingredients, which must be controlled, and many thousands of these are seriously underemployed and underpaid, creating some serious proliferation risks. In 1998, for example, a weapons expert from one of Russia's premier nuclear weapons laboratories was arrested on charges for spying for Iraq and Afghanistan—in this case on advanced conventional weapons. In October 2000, an official of Russia's Security Council confirmed that Russia had blocked Taliban efforts to recruit a former Soviet nuclear expert from a Central Asian state. A knowledgeable expert from a major state weapons of mass destruction program could substantially accelerate a proliferator's weapons of mass destruction program, or make it possible for a terrorist group to achieve a nuclear capability that would otherwise be beyond their reach.[14]

Radiological Attack

Radiological weapons are thought by many to be the likely choices for terrorists. Unlike nuclear weapons, they spread radioactive material, which contaminates equipment, facilities, land and acts as a toxic chemical, which can be harmful, and in some cases fatal.

A "dirty bomb" is the likely choice for terrorists and can kill or injure people by exposing them to radioactive materials, such as cesium-137, iridium-192 or cobalt-60.[15]

According to Dr. Henry Kelly, President of the Federation of American Scientists, "Radiological attacks constitute a credible threat." Radioactive materials that could be used for such attacks are stored in thousands of facilities around the US, many of which may not be adequately protected against theft by determined terrorists. Some of this material could be easily dispersed in urban areas by using conventional explosives or by other methods.

While radiological attacks would result in some deaths, they would not result in the hundreds of thousands of fatalities that could be caused by a crude nuclear weapon. Attacks could contaminate large urban areas with radiation levels that exceed the Environmental Protection Agency's health and toxic material guidelines.

Materials that could easily be lost or stolen from US research institutions and commercial sites could contaminate tens of city blocks at a level that would require prompt evacuation and create terror in large communities even if radiation casualties were low. Areas as large as tens of square miles could be contaminated at levels that exceed recommended civilian exposure limits. Since there are often no effective ways to decontaminate buildings that have been exposed at these levels, demolition may be the only practical solution. If such an event were to take place in a city like New York, it would result in

Radiological weapons are thought by many to be the likely choices for terrorists. Unlike nuclear weapons, they spread radioactive material, which contaminates equipment, facilities, land and acts as a toxic chemical, which can be harmful, and in some cases fatal.

losses of potentially trillions of dollars.

Because of the resultant high economic impact compared with the expected low loss of life, a "dirty bomb" is sometimes referred to as a "weapon of mass disruption." Radiological weapons have the advantage over nuclear weapons in as much as they don't require large quantities of restricted materials or specialized expertise for their fabrication. In fact, the required materials are readily available and used extensively throughout government and industry.

The radiation produced by radioactive materials provides a low-cost way to disinfect food, sterilize medical equipment, treat certain kinds of cancer, find oil, build sensitive smoke detectors, and provide other critical services to our economy. Radioactive materials are also widely used in university, corporate, and government research laboratories. As a result, significant amounts of radioactive materials are stored in laboratories, food irradiation plants, oil drilling facilities, medical centers, and many other sites.

Radioactive sources that emit intense gamma-rays, such as cobalt-60 and cesium-137, are useful in killing bacteria and cancer cells. Gamma-rays, like X-rays, can penetrate clothing, skin, and other materials, but they are more energetic and destructive. When these rays reach targeted cells, they cause lethal chemical changes inside the cell.

Significant quantities of radioactive material have been lost or stolen from US facilities during the past few years and thefts of foreign sources have led to fatalities. In the US, sources have been found abandoned in scrap yards, vehicles, and residential buildings.

Plutonium and americium also serve commercial and research purposes. When plutonium or americium decay, they throw off a very large particle called an alpha particle. Hence, they are referred to as alpha emitters. Plutonium, which is used in nuclear weapons, also has non-military functions. During the 1960s and 1970s the federal government encouraged the use of plutonium in university facilities studying nuclear engineering and nuclear physics. Americium is used in smoke detectors and in devices that find oil sources. These devices are lowered deep into oil wells and are used to detect fossil fuel deposits by measuring hydrogen content as they descend.

With the exception of nuclear reactors, commercial facilities do not have the types or volumes of materials usable for making nuclear weapons. Security concerns have focused on preventing thefts or accidents that could expose employees and the general public to harmful levels of radiation. A thief might, for example, take the material for its commercial value as a radioactive source, or it may be discarded as scrap by accident or as a result of neglect. This system works reasonably well when the owners have a vested interest in protecting commercially valuable material. However, once the materials are no longer needed and costs of appropriate disposal are high, security measures become lax, and the likelihood of abandonment or theft increases.

Significant quantities of radioactive material have been lost or stolen from US facilities during the past few years and thefts of foreign sources have led to fatalities. In the US, sources have been found abandoned in scrap yards, vehicles, and residential buildings. In September 1987, scavengers broke into an abandoned cancer clinic in Goiania, Brazil and stole a medical device containing large amounts of radioactive cesium. An estimated 250 people were exposed to the source, eight developed radiation sickness, and four died.

In almost all cases, the loss of radioactive materials has resulted from an accident or from a thief interested only in economic gain. In 1995, however, Chechen rebels placed a shielded container holding the cesium-137 core of a cancer treatment device in a Moscow park, and then tipped off Russian reporters of its location.

Gamma rays pose two types of health risks. Intense sources of gamma rays can cause immediate tissue damage, and lead to acute radiation poisoning. Fatalities can result from very high doses. Long-term exposure to low levels of gamma rays can also be harmful because it can cause genetic mutations leading to cancer. Triggering cancer is largely a matter of chance: the more radiation you're exposed to, the more often the dice are rolled. The risk is never zero since we are all constantly being bombarded by large amounts of gamma radiation produced by cosmic rays, which reach us from distant stars. We are also exposed to trace amounts of radioactivity in the soil, in building materials, and other parts of our environment. Any increase in exposure increases the risk of cancer.

Alpha particles emitted by plutonium, americium and other elements also pose health risks. Although these particles cannot penetrate clothing or skin, they are harmful if emitted by inhaled materials. If plutonium is in the environment in particles small enough to be inhaled, contaminated particles can lodge in the lung for extended periods. Inside the lung, the alpha particles produced by plutonium can damage lung tissue and lead to long-term cancers.

Impact of the release of radioactive material in a populated area will vary depending on a number of factors, many of which are not predictable. Consequences depend on the amount of material released, the nature of the material, the details of the device that distributes the material, the direction and speed of the wind, other weather conditions, the size of the particles released (which affects their ability to be carried by the wind and to be inhaled), and the location and size of buildings near the release site. Assuming the material is released on a calm day, and the material is distributed by an explosion creating a mist of fine particles to spread downwind in a cloud, then people will be exposed to radiation in several ways.

First, they will be exposed to material in the dust inhaled during the initial passage of the radiation cloud, if they have not been able to escape the area before the dust cloud arrives. If this material is plutonium or americium (or other alpha emitters), the material will stay in the body and lead to long term exposure.

Second, anyone living in the affected area will be exposed to material deposited from the dust that settles from the cloud. If the material contains cesium (or other gamma emitters) they will be continuously exposed to radiation from this dust, since the gamma rays penetrate clothing and skin. If the material contains plutonium (or other alpha emitters), dust that is pulled off the ground and into the air by wind, automobile movement, or other actions will continue to be inhaled, adding to exposure.

In a rural area, people would also be exposed to radiation from contaminated food and water sources.

The EPA has a series of recommendations for addressing radioactive contami-

Long-term exposure to low levels of gamma rays can also be harmful because it can cause genetic mutations leading to cancer. Triggering cancer is largely a matter of chance: the more radiation you're exposed to, the more often the dice are rolled. The risk is never zero.

nation that would likely guide official response to a radiological attack. Immediately after the attack, authorities would evacuate people from areas contaminated to levels exceeding these guidelines. People who received more than twenty-five times the threshold dose for evacuation would have to be taken in for medical supervision.

In the long term, the cancer hazard from the remaining radioactive contamination would have to be addressed. Typically, if decontamination could not reduce the danger of cancer death to about one-in-ten-thousand, the EPA would recommend the contaminated area be eventually abandoned. Decontaminating an urban area presents a variety of challenges. Several materials that might be used in radiological attack can chemically bind to concrete and asphalt, while other materials would become physically lodged in crevices on the surface of buildings, sidewalks and streets. Options for decontamination would range from sandblasting to demolition, with the latter likely being the only feasible option. Some radiological materials will also become firmly attached to soil in city parks, with the only disposal method being large scale removal of contaminated dirt. In short, there is a high risk that the area contaminated by a radiological attack would have to be deserted.

Consider if a medical gauge containing cesium was exploded in Washington, DC in a bomb using ten pounds of TNT. The initial passing of the radioactive cloud would be relatively harmless, and no one would have to evacuate immediately. But what area would be contaminated? Residents of an area about five city blocks, if they remained, would have a one-in-thousand chance of getting cancer. A swath about one mile long covering an area of forty city blocks would exceed EPA contamination limits, with remaining residents having a one-in-ten thousand chance of getting cancer. If decontamination were not possible, these areas would have to be abandoned for decades. If the device was detonated at the National Gallery of Art, the contaminated area might include the Capitol, Supreme Court, and Library of Congress.

Now imagine if a single piece of radioactive cobalt from a food irradiation plant was dispersed by an explosion at the lower tip of Manhattan. Typically, each of these cobalt "pencils" is about one inch in diameter and one foot long, with hundreds of such pieces often being found in the same facility. Again, no immediate evacuation would be necessary, but in this case, an area of approximately one-thousand square kilometers, extending over three states, would be contaminated. Over an area of about three hundred typical city blocks, there would be a one-in-ten risk of death from cancer for residents living in the contaminated area for forty years. The entire borough of Manhattan would be so contaminated that anyone living there would have a one-in-a-hundred chance of dying from cancer caused by the residual radiation. It would be decades before the city was inhabitable again, and demolition might be necessary.

A device that spreads materials like americium and plutonium would present an entirely different set of risks. Consider a typical americium source used in oil well surveying. If this were blown up with one pound of TNT, people in a region roughly ten times the area of the initial bomb blast would require medical supervision and monitoring. An area 30 times the size of the first area (a swath one kilometer long and covering twenty city blocks) would have to be evacuated within half an hour. After the initial passage of the cloud, most of

Options for decontamination would range from sandblasting to demolition, with the latter likely being the only feasible option. Some radiological materials will also become firmly attached to soil in city parks, with the only disposal method being large scale removal of contaminated dirt. In short, there is a high risk that the area contaminated by a radiological attack would have to be deserted.

the radioactive materials would settle to the ground. Of these materials, some would be forced back up into the air and inhaled, thus posing a long-term health hazard. A ten-block area contaminated in this way would have a cancer death probability of one-in-a-thousand. A region two kilometers long and covering sixty city blocks would be contaminated in excess of EPA safety guidelines. If the buildings in this area had to be demolished and rebuilt, the cost would exceed fifty billion dollars.[16]

Explosives Attack

An explosive is any material that, when ignited by heat or shock, undergoes rapid decomposition or oxidation. This process releases energy that is stored in the material in the form of heat and light, or by breaking down into gaseous compounds that occupy a much larger volume than the original piece of material. Because this expansion is very rapid, large volumes of air are displaced by the expanding gasses. This expansion occurs at a speed greater than the speed of sound, and so a sonic boom occurs. This explains the mechanics behind an explosion. Explosives occur in several forms: high-order explosives which detonate, low order explosives, which burn, and primers, which may do both.

High order explosives detonate. A detonation occurs only in a high order explosive. Detonations are usually incurred by a shockwave that passes through a block of the high explosive material. The shockwave breaks apart the molecular bonds between the atoms of the substance, at a rate approximately equal to the speed of sound traveling through that material. In a high explosive, the fuel and oxidizer are chemically bonded, and the shockwave breaks apart these bonds, and re-combines the two materials to produce mostly gasses. T.N.T., ammonium nitrate, and R.D.X. are examples of high order explosives.

Low order explosives do not detonate; they burn, or undergo oxidation when heated, the fuel(s) and oxidizer(s) combine to produce heat, light, and gaseous products. Some low order materials burn at about the same speed under pressure as they do in the open, such as black powder. Others, such as gunpowder, which is correctly called nitrocellulose, burn much faster and hotter when they are in a confined space, such as the barrel of a firearm; they usually burn much slower than black powder when they are ignited in unpressurized conditions. Black powder, nitrocellulose, and flash powder are good examples of low order explosives.

Primers are peculiarities to the explosive field. Some of them, such as mercury fulminate, will function as a low or high order explosive. They are usually more sensitive to friction, heat, or shock, than the high or low order explosives. Most primers perform like a high order explosive, except that they are much more sensitive. Still others merely burn, but when they are confined, they burn at a great rate and with a large expansion of gasses and a shockwave. Primers are usually used in a small amount to initiate, or cause to decompose, a high order explosive, as in an artillery shell. But they are also frequently used to ignite a low order explosive; the gunpowder in a bullet is ignited by the detonation of its primer.[17]

The production, storage, and distribution of explosive materials is regulated under Title 15 of US Code. Various regulatory organizations are responsible for enforcing the law. The Occupational Safety & Health Administration (OSHA) assures the safe and healthful working conditions for workers handling explosives in construction and manufacturing work. The Mine Safety & Health Administration (MSHA) protects the safety and health of miners while handling explosives, and enforces storage and record keeping rules at mining operations (surface and underground). The Department of Transportation (DOT) protects life and property against inherent risks of transporting hazardous materials in commerce. The Bureau of Alcohol Tobacco Firearms and Explosives (ATF) protects commerce and the public from the misuses and unsafe or insecure storage of explosives. The ATF investigates thefts, losses, and unexpected explosions to determine whether it was an accidental or criminal act. State and local fire and police authorities may also regulate explosive storage, transportation, and use.[18]

Despite intense government regulation, it's a matter of practical impossibility to prevent the proliferation of explosive materials since they may be easily manufactured from common materials using information that's widely available on the internet.

"The Terrorist's Handbook", available on the internet, includes recipes for twenty-three different types of explosives including impact, low order, high order, and other types of explosives. The handbook details methods for acquiring and fabricating materials, both legally and illegally.

Despite intense government regulation, it's a matter of practical impossibility to prevent the proliferation of explosive materials since they may be easily manufactured from common materials using information that's widely available on the internet.

For example, the handbook describes ammonium nitrate as a high explosive material that is often used as a commercial "safety explosive" because it's very stable, and difficult to ignite with a match. It explains how ammonium nitrate is used in "Cold-Paks" or "Instant Cold", available in most drug stores. To get the ammonium nitrate, simply cut off the top of the outside bag, remove the plastic bag of water, and save the ammonium nitrate in a well sealed, airtight container. The handbook also notes ammonium nitrate is the main ingredient in many fertilizers.[19] Indeed, Timothy McVeigh used ammonium nitrate found in fertilizer to build a truck bomb killing 168 people in the Alfred P. Murrah Federal Building, in Oklahoma City, Oklahoma, April 19, 1995.[20]

The handbook also describes methods for acquiring explosive materials illegally. Colleges, according to the handbook, are the best places to steal chemicals.

"Many state schools have all of their chemicals out on the shelves in the labs, and more in their chemical stockrooms. Evening is the best time to enter lab buildings, as there are the least number of people in the buildings, and most of the labs will be unlocked. One simply takes a book bag, wears a dress shirt and jeans, and tries to resemble a college freshman. If anyone asks what such a person is doing, the thief can simply say he is looking for the polymer chemistry lab, or some other chemistry-related department other than the one they are in. One can

usually find out where the various labs and departments in a building are by calling the university... as a rule, college campus security is pretty poor, and nobody suspects another person in the building of doing anything wrong, even if they are there at an odd hour."

— *The Terrorist's Handbook*

The First Amendment of the Constitution protects the existence of sources such as "The Terrorist's Handbook." Even if they could be eliminated, it wouldn't eliminate the threat from high explosives. The fact of the matter is that many common items can be made into high explosive devices. Consider that the terrorist attacks of September 11th 2001 used commercial aircraft as weapons of mass destruction by hijacking heavily fueled aircraft and ramming them into large buildings. Any other aircraft, train, ship, or truck could serve a similar purpose.

Conclusion

The knowledge, technology, and materials needed to build weapons of mass destruction are spreading. These capabilities have never been more accessible and the trends are not in our favor. If terrorist enemies acquire these weapons and the means to deliver them, they are likely to try to use them, with potential consequences far more devastating than those suffered on September 11.

Biological weapons, which release large quantities of living, disease-causing microorganisms, have extraordinary lethal potential. Biological weapons are relatively easy to manufacture, requiring straightforward technical skills, basic equipment, and a seed stock of pathogenic microorganisms. Biological weapons are especially dangerous because we may not know immediately that we have been attacked, allowing an infectious agent time to spread. Moreover, biological agents can serve as a means of attack against humans as well as livestock and crops, inflicting casualties as well as economic damage.

Chemical weapons are extremely lethal and capable of producing tens of thousands of casualties. They are also relatively easy to manufacture, using basic equipment, trained personnel, and precursor materials that often have legitimate dual uses. As the 1995 Tokyo subway attack revealed, even sophisticated nerve agents are within the reach of terrorist groups.

Nuclear weapons have enormous destructive potential. Terrorists who seek to develop a nuclear weapon must overcome two formidable challenges. First, acquiring or refining a sufficient quantity of fissile material is very difficult—though not impossible. Second, manufacturing a workable weapon requires a very high degree of technical capability—though terrorists could feasibly assemble the simplest type of nuclear device. To get around these significant though not insurmountable challenges, terrorists could seek to steal or purchase a nuclear weapon.

Radiological weapons, or "dirty bombs," combine radioactive material with conventional explosives. They can cause widespread disruption and fear, particularly in heavily populated areas.

Terrorists, both domestic and international, continue to use traditional methods of violence and destruction to inflict harm and spread fear. They have used knives, guns, and bombs to kill the innocent. They have taken hostages and spread propaganda. Given the low expense, ready availability of materials, and relatively high chance for successful execution, terrorists will continue to make use of conventional attacks.[21]

Questions

1. What is the definition of WMD according to Title 50, US Code?

2. What are the different classes of WMD?

3. Describe three different motives or rationales for terrorists to use WMD.

4. Of the various forms of WMD, which do you think is most destructive, and why?

5. Of the various forms of WMD, which do you think is most likely to be used, and why?

Part II: Organization Development

Chapter 7

Combating Terrorism

Objectives

- Know the definitions of antiterrorism, counterterrorism, and combating terrorism.
- Discuss the basic dilemma in combating terrorism.
- Explain some of the policy tools available for combating terrorism.
- Describe the U.S. organization for combating terrorism.
- Describe the U.S. strategy for combating terrorism.

Introduction

Antiterrorism (AT): Defensive measures used to reduce the vulnerability of individuals and property to terrorist acts, to include limited response and containment by local military forces.

Counterterrorism (CT): Offensive measures taken to prevent, deter, and respond to terrorism.

Combating Terrorism: Actions, including AT and CT, taken to oppose terrorism throughout the entire threat spectrum.

— DoD Instruction 2000.14

Reporting in July 2004, the National Commission on Terrorist Attacks Upon the United States, otherwise known as the 9/11 Commission, identified Islamist terrorism as the single most serious threat to the nation. The 9/11 Commission made it clear that the enemy is not Islam, the great world faith, but a perversion of Islam that draws on a long tradition of extreme intolerance within a minority strain and does not distinguish politics from religion, and distorts both. The 9/11 Commission recognized that the enemy goes beyond al Qaeda to include the radical ideological movement, inspired in part by al Qaeda, that has spawned other terrorist groups and violence. Thus, the 9/11 Commission proposed the following objectives and end states for the global war on terrorism:

1. Dismantle al Qaeda.

2. Prevail over the ideology that contributes to Islamist terrorism.

The 9/11 Commission acknowledged the first phase of post-9/11 efforts rightly included military action to topple the Taliban and pursue al Qaeda. But long-term success, according to the commission, demands the use of all elements of national power: diplomacy, intelligence, covert action, law enforcement, economic policy, foreign aid, public diplomacy, and homeland defense. The 9/11 Commission proposed using all these means to effect the desired ends in a strategy with three dimensions:

1. Attack terrorists and their organizations.

2. Prevent the continued growth of Islamist terrorism.

3. Protect against and prepare for terrorist attacks.

Attacking terrorists and their organizations means rooting out terrorist sanctuaries. According to the 9/11 Commission, the U.S. government should identify and prioritize actual or potential terrorist sanctuaries and have realistic country or regional strategies for each, utilizing every element of national power and reaching out to countries that can help.[1]

Unfortunately, the simplicity of these statements belie the difficulty entailed in actually going after the terrorists.

"Combating Terrorism: Actions, including AT and CT, taken to oppose terrorism throughout the entire threat spectrum."

— DoD Instruction 2000.14

U.S. Policy Response

The application of sanctions is one of the most frequently used anti-terrorist tools of U.S. policymakers. Governments supporting international terrorism (as identified by the Department of State) are prohibited from receiving U.S. economic and military assistance. Export of munitions to such countries is foreclosed, restrictions are imposed on exports of "dual use" equipment such as aircraft and trucks.

In the wake of the September 2001 World Trade Center and Pentagon attacks, President Bush, in addressing the nation, stressed that the United States in responding to the attacks will make no distinction between the terrorists who committed these acts and those who harbor them. The President characterized the incidents as "acts of war." Secretary of State Colin Powell called for a "full scale assault against terrorism" and announced plans to launch a world wide coalition against terrorism. A military response option, once perpetrators and/or supporters have been identified, became a strong probability.

Most experts agree that the most effective way to fight terrorism is to gather as much intelligence as possible; disrupt terrorist plans and organizations before they act; and organize multinational cooperation against terrorists and countries that support them. The U.N.'s role in mandating sanctions against Libya for its responsibility in the 1988 Pan Am 103 bombing was significant as the first instance when the world community imposed sanctions against a country in response to its complicity in an act of terrorism. Several factors made the action possible. First, terrorism has touched many more countries in recent years, forcing governments to put aside parochial interests. (Citizens from over 30 countries have reportedly died in Libyan-sponsored bombings.) Second, the end of the Cold War has contributed to increased international cooperation against terrorism. And third, U.S. determination to punish terrorist countries, by military force in some instances, once their complicity was established, was a major factor in spurring other countries to join U.S.-sponsored action.

In the past, governments have often preferred to handle terrorism as a national problem without outside interference. Some governments were also wary of getting involved in others battles and possibly attracting terrorism in the form of reprisals. Others were reluctant to join in sanctions if their own trade interests might be damaged or they sympathized with the perpetrator's cause. Finally, there is the persistent problem of extraditing terrorists without abandoning the long-held principle of asylum for persons fleeing persecution for legitimate political or other activity.

Most experts agree that the most effective way to fight terrorism is to gather as much intelligence as possible; disrupt terrorist plans and organizations before they act; and organize multinational cooperation against terrorists and countries that support them.

Dilemmas

In their desire to combat terrorism in a modern political context, nations often face conflicting goals and courses of action: (1) providing security from terrorist acts, i.e., limiting the freedom of individual terrorists, terrorist groups, and support networks to operate unimpeded in a relatively unregulated environment versus (2) maximizing individual freedoms, democracy, and human rights. Efforts to combat terrorism are complicated by a global trend toward deregulation, open borders, and expanded commerce. Particularly in democracies such as the United States, the constitutional limits within which policy must operate are often seen by some to conflict directly with the desire to secure the lives of citizens against terrorist activity more effectively.

Another dilemma for policymakers is the need to identify the perpetrators of particular terrorist acts and those who train, fund, or otherwise support or sponsor them. Moreover, as the international community increasingly demonstrates its ability to unite and apply sanctions against rogue states, states will become less likely to overtly support terrorist groups or engage in state sponsored terrorism.

Today a non-standard brand of terrorist may be emerging: individuals who do not work for any established terrorist organization and who are apparently not agents of any state sponsor. The worldwide threat of such individual or "boutique" terrorism, or that of "spontaneous" terrorist activity such as the bombing of bookstores in the United States after Ayatollah Khomeini's death edict against British author Salman Rushdie, appears to be on the increase. Thus, one likely profile of the terrorist of the 21st century may well be a private individual not affiliated with any established group. Another profile might be a group-affiliated individual acting independent of the group, but drawing on other similarly minded individuals for support. The difficulty in countering the non-standard brand of terrorist is that they are immune to the traditional methods of imposing state sanctions and dealing with state sponsors of terrorism.

Another problem surfacing in the wake of the number of incidents associated with Islamic fundamentalist groups is how to condemn and combat such terrorist activity, and the extreme and violent ideology of specific radical groups, without appearing to be anti-Islamic in general. A desire to punish a state for supporting international terrorism may also be subject to conflicting foreign policy objectives.

Nations often face conflicting goals and courses of action: (1) providing security from terrorist acts, i.e., limiting the freedom of individual terrorists, terrorist groups, and support networks to operate unimpeded in a relatively unregulated environment versus (2) maximizing individual freedoms, democracy, and human rights.

Policy Tools

The U.S. government has employed a wide array of policy tools to combat international terrorism, from diplomacy and international cooperation and constructive engagement to economic sanctions, covert action, protective security measures, and military force.

Diplomacy/Constructive Engagement

Most responses to international terrorism involve use of diplomacy in some form as governments seek cooperation to apply pressure on terrorists. One such initiative was the active U.S. role taken in the March 1996 Sharm al-Sheikh peacemaker/anti-terrorism summit. Another is the ongoing U.S. effort to get Japan and major European nations to join in U.S. trade and economic sanctions against Iran. Some argue that diplomacy holds little hope of success against determined terrorists or countries that support them. However, in most cases, diplomatic measures are considered least likely to widen the conflict and therefore are usually tried first.

In incidents of international terrorism by subnational groups, implementing a policy response of constructive engagement is complicated by the lack of existing channels and mutually accepted rules of conduct between government entities and the group in question. In some instances, as was the case with the Palestinian Liberation Organization (PLO), legislation may specifically prohibit official contact with a terrorist organization or its members. Increasingly, however, governments appear to be pursuing policies which involve verbal contact with terrorist groups or their representatives.

The media remain powerful forces in confrontations between terrorists and governments. Appealing to, and influencing, public opinion may impact not only the actions of governments but also those of groups engaged in terrorist acts. From the terrorist perspective, media coverage is an important measure of the success of a terrorist act or campaign. And in hostage type incidents, where the media may provide the only independent means a terrorist has of knowing the chain of events set in motion, coverage can complicate rescue efforts. Governments can use the media in an effort to arouse world opinion against the country or group using terrorist tactics. Public diplomacy and the media can be used to mobilize public opinion in other countries to pressure governments to take action against terrorism. An example would be to mobilize the tourist industry to pressure governments into participating in sanctions against a terrorist state.

Diplomatic measures are considered least likely to widen the conflict and therefore are usually tried first.

Economic Sanctions

In the past, use of economic sanctions was usually predicated upon identification of a nation as an active supporter or sponsor of international terrorism. On August 20, 1998, President Clinton signed an executive order freezing assets owned by Saudi-born Islamic terrorist leader Usama bin Laden, specific associates and their self-proclaimed Islamic Army Organization, prohibits U.S. individuals and firms from doing business with them. Previously, the Clinton Administration had frozen the assets of 12 alleged Middle East terrorist organizations and 18 individuals associated with those organizations. On October 8, 1997, the State Department released a list of 30 foreign terrorist organizations. The 1996 Antiterrorism and Effective Death Penalty Act makes it a crime to provide support to these organizations, and their members shall be denied entry visas into the United States.

Economic sanctions fall into six categories: restrictions on trading, technology transfer, foreign assistance, export credits and guarantees, foreign exchange and capital transactions, and economic access. Sanctions may include a total or partial trade embargo, embargo on financial transactions, suspension of foreign aid, restrictions on aircraft or ship traffic, or abrogation of a friendship, commerce, and navigation treaty. Sanctions usually require the cooperation of other countries to make them effective, and such cooperation is not always forthcoming.

The President has a variety of laws at his disposal, but the broadest in its potential scope is the International Emergency Economic Powers Act. The Act permits imposition of restrictions on economic relations once the President has declared a national emergency because of a threat to the U.S. national security, foreign policy, or economy. While the sanctions authorized must deal directly with the threat responsible for the emergency, the President can regulate imports, exports, and all types of financial transactions, such as the transfer of funds, foreign exchange, credit, and securities between the United States and the country in question. Specific authority for the Libyan trade embargo is Section 503 of the International Trade and Security Act of 1985, while Section 505 of the Act authorizes the banning of imports of goods and services from any country supporting terrorism. Other major laws that can be used against countries supporting terrorism are the Export Administration Act, the Arms Export Control Act, and the specific items or provisions of foreign assistance legislation.

Public Law 104-132 prohibits the sale of arms to any country the President certifies is not cooperating fully with the U.S. anti-terrorism efforts. The law also requires that aid be withheld to any nation providing lethal military aid to a country on the terrorism list.

[Economic] sanctions usually require the cooperation of other countries to make them effective, and such cooperation is not always forthcoming.

Covert Action

Intelligence gathering, infiltration of terrorist groups and military operations involve a variety of clandestine or so called "covert" activities. Much of this activity is of a passive monitoring nature. A more active form of covert activity occurs during events such as a hostage crisis or hijacking when a foreign country may quietly request advice, equipment or technical support during the conduct of operations, with no public credit to be given the providing country.

Some nations have periodically gone beyond monitoring or covert support activities and resorted to unconventional methods beyond their territory for the express purpose of neutralizing individual terrorists and/or thwarting preplanned attacks. Examples of activities might run the gamut from intercepting or sabotaging delivery of funding or weapons to a terrorist group to seizing and transporting a wanted terrorist to stand trial for assassination or murder. Arguably, such activity might be justified as preemptive self defense under Article 51 of the U.N. charter. On the other hand, it could be argued that such actions violate customary international law. Nevertheless, a July 1989 memorandum by the Department of Justice's Office of Legal Counsel advises that the President has the authority to violate customary international law and can delegate such authority to the Attorney General level, should the national interest so require.

Assassination is specifically prohibited by U.S. Executive Order (most recently, E.O. 12333), but bringing of wanted criminals to the United States for trial is not. There exists an established U.S. legal doctrine that allows an individual's trial to proceed regardless whether he is forcefully abducted from another country, or from international waters or airspace. For example, Fawaz Yunis, a Lebanese who participated in the 1985 hijacking of a Jordanian airliner with two Americans among its 70 passengers, was lured aboard a yacht in international waters off the coast of Cyprus in 1987 by federal agents, flown to the United States for trial, and convicted.

Experts warn that bringing persons residing abroad to U.S. justice by means other than extradition or mutual agreement with the host country, i.e., by abduction and their surreptitious transportation, can vastly complicate U.S. foreign relations, sometimes jeopardizing interests far more important than "justice," deterrence, and the prosecution of a single individual. For example, the abduction of a Mexican national in 1990 to stand trial in Los Angeles on charges relating to torture and death of a DEA agent led to vehement protests from the government of Mexico, a government subsequently plagued with evidence of high level drug related corruption. Subsequently, in November 1994, the two countries signed a Treaty to Prohibit Transborder Abductions. Notwithstanding the unpopularity of such abductions in nations that fail to apprehend and prosecute those accused, the "rendering" of such wanted criminals to U.S. courts is permitted under limited circumstances by a January 1993 Presidential Decision Directive issued under the first Bush Administration, and reaffirmed by former President Clinton. Such conduct, however, raises prospects of other nations using similar tactics against U.S. citizens.

Although conventional explosives—specifically car bombs—appear to be terrorism weapons of choice, the world is increasingly moving into an era in which terrorists may gain access to nuclear, chemical or biological weaponry. Faced with the potential of more frequent incidents and higher conventional casualty levels, or a nuclear or biological attack, nations may be more prone to consider covert operations designed to neutralize such threats.

Assassination is specifically prohibited by U.S. Executive Order.

Rewards for Information Program

Money is a powerful motivator. Rewards for information have been instrumental in Italy in destroying the Red Brigades and in Columbia in apprehending drug cartel leaders. A State Department program is in place, supplemented by the aviation industry, offering rewards of up to $5 million to anyone providing information that would prevent or resolve an act of international terrorism against U.S. citizens or U.S. property, or that leads to the arrest or conviction of terrorist criminals involved in such acts. This program was at least partly responsible for the arrest of Ramzi Yousef, the man accused of masterminding the World Trade Center bombing, and of the CIA personnel shooter, Mir Amal Kansi. The program was established by the 1984 Act to Combat International Terrorism (Public Law 98-533), and is administered by State's Diplomatic Security Service. Rewards over $250,000 must be approved by the Secretary of State. The program can pay to relocate informants and immediate family who fear for their safety. The 1994 "crime bill" (Public Law 103-322) helps relocate aliens and immediate family members in the U.S. who are reward recipients. Expanded participation by the private sector in funding and publicizing such reward programs has been suggested by some observers.

Extradition/Law Enforcement Cooperation

International cooperation in such areas as law enforcement, customs control, and intelligence activities is an important tool in combating international terrorism. One critical law enforcement tool in combating international terrorism is extradition of terrorists. International extradition traditionally has been subject to several limitations, including the refusal to extradite for political or extraterritorial offenses and the refusal of some countries to extradite their nationals. The United States has been encouraging the negotiation of treaties with fewer limitations, in part as a means of facilitating the transfer of wanted terrorists. Because much terrorism involves politically motivated violence, the State Department has sought to curtail the availability of the political offense exception, found in many extradition treaties, to avoid extradition. Increasingly, extradition is being employed by the U.S. as a vehicle for gaining physical custody over terrorist suspects.

Military Force

Although not without difficulties, military force, particularly when wielded by a superpower such as the United States, can carry substantial clout. Proponents of selective use of military force usually emphasize the military's unique skills and specialized equipment. The April 1986 decision to bomb Libya for its alleged role in the bombing of a German discotheque exemplifies the use of military force. Other examples are: (1) the 1993 bombing of Iraq's military intelligence headquarters by U.S. forces in response to Iraqi efforts to assassinate former President George Bush during a visit to Kuwait and (2) the August 1998 missile attacks against bases in Afghanistan and an alleged chemical production facility in Sudan.

Concerns about the terrorist threat prompted an extensive buildup of the military's counter-terrorist organization. A special unit known as "Delta Force" at Fort Bragg, NC, has been organized to perform anti-terrorist operations when needed. Details about the unit are secret, but estimates are that it has about 800 assigned personnel.

Use of military force presupposes the ability to identify a terrorist group or sponsor and its location, knowledge often unavailable to law enforcement officials. Risks of military force include (1) military casualties or captives, (2) foreign civilian casualties, (3) retaliation and escalation by terrorist groups, (4) holding the wrong parties responsible, (5) sympathy for the "bullied" victim, and (6) perception that the U.S. ignores rules of international law.

Public Law 104-264 includes a sense of the Senate statement that if evidence suggests "beyond a clear and reasonable doubt" that an act of hostility against any U.S. citizen was a terrorist act sponsored, organized, condoned or directed by any nation, then a state of war should be considered to exist between the United States and that nation.

International Conventions

To date, the United States has joined with the world community in developing all of the major anti-terrorism conventions. These conventions impose on their signatories an obligation either to prosecute offenders or extradite them to permit prosecution for a host of terrorism-related crimes including hijacking vessels and aircraft, taking hostages, and harming diplomats. An important

One critical law enforcement tool in combating international terrorism is extradition of terrorists.

convention is the Convention for the Marking of Plastic Explosives. Implementing legislation is in Public Law 104-132. On September 8, 1999 the U.S. signed the U.N. Convention on the Suppression of Terrorist Bombings; and on January 12, 2000, the U.N. Anti-Terrorism Financing Convention was signed as well.[2]

U.S. Organization and Program Response

Presidential Decision Directive 39 (PDD 39), signed in June 1995, is the foundation for current U.S. policy for combating terrorism. The document spells out three objectives for confronting terrorism:

1. Reduce the nation's international and domestic vulnerabilities to terrorism.

2. Deter terrorism.

3. Respond to terrorism rapidly and decisively.

PDD 39 designates Lead Federal Agencies (LFA's) for international and domestic terrorism policy. The Lead Federal Agency for combating terrorism overseas is the Department of State (DoS), and the agency designated to respond to terrorist attacks on U.S. soil is the Department of Justice (DoJ) through the Federal Bureau of Investigation (FBI). The Federal Emergency Management Agency (FEMA) has the primary responsibility to lead federal efforts to deal with the consequences and collateral second and third order effects of terrorist WMD attacks on American soil.[3]

In the wake of 9-11, The Homeland Security Act of November 25, 2002, established the Department of Homeland Security to (1) prevent terrorist attacks within the United States, (2) reduce the vulnerability of the United States to terrorism, and (3) minimize the damage, and assist in the recovery, from terrorist attacks that do occur within the United States. The Homeland Security Act preserved the roles for combating terrorism assigned to Lead Federal Agencies in PDD 39 by explicitly stating "primary responsibility for investigating and prosecuting acts of terrorism shall be vested not in the Department [of Homeland Security], but rather in Federal, State, and local law enforcement agencies with jurisdiction over the acts in question."[4]

Prior to 9-11, the job of coordinating the actions of the Lead Federal Agencies rested with the National Security Council. The chain of command on anti-terrorism planning ran from the President through the National Security Council's (NSC's) Principals Committee, through the NSC's Deputies Committee, a representative of which chaired a senior interagency Counterterrorism & National Preparedness Policy Coordinating Committee (PCC). The PCC oversaw four working groups charged with overseeing policy in four generic areas: (1) continuity of federal operations; (2) preventing and responding to foreign terrorism; (3) preventing and responding to weapons of mass destruction (WMD) attacks; and (4) preventing and responding to cyber threats.[5]

Following the attacks of 9-11, President George W. Bush issued Executive Order 13228, October 8, 2001, establishing the Whitehouse Office of Homeland Security (OHS) and Homeland Security Council (HSC) to assume the anti-

The Lead Federal Agency for combating terrorism overseas is the Department of State (DoS), and the agency designated to respond to terrorist attacks on U.S. soil is the Department of Justice (DoJ) through the Federal Bureau of Investigation (FBI). The Federal Emergency Management Agency (FEMA) has the primary responsibility to lead federal efforts to deal with the consequences and collateral second and third order effects of terrorist WMD attacks on American soil.

terrorism roles previously assigned to the National Security Council.[6] OHS responsibilities were subsequently transferred to the Department of Homeland Security (DHS) and OHS closed in October 2005. Unlike the NSC, the HSC and DHS must deal with a far broader spectrum of U.S. agencies and organizations. The strategy acknowledges that there is a vital need for cooperation between the federal government and state and local governments on a scale never before seen in the United States. Cooperation must occur both horizontally (within each level of government) and vertically (among various levels of government). While the President has only one jurisdiction on the international side in the NSC, he has over 180 jurisdictions on the homeland side through federal, state, and local levels, while the DHS consolidates over 22 organizations with critical homeland security missions.[7] The Department of Homeland Security, develops and coordinates the implementation of a comprehensive national strategy to secure the United States from terrorist threats or attacks by coordinating the executive branch's efforts to detect, prepare for, prevent, protect against, respond to, and recover from terrorist attacks within the United States. The purpose of the Homeland Security Council is to advise the President with respect to all aspects of homeland security, and serve as the mechanism for ensuring coordination of homeland security-related activities of executive departments and agencies in the implementation of homeland security policies.

The Homeland Security Council (HSC) was modeled on the structure of the National Security Council, and the two organizations share overlapping areas of responsibility. Today, the chain of command on anti-terrorism planning runs from the President through the HSC's Principals Committee, through the HSC's Deputies Committee, to the HSC's Policy Coordination Committees.

The HSC Principals Committee (HSC/PC) is the senior interagency forum under the HSC for homeland security issues. The HSC/PC is composed of the following members: the Secretary of the Treasury; the Secretary of Defense; the Attorney General; the Secretary of Health and Human Services; the Secretary of Transportation; the Director of the Office of Management and Budget; the Assistant to the President for Homeland Security (who serves as Chairman); the Assistant to the President and Chief of Staff; the Director of Central Intelligence; the Director of the Federal Bureau of Investigation; the Director of the Federal Emergency Management Agency; and the Assistant to the President and Chief of Staff to the Vice President.

The HSC Deputies Committee (HSC/DC) serves as the senior sub-Cabinet interagency forum for consideration of policy issues affecting homeland security. The HSC/DC can task and review the work of the HSC interagency groups. The HSC/DC ensures that issues brought before the HSC Principals Committee have been properly analyzed and prepared for action. The HSC/DC is comprised of representatives from the same federal agencies who are members of the HSC Principals Committee.

HSC Policy Coordination Committees (HSC/PCCs) coordinate the development and implementation of homeland security policies by multiple departments and agencies throughout the federal government, and coordinate those policies with state and local government. The HSC/PCCs are the main day-to-day forum for interagency coordination of homeland security policy. The HSC/PCCs

Today, the chain of command on anti-terrorism planning runs from the President through the Homeland Security Council's (HSC's) Principals Committee, through the HSC's Deputies Committee, to the HSC's Policy Coordination Committees.

provide policy analysis for consideration by the more senior committees of the HSC system and ensure timely responses to decision by the President. There are eleven assigned HSC Policy Coordination Committees:

1. Detection, Surveillance, and Intelligence

2. Plans, Training, Exercises, and Evaluation

3. Law Enforcement and Investigation

4. Weapons of Mass Destruction

5. Key Asset, Border, Territorial Water, and Airspace Security

6. Domestic Transportation Security

7. Research and Development

8. Medical and Public Health

9. Domestic Threat Response and Incident Management

10. Economic Consequences

11. Public Affairs[8]

National Strategy for Combating Terrorism

In February 2003, the Whitehouse released the National Strategy for Combating Terrorism, defining the U.S. war plan against international terrorism. The intent of the national strategy is to stop terrorist attacks against the United States, its citizens, its interests, and our friends and allies around the world and ultimately, to create an international environment inhospitable to terrorists and all those who support them. To accomplish these tasks the nation will simultaneously act on four fronts.

The National Strategy for Combating Terrorism:
- *Defeat*
- *Deny*
- *Diminish*
- *Defend*

The United States and its partners will *defeat* terrorist organizations of global reach by attacking their sanctuaries; leadership; command, control, and communications; material support; and finances. This approach will have a cascading effect across the larger terrorist landscape, disrupting the terrorists' ability to plan and operate. As a result, it will force these organizations to disperse and then attempt to reconsolidate along regional lines to improve their communications and cooperation.

As this dispersion and organizational degradation occurs, The U.S. will work with regional partners to implement a coordinated effort to squeeze, tighten, and isolate the terrorists. Once the regional campaign has localized the threat, America will help states develop the military, law enforcement, political, and financial tools necessary to finish the task. However, this campaign need not be sequential to be effective; the cumulative effect across all geographic regions will help achieve the desired results.

The U.S. will *deny* further sponsorship, support, and sanctuary to terrorists by ensuring other states accept their responsibilities to take action against these international threats within their sovereign territory. UNSCR 1373 and the 12 UN counterterrorism conventions and protocols establish high standards that the U.S. and our international partners expect others to meet in deed as well as word.

Where states are willing and able, the U.S. will reinvigorate old partnerships and forge new ones to combat terrorism and coordinate actions to ensure that they are mutually reinforcing and cumulative.

Where states are weak but willing, America will support them vigorously in their efforts to build the institutions and capabilities needed to exercise authority over all their territory and fight terrorism where it exists.

Where states are reluctant, the U.S. will work with our partners to convince them to change course and meet their international obligations.

Where states are unwilling, the U.S. will act decisively to counter the threat they pose and, ultimately, to compel them to cease supporting terrorism.

The U.S. will *diminish* the underlying conditions that terrorists seek to exploit by enlisting the international community to focus its efforts and resources on the areas most at risk. The nation will maintain the momentum generated in response to the September 11 attacks by working with our partners abroad and various international forums to keep combating terrorism at the forefront of the international agenda.

Most importantly, the government will *defend* the United States, its citizens, and its interests at home and abroad by both proactively protecting our homeland and extending our defenses to ensure we identify and neutralize the threat as early as possible.[10]

Conclusion

Victory against terrorism will not occur as a single, defining moment. It will not be marked by the likes of the surrender ceremony on the deck of the USS Missouri that ended World War II. However, through the sustained effort to compress the scope and capability of terrorist organizations, isolate them regionally, and destroy them within state borders, the United States and its friends and allies will secure a world in which our children can live free from fear and where the threat of terrorist attacks does not define our daily lives.

Victory, therefore, will be secured only as long as the United States and the international community maintain their vigilance and work tirelessly to prevent terrorists from inflicting horrors like those of September 11, 2001.[10]

Questions

1. What is the definition of "combating terrorism" according to DoD Instruction 2000.14?

2. What is the basic dilemma in combating terrorism.

3. List and describe two different policy tools for combating terrorism.

4. Who are the lead federal agencies responsible for combating terrorism?

5. What is the U.S. strategy for combating terrorism?

## Chapter 8

DHS Origins

Objectives

- Know the difference between crisis management and consequence management.

- Understand the organization for homeland security before 9-11.

- Describe some of the security shortcomings prior to 9-11.

- Explain the sequence of events leading to the establishment of the Department of Homeland Security.

"A direct attack against American citizens on American Soil is likely over the next quarter century. The risk is not only death and destruction but also demoralization that could undermine U.S. global leadership. In the face of this threat, our nation has no coherent or integrated governmental structures. We therefore recommend the creation of an independent National Homeland Security Agency (NHSA) with responsibility for planning, coordinating, and integrating various U.S. government activities involved in homeland security."

— *Phase III Report of the U.S. Commission on National Security/21st Century, February 15, 2001*

Introduction

The United Stated Department of Homeland Security (DHS) is a Cabinet department of the federal government of the United States that is concerned with protecting the American homeland and the safety of American citizens. The department was created primarily from a conglomeration of existing federal agencies in response to the terrorist attacks of September 11th, 2001.

The department was established on November 25th, 2002, by the Homeland Security Act and officially began operation January 24th, 2003. After months of discussion about employee rights and benefits and "rider" portions of the bill, Congress passed it shortly after the midterm elections, and it was signed into law by U.S. President George W. Bush. It was intended to consolidate U.S. executive branch organizations related to "homeland security" into a single cabinet agency.

It was the largest government reorganization in 50 years (since the United States Department of Defense was created). The department assumed a number of government functions previously in other departments.[1]

Evolution

The concept of operations for a federal response to a terrorist threat or incident provides for an overall lead federal agency to ensure multi-agency coordination and a tailored, time-phased deployment of specialized federal assets. Prior to 9-11, the U.S. strategy for combating terrorism consisted of crisis management and consequence management:

- Crisis management involved efforts to prevent and deter a terrorist attack, protect public health and safety, arrest terrorists, and gather evidence for criminal prosecution.

- Consequence management included efforts to provide medical treatment and emergency services, evacuate people from dangerous areas, and restore government services.

The government strategy for combating terrorism had evolved into a complex framework of programs and activities across more than 40 federal agencies, bureaus, and offices. The evolution of theses programs came from a variety of presidential decision directives, implementing guidance, executive orders, interagency agreements and legislation.[2]

National Security Decision Directive (NSDD) 30 signed by President Ronald Reagan, April 10th 1982, established a Special Security Group inside the National Security Council to advise the President with respect to decision options in the event of a terrorist incident or situation. NSDD 30 designated lead federal agencies to coordinate federal responses to federal agencies with the most direct operational role in dealing with the incident at hand. NSDD 30 appointed the Department of State (DoS) as the lead federal agency for international terrorist incidents taking place outside U.S. territory. NSDD 30 appointed the Federal Bureau of Investigation (FBI) under the Department of Justice (DoJ) as the lead federal agency for domestic terrorist incidents taking place within U.S. territory. The Federal Aviation Administration was appointed the lead federal agency for hijackings within the jurisdiction of the United States, and the Federal Emergency Management Agency (FEMA) assigned responsibility for planning and managing the public health aspects of a terrorist incident and recovery from the consequences of such incidents.

U.S. policy for combating terrorism for terrorist incidents overseas was formalized in 1986 under National Security Decision 207. The Department of State was reaffirmed as the lead federal agency for international terrorism policy, procedures, and programs. The FBI, through the Department of Justice, was reaffirmed as the lead federal agency for handling domestic terrorist threats.

Presidential Decision Directive 39 (PDD 39), issued in June 1995 in the aftermath of the bombing of the federal building in Oklahoma City, reaffirmed the Department of Justice, through the FBI, as the lead federal agency responsible for crisis management of domestic terrorist incidents. Although state and local governments have the primary responsibility for managing the consequence of a domestic terrorist incident, the 1995 directive designated the Federal Emergency Management Agency (FEMA) as the lead agency responsible for coordinating federal agencies' responses and activities when state and local authorities requested assistance.[3]

The federal response to a terrorist incident was seen as a highly coordinated interagency operation that included federal, state, and local participation. Primary federal agencies besides the DoJ, FBI, and FEMA included the Department of Defense (DoD), Department of Energy (DoE), the Environmental Protection Agency (EPA), and the Department of Health and Human Services (DHHS).

The National Security Council was the center of U.S. government efforts to coordinate the national response to threats or acts of domestic terrorism. The NSC Principals Committee, the Deputies Committee, and the Counterterrorism and National Preparedness Policy Coordination Committee (PCC) constituted the major policy and decision making bodies involved in the federal response to terrorism.

The PCC had four standing subordinate groups to coordinate policy in specific areas. The Counterterrorism and Security Group (CSG) coordinated policy for preventing and responding to foreign terrorism, either internationally or domestically. The Preparedness and Weapons of Mass Destruction Group provided policy coordination for preventing WMD attacks in the United States

NSDD 30 signed by President Reagan designated lead federal agencies to coordinate federal responses to federal agencies with the most direct operational role in dealing with the incident at hand.

and developing response and consequence management capabilities to deal with domestic WMD incidents. The Information Infrastructure Protection and Assurance Group handled policy for preventing and responding to major threats to America's cyberspace, and the Continuity of Federal Operations Group was charged with policy coordination for assuring the continued operation of Constitutional offices and federal departments and agencies.

When the NSC was advised of the threat of a terrorist incident or actual event, the appropriate subordinate group would convene to formulate recommendations for the Counterterrorism and Preparedness PCC who in turn would provide policy analysis for the Deputies Committee. The Deputies Committee would ensure that the issues being brought before the Principals Committee and NSC were properly analyzed and prepared for a decision by the President.[4]

In May 1998, President Clinton issues PDD 62 establishing the position of a National Coordinator for Security, Infrastructure Protection, and Counterterrorism within the NSC. Part of the rationale for creating this National Coordinator was to improve leadership and coordination among the various federal agencies. The directive enumerated responsibilities for the coordinator that included general coordination of federal efforts, chairing certain meetings, sponsoring interagency working groups, and providing budget advice.

When the NSC was advised of the threat of a terrorist incident or actual event, the appropriate subordinate group would convene to formulate recommendations for the Counterterrorism and Preparedness PCC who in turn would provide policy analysis for the Deputies Committee.

Shortcomings

Other than the general responsibilities identified in PDD 62, the functions of the National Coordinator were never detailed in either an executive order or legislation. Many critical leadership functions were not given to the National Coordinator:

- Overall Accountability. In some cases, the President and Congress held different officials accountable for interagency functions. For example, while the President appointed a national coordinator, Congress directed a different official, the Attorney General, to develop an interagency strategy.

- Threat and Risk Assessment. The FBI made only limited progress to perform an assessment while agencies expended resources on less likely threats and scenarios.

- National Strategy. There was no unified effort. Agencies developed competing "national strategies".

- Monitoring Budgets. While the OMB attempted to track and analyze agency funding to combat terrorism, there was no effort to eliminate duplication and no linkage to national strategy.

- Tracking and Implementing Lessons Learned. There was no standard for tracking lessons learned from state and local exercises.

- Coordinating Agency Implementation. Different agencies developed programs to provide assistance to state and local governments that were similar and potentially duplicative. These multiple programs created confusion and frustration among state and local officials.

Concerned about the overall leadership and coordination of programs to combat terrorism, Congress established three separate commissions to include the Advisory Panel to Assess Domestic Response Capabilities for Terrorism Involving Weapons of Mass Destruction (also known as the Gilmore Panel because it was chaired by Governor James Gilmore III of Virginia); the United States Commission on National Security in the 21st Century (also known as the Hart-Rudman Commission because it was chaired by former Senators Gary Hart and Warren Rudman); and the National Commission on Terrorism (also known as the Bremer Commission because it Chairman was former Ambassador Paul Bremer).[5]

The Bremer Commission raised the issue that the National Coordinator, the senior official responsible for coordinating all U.S. counterterrorism efforts, didn't have sufficient authority to ensure the President's priorities were reflected in agencies' budgets. The United States didn't have a single counterterrorism budget. Instead, counterterrorism programs existed in the individual budgets of 45 departments and agencies of the federal government.[6]

In December 2000, the second report of the Gilmore Commission issued a finding that the organization of the federal government's programs for combating terrorism was fragmented, uncoordinated, and politically unaccountable. It linked the lack of a national strategy to the fact that no entity had the authority to direct all of the agencies that may be engaged. At the federal level, no entity had the authority even to direct the coordination of relevant federal efforts. As a consequence, the Gilmore Commission recommended that the next President should establish a National Office for Combating Terrorism in the Executive Office of the President, and should seek a statutory basis for this office.

The United States didn't have a single counterterrorism budget. Instead, counterterrorism programs existed in the individual budgets of 45 departments and agencies of the federal government.

The Gilmore Commission recommended that the National Office for Combating Terrorism should have a broad and comprehensive scope, with responsibility for the full range of deterring, preventing, preparing for, and responding to international as well as domestic terrorism. The director of the office should be the principal spokesman of the Executive Branch on all matters related to federal programs for combating terrorism and should be appointed by the President and confirmed by the Senate. The office should have a substantial and professional staff, drawn from existing National Security Council offices and other relevant agencies. The Gilmore Commission argued that the office should have at least five major sections, each headed by an Assistant Director:

1. Domestic Preparedness Programs

2. Intelligence

3. Health and Medical Programs

4. Research, Development, Test, and Evaluation (RDT&E), and National Standards

5. Management and Budget[7]

The Hart-Rudman Commission decried the fact that responsibility for homeland security resided at all levels of the U.S. government—local, state, and federal. That within the federal government, almost every agency and department was involved in some aspect of homeland security, but none was organized to focus on the scale of the contemporary threat to the homeland. The Hart-Rudman Commission recommended an organizational realignment that:

- Designated a single person, accountable to the President, to be responsible for coordinating and overseeing various U.S. government activities related to homeland security;

- Consolidated certain homeland security activities to improve their effectiveness and coherence;

- Established planning mechanisms to define clearly specific responses to specific types of threats; and

- Ensured that the appropriate resources and capabilities were available.

In February 2001, the Hart-Rudman Commission recommended the creation of a National Homeland Security Agency (NHSA) with responsibility for planning, coordinating, and integrating various U.S. government activities involved in homeland security.[8]

On October 8th, 2001, President George W. Bush issued Executive Order 13228, establishing the Office of Homeland Security within the Executive Office of the President to coordinate a comprehensive national strategy to secure the United States from terrorist threats and attacks.

Impetus for Change

On September 20th, 2001, the General Accounting Office completed an independent analysis of the national framework for combating terrorism and issued the following recommendations:

> *"Based upon numerous evaluations, the identification of recurring problems in the overall leadership and coordination programs, and an analysis of various proposals, GAO believes a single focal point, with all critical functions and responsibilities, should be assigned to lead and coordinate these programs. This focal point, for example, could be an individual, an executive office, or a council. Furthermore, this focal point should be in the Executive Office of the President and be independent of any existing federal agency. A focal point within the Executive Office of the President would be independent above the interests of any of several individual agencies involved. The focal point needs to have the time, responsibility, authority, and resources for coordinating both crisis management and consequence management activities. Current proposals to create a new agency to combine functions currently in several agencies still would not contain all the government agencies and functions needed to combat terrorism. While not endorsing any specific organizational structure for the single focal point, GAO has identified basic functions that any focal point should perform."[9]*

On October 8th, 2001, President George W. Bush issued Executive Order 13228, establishing the Office of Homeland Security within the Executive Office of the President to coordinate a comprehensive national strategy to secure the United States from terrorist threats and attacks. Thomas Ridge, former Governor of Pennsylvania, was appointed Assistant to the President.

Immediately following the 9-11 the attacks, many Members of Congress sought to address the government's organizational problems by introducing legislation to rearrange the federal government. However, the President preferred instead to focus on faster ways to improve coordination. He established the Office of Homeland Security and initiated a strategic assessment of U.S. capabilities for security of the homeland.

Congress's deliberations on reorganizing the government's homeland security functions were largely built on the recommendations of the U.S. Commission on National Security for the 21st Century (Hart-Rudman Commission) which proposed creating a new federal agency by consolidating the Coast Guard, the Customs Service, the Immigration and Naturalization Service (INS) and FEMA into a new National Homeland Security Agency.

In April 2001, Representative William (Mac) Thornberry (R-TX) introduced HR 1158 to create that agency. Shortly after September 11, Senator Joseph Lieberman (D-CT) proposed similar legislation (S. 1534) to create a National Homeland Security Department (NHSD). Other Members, such as Representative Alcee Hastings (D-FL) and Senator Bob Graham (D-FL) promoted the findings of the Advisory Panel to Assess Domestic Response Capabilities for Terrorism Involving Weapons of Mass Destruction (Gilmore Commission) in HR 3078. The Gilmore Commission had concluded that a White House office with detailed statutory authority, modeled after the Office of National Drug Control Policy (ONDCP), would be best situated to solve the federal government's coordination problems.

After introducing HR 1158 and S. 1534, Representative Thornberry and Senator Lieberman refined their proposals to gain the support of more Members of Congress, and in May 2002 introduced the National Homeland Security and Combating Terrorism Act of 2002 (HR 4660).[10] The new bill chose to exclude the Transportation Security Administration (TSA) in the reorganization, and focused more narrowly on border security and emergency preparedness and response. [11]

On June 6, 2002, President Bush proposed establishment of a Cabinet-level Department of Homeland Security (DHS).

On June 6, 2002, President Bush proposed establishment of a Cabinet-level Department of Homeland Security (DHS). His initiative called for consolidating most federal agencies with homeland security missions in one department to focus the government's resources more efficiently and effectively on domestic security. The President's plan built on the recommendations of the various national commissions and legislative proposals already submitted before Congress.

Following President Bush's call to Congress, Representative Richard Armey (R-TX) submitted House Resolution 5005 (HR 5005) calling for the establishment of a Department of Homeland Security, June 24th, 2002. HR 5005 incorporated most provisions set forth in HR 4660, plus the President's request to transfer TSA from the Department of Transportation (DOT) to DHS. HR 5005 passed the House July 26th, and was handed over to the Senate on July 30th. HR 5005 wasn't without its detractors, and stalled in the Senate.[12]

Controversy centered on whether the FBI and the CIA should be incorporated in part or in whole (both were not). The bill itself was also controversial for the presence of unrelated riders, as well as eliminating some standard civil service and labor protections from employees of the department. President Bush wanted the right to fire an employee within Homeland Security immediately for security reasons, for incompetence, or insubordination. Senate Minority Leader Tom Daschle wanted an appeals process that could take up to 18 months or as little as one month.[13]

The impasse was broken when both the House and Senate agreed to a compromise resolution, HR 5710 incorporating provisions by Senator Joseph Lieberman authorizing the President to bypass traditional civil service procedures provided he first consult with Congress and mediate with the federal employees union.[14]

Conclusion

President Bush signed [the Homeland Security Act establishing the Department of Homeland Security], Public Law 107-296, November 25th, 2002.

On November 20th 2002, the Senate passed HR 5005 by a vote of 90-9 authorizing the creation of a Department of Homeland Security consolidating 22 federal agencies under a single executive department with an initial budget appropriation of $34 billion.

President Bush signed the bill into law, Public Law 107-296, November 25th, 2002. Tom Ridge was made secretary of the new department. President Bush signed Executive Order 13284 activating the Department of Homeland Security effective January 23rd, 2003.

Questions

1. What is the difference between crisis management and consequence management?

2. What was perceived as the biggest impediment to anti-terrorist activity prior to 9-11?

3. What was the purpose for establishing the Department of Homeland Security?

## Chapter 9

Homeland Security Strategy

Objectives

- Comprehend the relationship between homeland security and national security.
- Understand the purpose of homeland security.
- Know the critical mission areas identified in the National Strategy for Homeland Security.

Introduction

In the wake of the attacks of September 11th, President George W. Bush issued Executive Order 13228 October 8th 2001 establishing the Office of Homeland Security within the Executive Office of the President to coordinate the implementation of a comprehensive national strategy to secure the United States from terrorist threats or attacks. As HR 5005 went before Congress seeking to establish the Department of Homeland Security, the Office of Homeland Security under the direction of Tom Ridge issued the nation's first National Strategy for Homeland Security July 16th, 2002.

Homeland Security and National Security

The Preamble to the Constitution defines our federal government's basic purposes as *"... to form a more perfect Union, establish justice, insure domestic Tranquility, provide for the common defense, promote the general Welfare, and secure the Blessings of Liberty to ourselves and our Posterity."* The requirement to provide for the common defense remains as fundamental today as it was when these words were written, more than two hundred years ago.

For six decades, National Security Strategy has sought to protect America's sovereignty and independence through global presence and engagement. Unable to match our great power, our enemies have sought to take advantage of America's freedom and openness to attack her from within. Homeland Security Strategy seeks to deny this avenue of attack to our enemies, and thus to provide a secure foundation for America's ongoing global engagement.

Since 1986 Congress has required the President to enunciate the National Security Strategy of the United States detailing how he aims to guarantee the sovereignty and independence of the United States. The National Security Strategy provides a framework for creating and seizing opportunities that strengthen our security and prosperity. The National Strategy for Homeland Security complements the National Security Strategy of the United States by addressing a very specific and uniquely challenging threat – terrorism in the United States – and by providing a comprehensive framework for organizing the efforts of federal, state, local and private organizations whose primary functions are often unrelated to national security.

The link between national security and homeland security is a subtle but important one. For more than six decades, America has sought to protect its own sovereignty and independence through a strategy of global presence and engagement. In so doing, America has helped many other countries and peoples advance along the path of democracy, open markets, individual liberty, and peace with their neighbors. Yet there are those who oppose America's role in the world, and who are willing to use violence against us and our friends. Our great power leaves these enemies with few conventional options for doing us harm. One such option is to take advantage of our freedom and openness by secretly inserting terrorists into our country to attack our homeland. Homeland security seeks to deny this avenue of attack to our enemies and thus to provide a secure foundation for America's ongoing global engagement. Thus the National Security Strategy of the United States and National Strategy for Homeland Security work as mutually supporting documents, providing guidance to the executive branch departments and agencies.

There are also a number of other, more specific strategies maintained by the United States that are subsumed within the twin concepts of national security and homeland security. The National Strategy for Combating Terrorism defines the U.S. war plan against international terrorism. The National Strategy to Combat Weapons of Mass Destruction coordinates America's many efforts to deny terrorists and states the materials, technology, and expertise to make and deliver weapons of mass destruction. The National Strategy to Secure Cyberspace describes our initiatives to secure our information systems against deliberate, malicious disruption. The National Money Laundering Strategy aims to undercut the illegal flow of money that supports terrorism and international criminal activity. The National Defense Strategy sets priorities for our most powerful national security instrument. The National Drug Control Strategy lays out a comprehensive U.S. effort to combat drug smuggling and consumption. All of these documents fit into the framework established by the National Security Strategy of the United States and National Strategy for Homeland Security, which together take precedence over all other national strategies, programs, and plans.

Securing the Homeland

Homeland security is a concerted national effort to prevent terrorist attacks within the United States, reduce America's vulnerability to terrorism, and minimize the damage and recover from attacks that do occur.

The National Strategy for Homeland Security establishes the foundation for organizing efforts and prioritizing work to:

1. Prevent terrorist attacks within the United States.

2. Reduce America's vulnerability to terrorism.

3. Minimize the damage and recover from attacks that do occur.

The National Strategy for Homeland Security aligns and focuses homeland security functions into six critical mission areas:

1. Intelligence and Warning.

2. Border and Transportation Security.

3. Domestic Counterterrorism.

4. Protecting Critical Infrastructure.

5. Defending Against Catastrophic Terrorism.

6. Emergency Preparedness and Response.

The first three mission areas focus primarily on preventing terrorist attacks; the next two on reducing the nation's vulnerabilities, and the final one on minimizing the damage and recovering from attacks that do occur. The Strategy provides a framework to align the resources of the federal budget directly to the task of securing the homeland.

Intelligence and Warning

Terrorism depends on surprise. With it, a terrorist attack has the potential to do massive damage to an unwitting and unprepared target. Without it, the

Homeland security is a concerted national effort to prevent terrorist attacks within the United States, reduce America's vulnerability to terrorism, and minimize the damage and recover from attacks that do occur.

terrorists stand a good chance of being preempted by authorities, and even if they are not, the damage that results from their attacks is likely to be less severe. The United States needs an intelligence and warning system that can detect terrorist activity before it manifests itself in an attack so that proper preemptive, preventative, and protective action can be taken. The National Strategy for Homeland Security identifies five major initiatives in this area:

1. Enhance the analytic capabilities of the FBI.

2. Build new capabilities through the Information Analysis and Infrastructure Protection Division of the Department of Homeland Security.

3. Implement the Homeland Security Advisory System.

4. Utilize dual-use analysis to prevent attacks.

5. Employ "red team" techniques.

Border and Transportation Security

The National Strategy for Homeland Security aligns and focuses homeland security functions into six critical mission areas:

1. *Intelligence and Warning*
2. *Border and Transportation Security*
3. *Domestic Counterterrorism*
4. *Protecting Critical Infrastructure*
5. *Defending Against Catastrophic Terrorism*
6. *Emergency Preparedness and Response*

America historically has relied heavily on two vast oceans and two friendly neighbors for border security, and on the private sector for most forms of domestic transportation security. The increasing mobility and destructive potential of modern terrorism has required the United States to conceive of border security and transportation security as fully integrated requirements because our domestic transportation systems are inextricably intertwined with the global transport infrastructure. Virtually every community in America is connected to the global transportation network by the seaports, airports, highways, pipelines, railroads, and waterways that move people and goods into, within, and out of the nation. It is necessary therefore to promote the efficient and reliable flow of people, goods, and services across borders, while preventing terrorists from using transportation conveyances or systems to deliver implements of destruction. The National Strategy for Homeland Security identifies six major initiatives in this area:

1. Ensure accountability in border and transportation security.

2. Create "smart borders".

3. Increase the security of international shipping containers.

4. Implement the Aviation and Transportation Security Act of 2001.

5. Recapitalize the U.S. Coast Guard.

6. Reform immigration services.

Domestic Counterterrorism

The attacks of September 11 and the catastrophic loss of life and property that resulted have redefined the mission of federal, state, and local law enforcement authorities. While law enforcement agencies will continue to investigate and prosecute criminal activity, they should now assign priority to preventing and interdicting terrorist activity within the United States. The nation's state and local law enforcement officers will be critical to this effort. Our nation will use all legal means—both traditional and nontraditional—to identify, halt, and where appropriate, prosecute terrorists in the United States. We will pursue not only the individuals directly involved in terrorist activity but also their sources of support: the people and organizations that knowingly fund the terrorists and those that provide them with logistical assistance.

Effectively reorienting law enforcement organizations to focus on counterterrorism objectives requires decisive action in a number of areas. The National Strategy for Homeland Security identifies six major initiatives in this area:

1. Improve intergovernmental law enforcement coordination.

2. Facilitate apprehension of potential terrorists.

3. Continue ongoing investigations and prosecutions.

4. Complete FBI restructuring to emphasize prevention of terrorist attacks.

5. Target and attack terrorist financing.

6. Track foreign terrorists and bring them to justice.

Protecting Critical Infrastructure and Key Assets

American society and modern way of life are dependent on networks of infrastructure—both physical networks such as energy and transportation systems, and virtual networks such as the Internet. If terrorists attack one or more pieces of critical infrastructure, they may disrupt entire systems and cause significant damage to the nation. It is important therefore to improve protection of the individual pieces and interconnecting systems that make up the critical infrastructure. Protecting America's critical infrastructure and key assets will not only make us more secure from terrorist attacks, but will also reduce our vulnerability to natural disasters, organized crime, and computer hackers.

America's critical infrastructure encompasses a large number of sectors. The U.S. government will seek to deny terrorists the opportunity to inflict lasting harm to our nation by protecting the assets, systems, and functions vital to our national security, governance, public health and safety, economy, and national morale.

The National Strategy for Homeland Security identifies eight major initiatives in this area:

1. Unify America's infrastructure protection effort in the Department of Homeland Security.

2. Build and maintain a complete and accurate assessment of America's critical infrastructure and key assets.

3. Enable effective partnership with state and local governments and the private sector.

4. Develop a national infrastructure protection plan.

5. Secure cyberspace.

6. Harness the best analytic and modeling tools to develop effective protective solutions.

7. Guard America's critical infrastructure and key assets against "inside" threats.

8. Partner with the international community to protect our transnational infrastructure.

Defending Against Catastrophic Threats

The expertise, technology, and material needed to build the most deadly weapons known to mankind—including chemical, biological, radiological, and nuclear weapons—are spreading inexorably. If our enemies acquire these weapons, they are likely to try to use them. The consequences of such an attack could be far more devastating than those we suffered on September 11—a chemical, biological, radiological, or nuclear terrorist attack in the United States could cause large numbers of casualties, mass psychological disruption, contamination, and significant economic damage, and could overwhelm local medical capabilities.

Currently, chemical, biological, radiological, and nuclear detection capabilities are modest and response capabilities are dispersed throughout the country at every level of government. While current arrangements have proven adequate for a variety of natural disasters and even the September 11 attacks, the threat of terrorist attack using chemical, biological, radiological, and nuclear weapons requires new approaches, a focused strategy, and a new organization.

The National Strategy for Homeland Security identifies six major initiatives in this area:

1. Prevent terrorist use of nuclear weapons thorough better sensors and procedures.

2. Detect chemical and biological materials and attacks.

3. Improve chemical sensors and decontamination.

4. Develop broad spectrum vaccines, antimicrobials, and antidotes.

5. Harness the scientific knowledge and tools to counter terrorism.

6. Implement the Select Agent Program.

Emergency Preparedness and Response

The United States must prepare to minimize the damage and recover from any future terrorist attacks that may occur despite our best efforts at prevention. An effective response to a major terrorist incident—as well as a natural disaster—depends on being prepared. Therefore, we need a comprehensive national system to bring together and coordinate all necessary response assets quickly and effectively. We must plan, equip, train, and exercise many different response units to mobilize without warning for any emergency.

Many pieces of this national emergency response system are already in place. America's first line of defense in the aftermath of any terrorist attack is its first responder community—police officers, firefighters, emergency medical providers, public works personnel, and emergency management officials. Nearly three million state and local first responders regularly put their lives on the line to save the lives of others and make our country safer.

Yet multiple plans currently govern the federal government's support of first responders during an incident of national significance. These plans which form the government's overarching policy for counterterrorism are based on an artificial and unnecessary distinction between "crisis management" and "consequence management." Under the President's proposal, the Department of Homeland Security will consolidate federal response plans and build a national system for incident management in cooperation with state and local government. Our federal, state, and local governments would ensure that all response personnel and organizations are properly equipped, trained, and exercised to respond to all terrorist threats and attacks in the United States. Our emergency preparedness and response efforts would also engage the private sector and the American people.

The National Strategy for Homeland Security identifies twelve major initiatives in this area:

1. Integrate separate federal response plans into a single all-discipline incident management plan.

2. Create a national incident management system.

3. Improve tactical counterterrorist capabilities.

4. Enable seamless communication among all responders.

5. Prepare health care providers for catastrophic terrorism.

6. Augment America's pharmaceutical and vaccine stockpiles.

7. Prepare for chemical, biological, radiological, and nuclear decontamination.

8. Plan for military support to civil authorities.

9. Build the Citizen Corps.

10. Implement the First Responder Initiative of Fiscal Year 2003 Budget.

11. Build a national training and evaluation system.

12. Enhance the victim support system.

Foundations for Homeland Security

The National Strategy for Homeland Security describes four foundations—unique American strengths that cut across all of the mission areas, across all levels of government, and across all sectors of our society:

1. Law

2. Science and Technology

3. Information Sharing and Systems

4. International Cooperation

These foundations provide a useful framework for evaluating homeland security investments across the federal government.

Law

Throughout our nation's history, we have used laws to promote and safeguard our security and our liberty. The law will both provide mechanisms for the government to act and will define the appropriate limits of action.

The National Strategy for Homeland Security outlines legislative actions that would help enable our country to fight the war on terrorism more effectively. New federal laws should not preempt state law unnecessarily or overly federalize the war on terrorism. We should guard scrupulously against incursions on our freedoms.

The Strategy identifies twelve major initiatives in this area:

Federal Level

1. Enable critical infrastructure information sharing.

2. Streamline information sharing among intelligence and law enforcement agencies.

3. Expand existing extradition authorities.

4. Review authority for military assistance in domestic security.

5. Revive the President's reorganization authority.

6. Provide substantial management flexibility for the Department of Homeland Security.

State Level

7. Coordinate suggested minimum standards for state driver's licenses.

8. Enhance market capacity for terrorism insurance.

9. Train for prevention of cyber attacks.

10. Suppress money laundering.

11. Ensure continuity of the judiciary.

12. Review quarantine authorities.

Science and Technology

The nation's advantage in science and technology is a key to ensuring the safety of the homeland. New technologies for analysis, information sharing, detection of attacks, and countering chemical, biological, radiological, and nuclear weapons will help prevent and minimize the damage from future terrorist attacks. Just as science has helped us defeat past enemies overseas, so too will it help us defeat the efforts of terrorists to attack our homeland and disrupt our way of life.

The federal government is launching a systematic national effort to harness science and technology in support of homeland security. We will build a national research and development enterprise for homeland security sufficient to mitigate the risk posed by modern terrorism. The federal government will consolidate most federally funded homeland security research and development under the Department of Homeland Security to ensure strategic direction and avoid duplicative efforts. We will create and implement a long-term research and development plan that includes investment in revolutionary capabilities with high payoff potential. The federal government will also seek to harness the energy and ingenuity of the private sector to develop and produce the devices and systems needed for homeland security.

The National Strategy for Homeland Security identifies eleven major initiatives in this area:

1. Develop chemical, biological, radiological, and nuclear countermeasures.

2. Develop systems for detecting hostile intent.

3. Apply biometric technology to identification devices.

4. Improve the technical capabilities of first responders.

5. Coordinate research and development of the homeland security apparatus.

6. Establish a national laboratory for homeland security.

7. Solicit independent and private analysis for science and technology research.

8. Establish a mechanism for rapidly producing prototypes.

9. Conduct demonstrations and pilot deployments.

10. Set standards for homeland security technology.

11. Establish a system for high-risk, high-payoff homeland security research.

Information Sharing and Systems

Information systems contribute to every aspect of homeland security. Although American information technology is the most advanced in the world, our country's information systems have not adequately supported the homeland security mission. Databases used for federal law enforcement, immigration, intelligence, public health surveillance, and emergency management have not been connected in ways that allow us to comprehend where information gaps or redundancies exist. In addition, there are deficiencies in the communications systems used by states and municipalities throughout the country; most state and local first responders do not use compatible communications equipment. To secure the homeland better, we must link the vast amounts of knowledge residing within each government agency while ensuring adequate privacy.

The National Strategy for Homeland Security identifies five major initiatives in this area:

1. Integrate information sharing across the federal government

2. Integrate information sharing across state and local governments, private industry, and citizens

3. Adopt common "meta-data" standards for electronic information relevant to homeland security

4. Improve public safety emergency communications

5. Ensure reliable public health information

International Cooperation

In a world where the terrorist threat pays no respect to traditional boundaries, the strategy for homeland security cannot stop at the borders. America must pursue a sustained, steadfast, and systematic international agenda to counter the global terrorist threat and improve our homeland security. Our international anti-terrorism campaign has made significant progress since September 11.

The National Strategy for Homeland Security identifies nine major initiatives in this area:

1. Create "smart borders".

2. Combat fraudulent travel documents.

3. Increase the security of international shipping containers.

4. Intensify international law enforcement cooperation.

5. Help foreign nations fight terrorism.

6. Expand protection of transnational critical infrastructure.

7. Amplify international cooperation on homeland security science and technology.

8. Improve cooperation in response to attacks.

9. Review obligations to international treaties and law.

Conclusion

The National Strategy for Homeland Security sets a broad and complex agenda for the United States. The Strategy has defined many different goals that need to be met, programs that need to be implemented, and responsibilities that need to be fulfilled. But creating a strategy is, in many respects, about setting priorities—about recognizing that some actions are more critical or more urgent than others.

The President's Fiscal Year 2003 Budget proposal, released in February 2002, identified four priority areas for additional resources and attention in 2003:

1. Support first responders.

2. Defend against bioterrorism.

3. Secure America's borders.

4. Use 21st-century technology to secure the homeland.

Furthermore, at the time National Strategy for Homeland Security was published, it was expected that the Fiscal Year 2004 Budget would attach priority to the following specific items for substantial support:

- Enhance the analytic capabilities of the FBI.

- Build new capabilities through the Information Analysis and Infrastructure Protection Division of the proposed Department of Homeland Security.

- Create "smart borders".

- Improve the security of international shipping containers.

- Recapitalize the U.S. Coast Guard.

- Prevent terrorist use of nuclear weapons through better sensors and procedures.

- Develop broad spectrum vaccines, antimicrobials, and antidotes.

- Integrate information sharing across the federal government.

In the intervening months, the executive branch will prepare detailed implementation plans for these and many other initiatives contained within the National Security Strategy for Homeland Security. These plans will ensure that the taxpayer's money is spent only in a manner that achieves specific objectives with clear performance-based measures of effectiveness.[1]

Questions

1. What is the relationship between homeland security and national security?

2. What is the purpose of homeland security?

3. List the six critical mission areas identified in the National Strategy for Homeland Security.

## Chapter 10

DHS Organization

Objectives

- Know the mission of DHS.

- Describe the relationship between HSC and DHS.

- Understand the basic structure of DHS.

- Relate the DHS structure to the National Strategy for Homeland Security.

- Relate the DHS structure to the events of 9-11.

Introduction

The U.S. Department of Homeland Security (DHS or Department) was established by the Homeland Security Act of 2002 (the Act), Public Law 107-296 (the Law), dated November 25, 2002, as an executive department of the United States government. The primary mission of DHS is to:

- Prevent terrorist attacks within the United States;

- Reduce the vulnerability of the United States to terrorism;

- Minimize the damage, and assist in the recovery, from terrorist attacks and natural disasters that occur within the United States;

- Carry out all functions of entities transferred to the Department, including acting as a focal point regarding natural and manmade crises and emergency planning;

- Ensure that the functions of the agencies and subdivisions within the Department that are not related directly to securing the homeland are not diminished or neglected except by a specific, explicit Act of Congress;

- Ensure that the overall economic security of the United States is not diminished by efforts, activities, and programs aimed at securing the homeland; and

- Monitor connections between illegal drug trafficking and terrorism, coordinate efforts to sever such connections, and otherwise contribute to efforts to interdict illegal drug trafficking.

The Law was implemented according to the President's Department of Homeland Security Reorganization Plan (Reorganization Plan), dated November 25, 2002. On January 24, 2003, the effective date of the Law, and in accordance with the Reorganization Plan, the Office of the Secretary of DHS (the Secretary) was established, as well as other key managerial positions. In addition, pursuant to the Law and Reorganization Plan, the Secretary established the following four DHS Directorates:

1. Science and Technology

2. Border and Transportation Security

3. Emergency Preparedness and Response

4. Information Analysis and Infrastructure

In addition, the Secretary established Bureaus or sub organizations including:

1. U.S. Citizenship and Immigration Services

2. U.S. Secret Service

3. U.S. Coast Guard

4. Management

5. Office of Inspector General[1]

Even after creation of the new Department, homeland security would still involve the efforts of other Cabinet departments. The Department of Justice (DoJ) and the FBI would remain the lead law enforcement agencies for preventing terrorist attacks. The Department of Defense (DoD) would continue to play a crucial support role in the case of a catastrophic incident. The Department of Transportation (DoT) would continue to be responsible for highway and rail safety, and air traffic control. The Central Intelligence Agency (CIA) would continue to gather and analyze overseas intelligence. Homeland security would continue to require interagency coordination, and the President would still need a close advisor on homeland security related issues.[2]

White House Office of Homeland Security

Accordingly, the President intended a strong continuing role for the White House Office of Homeland Security (OHS) and the Homeland Security Council (HSC) established by Executive Order 13228, October 8th, 2001. When signing the Homeland Security Act into law on November 25th, 2002, President Bush said he intended to nominate Tom Ridge, then acting as Assistant to the President for Homeland Security, as the first Secretary of Homeland Security. The Senate confirmed Ridge in this new role on January 24th, 2003, the day the Homeland Security Act took effect. His deputy, Steve Abbot, assumed direction of OHS. On April 29th, 2003, the White House announced that President Bush was appointing retired general John A. Gordon—who held high-level intelligence, energy security, and counterterrorism positions—to be Assistant to the President and Homeland Security Advisor, which brought him the directorship of OHS. However, some of the functions of OHS—incident management, budget review, alert advisory determinations, and various coordination efforts—were, or soon would be, performed by the new department. The director of OHS was not a statutory member of the new Homeland Security Council mandated by the Homeland Security Act. In late July 2004, House appropriators revealed that the Bush Administration had changed the "Office of Homeland Security" account to one for the "Homeland Security Council." The President's FY2005 budget made no mention of OHS, which while not formally abolished, has become dormant, like the council of National Defense of World War I, and the Office for Emergency Management of World War II. The Homeland Security Council remains, however, to help the President develop policy and coordinate interagency action.

The President's FY2005 budget made no mention of OHS, which while not formally abolished, has become dormant, like the council of National Defense of World War I, and the Office for Emergency Management of World War II.

Consolidating the New Department

The Department of Homeland Security was meant to mobilize and focus the resources of the federal government, state and local government, the private sector, and the American people. The creation of the Department of Homeland Security empowered a single Cabinet official whose primary mission is to protect the American homeland from terrorism.[3]

Transfers of personnel, facilities, records, assets (including technology systems), obligations, and functions (e.g., authorities, powers, rights, privileges, immunities, programs, projects, activities, duties and responsibilities) from 22 existing Federal agencies and programs, began on March 1, 2003 – the inception date of DHS operations – pursuant to guidance provided to the legacy agencies from the Office of Management and Budget (OMB) and the U.S. Department of Treasury (Treasury).

The Department of Homeland Security faced the unprecedented challenge of reorganizing 22 agencies, 180,000 employees and numerous financial management systems, compensation structures and information systems.[4] The agencies slated to become part of the Department of Homeland Security would be housed in one of four major directorates: Border and Transportation Security, Emergency Preparedness and Response, Science and Technology, and Information Analysis and Infrastructure Protection.

The Border and Transportation Security directorate would bring the major border security and transportation operations under one roof, including:

- The U.S. Customs Service (Treasury)

- The Immigration and Naturalization Service (part) (Justice)

- The Federal Protective Service

- The Transportation Security Administration (Transportation)

- Federal Law Enforcement Training Center (Treasury)

- Animal and Plant Health Inspection Service (part) (Agriculture)

- Office for Domestic Preparedness (Justice)

The Emergency Preparedness and Response directorate would oversee domestic disaster preparedness training and coordinate government disaster response. It would bring together:

- The Federal Emergency Management Agency (FEMA)

- Strategic National Stockpile and the National Disaster Medical System (HHS)

- Nuclear Incident Response Team (Energy)

- Domestic Emergency Support Teams (Justice)

- National Domestic Preparedness Office (FBI)

The Science and Technology directorate would seek to utilize all scientific and technological advantages when securing the homeland. The following assets would be part of this effort:

- CBRN Countermeasures Programs (Energy)

- Environmental Measurements Laboratory (Energy)

- National BW Defense Analysis Center (Defense)

- Plum Island Animal Disease Center (Agriculture)

The Information Analysis and Infrastructure Protection directorate would analyze intelligence and information from other agencies (including the CIA, FBI, DIA and NSA) involving threats to homeland security and evaluate vulnerabilities in the nation's infrastructure. It would bring together:

- Federal Computer Incident Response Center (GSA)

- National Communications System (Defense)

- National Infrastructure Protection Center (FBI)

- Energy Security and Assurance Program (Energy)

The Secret Service and the Coast Guard would also be located in the Department of Homeland Security, remaining intact and reporting directly to the Secretary. In addition, the INS adjudications and benefits programs would report directly to the Deputy Secretary as the U.S. Citizenship and Immigration Services.[5]

New Headquarters

On December 17, 2002, the General Services Administration (GSA), which is responsible for finding office space for government agencies, issued a solicitation for approximately 275,000 rentable square feet of space for the Department of Homeland Security. The deadline for submission of proposals, or offers, was 3:00 p.m. on December 23, 2002. Paragraph 1.2 of the solicitation identified the area of consideration:

> "All properties offered must be located within the Metropolitan Area of Washington, DC. For purposes of this solicitation, the Metropolitan Area of Washington, DC is limited to the District of Columbia, Prince Georges and Montgomery Counties of Maryland, and Alexandria City, and Fairfax, Loudoun, Arlington Counties of Virginia and their incorporated cities."

During the first week of the 108th Congress, both chambers passed, and the President signed, P.L. 108-2 (H.J. Res. 1), which included a section that refers to a prospectus for leasing office space for DHS. Section 5(a) stated:

> "For purposes of section 3307(a) of title 40, United States Code, the prospectus of General Services Administration entitled 'Prospectus — Lease, Department of Homeland Security, Washington, DC Metropolitan Area', prospectus number PDC-08W03, as submitted on December 24, 2002, is deemed approved by the Committee on Environment and Public Works of the Senate and the Committee on Transportation and Infrastructure of the House of Representatives on the date of enactment of this Act."

As reported in the *Washington Post on* January 8, 2003, and the *Washington Times on* January 9, 2003, three sites in northern Virginia (one in Chantilly, two in Tysons Corner) were, at the time, likely candidates for the new department.

However, DHS chose the U.S. Naval Security Station, which is located at Nebraska and Massachusetts Avenues in the District of Columbia and which is also known as the Nebraska Avenue complex. DHS began operations at the complex on January 27, 2003. With the enactment of P.L. 108-268 (H.R. 4322) on July 2, 2004, it appears that the Nebraska Avenue complex has been selected, for the time being, as the location for the headquarters of DHS. Section 1(a) requires the Secretary of the Navy to transfer the jurisdiction, custody, and control of the Nebraska Avenue complex to the Administrator of General Services for the purpose of permitting the Administrator to use the complex to accommodate the Department of Homeland Security. The transfer was to be completed within nine months of the date of enactment.[6]

Transition

With the exception of the new headquarters, management, and staff, most elements of the new Department remained in place: there wasn't a massive shift of personnel or resources to Washington DC.

With the exception of the new headquarters, management, and staff, most elements of the new Department remained in place: there wasn't a massive shift of personnel or resources to Washington DC. The transition, for the most part, involved transferring lines of authority to the new Secretary of Homeland Security. Given the incoming entities' widely disparate policies, procedures and information systems, the change was complex and required a high degree of cooperation and coordination. An important step in the establishment of the Department was the determination order process. Through the determination order, agencies documented key financial, logistical, and human resources to be transferred to the Department. The President's November 25th, 2002, Reorganization Plan for the Department outlined the transfer of most component agencies and programs to the Department by March 1st, 2003. In the short span of two months, the Under Secretary for Management coordinated the transfers of personnel and resources into the Department. These efforts included the transfer of the following:

- Unexpended Budgetary Resources totaling: $37 billion. In advance of these transfers, the Department worked with the Office of Management and Budget (OMB) and the Treasury to establish an entirely new appropriation account structure and bureau structure. This effort involved over 19 accounting offices processing over 330 separate transfers and created the budgetary resources to fund Department operations.

- Personnel. This effort involved 180,000 full time employees. In advance of these transfers, the Department worked with the Office of Personnel Management (OPM) to design and implement a personnel management structure impacting seven Federal separate payroll providers. As a result, all personnel were transferred as of the effective date of the Homeland Security Act.

- Accounting Location Codes. This effort involved the establishment of approximately 100 locations certifying disbursements and depositing re-

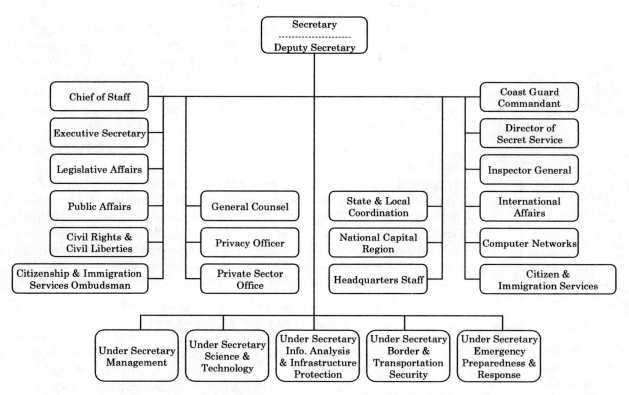

Figure 10.1: Organization of the Department of Homeland Security.

ceipts. This effort alone ensured the Department would have the capability to process commercial payments to vendors and reimburse employees for travel and other expenses and deposit billions of dollars in collections.

- Real Estate. The Department of Homeland Security owns 8,500 buildings amounting to a total 34,700,000 square feet of space. In addition, the Department leased 3,600 buildings amounting to a total of 33,800,000 square feet of space.

Directorates

To accomplish its mission, the Department of Homeland Security organized into five directorates.

1. Information Analysis and Infrastructure Protection (IAIP) Directorate identifies and assesses a broad range of intelligence information concerning threats to the homeland, issues timely warnings and takes appropriate preventive and protective action. IAIP functions include:

    - Information Analysis provides actionable intelligence essential for preventing acts of terrorism and, with timely and thorough analysis and dissemination of information about terrorists and their activities, improves the government's ability to disrupt and prevent terrorist acts and to provide useful warning to state and local government, the private sector and our citizens; and

- Infrastructure Protection coordinates national efforts to secure America's critical infrastructure, including vulnerability assessments, strategic planning efforts and exercises. Protecting America's critical infrastructure is the shared responsibility of federal, state and local governments, in active partnership with the private sector, which owns approximately 85 percent of our nation's critical infrastructure.

2. Border and Transportation Security (BTS) Directorate ensures the security of our nation's borders and transportation systems. Its first priority is to prevent the entry of terrorists and the instruments of terrorism while simultaneously ensuring the efficient flow of lawful traffic and commerce. BTS manages and coordinates port of entry activities and lead efforts to create borders that feature greater security through better intelligence, coordinated national efforts and international cooperation against terrorists and the instruments of terrorism and other international threats. BTS includes the following organizations:

   - U.S. Customs and Border Protection (CBP) provides security at America's borders and ports of entry as well as extending our zone of security beyond our physical borders—so that American borders are the last line of defense, not the first. CBP also is responsible for apprehending individuals attempting to enter the United States illegally, stemming the flow of illegal drugs and other contraband; protecting our agricultural and economic interests from harmful pests and diseases; protecting American businesses from theft of intellectual property; regulating and facilitating international trade; collecting import duties; and enforcing United States trade laws;

   - U.S. Immigration and Customs Enforcement (ICE), the largest investigative arm of the Department, enforces federal immigration, customs and air security laws. ICE's primary mission is to detect vulnerabilities and prevent violations that threaten national security. ICE works to protect the United States and its people by deterring, interdicting and investigating threats arising from the movement of people and goods into and out of the United States; and by policing and securing federal government facilities across the Nation;

   - Transportation Security Administration (TSA) protects the Nation's transportation systems to ensure freedom of movement for people and commerce. TSA sets the standard for excellence in transportation security through its people processes and technologies;

   - Federal Law Enforcement Training Center (FLETC) is the Federal Government's leader for and provider of world-class law enforcement training. FLETC prepares new and experienced law enforcement professionals to fulfill their responsibilities safely and at the highest level of proficiency, ensuring that training is provided in the most cost-effective manner; and

DHS is organized into five directorates:

1. *Information Analysis and Infrastructure Protection*
2. *Border and Transportation Security*
3. *Emergency Preparedness and Response*
4. *Science and Technology*
5. *Management*

3. Emergency Preparedness and Response (EP&R) Directorate ensures that our nation is prepared for, and able to recover from terrorist attacks and natural disasters. EP&R provides domestic disaster preparedness training and coordinates government disaster response. The core of emergency preparedness includes the Federal Emergency Management Agency (FEMA), responsible for reducing the loss of life and property and protecting our nation's institutions from all types of hazards through a comprehensive, emergency management program of preparedness, prevention, response and recovery.

4. Science and Technology (S&T) Directorate provides federal, state and local operators with the technology and capabilities needed to protect the Nation from catastrophic terrorist attacks, including threats from weapons of mass destruction. The S&T Directorate develops and deploys state-of-the-art, high performance, low operating cost systems to detect and rapidly mitigate the consequences of terrorist attacks, including those that may use chemical, biological, radiological and nuclear materials.

5. Management Directorate oversees the budget; appropriations; expenditure of funds; accounting and finance; procurement; human resources and personnel; information technology systems; facilities, property, equipment and other material resources; and identification and tracking of performance measures aligned with the mission of the Department. The Chief Financial Officer, Chief Information Officer, Chief Human Capital Officer, Chief Procurement Officer and the Chief of Administrative Services report to the Undersecretary for Management as allowed by the Homeland Security Act of 2002.

Agencies

Besides the five major Directorates, the following are critical agencies within the Department.

- The United States Coast Guard (USCG) ensures maritime safety, mobility and security and protects our natural marine resources. Its mission is to protect the public, the environment and the United States economic interests—in the Nation's ports and waterways, along the coast, on international waters, or in any maritime region as required to support our national security. The Coast Guard also prevents Maritime terrorist attacks; halts the flow of illegal drugs and contraband; prevents individuals from entering the United States illegally; and prevents illegal incursion of our exclusive economic zone. Upon declaration of war, or when the President so directs, the USCG will operate as an element of the Department of Defense, consistent with existing law.

- The United States Secret Service (USSS) protects the President and Vice President, their families, heads of state and other designated individuals; investigates threats against these protectees; protects designated buildings within Washington, D.C.; and plans and implements security for designated National Special Security Events (NSSEs). The USSS also investigates violations of laws relating to counterfeiting and financial crimes, including computer fraud and computer-based attacks on our nation's financial, banking, and telecommunications infrastructure.

- The U.S. Citizenship and Immigration Services (USCIS) directs the Nation's immigration benefit system and promotes citizenship values by providing immigration services such as immigrant and nonimmigrant sponsorship; adjustment of status; work authorization and other permits; naturalization of qualified applicants for United States citizenship; and asylum or refugee processing. USCIS makes certain that America continues to welcome visitors and those who seek opportunity within our shores while excluding terrorists and their supporters.

- The Office of Inspector General (OIG) serves as an independent and objective inspection, audit, and investigative body to promote effectiveness, efficiency, and economy in the Department's programs and operations. OIG seeks to prevent and detect fraud, abuse, mismanagement and waste.

- Office of State and Local Coordination (OSLC) including the Office for Domestic Preparedness (ODP) coordinates with State and local government personnel, agencies, and authorities, and with the private sector, to ensure adequate planning, equipment, training, and exercise activities; consolidate the Federal Government's communications with State and local governments and the public; and distribute or, as appropriate, coordinate the distribution of, warnings and information to State and local government and to the public.[7]

On July 13, 2005 the new Secretary of Homeland Security, Michael Chertoff, announced a six-point agenda for the Department of Homeland Security designed to ensure that the Department's policies, operations, and structures are aligned in the best way to address the potential threats – both present and future – that face our nation.

Six-Point Agenda

The Homeland Security Act of 2002 provided certain flexibility for the Secretary of Homeland Security to establish, consolidate, alter or discontinue organizational units within the Department. The mechanism for implementing these changes is a notification to Congress, required under section 872 of the Homeland Security Act, allowing for the changes to take effect after 60 days.

On July 13, 2005 the new Secretary of Homeland Security, Michael Chertoff, announced a six-point agenda for the Department of Homeland Security designed to ensure that the Department's policies, operations, and structures are aligned in the best way to address the potential threats – both present and future – that face our nation:[8]

1. Increase overall preparedness, particularly for catastrophic events

2. Create better transportation security systems to move people and cargo more securely and efficiently

3. Strengthen border security and interior enforcement and reform immigration processes;

4. Enhance information sharing with DHS partners

5. Improve DHS financial management, human resource development, procurement and information technology

6. Realign the DHS organization to maximize mission performance.

The agenda is based on conclusions drawn as a result of the Second Stage Review. The review, initiated by the Secretary, examined nearly every element of the Department of Homeland Security in order to recommend ways that DHS could better:

- Manage risk in terms of threat, vulnerability and consequence;

- Prioritize policies and operational missions according to a risk-based approach;

- Establish a series of preventive and protective steps that would increase security at multiple levels.

Eighteen action teams composed of 10-12 subject matter experts and hundreds of public and private partners at the federal, state, local, tribal and international levels examined a wide range of issues, including:

- Risk/Readiness

- Information and Intelligence Sharing

- Performance Metrics

- Law Enforcement Activities

- Listening to External Partners

- Supply Chain Security

- Internal Communications and DHS Culture

- Research, Technology & Detection

To support the six-point agenda, Secretary Chertoff proposed realigning the Department of Homeland Security to increase its ability to prepare, prevent, and respond to terrorist attacks and other emergencies by:

- Centralizing and improving policy development and coordination.

- Strengthening intelligence functions and information sharing.

- Improving coordination and efficiency of operations.

- Enhancing coordination and deployment of preparedness assets.

- Realigning other departments.

Centralizing and Improving Policy Development and Coordination. A new Directorate of Policy will become the primary Department-wide coordinator for policies, regulations, and other initiatives to ensure consistency of policy and regulatory development across the department. It will perform long-range strategic policy planning and assume the policy coordination functions previously performed by the Border and Transportation Security (BTS) Directorate. The new Policy Directorate will include:

To support the six-point agenda, Secretary Chertoff proposed realigning the Department of Homeland Security by:

- *Centralizing and improving policy development and coordination.*
- *Strengthening intelligence functions and information sharing.*
- *Improving coordination and efficiency of operations.*
- *Enhancing coordination and deployment of preparedness assets.*
- *Realigning other departments.*

- The Office of International Affairs

- Office of Private Sector Liaison

- Homeland Security Advisory Council

- Office of Immigration Statistics

- The Senior Asylum Officer

Strengthen Intelligence Functions and Information Sharing. A new Office of Intelligence and Analysis will be created to ensure that information is gathered from all relevant field operations and other parts of the intelligence community and analyzed with a mission-oriented focus informative to senior decision-makers, and disseminated to the appropriate federal, state, local, and private sector partners. The new office will be led by a Chief Intelligence Officer reporting directly to the Secretary, and comprised of analysts within the former Information Analysis directorate. It will also draw on the expertise of other department components with intelligence collection and analysis operations.

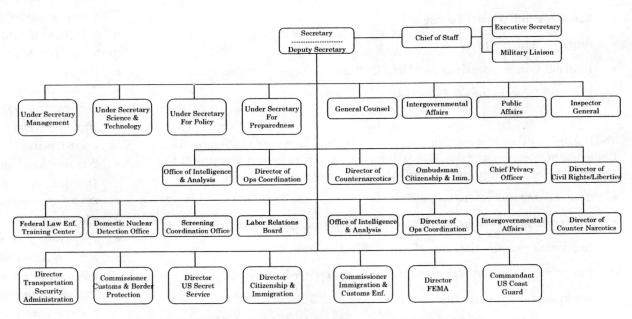

Figure 10.2: Proposed Six-Point Agenda DHS Realignment .

Improve Coordination and Efficiency of Operations. A new Director of Operations Coordination will be created to conduct joint operations across all organizational elements, coordinate incident management activities, and use all resources within the Department to translate intelligence and policy into immediate action. The Homeland Security Operations Center, which serves as the nation's nerve center for information sharing and domestic incident management on a 24/7/365 basis, will become a critical part of this new office.

Enhance Coordination and Deployment of Preparedness Assets. A new Directorate for Preparedness will consolidate preparedness assets from across the Department to facilitate grants and oversee nationwide preparedness efforts supporting first responder training, citizen awareness, public health, infrastructure and cyber security and ensure proper steps are taken to protect high-risk targets. The new department will focus on cyber security and telecommunications, and include a new Chief Medical Officer, responsible for carrying out the Department's responsibilities to coordinate the response to biological attacks. Managed by an Under Secretary, this Directorate will include infrastructure protection, assets of the Office of State and Local Government Coordination and Preparedness responsible for grants, training and exercises, the U.S. Fire Administration, and the Office of National Capitol Region Coordination.

Other Department Realignments.

- Improve National Response and Recovery Efforts by Focusing FEMA on Its Core Functions. FEMA will report directly to the Secretary of Homeland Security. In order to strengthen and enhance our Nation's ability to respond to and recover from manmade or natural disasters, FEMA will now focus on its historic and vital mission of response and recovery.

- Integrate Federal Air Marshal Service (FAMS) into Broader Aviation Security Efforts. The Federal Air Marshal Service will be moved from the Immigration and Customs Enforcement (ICE) bureau to the Transportation Security Administration to increase operational coordination and strengthen efforts to meet this common goal of aviation security.

- Merge Legislative and Intergovernmental Affairs. This new Office of Legislative and Intergovernmental Affairs will merge certain functions among the Office of Legislative Affairs and the Office of State and Local Government Coordination in order to streamline intergovernmental relations efforts and better share homeland security information with members of Congress as well as state and local officials.

- Assign Office of Security to Management Directorate. The Office of Security will be moved to return oversight of that office to the Under Secretary for Management in order to better manage information systems, contractual activities, security accreditation, training and resources.[9]

Conclusion

The Department of Homeland Security was designed to make Americans safer by providing the Nation with:

- One department whose primary mission is to protect the American homeland;

- One department to secure our borders, transportation sector, ports, and critical infrastructure;

- One department to synthesize and analyze homeland security intelligence from multiple sources;

- One department to coordinate communications with state and local governments, private industry, and the American people about threats and preparedness;

- One department to coordinate our efforts to protect the American people against bioterrorism and other weapons of mass destruction;

- One department to help train and equip first responders;

- One department to manage federal emergency response activities; and

- More security officers in the field working to stop terrorists and fewer resources in Washington managing duplicative and redundant activities that drain critical homeland security resources.[10]

Questions

1. What is the purpose and mission of DHS?

2. Why do we still need an HSC?

3. What are the five DHS directorates?

4. Compare the critical mission areas of the Homeland Security Strategy with the organization of DHS.

Part III:
Critical Mission Areas

Chapter 11

Information Analysis & Warning

Objectives

- Explain the rationale for creating a DHS information analysis and warning capability.

- Understand the issues with investing an intelligence capability in DHS.

- Describe some of the concerns regarding civil liberties.

- Know which organization in DHS is responsible for analyzing and issuing warnings.

- List the five terrorist alert conditions.

- Describe some of the drawbacks to the Homeland Security Advisory System.

Intelligence and Warning. Terrorism depends on surprise. With it, a terrorist attack has the potential to do massive damage to an unwitting and unprepared target. Without it, the terrorists stand a good chance of being preempted by authorities, and even if they are not, the damage that results from their attacks is likely to be less severe. The United States will take every necessary action to avoid being surprised by another terrorist attack. We must have an intelligence and warning system that can detect terrorist activity before it manifests itself in an attack so that proper preemptive, preventive, and protective action can be taken.

— Critical Mission Area #1, National Strategy for Homeland Security, July 2002

Introduction

Better intelligence is held by many observers to be a crucial factor in preventing terrorist attacks. Concerns have been expressed that no single agency or office in the federal government prior to September 11, 2001 was in a position to "connect the dots" between diffuse bits of information that might have provided clues to the planned attacks. Testimony before the two intelligence committees' Joint Inquiry on the September 11 attacks indicated that significant information in the possession of intelligence and law enforcement agencies was not fully shared with other agencies and that intelligence on potential terrorist threats against the United States was not fully exploited.

Better intelligence is held by many observers to be a crucial factor in preventing terrorist attacks.

For many years, the sharing of intelligence and law enforcement information was circumscribed by administrative policies and statutory prohibitions. Beginning in the early 1990s, however, much effort has gone into improving interagency coordination.

After the September 11 attacks, a number of statutory obstacles were addressed by the USA-Patriot Act of 2001 and other legislation. Nevertheless, there has been no one place where the analytical effort is centered; the Department of Homeland Security (DHS) was designed to remedy that perceived deficiency as is the new Terrorist Threat Integration Center announced by the President in his January 2003 State of the Union address.

Background

The Bush Administration's legislative proposal for a Department of Homeland Security, released July 16, 2002, was incorporated in H.R. 5005, introduced on June 24, 2002 by Representative Armey. Title II of the bill, Information Analysis and Infrastructure Protection, as subsequently amended and passed by the House on July 26, included provisions to establish an Intelligence Analysis Center to give intelligence support to the homeland security effort and to identify priorities for measures to protect key sources and critical infrastructures. In the Senate, Senator Lieberman had introduced legislation (S. 2452) to establish a Department of National Homeland Security on May 2, 2002. The original version of S. 2452 did not address the intelligence function, but subsequent amendments in the nature of a substitute included provisions establishing a Directorate of Intelligence as an integral part of the new department. After the November 2002 elections a modified version of homeland security legislation was introduced by Representative Armey and passed by the House on November 13, 2002. Subsequently, both House and Senate passed an amended version of H.R. 5005, and the bill was signed by the President on November 25, 2002, becoming P.L. 107-296.

The final version of the Homeland Security Act established a Directorate for Information Analysis and Infrastructure Protection headed by an Under Secretary for Information Analysis and Infrastructure Protection (appointed by the President by and with the advice and consent of the Senate) with an Assistant Secretary of Information Analysis (appointed by the President). The legislation, especially the Information Analysis section, seeks to promote close ties between intelligence analysts and those responsible for assessing vulnerabilities of key U.S. infrastructure. The bill envisions an intelligence entity focused on receiving and analyzing information from other government agencies and using it to provide warning of terrorist attacks and for addressing vulnerabilities that terrorists could exploit.

DHS is not intended to duplicate the collection effort of intelligence agencies; it will not have its own agents, satellites, or signals intercept sites. Major intelligence agencies are not transferred to the DHS, although some DHS elements, including Customs and the Coast Guard, will continue to collect information that is crucial to analyzing terrorist threats.

DHS is not intended to duplicate the collection effort of intelligence agencies; it will not have its own agents, satellites, or signals intercept sites.

The legislation establishing DHS envisioned an information analysis element with the responsibility for acquiring and reviewing information from the agencies of the Intelligence Community, from law enforcement agencies, state and local government agencies, and unclassified publicly available information (known as open source information or "OSINT") from books, periodicals, pamphlets, the Internet, media, etc. The legislation is explicit that, "Except as otherwise directed by the President, the Secretary [of DHS] shall have such access as the Secretary considers necessary to all information, including reports, assessments, analyses, and unevaluated intelligence relating to threats of terrorism against the United States and to other areas of responsibility assigned by the Secretary, and to all information concerning infrastructures or other vulnerabilities of the United States to terrorism, whether or not such information has been analyzed, that may be collected, possessed, or prepared by any agency of the Federal Government."

DHS analysts are charged with using this information to identify and assess the nature and scope of terrorist threats; producing comprehensive vulnerability assessments of key resources and infrastructure; identifying priorities for protective and support measures by DHS, by other agencies of the federal government, state and local government agencies and authorities, the private sector, and other entities. They will disseminate information to assist in the deterrence, prevention, preemption of, or response to, terrorist attacks against the U.S. The intelligence element is also charged with recommending measures necessary for protecting key resources and critical infrastructure in coordination with other federal agencies.

DHS is responsible for ensuring that any material received is protected from unauthorized disclosure and handled and used only for the performance of official duties. (This provision addresses a concern that sensitive personal information made available to DHS analysts could be misused.) As is the case for other federal agencies that handle classified materials, intelligence information is transmitted, retained, and disseminated consistent with policies established under the authority of the Director of Central Intelligence (DCI) to protect intelligence sources and methods and similar authorities of the Attorney General concerning sensitive law enforcement information.

Concerns about DHS Intelligence

Despite enactment of the Homeland Security Act, it is clear that significant concerns persisted within the Administration about the new department's ability to analyze intelligence and law enforcement information. Media accounts suggest that these concerns center on DHS' status as a new and untested agency and the potential risks involved in forwarding "raw" intelligence to the DHS intelligence component. Another concern is that a new entity, rather than long-established intelligence and law enforcement agencies, would be relied on to produce all-source intelligence relating to the most serious threats facing the country.

Significant concerns persist about the new department's ability to analyze intelligence and law enforcement information. Media accounts suggest that these concerns center on DHS' status as a new and untested agency and the potential risks involved in forwarding "raw" intelligence to the DHS intelligence component.

DHS Role in the Intelligence Community

The U.S. Intelligence Community consists of the Central Intelligence Agency (CIA) and some 14 other agencies; it provides information in various forms to the White House and other federal agencies (as well as to Congress). In addition, law enforcement agencies, such as the Federal Bureau of Investigation (FBI), also collect information for use in the federal government. Within the Intelligence Community, priorities for collection (and to some extent for analysis) are established by the DCI, based in practice on inter-agency discussions. Being "at the table" when priorities are discussed, it is widely believed, helps ensure equitable allocations of limited collection resources.

The Homeland Security Act makes the DHS information analysis element a member of the Intelligence Community, thus giving DHS a formal role when intelligence collection and analysis priorities are being addressed. It is also intended to facilitate access to intelligence databases and other analytical resources. Nonetheless, the relationship of DHS to the Intelligence Community will probably not be as close — at least initially — as that of other intelligence agencies that have long experience in dealing with national security questions and in dealing with jurisdictional issues.

The Question of "Raw" Intelligence

There has been discussion in the media whether DHS will have access to "raw" intelligence or only to finished analytical products, but these reports may reflect uncertainty regarding the definition of "raw" intelligence. A satellite photograph standing by itself might be considered "raw" data, but it would be useless unless something were known about where and when it was taken. Thus, satellite imagery supplied to DHS would under almost any circumstances have to include some analysis. The same would apply to signals intercepts. Reports from human agents present special challenges. Some assessment of the reliability of the source would have to be provided, but information that would identify a specific individual is normally retained within a very small circle of intelligence officials so as to reduce the risk of unauthorized disclosure and harm to the source.

The issue of the extent and nature of information forwarded to DHS has proved to be difficult. Reviewing copies of summary reports prepared by existing agencies is seen by some observers as inadequate for the task of putting together a meaningful picture of terrorist capabilities and intentions and providing timely warning. On the other hand, there is a need to ensure that DHS would not be inundated with vast quantities of data and that highly sensitive information is not given wider dissemination than absolutely Necessary.

Analytical Quality

The key test for homeland security will of course be the quality of the analytical product — whether terrorist groups can be identified and timely warning given of plans for attacks on the U.S. While most observers acknowledge that focusing in one office the responsibility for identifying terrorist threats will remedy a fundamental limitation of existing arrangements, it is also understood that establishing such an office in a new agency may have complications. The types of information that have to be analyzed come from disparate sources and require a variety of analytical skills that are not in plentiful supply. Academic institutions prepare significant numbers of linguists and area specialists, but training in the inner workings of clandestine terrorist entities is less often undertaken. Analysts with law enforcement backgrounds may not be attuned to the foreign environments from which terrorist groups emerge. DHS would begin with analysts detailed from existing intelligence and law enforcement agencies along with, presumably, some newly hired personnel. There is concern about previous bureaucratic competitors merging effectively and a culture of objectivity and adherence to high standards being established from the outset.[1]

Homeland security measures often involve striking a balance between greater safety and infringements on civil liberties, such as invasions of privacy, discrimination, and other curtailments of individual freedom.

Security Versus Freedom

Homeland security measures often involve striking a balance between greater safety and infringements on civil liberties, such as invasions of privacy, discrimination, and other curtailments of individual freedom. As USA Today's Gene Stephens explains, *"We cannot truly be free unless we have a reasonable degree of safety, but we cannot truly feel safe unless we are also secure from undue prying into our personal lives."* Baggage searches at airports, for example, may deter potential hijackers, but they also invade the privacy of countless non-terrorists. Similarly, granting broader investigative powers to the FBI could help thwart future attacks but may also result in unwarranted government surveillance or harassment of many innocent people. Evaluating homeland security efforts thus becomes a question of trade-offs; security experts must decide to what degree civil liberties should be curtailed in order to strengthen homeland security.

While homeland security encompasses a vast array of efforts at the local, state, and national levels, three centerpieces of the federal government's homeland security strategy have been intelligence gathering, intelligence sharing, and immigration control. The Bush administration's efforts to improve the government's capabilities in each of these three areas have been among the most controversial issues surrounding homeland security.

Intelligence Gathering

In the aftermath of September 11, a consensus quickly emerged that the tragedies were due in part to a breakdown in intelligence. Leaders from across the political spectrum questioned how al-Qaeda—a known terrorist network—had been able to plan and execute the September 11 attacks without attracting the attention of the CIA, the FBI, the National Security Agency (NSA), the Department of Defense, and other agencies charged with tracking terrorist threats. A key to preventing future attacks, it seemed, was to revitalize U.S. intelligence efforts.

To this end Congress passed, and President George W. Bush signed, the USA Patriot Act on October 26, 2001. The act gave new investigative powers to domestic law enforcement and international intelligence agencies. For example, it expanded federal agents' power to conduct telephone and e-mail surveillance of suspected terrorists—measures that have alarmed some civil libertarians and privacy advocates.

Controversy over the Patriot Act highlights a fundamental theme in homeland security debates: In general Americans want the government to use its power to investigate and avert terrorist threats, but at the same time they oppose the idea of a "police state" in which the government continuously monitors average people. The challenge facing the government, according to William Webster, former FBI director and CIA chief, is *"getting as much information as possible without impairing the rights of privacy that Americans have always considered dear. Everyone has a right to question, 'Why are they doing these things?'"*

Intelligence Sharing

Related to, but distinct from, the challenge of intelligence gathering is the issue of intelligence sharing. Critics of the government's counterterrorism measures have laid part of the blame for September 11 on a lack of communication between the FBI, CIA, and other federal agencies. According to this view, there were significant warning signs that, had they been heeded, could have averted the September 11 attacks. However, because of the compartmentalized nature of the U.S. intelligence apparatus, the various agencies charged with tracking terrorist threats were unable to recognize the warning signs because they were not communicating with one another. As former FBI agent David

Major put it, *"If you don't share intelligence, you don't connect the dots."*

To better "connect the dots"—the countless bits of information gathered through separate intelligence operations—Congress passed the Homeland Security Act, which became law on November 25, 2002. The act created a new cabinet-level agency, the Department of Homeland Security (DHS), to coordinate homeland security efforts. The DHS incorporated twenty-two federal agencies, including the Immigration and Naturalization Service, Coast Guard, and the Border Patrol—but not the FBI or CIA—and constitutes the biggest reorganization in the federal government since the Department of Defense was created in 1947. One of the primary roles of the DHS is to collect and coordinate intelligence from the FBI, CIA, NSA, and other agencies so that they can more easily recognize patterns and threats.

From a civil libertarian point of view, the problem with intelligence sharing—as with intelligence gathering—is its potential for abuse. By its very nature intelligence gathering—or more colloquially, spying—involves invasions of privacy that run counter to the Fourth Amendment's protection against unwarranted government searches. For this reason, spying has historically been justified as a tool of national security rather than law enforcement, to be used against foreign governments rather than U.S. citizens. Domestic law enforcement agencies, such as the FBI, who wish to conduct wiretaps or property searches in criminal investigations must obtain warrants and observe other rules of procedure that foreign intelligence agencies such as the CIA do not. The CIA, in turn, is prohibited from engaging in law enforcement or internal security functions. Many analysts worry that the DHS's emphasis on intelligence sharing may serve to remove the prohibitions on domestic spying and erode the regulatory framework that governs the use of sensitive information gained through intelligence operations.[2]

Threat Analysis and Warning

The Department of Homeland Security merged under one roof the capability to identify and assess current and future threats to the homeland, map those threats against current vulnerabilities, inform the President, issue timely warnings, and immediately take or effect appropriate preventive and protective action.

Actionable intelligence is essential for preventing acts of terrorism. The timely and thorough analysis and dissemination of information about terrorists and their activities will improve the government's ability to disrupt and prevent terrorist acts and to provide useful warning to the private sector and population. DHS, working together with enhanced capabilities in other agencies such as the FBI, sees itself as making America safer by pulling together information and intelligence from a variety of sources.

The Department fuses and analyzes legally accessible information from multiple available sources pertaining to terrorist threats to the homeland to provide early warning of potential attacks. This information includes foreign intelligence, law enforcement information, and publicly available information. The Department is a full partner and consumer of all intelligence-generating agen-

From a civil libertarian point of view, the problem with intelligence sharing—as with intelligence gathering—is its potential for abuse. By its very nature intelligence gathering—or more colloquially, spying—involves invasions of privacy that run counter to the Fourth Amendment's protection against unwarranted government searches.

cies, such as the CIA, the NSA, and the FBI. By obtaining and analyzing this information, the Department has the ability to view the dangers facing the homeland comprehensively, ensure that the President is briefed on relevant information, and take necessary protective action.

The Attorney General revised the guidelines governing how the FBI gathers information and conducts investigations. The new guidelines reflect the President's commitment to preventing terrorism by allowing the FBI to intervene and investigate promptly, while also protecting American's constitutional rights, when information suggests the possibility of terrorism. The revised guidelines empower FBI agents with new investigative authority at the early stage of preliminary inquiries, as well as the ability to search public sources for information on future terrorist threats. The FBI can identify and track foreign terrorists by combining information obtained from lawful sources, such as foreign intelligence and commercial data services, with the information derived from FBI investigations. In addition, the revised guidelines removed a layer of "red tape" by allowing FBI field offices to approve and renew terrorism enterprise investigations rather than having to obtain approval from headquarters.

The Department of Homeland Security complements the FBI's enhanced emphasis on counterterrorism law enforcement by ensuring that information from the FBI is analyzed side-by-side with all other intelligence. The Department and the Bureau ensure cooperation by instituting standard operating procedures to ensure the free and secure flow of information and exchanging personnel as appropriate.

The Department's threat analysis and warning functions support the President and, as he directs, other national decision-makers responsible for securing the homeland from terrorism. It coordinates and, as appropriate, consolidates the federal government's lines of communication with state and local public safety agencies and with the private sector, creating a coherent and efficient system for conveying actionable intelligence and other threat information. The Department administers the Homeland Security Advisory System and is responsible for public alerts.[3]

DHS translates analysis into action in the shortest possible time – a critical factor in preventing or mitigating terrorist attacks, particularly those involving weapons of mass destruction.

Homeland Security Operations Center

On July 8, 2004, the Department of Homeland Security stood up the Homeland Security Operations Center (HSOC) to serve as the primary, national-level nerve center for real-time threat monitoring, domestic incident management, and vertical and horizontal information sharing. Operating 24 hours a day, seven days a week, 365 days a year, the HSOC provides situational awareness and monitoring of the homeland, coordinates incidents and response activities, and issues advisories and bulletins to homeland security partners as well as specific protective and counter measure guidance.

As a single point of information integration, the HSOC maintains daily situational awareness on the security of the homeland and coordinates activities with other departments and agencies. The cornerstone of the HSOC is its ability to share threat information and provide real-time interactive connectivity with Governors, Homeland Security Advisors, law enforcement partners and critical infrastructure operators in all 50 States and more than 50 major urban areas through the Homeland Security Information Network. The HSIN system was launched on February 25, 2004, with all states receiving connectivity by July 2004.[4]

The HSOC includes representatives from over 35 agencies ranging from state and local law enforcement to federal intelligence agencies. Receiving hundreds of calls, they address about 22 incidents or cases per day. Information is shared and fused on a daily basis by the two halves of the HSOC that are referred to as the "Intelligence Side" and the "Law Enforcement Side." Each half is identical and functions in tandem with the other but requires a different level of clearance to access information. The "Intelligence Side" focuses on pieces of highly classified intelligence and how the information contributes to the current threat picture for any given area. The "Law Enforcement Side" is dedicated to tracking the different enforcement activities across the country that may have a terrorist nexus. The two pieces fused together create a real-time snap shot of the nation's threat environment at any moment.

1. Alcohol, Tobacco, & Firearms	19. Federal Air Marshal Service
2. Central Intelligence Agency	20. Federal Bureau of Investigation
3. Customs and Border Protection	21. Federal Emergency Management Agency
4. DC Metropolitan Police Dept.	22. Federal Protective Service
5. Defense Intelligence Agency	23. Immigration Customs Enforcement
6. Department of Defense	24. LA Police Department
7. Department of Energy	25. National Capitol Region
8. Dept. of Health and Human Services	26. National Geospatial Intelligence Agency
9. Department of State	27. National Oceanic & Atmospheric Admin.
10. Department of Transportation	28. National Security Agency
11. Department of Veterans Affairs	29. NY Police Department
12. DHS Geo-spatial Mapping Office	30. Postal Inspection Service
13. DHS Information Analysis Office	31. State & local Coordination Offices
14. DHS Infrastructure Protection Office	32. Transportation Security Administration
15. DHS Public Affairs	33. US Coast Guard
16. DHS Science & Technology Directorate	34. US Park Police
17. Drug Enforcement Agency	35. US Secret Service
18. Environmental Protection Agency	

Table 11.1: HSOC Watchstanders.

The HSOC monitors vulnerabilities and compares them against threats, providing a centralized, real-time flow of information between homeland security partners. This data collected from across the country is then fused into a master template which allows the HSOC to provide a visual picture of the nation's current threat status. The HSOC has the capability to:

- Perform initial (first phase) assessment of the information to gauge the terrorist nexus.

- Track operational actions taking place across the country in response to the intelligence information.

- Disseminate notifications and alerts about the information and any decisions made.

As information is shared across agencies, HSOC staff can apply imagery capabilities by cross-referencing informational data against geospatial data that can then pinpoint an image down to an exact location. Satellite technology is able to transmit pictures of the site in question directly into the HSOC. This type of geographic data can then be stored to create a library of images that can be mapped against future threats and shared with our state and local partners.

The "current operational picture" can be viewed using the geographical and mapping capabilities of 16 flat panel fifty-inch screens to monitor the threat environment in real time. Access to a significant portion of the District of Columbia's traffic cameras for real-time view of various transportation hubs.

The HSOC is in constant communication with the White House, acting as the situational awareness conduit for the White House Situation Room by providing information needed to make decisions and define courses of action.

In crisis or emergencies the HSOC hosts the Interagency Incident Management Group (IIMG). The IIMG is a headquarters-level group comprised of senior representatives from DHS components, other federal departments and agencies, and non-governmental organizations. The IIMG provides strategic situational awareness, synthesizes key intelligence and operational information, frames operational courses of action and policy recommendations, anticipates evolving requirements, and provides decision support to the Secretary of Homeland Security and other national authorities during periods of elevated alert and national domestic incidents. During incidents such as Hurricane Isabel, the December 2003 Orange Alert, and the black-out in New York City, the IIMG was "stood-up" in less than 90 minutes and hosted Assistant Secretary-level members of the represented agencies to provide strategic leadership.

The HSOC communicates in real-time to its partners by utilizing the Homeland Security Information Network's (HSIN) internet-based counterterrorism communications tool, supplying information to all 50 states, Washington, D.C., and more than 50 major urban areas. Threat information is exchanged with state and local partners at the Sensitive-but-Unclassified level (SBU). Future program expansion will include linking additional cities and counties, communication capabilities at the classified SECRET level, and increasing the involvement and integration of the private sector. The system is encrypted using a secure network that includes a suite of applications including mapping

The HSOC is in constant communication with the White House, acting as the situational awareness conduit for the White House Situation Room by providing information needed to make decisions and define courses of action.

and imaging capabilities. System participants include governors, mayors, Homeland Security Advisors, state National Guard offices, Emergency Operations Centers, First Responders and Public Safety departments, and other key homeland security partners. Each receives training to participate in the information sharing network to combat terrorism and increase anti-terrorism situational awareness. HSIN-CI was specially designed to communicate real-time information to critical infrastructure owners and operators – 80 percent of whom are part of the private sector.

The HSOC regularly disseminates domestic terrorism-related information generated by the Information Analysis and Infrastructure Protection Directorate, known as "products" to federal, state, and local governments, as well as private-sector organizations and international partners. Threat products come in two forms:

1. Homeland Security Threat Advisories are the result of information analysis and contain actionable information about an incident involving, or a threat targeting, critical national networks, infrastructures, or key assets. They often relay newly developed procedures that, when implemented, significantly improve security and protection. Advisories also often suggest a change in readiness posture, protective actions, or response.

2. Homeland Security Information Bulletins are infrastructure protection products that communicate information of interest to the nation's critical infrastructures that do not meet the timeliness, specificity, or significance thresholds of warning messages. Such information may include statistical reports, periodic summaries, incident response or reporting guidelines, common vulnerabilities and patches, and configuration standards or tools.

Raising the threat condition has economic, physical, and psychological effects on the nation.

Homeland Security Advisory System

On March 11, 2002, President Bush unveiled the Homeland Security Advisory System (HSAS) as a tool to improve coordination and communication among all levels of government, the private sector, and the American public in the fight against terrorism. The Advisory System not only identifies the Threat Condition, but also outlines protective measures that can be taken. The federal government, states, and the private sector each have a set of plans and protective measures that are implemented as the Threat Condition is raised or lowered, thus reducing vulnerability to attack. The HSOC is the distributor of the recommended security measures to state and local partners when the threat level is raised or lowered.[5]

A color-coded threat level system is used to communicate with public safety officials and the public at-large through a threat-based, color-coded system so that protective measures can be implemented to reduce the likelihood or impact of an attack. Raising the threat condition has economic, physical, and psychological effects on the nation; so, the Homeland Security Advisory System can place specific geographic regions or industry sectors on a higher alert status than other regions or industries, based on specific threat information.[6]

1. Condition Green. This condition is declared when there is a low risk of terrorist attacks.

2. Condition Blue ("Guarded"). This condition is declared when there is a general risk of terrorist attack.

3. Condition Yellow. This condition is declared when there is an elevated risk of terrorist attacks.

4. Condition Orange. This condition is declared when there is a high risk of terrorist attacks.

5. Condition Red. This condition is declared when there is a severe risk of terrorist attacks.[7]

The higher the Threat Condition, the greater the risk of a terrorist attack. Risk includes both the probability of an attack occurring and its potential gravity. Threat Conditions are assigned by the Attorney General in consultation with the Secretary for Homeland Security. Except in exigent circumstances, the Attorney General shall seek the views of the appropriate Homeland Security Principals or their subordinates, and other parties as appropriate, on the Threat Condition to be assigned. Threat Conditions may be assigned for the entire Nation, or they may be set for a particular geographic area or industrial sector. Assigned Threat Conditions are reviewed at regular intervals to determine whether adjustments are warranted.

For facilities, personnel, and operations inside the territorial United States, all Federal departments, agencies, and offices other than military facilities must conform their threat advisory systems to this system and administer their systems consistent with the determination of the Attorney General with regard to the Threat Condition in effect.

The assignment of a Threat Condition should prompt the implementation of an appropriate set of Protective Measures. Protective Measures are the specific steps an organization should take to reduce its vulnerability or increase its ability to respond during a period of heightened alert. The authority to craft and implement Protective Measures rests with the Federal departments and agencies. It is recognized that departments and agencies may have several preplanned sets of responses to a particular Threat Condition to facilitate a rapid, appropriate, and tailored response. Department and agency heads are responsible for developing their own Protective Measures and other antiterrorism or self-protection and continuity plans, and resourcing, rehearsing, documenting, and maintaining these plans. Likewise, they retain the authority to respond, as necessary, to risks, threats, incidents, or events at facilities within the specific jurisdiction of their department or agency, and, as authorized by law, to direct agencies and industries to implement their own Protective Measures. They are responsible for taking all appropriate proactive steps to reduce the vulnerability of their personnel and facilities to terrorist attack. Federal department and agency heads must submit an annual written report to the President, through the Department of Homeland Security, describing the steps they have taken to develop and implement appropriate Protective Measures for each Threat Condition. Governors, mayors, and the leaders of other organizations are encouraged to conduct a similar review of their organizations.

The decision whether to publicly announce Threat Conditions is made on a case-by-case basis by the Attorney General in consultation with the Secretary for Homeland Security. Every effort is made to share as much information regarding the threat as possible, consistent with the safety of the Nation. The Attorney General shall ensure, consistent with the safety of the Nation, that State and local government officials and law enforcement authorities are provided the most relevant and timely information. The Attorney General is responsible for identifying any other information developed in the threat assessment process that would be useful to State and local officials and others and conveying it to them as permitted consistent with the constraints of classification. The Attorney General has a process and a system for conveying relevant information to Federal, State, and local government officials, law enforcement authorities, and the private sector expeditiously.

The Director of Central Intelligence (DCI) and the Attorney General ensure that a continuous and timely flow of integrated threat assessments and reports is provided to the President, the Vice President, Assistant to the President and Chief of Staff, the Secretary for Homeland Security, and the Assistant to the President for National Security Affairs. Whenever possible and practicable, these integrated threat assessments and reports are reviewed and commented upon by the wider interagency community.

A decision on which Threat Condition to assign integrates a variety of considerations. This integration relies on qualitative assessment, not quantitative calculation. Higher Threat Conditions indicate greater risk of a terrorist act, with risk including both probability and gravity. Despite best efforts, there can be no guarantee that, at any given Threat Condition, a terrorist attack will not occur. An initial and important factor is the quality of the threat information itself. The evaluation of this threat information includes, but not be limited to, the following factors:

Despite best efforts, there can be no guarantee that, at any given Threat Condition, a terrorist attack will not occur.

1. To what degree is the threat information credible?

2. To what degree is the threat information corroborated?

3. To what degree is the threat specific and/or imminent?

4. How grave are the potential consequences of the threat?[8]

Growing Pains

When the color-coded alert system was announced in March 2002, the government listed a number of precautions citizens should be aware of at the orange alert level. According to the Department of Homeland Security, citizens should have on hand three days worth of food and water, extra batteries, a disaster supply kit, a battery powered radio, and a supply of duct tape and plastic sheeting to protect against biological and chemical agents.

Americans were also asked to create a system to make sure all family members could communicate with one another and evacuate in the event of an attack and to be especially aware of one's surroundings. People were asked not to cancel any travel plans or events that they might have scheduled, just to have a heightened sense of security.

In February 2003, Americans prepared themselves for imminent terrorist attack, stocking up on essentials and outfitting their homes with duct tape and plastic sheeting to protect against chemical and biological weapons.

The heightened preparedness came as a result of the Homeland Security Department raising the terror warning system from yellow, or "elevated risk," to orange or "high risk" on February 11, 2003. The government raised the terror alert level because of intelligence reports that showed an increase in chatter among terror groups.

Major cities saw an increase in military patrols both by land and by air, and military vehicles with anti-aircraft missiles were deployed around the Washington region.

Military bases across the country increased security levels from Threat Condition Alpha to Threat Condition Bravo. The Pentagon was placed at a still-higher state of alert and universities took special precautions as military officials labeled them as possible targets.

In Congress, both parties criticized the move by the Bush administration with Rep. Porter J. Goss, R-FL., a former CIA officer and chairman of the House Intelligence Committee, telling citizens *"not (to) fall for hysteria and rumor."*

Other lawmakers were cautious. According to The Washington Post, Sen. Pat Roberts, R-Kan., chairman of the Senate Intelligence Committee, said the threat information was "serious and specific."[9]

But four days after telling Americans to assemble emergency supply kits, a move that had people from Washington to New York stripping hardware stores of supplies, Homeland Security Secretary Tom Ridge was forced to clarify his instructions for how Americans should prepare for potential terrorism.

His new guidance: Buy the duct tape. Just don't use it without a signal from the government. And wait for further instructions next week.

It was an example of the difficulty federal officials were facing in making the public prepared but not panicked about terrorism. It came in a week that saw schools purchase gas masks, businesses review evacuation plans and antiaircraft missile batteries return to key posts around the capital.

The administration's advice on February 11, 2003, moved thousands of Americans, mostly in the New York-to-Washington corridor, to stock up on disaster supplies. But it also drew questions from many residents, as well as ridicule from Congress.[10]

The Terrorist Threat Integration Center

President Bush, in his State of the Union address delivered on January 28, 2003, called for the establishment of a new Terrorist Threat Integration Center (TTIC) that would merge and analyze all threat information in a single location under the direction of the DCI. According to Administration spokesmen, TTIC will eventually encompass CIA's Counterterrorist Center (CTC) and the FBI's Counterterrorism Division, along with elements of other agencies, including DoD and DHS. TTIC's stated responsibilities are to "integrate terrorist-related information collected domestically and abroad" and to provide "terrorist threat assessments for our national leadership." On May 1, 2003, TTIC began operations at CIA Headquarters under the leadership of John O. Brennan, who had previously served as the CIA's Deputy Executive Director. Initially it consisted of some 50 officers from various intelligence agencies and federal departments; it was expected to move to a separate facility in May 2004.

TTIC appears to be designed to assume at least some of the functions intended for DHS' information analysis division. Making the DCI responsible for TTIC will facilitate its ability to use highly sensitive classified information and TTIC can expand upon the relationships that have evolved in the CTC that was established in CIA's Operations Directorate in the mid-1980s. According to testimony by Administration officials to the Senate Government Affairs Committee on February 26, 2003, TTIC will in effect function as an information analysis center for DHS and DHS will require a smaller number of analysts with less extensive responsibilities.

Some observers express concern that the DCI's role in the TTIC — responsibility for the analysis of domestically collected information and for maintaining "an up-to-date database of known and suspected terrorists that will be accessible to federal and nonfederal officials and entities,"— may run counter to the statutory provision that excludes the CIA from "law enforcement or internal security functions." There are also questions about transferring the FBI's Counterterrorism Division to the DCI. Some express concern about how the TTIC under the DCI will coordinate with state and local officials and with private industry.

A major concern for some observers is that TTIC may just become an expanded version of the CTC that has long had representatives from the FBI and other agencies. They argue that the CTC did not provide advance warning of the September 11 attacks and that a different approach (such as that envisioned in the Homeland Security Act) is called for. Some in Congress may consider modifications of the Homeland Security Act that could encompass the analytical efforts of DHS.[11]

Conclusion

Legislation creating a homeland security department recognized the crucial importance of intelligence to the counterterrorist effort. It proposed an analytical office within DHS that would be able to draw upon the information gathering resources of other government agencies and of the private sector. It envisioned the DHS information analysis entity working closely with other DHS offices, other federal agencies, state and local officials, and the private sector to devise strategies and programs to protect U.S. vulnerabilities and to provide warning of specific attacks.

The Bush Administration appears to prefer a modification to the approach originally envisioned in the legislation that created DHS. TTIC, under the direction of the DCI, will provide the integrative analytical effort that the drafters of homeland security legislation and others in Congress have felt to be essential in light of breakdowns in communication that occurred prior to September 11, 2001. Whether TTIC is consistent with the intent of Congress in passing the Homeland Security Act and whether it is ultimately the best place for the integrative effort is currently a matter of discussion in Congress. Regardless of where the integrative effort is ultimately located, the task will remain fundamentally the same. Pulling together vast amounts of data from a wide variety of sources concerning terrorist groups, analyzing them, and reporting threat warnings in time to prevent attacks is and will remain a daunting challenge.

Pulling together vast amounts of data from a wide variety of sources concerning terrorist groups, analyzing them, and reporting threat warnings in time to prevent attacks is and will remain a daunting challenge.

Questions

1. Why did DHS incorporate an information analysis and warning capability?

2. What is the purpose of this capability?

3. Why are some intelligence experts skeptical of DHS?

4. Why are some civil libertarians concerned with DHS?

5. What is the purpose of the Homeland Security Operations Center?

6. How does the Homeland Security Advisory System work?

## Chapter 12

U.S. Secret Service

Objectives

- Know the two primary missions of the Secret Service.
- Describe the three investigative missions of the Secret Service.

Introduction

The United States Secret Service is mandated by statute and executive order to carry out two significant missions: protection and criminal investigations. The Secret Service protects the President and Vice President, their families, heads of state, and other designated individuals; investigates threats against these protectees; protects the White House, Vice President's Residence, Foreign Missions, and other buildings within Washington, D.C.; and plans and implements security designs for designated National Special Security Events (NSSEs). The Secret Service also investigates violations of laws relating to counterfeiting of obligations and securities of the United States; financial crimes that include, but are not limited to, access device fraud, financial institution fraud, identity theft, computer fraud; and computer-based attacks on our nation's financial, banking, and telecommunications infrastructure.

Protective Mission

After the assassination of President William McKinley in 1901, Congress directed the Secret Service to protect the President of the United States. Protection remains the primary mission of the United States Secret Service.

Today, the Secret Service is authorized by law to protect:

- The President, the Vice President, (or other individuals next in order of succession to the Office of the President), the President-elect and Vice President-elect;

- The immediate families of the above individuals;

- Former Presidents, their spouses for their lifetimes, except when the spouse re-marries. In 1997, Congressional legislation became effective limiting Secret Service protection to former Presidents for a period of not more than 10 years from the date the former President leaves office.

- Children of former presidents until age 16;

- Visiting heads of foreign states or governments and their spouses traveling with them, other distinguished foreign visitors to the United States, and official representatives of the United States performing special missions abroad;

- Major Presidential and Vice Presidential candidates, and their spouses within 120 days of a general Presidential election.[1]

Investigative Mission

The Secret Service was established as a law enforcement agency in 1865. While most people associate the Secret Service with Presidential protection, the original mandate was to investigate the counterfeiting of U.S. currency— which they still do. Today the primary investigative mission is to safeguard the payment and financial systems of the United States. This has been historically accomplished through the enforcement of the counterfeiting statutes to

The United States Secret Service is mandated by statute and executive order to carry out two significant missions: protection and criminal investigations.

preserve the integrity of United States currency, coin and financial obligations. Since 1984, investigative responsibilities have expanded to include crimes that involve financial institution fraud, computer and telecommunications fraud, false identification documents, access device fraud, advance fee fraud, electronic funds transfers, and money laundering as it relates to core violations.

The Secret Service believes that its primary enforcement jurisdictions will only increase in significance in the 21st Century. For this reason, the Secret Service has adopted a proactive approach to monitor the development of technology and continue to use it in the interest of federal, state, and local law enforcement. There are three Investigative Missions: Counterfeit, Financial Crimes, and Forensic Services.[2]

Counterfeit Division

The Secret Service has exclusive jurisdiction for investigations involving the counterfeiting of United States obligations and securities. This authority to investigate counterfeiting is derived from Title 18 of the United States Code, Section 3056. Some of the counterfeited United States obligations and securities commonly dealt with by the Secret Service include U.S. currency and coins; U.S. Treasury checks; Department of Agriculture food coupons and U.S. postage stamps. The Secret Service remains committed to the mission of combating counterfeiting by working closely with state and local law enforcement agencies, as well as foreign law enforcement agencies, to aggressively pursue counterfeiters. To perform at the highest level, the Secret Service constantly reviews the latest reprographic/lithographic technologies to keep a step ahead of the counterfeiters. The Secret Service maintains a working relationship with the Bureau of Engraving and Printing and the Federal Reserve System to ensure the integrity of our currency.

There are three Investigative Missions: Counterfeit, Financial Crimes, and Forensic Services.

History of Counterfeiting

The counterfeiting of money is one of the oldest crimes in history. At some periods in early history, it was considered treasonous and was punishable by death.

During the American Revolution, the British counterfeited U.S. currency in such large amounts that the Continental currency soon became worthless. "Not worth a Continental" became a popular expression that is still heard today.

During the Civil War, one-third to one-half of the currency in circulation was counterfeit. At that time, approximately 1,600 state banks designed and printed their own bills. Each bill carried a different design, making it difficult to detect counterfeit bills from the 7,000 varieties of real bills.

A national currency was adopted in 1862 to resolve the counterfeiting problem. However, the national currency was soon counterfeited and circulated so extensively that it became necessary to take enforcement measures. Therefore, on July 5, 1865, the United States Secret Service was established to suppress the wide-spread counterfeiting of this nation's currency.

Although the counterfeiting of money was substantially suppressed after the establishment of the Secret Service, this crime still represents a potential danger to the Nation's economy.

Today, counterfeiting once again is on the rise. One reason for this is the ease and speed with which large quantities of counterfeit currency can be produced using modern photographic and printing equipment.[3]

Financial Crimes Division

The Secret Service investigates crimes associated with financial institutions. Today, this jurisdiction includes bank fraud, access device fraud involving credit and debit cards, telecommunications and computer crimes, fraudulent identification, fraudulent government and commercial securities, and electronic funds transfer fraud.

Financial Institution Fraud (FIF) and Related Criminal Investigations

On November 5, 1990, Congress enacted legislation that gave the Secret Service concurrent jurisdiction with the Department of Justice to investigate fraud, both civil and criminally against any federally insured financial institution or the Resolution Trust Corporation. Annually, agents of the Secret Service review thousands of criminal referrals submitted by Treasury Department regulators. The Secret Service promotes an aggressive policy toward conducting these investigations in an effort to safeguard the soundness of our financial institutions.

The Secret Service has concurrent jurisdiction with the Department of Justice to investigate fraud, both civil and criminal, against federally insured financial (FIF) institutions. The Crime Bill of 1994 extended FIF investigative authority to the year 2004.

The FIF program distinguishes itself from other such programs by recognizing the need to balance traditional law enforcement operations with a program management approach designed to prevent recurring criminal activity.

A recent American Banking Association (ABA) survey concluded that the two major problems in the area of bank fraud today are: (1) the fraudulent production of negotiable instruments through the use of what has become known as "desktop publishing," and (2) access device fraud.

Recent Secret Service investigations indicate that there has been an increase in credit card fraud, fictitious document fraud, and fraud involving the counterfeiting of corporate checks and other negotiable instruments, as well as false identification documents created with the use of computer technology.

Title 18 United States Code, Section 514 was enacted into law in 1996 to prevent the increasing amount of fraud through the use of fictitious instruments. Congress passed this law through the joint efforts of the Department of Justice and the Department of Treasury. The Financial Crimes Division (FCD) is responsible for the investigations of Title 18, United States Code Section 514 (Fictitious Instruments).

Access Device Fraud

Financial industry sources estimate that losses associated with credit card fraud are in the billions of dollars annually. The Secret Service is the primary federal agency tasked with investigating access device fraud and its related activities under Title 18, United States Code, Section 1029. Although it is commonly called the credit card statute, this law also applies to other crimes involving access device numbers including debit cards, automated teller machine (ATM) cards, computer passwords, personal identification numbers (PINs) used to activate ATMs, credit card or debit card account numbers, long-distance access codes, and the computer chips in cellular phones that assign billing. During fiscal year 1996, the Secret Service opened 2,467 cases, closed 2,963 cases, and arrested 2,429 individuals for access device fraud. Industry sources estimate that losses associated with credit card fraud are in the billions of dollars annually.

Counterfeit and Fraudulent Identification

Since 1982, the Secret Service has enforced laws involving counterfeit and fraudulent identification. Title 18, United States Code, Section 1028, defines this criminal act as someone who knowingly and without lawful authority produces, transfers, or possesses a false identification document to defraud the U.S. Government. The use of desktop publishing software/hardware to counterfeit and produce different forms of identification used to obtain funds illegally remains one of the Secret Service's strongest core violations.

Money Laundering

The Money Laundering Control Act makes it a crime to launder proceeds of certain criminal offenses called "specified unlawful activities" (SUA), which are defined in Title 18, United States Code,1956, 1957 and Title 18,United States Code, 1961, the Racketeer Influenced and Corrupt Organizations Act (RICO).

The Secret Service has observed an increase in money laundering activities as they relate to these specified unlawful activities. This is especially true in the area of financial institution fraud, access device fraud (credit card, telecommunications and computer investigations), food stamp fraud, and counterfeiting of U.S. currency.

Computer Fraud

In 1986, Congress revised Title 18 of the United States Code to include the investigation of fraud and related activities concerning computers that were described as "federal interest computers," as defined in Title 18, United States

Code, Section 1030. The Secret Service has also investigated cases where computer technology has been used in traditional Secret Service violations, such as counterfeiting and the creation of false identification documents.

Computers are being used extensively in financial crimes, not only as an instrument of the crime, but to "hack" into databases to retrieve account information; store account information; clone microchips for cellular telephones; and scan corporate checks, bonds and negotiable instruments, that are later counterfeited using desktop publishing methods.

Because computers are a tremendous source of both investigative leads and evidentiary material, the Secret Service has established the Electronic Crimes Special Agent Program (ECSAP), that trains agents to conduct forensic examinations of computers that were used in criminal endeavors. So trained, these agents can preserve any investigative leads within the computer, as well as any evidence needed for subsequent prosecutions.

Telecommunications Fraud

Telecommunication fraud losses are estimated at more than a billion dollars yearly. One of the largest "markets" for this type of fraud is the cloning of cellular telephones, a relatively simple procedure that can be done with the purchase of over-the-counter electronic equipment. When an individual transmits with a cellular telephone, the telephone emits a burst of electronic information. Within this burst of information is the electronic serial number (ESN), the mobile identification number (MIN) and other electronic identification signals, all of which can be illegally captured through the use of an ESN reader. Once captured, this information is transported through a computer onto microchips in the cellular telephones. These new telephones can be used for up to 30 days before the fraudulent charges are discovered. Cell telephones are being used extensively by organized criminal groups and drug cartels, as well as several Middle Eastern groups. Using acquired investigative expertise and state-of-the-art electronic equipment, the Secret Service now has the ability to effectively investigate the use of such telephones. This is another example of law enforcement using technology to target criminal enterprise.

The Secret Service has become the recognized law enforcement expert in the field of telecommunications fraud. It works closely with other law enforcement agencies, as well as representatives of the telecommunications industry in conducting telecommunications fraud investigations. These types of investigations, in many instances, act as a nexus to other criminal enterprises, such as access device fraud, counterfeiting, money laundering, and the trafficking of narcotics. During fiscal year 1996, the Secret Service opened 555 cases and arrested 556 individuals for telecommunications fraud.

Electronic Benefits Transfer (EBT) Card

The Vice President's National Performance Review designated the Electronic Benefits Transfer (EBT) card as the method of payment for the delivery of recurring government cash benefit payments to individuals without a bank account and for the delivery of non-cash benefits such as Food Stamps. For individuals with bank accounts, Electronic Funds Transfer will continue as the preferred method of making federal benefit payments. As with any recurring payment system, EBT is open to a wide variety of fraud, including multiple false applications for benefits, counterfeiting of the EBT card and trafficking of non-cash benefits for cash or contraband. The Financial Crimes Division is taking a proactive approach by recommending fraud deterrent features to this new system as it is designed.

In an attempt to combat potential attacks, Financial Crimes Division has suggested the use of: biometric identifiers to verify applicants' identities and prevent application fraud; counterfeit deterrents such as four-color graphics and fine-line printing, and the use of holograms and embossing in the design of the card; and features that allow investigators to monitor transactions and use the audit trail to identify criminals who illegally traffic food benefit payments.[4]

Forensic Services Division

Forensic examiners in the Secret Service Forensic Services Division (FSD) provide analysis for questioned documents, fingerprints, false identification, credit cards, and other related forensic science areas. Examiners use both instrumental and chemical analysis when reviewing evidence. FSD also manages the Secret Service's polygraph program nationwide. The division coordinates photographic, graphic, video, and audio and image enhancement service, as well as the Voice Identification Program. In addition, FSD is responsible for handling the Forensic Hypnosis Program. Much of the forensic assistance the Secret Service offers is unique technology operated in this country only by FSD.

Instrument Analysis Services Section

The Instrument Analysis Services Section houses the International Ink Library - the most complete forensic collection of writing inks world-wide that contains over 7,000 samples. This collection is used to identify the source of suspect writing by not only providing the type and brand of writing instrument, but the earliest possible date that a document could have been produced. This Section also maintains a watermark collection of over 22,000 images as well as collections of plastics, toners and computer printer inks.

Fingerprint Identification Services Section

FSD also operates a hybrid Automated Fingerprint Identification System (AFIS). As of 1999, this network is the largest of its kind and is composed of remote latent fingerprint terminals providing a connection to fingerprint databases with access to more than 30 million fingerprints. This enables the fingerprint specialist to digitize a single latent fingerprint from an item of evidence and to search for its likeness from fingerprint databases throughout the country. These findings often provide the investigator with a suspect's name.

Polygraph Examination Program

The Polygraph Examination Program is known as a forerunner in the law enforcement community for advancing the fine art of physiologically detecting deception. Polygraph examinations are a major investigative tool for all cases under the Secret Service jurisdiction. Through proper use of the polygraph, the agency maintains a high resolution of its investigations, resulting in a significant savings in the expenditure of man-hours, equipment, and money. The Polygraph Program has a host of examiners who are highly trained in interview and interrogation techniques. Each examiner is capable of conducting a reliable polygraph examination on issues involving criminal, national security, and employee-screening matters.[5]

Origin of the U.S. Secret Service

The U.S. Secret Service, one of the nation's oldest federal investigative law enforcement agencies, was founded in 1865 as a branch of the U.S. Treasury Department. The original mission was to investigate counterfeiting of U.S. currency. It was estimated that one-third to one-half of the currency in circulation at that time was counterfeit. In 1901, following the assassination of President William McKinley in Buffalo, New York, the Secret Service was assigned the responsibility of protecting the President. Today, the Secret Service's mission is two fold: protection of the President, Vice President and others; and protection of our nation's financial system.

Legal Authority

Under Title 18, Section 3056, United States Code, agents and officers of the Secret Service can carry firearms; execute warrants issued under the laws of the United States; make arrests without warrants for any offense against the United States committed in their presence, or for any felony recognizable under the laws of the United States if they have reasonable grounds to believe that the person to be arrested has committed such felony; offer and pay rewards for services and information leading to the apprehension of persons involved in the violation of the law that the Secret Service is authorized to enforce; investigate fraud in connection with identification documents, fraudulent commerce, fictitious instruments and foreign securities; perform other functions and duties authorized by law. The Secret Service works closely with the United States Attorney's Office in both protective and investigative matters.

Title 18, United States Code, Section 504 permits black and white reproductions of currency and other obligations, provided such reproductions meet the size requirement.

Protection of Former Presidents

In 1965, Congress authorized the Secret Service (Public Law 89-186) to protect a former president and his/her spouse during their lifetime, unless they decline protection. Congress recently enacted legislation that limits Secret Service protection for former presidents to ten years after leaving office. Under this new law, individuals who are in office before January 1, 1997, will continue to receive Secret Service protection for their lifetime. Individuals elected to office after that time will receive protection for ten years after leaving office. Therefore, former president Clinton will be the last President to receive lifetime protection.

Title 18, Section 3056 of the U.S. Code states, "The United States Secret Service is authorized to protect former presidents and their spouses for their lifetimes, except that protection of a spouse shall terminate in the event of remarriage unless the former president did not serve as president prior to January 1, 1997, in which case, former president and their spouses for a period of not more than ten years from the date a former president leaves office, except that—

- Protection of a spouse shall terminate in the event of remarriage or the divorce from, or death of a former president; and

- Should the death of a president occur while in office or within one year after leaving office, the spouse shall receive protection for one year from the time of such death.

- Children of a former president who are under 16 years of age for a period not to exceed ten years or upon the child becoming 16 years of age, whichever comes first."[6]

Conclusion

The primary mission of the United States Secret Service is to protect the President, Vice President, and other national leaders. The Service also contributes its specialized protective expertise to planning for events of national significance (National Special Security Events). In addition, the Service combats counterfeiting, cyber-crime, identity fraud, and access device fraud, all closely tied to the terrorist threat. The Homeland Security Act of 2002 transferred the Secret Service from the Treasury Department to the Department of Homeland Security. The Service remained intact and was not merged with any other Department function to take advantage of the Service's unique and highly specialized expertise to complement the core mission of the new Department.[7]

The Homeland Security Act of 2002 transferred the Secret Service from the Treasury Department to the Department of Homeland Security to take advantage of the Service's unique and highly specialized expertise to complement the core mission of the new Department.

Questions

1. What are the two primary missions of the Secret Service?

2. What are the three investigative missions of the Secret Service?

## Chapter 13

Infrastructure Protection

Objectives

- Describe what is meant by "critical infrastructure".

- Explain the threat to critical infrastructure posed by terrorism.

- Know the national strategy for protecting critical infrastructure.

- Understand the role of DHS in protecting critical infrastructure.

- Describe the mission of the National Cyber Security Division.

Protecting Critical Infrastructure and Key Assets. Our society and modern way of life are dependent on networks of infrastructure—both physical networks such as our energy and transportation systems and virtual networks such as the Internet. If terrorists attack one or more pieces of our critical infrastructure, they may disrupt entire systems and cause significant damage to the Nation. We must therefore improve protection of the individual pieces and interconnecting systems that make up our critical infrastructure. Protecting America's critical infrastructure and key assets will not only make us more secure from terrorist attack, but will also reduce our vulnerability to natural disasters, organized crime, and computer hackers.

- Critical Mission Area #4, National Strategy for Homeland Security, July 2002

Introduction

The National Strategy for the Physical Protection of Critical Infrastructures and Key Assets defines the road ahead for reducing the Nation's vulnerability to acts of terrorism by protecting our critical infrastructures and key assets from physical attack.

The National Strategy for the Physical Protection of Critical Infrastructures and Key Assets identifies national goals and objectives and outlines the guiding principles underpinning efforts to secure the infrastructures and assets vital to our national security, governance, public health and safety, economy, and public confidence. The Strategy provides a unifying organization and identifies specific initiatives to drive our near-term national protection priorities and inform the resource allocation process. Most importantly, it establishes a foundation for building and fostering a cooperative environment in which government, industry, and private citizens can carry out their respective protection responsibilities more effectively and efficiently.

A New Mission

The September 11 attacks demonstrated our national level physical vulnerability to the threat posed by an enemy-focused, mass destruction terrorism. The events of that day revealed how determined, patient, and sophisticated—in both planning and execution—terrorist enemies have become. The basic nature of our free society greatly enables terrorist operations and tactics, while, at the same time, hinders our ability to predict, prevent, or mitigate the effects of terrorist acts. Given these realities, it is imperative to develop a comprehensive national approach to physical protection.

Defining the End State: Strategic Objectives

The strategic objectives that underpin our national critical infrastructure and key asset protection effort include:

- Identifying and assuring the protection of those infrastructures and assets that are deemed most critical in terms of national-level public health and safety, governance, economic and national security, and public confidence consequences;

- Providing timely warning and assuring the protection of those infrastructures and assets that face a specific, imminent threat; and

- Assuring the protection of other infrastructures and assets that may become terrorist targets over time by pursuing specific initiatives and enabling a collaborative environment in which federal, state, and local governments and the private sector can better protect the infrastructures and assets they control.

Traditionally, national security has been recognized largely as the responsibility of the federal government. National security is underpinned by the collective efforts of the military, foreign policy establishment, and intelligence community in the defense of our airspace and national borders, as well as operations overseas to protect our national interests.

Homeland security, particularly in the context of critical infrastructure and key asset protection, is a shared responsibility that cannot be accomplished by the federal government alone. It requires coordinated action on the part of federal, state, and local governments; the private sector; and concerned citizens across the country.

The Importance of Key Assets

Key assets and high profile events are individual targets whose attack—in the worst-case scenarios—could result in not only large-scale human casualties and property destruction, but also profound damage to our national prestige, morale, and confidence.

Individually, key assets like nuclear power plants and dams may not be vital to the continuity of critical services at the national level. However, a successful strike against such targets may result in a significant loss of life and property in addition to long-term, adverse public health and safety consequences. Other key assets are symbolically equated with traditional American values and institutions or U.S. political and economic power. Our national icons, monuments, and historical attractions preserve history, honor achievements, and represent the natural grandeur of our country. They celebrate our American ideals and way of life and present attractive targets for terrorists, particularly when coupled with high profile events and celebratory activities that bring together significant numbers of people.

Key assets and high profile events are individual targets whose attack—in the worst-case scenarios—could result in not only large-scale human casualties and property destruction, but also profound damage to our national prestige, morale, and confidence.

Understanding the Threat

The September 11 attacks on the World Trade Center and the Pentagon underscore the determination of our terrorist enemies. Terrorists are relentless and patient, as evidenced by their persistent targeting of the World Trade Center towers over the years. Terrorists are also opportunistic and flexible. They learn from experience and modify their tactics and targets to exploit perceived vulnerabilities and avoid observed strengths. As security increases around more predictable targets, they shift their focus to less protected assets. Enhancing countermeasures for any one terrorist tactic or target, therefore, makes it more likely that terrorists will favor another.

Terrorists' pursuit of their long-term strategic objectives includes attacks on critical infrastructures and key assets. Terrorists target critical infrastructures to achieve three general types of effects:

1. Direct infrastructure effects: Cascading disruption or arrest of the functions of critical infrastructures or key assets through direct attacks on a critical node, system, or function.

2. Indirect infrastructure effects: Cascading disruption and financial consequences for government, society, and economy through public- and private-sector reactions to an attack.

3. Exploitation of infrastructure: Exploitation of elements of a particular infrastructure to disrupt or destroy another target.

Statement of National Policy

As a Nation we remain committed to protecting our critical infrastructures and key assets from acts of terrorism that would:

- Impair the federal government's ability to perform essential national and homeland security missions and ensure the general public's health and safety;

- Undermine state and local government capacities to maintain order and to deliver minimum essential public services;

- Damage the private sector's capability to ensure the orderly functioning of the economy and the delivery of essential services; and

- Undermine the public's morale and confidence in our national economic and political institutions.

We must work collaboratively to employ the tools necessary to implement such protection. Eight guiding principles underpin this Strategy:

1. Assure public safety, public confidence, and services;

2. Establish responsibility and accountability;

3. Encourage and facilitate partnering among all levels of government and between government and industry;

4. Encourage market solutions wherever possible and compensate for market failure with focused government intervention;

5. Facilitate meaningful information sharing;

6. Foster international cooperation;

7. Develop technologies and expertise to combat terrorist threats; and

8. Safeguard privacy and constitutional freedoms.

Organizing and Partnering for Protection

Implementing this Strategy requires a unifying organization, a clear purpose, a common understanding of roles and responsibilities, accountability, and a set of well-understood coordinating processes.

Federal Government Responsibilities

Every terrorist event has a potential national impact. The federal government will, therefore, take the lead to ensure that three principal objectives are met:

- Preventing terrorist attacks in the United States.

- Reducing America's vulnerability to terrorism.

- Minimizing the damage and recovering from attacks that do occur.

This leadership role involves:

- Taking stock of our most critical facilities, systems, and functions and monitoring their preparedness across economic sectors and governmental jurisdictions;

- Assuring that federal, state, local, and private entities work together to protect critical facilities, systems, and functions that face an imminent threat and/or whose loss could have significant national consequences;

- Providing and coordinating national-level threat information, assessments, and warnings that are timely, actionable, and relevant to state, local, and private sector partners;

- Creating and implementing comprehensive, multi-tiered protection policies and programs;

- Exploring potential options for enablers and incentives to encourage stakeholders to devise solutions to their unique protection impediments;

- Developing cross-sector and cross-jurisdictional protection standards, guidelines, criteria, and protocols;

- Facilitating the sharing of critical infrastructure and key asset protection best practices and processes and vulnerability assessment methodologies;

- Conducting demonstration projects and pilot programs;

- Seeding the development and transfer of advanced technologies while taking advantage of private sector expertise and competencies;

- Promoting national-level critical infrastructure and key asset protection education and awareness; and

- Improving the federal government's ability to work with state and local responders and service providers.

Federal Lead Departments and Agencies

The National Strategy for Homeland Security provides a sector-based organizational scheme for protecting critical infrastructure and key assets. It identifies the federal lead departments and agencies responsible for coordinating protection activities and developing and maintaining collaborative relationships with their state and local government and industry counterparts in the critical sectors.

Sector	Lead Agency
Agriculture	Department of Agriculture
Food:	
Meat and poultry	Department of Agriculture
All other food products	Department of Health & Human Services
Water	Environmental Protection Agency
Public Health	Department of Health & Human Services
Emergency Services	Department of Homeland Security
Government:	
Continuity of government	Department of Homeland Security
Continuity of operations	All departments and agencies
Defense Industrial Base	Department of Defense
Energy	Department of Energy
Transportation	Department of Homeland Security (TSA)
Banking and Finance	Department of Treasury
Chemical Industry & Hazardous Materials	Environmental Protection Agency
Postal and Shipping	Department of Homeland Security
National Monuments and Icons	Department of the Interior

Table 13.1: Federal Organization to Protect Critical Infrastructure and Key Assets.

In addition to securing federally owned and operated infrastructures and assets, the role of the federal lead departments and agencies is to assist state and local governments and private-sector partners in their efforts to:

- Organize and conduct protection and continuity of government and operations planning, and elevate awareness and understanding of threats and vulnerabilities to their critical facilities, systems, and functions;

- Identify and promote effective sector-specific protection practices and methodologies; and

- Expand voluntary security-related information sharing among private entities within the sector, as well as between government and private entities.

Department of Homeland Security

The Department of Homeland Security (DHS) provides overall cross-sector coordination in this organizational scheme, serving as the primary liaison and facilitator for cooperation among federal agencies, state and local governments, and the private sector. As the cross-sector coordinator, DHS is also responsible for the detailed refinement and implementation of the core elements of this Strategy.

Other Federal Departments and Agencies

Besides the designated federal lead departments and agencies, the federal government will rely on the unique expertise of other departments and agencies to enhance the physical protection dimension of homeland security. Additionally, overall sector initiatives will often include an international component or requirement, require the development of a coordinated relationship with other governments or agencies, and entail information sharing with foreign governments. Accordingly, the Department of State (DoS) will support the development and implementation of sector protection initiatives by laying the groundwork for bilateral and multilateral infrastructure protective agreements with our international allies.

State and Local Government Responsibilities

The 50 states, 4 territories, and 87,000 local jurisdictions that comprise this Nation have an important and unique role to play in the protection of our critical infrastructures and key assets. State and local governments, like the federal government, should identify and secure the critical infrastructures and key assets they own and operate within their jurisdictions.

States should also engender coordination of protective and emergency response activities and resource support among local jurisdictions and regions in close collaboration with designated federal lead departments and agencies. States should further facilitate coordinated planning and preparedness for critical infrastructure and key asset protection, applying unified criteria for determining criticality, prioritizing protection investments, and exercising preparedness within their jurisdictions. States should also act as conduits for requests for federal assistance when the threat at hand exceeds the capabilities of local jurisdictions and private entities within those jurisdictions. Finally, states should facilitate the exchange of relevant security information and threat alerts down to the local level.

State and local governments look to the federal government for coordination, support, and resources when national requirements exceed local capabilities. Protecting critical infrastructures and key assets requires a close and extensive cooperation among all three levels of government. DHS, in particular, is designed to provide a single point of coordination with state and local governments for homeland security issues, including the critical infrastructure and key asset protection mission area. Other federal lead departments and agencies and law enforcement organizations will provide support as needed and appropriate for specific critical infrastructure and key asset protection requirements.

Private Sector Responsibilities

The lion's share of our critical infrastructures and key assets are owned and operated by the private sector.

The lion's share of our critical infrastructures and key assets are owned and operated by the private sector. Customarily, private sector firms prudently engage in risk management planning and invest in security as a necessary function of business operations and customer confidence. Moreover, in the present threat environment, the private sector generally remains the first line of defense for its own facilities. Consequently, private sector owners and operators should reassess and adjust their planning, assurance, and investment programs to better accommodate the increased risk presented by deliberate acts of violence. Since the events of September 11, many businesses have increased their threshold investments and undertaken enhancements in security in an effort to meet the demands of the new threat environment.

For most enterprises, the level of investment in security reflects implicit risk-versus-consequence tradeoffs, which are based on: (1) what is known about the risk environment; and (2) what is economically justifiable and sustainable in a competitive marketplace or in an environment of limited government resources. Given the dynamic nature of the terrorist threat and the severity of the consequences associated with many potential attack scenarios, the private sector naturally looks to the government for better information to help make its crucial security investment decisions.

Similarly, the private sector looks to the government for assistance when the threat at hand exceeds an enterprise's capability to protect itself beyond a reasonable level of additional investment. In this light, the federal government collaborates with the private sector (and state and local governments) to assure the protection of nationally critical infrastructures and assets; provide timely warning and assure the protection of infrastructures and assets that face a specific, imminent threat; and promote an environment in which the private sector can better carry out its specific protection responsibilities.

Near-term Roadmap: Cross-Sector Security Priorities

Cross-Sector Security Priorities represent important, near-term national priorities. They are focused on impediments to physical protection that significantly impact multiple sectors of our government, society, and economy. Potential solutions to the problems identified—such as information sharing and threat indications and warning—are high leverage areas that, when realized, will enhance the Nation's collective ability to protect critical infrastructures and key assets across the board. Accordingly, DHS and designated federal lead departments and agencies are preparing detailed implementation plans to support the activities outlined in this strategy.

This Strategy identifies major cross-sector initiatives in five areas:

1. Planning and Resource Allocation:

    *   Create collaborative mechanisms for government-industry critical infrastructure and key asset protection planning;

    *   Identify key protection priorities and develop appropriate supporting mechanisms for these priorities;

    *   Foster increased sharing of risk-management expertise between the public and private sectors;

    *   Identify options for incentives for private organizations that proactively implement enhanced security measures;

    *   Coordinate and consolidate federal and state protection plans;

    *   Establish a task force to review legal impediments to reconstitution and recovery in the aftermath of an attack against a critical infrastructure or key asset;

    *   Develop an integrated critical infrastructure and key asset geospatial database; and

    *   Conduct critical infrastructure protection planning with our international partners.

2. Information Sharing and Indications and Warnings:

    *   Define protection-related information sharing requirements and establish effective, efficient information sharing processes;

    *   Implement the statutory authorities and powers of the Homeland Security Act of 2002 to protect security and proprietary information regarded as sensitive by the private sector;

    *   Promote the development and operation of critical sector Information Sharing Analysis Centers;

    *   Improve processes for domestic threat data collection, analysis, and dissemination to state and local government and private industry;

The National Strategy for the Physical Protection of Critical Infrastructure and Key Assets identifies five major cross-sector initiatives:

1. *Planning and Resource Allocation.*
2. *Information Sharing and Indications and Warnings.*
3. *Personnel Surety, Building Human Capital and Awareness.*
4. *Technology and Research & Development.*
5. *Modeling, Simulation, and Analysis.*

- Support the development of interoperable secure communications systems for state and local governments and designated private sector entities; and

- Complete implementation of the Homeland Security Advisory System.

3. Personnel Surety, Building Human Capital, and Awareness:

- Coordinate the development of national standards for personnel surety;

- Develop a certification program for background screening companies;

- Explore establishment of a certification regime or model security training program for private security officers;

- Identify requirements and develop programs to protect critical personnel;

- Facilitate the sharing of public- and private-sector protection expertise; and

- Develop and implement a national awareness program for critical infrastructure and key asset protection.

4. Technology and Research & Development:

- Coordinate public- and private-sector security research and development activities;

- Coordinate interoperability standards to ensure compatibility of communications systems;

- Explore methods to authenticate and verify personnel identity; and

- Improve technical surveillance, monitoring and detection capabilities.

5. Modeling, Simulation, and Analysis:

- Enable the integration of modeling, simulation, and analysis into national infrastructure and asset protection planning and decision support activities;

- Develop economic models of near- and long-term effects of terrorist attacks;

- Develop critical node/chokepoint and interdependency analysis capabilities;

- Model interdependencies across sectors with respect to conflicts between sector alert and warning procedures and actions;

- Conduct integrated risk modeling of cyber and physical threats, vulnerabilities, and consequences; and

- Develop models to improve information integration.

Unique Protection Areas

In addition to the cross-sector themes addressed in this Strategy, the individual critical infrastructure sectors and special categories of key assets have unique issues that require action:

1. Securing Critical Infrastructures: This Strategy identifies major protection initiatives for the following critical infrastructure sectors:

   - Agriculture and Food
   - Water
   - Public Health
   - Emergency Services
   - Defense Industrial Base
   - Telecommunications
   - Energy
   - Transportation
   - Banking and Finance
   - Chemicals and Hazardous Materials
   - Postal and Shipping

2. Protecting Key Assets: This Strategy identifies major protection initiatives for the following key asset categories:

   - National Monuments and Icons
   - Nuclear Power Plants
   - Dams
   - Government Facilities
   - Commercial Key Assets[1]

The Department of Homeland Security coordinates the national effort to secure America's critical infrastructure.

Coordinating the National Effort

The Department of Homeland Security coordinates the national effort to secure America's critical infrastructure. Protecting America's critical infrastructure is the shared responsibility of federal, state, and local government, in active partnership with the private sector, which owns approximately 85 percent of our nation's critical infrastructure. The Department of Homeland Security concentrates this partnership in a single government agency responsible for coordinating a comprehensive national plan for protecting our infrastructure. The Department gives state, local, and private entities one primary contact instead of many for coordinating protection activities with the federal government, including vulnerability assessments, strategic planning efforts, and exercises.

The Department builds and maintain a comprehensive assessment of our nation's infrastructure sectors: food, water, agriculture, health systems and emergency services, energy (electrical, nuclear, gas and oil, dams), transportation (air, road, rail, ports, waterways), information and telecommunications, banking and finance, energy, transportation, chemical, defense industry, postal and shipping, and national monuments and icons. The Department develops and harnesses the best modeling, simulation, and analytic tools to prioritize effort, taking as its foundation the National Infrastructure Simulation and Analysis Center. The Department directs or coordinates action to protect significant vulnerabilities, particularly targets with catastrophic potential such as nuclear power plants, chemical facilities, pipelines, and ports, and establishes policy for standardized, tiered protective measures tailored to the target and rapidly adjusted to the threat.

The nation's information and telecommunications systems are directly connected to many other critical infrastructure sectors, including banking and finance, energy, and transportation. The consequences of an attack on our cyber infrastructure can cascade across many sectors, causing widespread disruption of essential services, damaging our economy, and imperiling public safety. The speed, virulence, and maliciousness of cyber attacks have increased dramatically in recent years. Accordingly, the Department of Homeland Security places an especially high priority on protecting the cyber infrastructure from terrorist attack by unifying and focusing the key cyber security activities performed by the Critical Infrastructure Assurance Office and the National Infrastructure Protection Center. The Department augments those capabilities with the response functions of the Federal Computer Incident Response Center. Because the information and telecommunications sectors are increasingly interconnected, the Department also assumes the functions and assets of the National Communications System, which coordinates emergency preparedness for the telecommunications sector.[2]

PCII Program

On February 18, 2004, the U.S. Department of Homeland Security announced the launch of the Protected Critical Infrastructure Information (PCII) Program. The PCII Program enables the private sector to voluntarily submit infrastructure information to the Federal government to assist the Nation in reducing its vulnerability to terrorist attacks.

Critical infrastructure includes the assets and systems that, if disrupted, would threaten national security, public health and safety, economy, and our way of life. Although these industries, services and systems may be found in both the public and private sectors, the Department of Homeland Security estimates that more than 85 percent falls within the private sector. Recognizing that the private sector may be reluctant to share information with the Federal Government if it could be publicly disclosed, Congress passed the CII Act in

2002 with its provisions for protection from public disclosure.[3]

The Protected Critical Infrastructure Information (PCII) Program, established pursuant to the Critical Infrastructure Information Act of 2002 (CII Act), created a framework which enables members of the private sector to voluntarily submit sensitive information regarding the nation's critical infrastructure to the Department of Homeland Security (DHS) with the assurance that the information will be protected from public disclosure.

The PCII Program seeks to facilitate greater sharing of critical infrastructure information among the owners and operators of the critical infrastructures and government entities with infrastructure protection responsibilities, thereby reducing the nation's vulnerability to terrorism.

To implement and manage the program, DHS created the PCII Program Office within the Information Analysis and Infrastructure Protection (IAIP) Directorate. The PCII Program Office receives, validates, disseminates and safeguards critical infrastructure information in accordance with the CII Act and implementing regulations at 6 CFR Part 29.

The security and protection of the nation's critical infrastructure are of paramount importance, not only to the federal, state and local governments, but also to private utilities, businesses, and industries. There are several benefits for private sector participants in the PCII program:

PCII focuses primarily on analyzing and securing critical infrastructure and protected systems, risk and vulnerabilities assessments, and assisting with recovery as appropriate.

- Proprietary or sensitive infrastructure information can now be shared with governmental entities who share the private sector's commitment to a more secure homeland.

- Information sharing will result in better identification of risks and vulnerabilities, which will help industry partner with others in protecting their assets.

- By voluntarily submitting CII to the Federal Government, industry is helping to safeguard and prevent disruption to the American economy and way of life.

- Private industry is demonstrating good corporate citizenship that may save lives and protect communities.

PCII may be used for many purposes, focusing primarily on analyzing and securing critical infrastructure and protected systems, risk and vulnerabilities assessments, and assisting with recovery as appropriate. The IAIP Directorate plays a critical role in securing the homeland by identifying and assessing threats and mapping those threats against vulnerabilities such as critical infrastructure.[4]

Securing Cyberspace

The Nation's critical infrastructures are composed of public and private institutions in the sectors of agriculture, food, water, public health, emergency services, government, defense industrial base, information and telecommunications, energy, transportation, banking and finance, chemicals and hazardous materials, and postal and shipping. Cyberspace is their nervous system—the control system of our country. Cyberspace is composed of hundreds of thousands of interconnected computers, servers, routers, switches, and fiber optic cables that allow our critical infrastructures to work. Thus, the healthy functioning of cyberspace is essential to our economy and our national security.

National Strategy to Secure Cyberspace

The National Strategy to Secure Cyberspace is part an implementing component of the National Strategy for Homeland Security complemented by the National Strategy for the Physical Protection of Critical Infrastructures and Key Assets. The purpose of the Strategy is to engage and empower Americans to secure the portions of cyberspace that they own, operate, control, or with which they interact. Securing cyberspace is a difficult strategic challenge that requires coordinated and focused effort from our entire society—the federal government, state and local governments, the private sector, and the American people.

Cyberspace is composed of hundreds of thousands of interconnected computers, servers, routers, switches, and fiber optic cables that allow our critical infrastructures to work.

The National Strategy to Secure Cyberspace outlines an initial framework for both organizing and prioritizing efforts. It provides direction to the federal government departments and agencies that have roles in cyberspace security. It also identifies steps that state and local governments, private companies and organizations, and individual Americans can take to improve our collective cybersecurity. The Strategy highlights the role of public-private engagement. The document provides a framework for the contributions that we all can make to secure our parts of cyberspace. The dynamics of cyberspace will require adjustments and amendments to the Strategy over time.

Cyber Threat

The speed and anonymity of cyber attacks makes distinguishing among the actions of terrorists, criminals, and nation states difficult, a task which often occurs only after the fact, if at all. Therefore, the National Strategy to Secure Cyberspace helps reduce our Nation's vulnerability to debilitating attacks against our critical information infrastructures or the physical assets that support them.

Consistent with the National Strategy for Homeland Security, the strategic objectives of this National Strategy to Secure Cyberspace are to:

- Prevent cyber attacks against America's critical infrastructures;

- Reduce national vulnerability to cyber attacks; and

- Minimize damage and recovery time from cyber attacks that do occur.

Our economy and national security are fully dependent upon information technology and the information infrastructure. At the core of the information infrastructure upon which we depend is the Internet, a system originally designed to share unclassified research among scientists who were assumed to be uninterested in abusing the network. It is that same Internet that today connects millions of other computer networks making most of the nation's essential services and infrastructures work. These computer networks also control physical objects such as electrical transformers, trains, pipeline pumps, chemical vats, radars, and stock markets, all of which exist beyond cyberspace.

A spectrum of malicious actors can and do conduct attacks against our critical information infrastructures. Of primary concern is the threat of organized cyber attacks capable of causing debilitating disruption to our Nation's critical infrastructures, economy, or national security. The required technical sophistication to carry out such an attack is high—and partially explains the lack of a debilitating attack to date.

We should not, however, be too sanguine. There have been instances where organized attackers have exploited vulnerabilities that may be indicative of more destructive capabilities.

Uncertainties exist as to the intent and full technical capabilities of several observed attacks. Enhanced cyber threat analysis is needed to address long-term trends related to threats and vulnerabilities. What is known is that the attack tools and methodologies are becoming widely available, and the technical capability and sophistication of users bent on causing havoc or disruption is improving.

In peacetime America's enemies may conduct espionage on our Government, university research centers, and private companies. They may also seek to prepare for cyber strikes during a confrontation by mapping U.S. information systems, identifying key targets, and lacing our infrastructure with back doors and other means of access. In wartime or crisis, adversaries may seek to intimidate the Nation's political leaders by attacking critical infrastructures and key economic functions or eroding public confidence in information systems.

Cyber attacks on United States information networks can have serious consequences such as disrupting critical operations, causing loss of revenue and intellectual property, or loss of life.

Cyber Security

Cyber attacks on United States information networks can have serious consequences such as disrupting critical operations, causing loss of revenue and intellectual property, or loss of life. Countering such attacks requires the development of robust capabilities where they do not exist today if we are to reduce vulnerabilities and deter those with the capabilities and intent to harm our critical infrastructures.

In general, the private sector is best equipped and structured to respond to an evolving cyber threat. There are specific instances, however, where federal government response is most appropriate and justified. Looking inward, providing continuity of government requires ensuring the safety of its own cyber infrastructure and those assets required for supporting its essential missions and services. Externally, a government role in cybersecurity is warranted in cases where high transaction costs or legal barriers lead to significant coordination problems; cases in which governments operate in the absence of private sector forces; resolution of incentive problems that lead to under provisioning of critical shared resources; and raising awareness.

Public-private engagement is a key component of our Strategy to secure cyberspace. This is true for several reasons. Public-private partnerships can usefully confront coordination problems. They can significantly enhance information exchange and cooperation. Public-private engagement takes a variety of forms and addresses awareness, training, technological improvements, vulnerability remediation, and recovery operations.

A federal role in these and other cases is only justified when the benefits of intervention outweigh the associated costs. This standard is especially important in cases where there are viable private sector solutions for addressing any potential threat or vulnerability. For each case, consideration should be given to the broad based costs and impacts of a given government action, versus other alternative actions, versus non-action, taking into account any existing or future private solutions.

Federal actions to secure cyberspace are warranted for purposes including: forensics and attack attribution, protection of networks and systems critical to national security, indications and warnings, and protection against organized attacks capable of inflicting debilitating damage to the economy. Federal activities should also support research and technology development that will enable the private sector to better secure privately-owned portions of the Nation's critical infrastructure.[5]

Federal actions to secure cyberspace are warranted for purposes including: forensics and attack attribution, protection of networks and systems critical to national security, indications and warnings, and protection against organized attacks capable of inflicting debilitating damage to the economy.

National Cyber Security Division

The Department of Homeland Security (DHS) in implementing the President's National Strategy to Secure Cyberspace and the Homeland Security Act of 2002, created the National Cyber Security Division (NCSD) under the Department's Information Analysis and Infrastructure Protection Directorate, June 6, 2003. The NCSD provides for 24 x7 functions, including conducting cyberspace analysis, issuing alerts and warning, improving information sharing, responding to major incidents, and aiding in national-level recovery efforts. This Division represents a significant step toward advancing the Federal government's interaction and partnership with industry and other organizations in this critical area.

The NCSD identifies, analyzes and reduces cyber threats and vulnerabilities; disseminate threat warning information; coordinates incident response; and provides technical assistance in continuity of operations and recovery planning.

The NCSD builds upon the existing capabilities transferred to DHS from the former Critical Infrastructure Assurance Office, the National Infrastructure Protection Center, the Federal Computer Incident Response Center, and the National Communications System. The creation of the NCSD both strengthens government-wide processes for response and improves protection of critical cyber assets through maximizing and leveraging the resources of these previously separate offices.

With 60 employees, the Division is organized around three units designed to:

- Identify risks and help reduce the vulnerabilities to government's cyber assets and coordinate with the private sector to identify and help protect America's critical cyber assets;

- Oversee a consolidated Cyber Security Tracking, Analysis, & Response Center (CSTARC), which will detect and respond to Internet events; track potential threats and vulnerabilities to cyberspace; and coordinate cyber security and incident response with federal, state, local, private sector and international partners; and

- Create, in coordination with other appropriate agencies, cyber security awareness and education programs and partnerships with consumers, businesses, governments, academia, and international communities.

Consistent with law and policy, DHS's NCSD coordinates closely with the Office of Management and Budget and National Institute of Standards and Technology regarding the security of Federal systems, and coordinates with Federal law enforcement authorities, as appropriate. NCSD leverages other DHS components including the Science and Technology Directorate, the U.S. Secret Service and the Department's Privacy Officer.

The NCSD works closely with the DHS Science & Technology (S&T) Directorate to implement all required programs for research and development in cyber security. While S&T provides the actual research and development functions and execution, the NCSD provides detailed requirements into the direction of this R&D in response to needs of our public and private sectors partners.[6]

Conclusion

Terrorists are opportunistic. They exploit vulnerabilities we leave exposed, choosing the time, place, and method of attack according to the weaknesses they observe or perceive. Protecting America's critical infrastructure and key assets is thus a formidable challenge. Our open and technologically complex society presents an almost infinite array of potential targets, and our critical infrastructure changes as rapidly as the marketplace. It is impossible to protect completely all targets, all the time. On the other hand, we can help deter or deflect attacks, or mitigate their effects, by making strategic improvements in protection and security. Thus, while we cannot assume we will prevent all terrorist attacks, we can substantially reduce America's vulnerability, particularly to the most damaging attacks.

All elements of our society have a crucial stake in reducing our vulnerability to terrorism; and all have highly valuable roles to play. Protecting America's critical infrastructure and key assets requires an unprecedented level of cooperation throughout all levels of government-with private industry and institutions, and with the American people. The federal government has the crucial task of fostering a collaborative environment, and enabling all of these entities to work together to provide America the security it requires.[7]

Questions

1. What is "critical infrastructure"?

2. Why must we protect it?

3. List the five major cross-sector initiatives to protect our critical infrastructure.

4. What is the role of DHS in protecting our nation's critical infrastructure?

5. What is the mission of the National Cyber Security Division?

## Chapter 14

Border & Transportation Security

Objectives

- Know the three subcomponents of Border and Transportation Security directorate.
- Know the five offices of the Immigration and Customs Enforcement agency.
- Explain the U.S. Coast Guard's relationship to the Department of Homeland Security.
- Explain the relationship between the ICE and USCIS.

Border and Transportation Security. America historically has relied heavily on two vast oceans and two friendly neighbors for border security, and on the private sector for most forms of domestic transportation security. The increasing mobility and destructive potential of modern terrorism has required the United States to rethink and renovate fundamentally its systems for border and transportation security. Indeed, we must now begin to conceive of border security and transportation security as fully integrated requirements because our domestic transportation systems are inextricably intertwined with the global transport infrastructure. Virtually every community in America is connected to the global transportation network by the seaports, airports, highways, pipelines, railroads, and waterways that move people and goods into, within, and out of the Nation. We must therefore promote the efficient and reliable flow of people, goods, and services across borders, while preventing terrorists from using transportation conveyances or systems to deliver implements of destruction.

- Critical Mission Area #2, National Strategy for Homeland Security, July 2002

Introduction

Securing the nation's air, land, and sea borders is a difficult yet critical task. The United States has 5,525 miles of border with Canada and 1,989 miles with Mexico. Our maritime border includes 95,000 miles of shoreline, and a 3.4 million square mile exclusive economic zone. Each year, more than 500 million people cross the borders into the United States, some 330 million of whom are non-citizens.

On March 1st, 2003, the Department of Homeland Security, through the Directorate of Border and Transportation Security (BTS), assumed responsibility for securing our nation's borders and transportation systems, which straddle 350 official ports of entry and connect our homeland to the rest of the world. BTS also assumed responsibility for enforcing the nation's immigration laws.

The Department's first priority is to prevent the entry of terrorists and the instruments of terrorism while simultaneously ensuring the efficient flow of lawful traffic and commerce. BTS manages and coordinates port of entry activities and leads efforts to create a border of the future that provides greater security through better intelligence, coordinated national efforts, and international cooperation against terrorists, the instruments of terrorism, and other international threats.

To carry out its border security mission, BTS incorporates the United States Customs Service (previously part of the Department of Treasury), the enforcement division of the Immigration and Naturalization Service (Department of Justice), the Animal and Plant Health Inspection Service (Department of Agriculture), the Federal Law Enforcement Training Center (Department of Treasury) and the Transportation Security Administration (Department of Transportation). BTS also incorporates the Federal Protective Service (General Services Administration) to perform the additional function of protecting government buildings, a task closely related to the Department's infrastructure protection responsibilities.[1]

The BTS organized these capabilities under three major subcomponents:

1. Transportation Security Administration (TSA)

2. Customs and Border Protection (CBP)

3. Immigration and Customs Enforcement (ICE)[2]

Transportation Security Administration

The Transportation Security Administration (TSA) has statutory responsibility for security of all of the nation's airports. Tools it uses include intelligence, regulation, enforcement, inspection, and screening and education of carriers, passengers and shippers. The incorporation of TSA into the Department of Homeland Security allows the Department of Transportation to remain focused on its core mandate of ensuring that the nation has a robust and efficient transportation infrastructure that keeps pace with modern technology and the nation's demographic and economic growth.[3]

On November 19, 2001 President Bush signed Public Law 107-71, the Aviation and Transportation Security Act (ATSA) which among other things established the new Transportation Security Administration (TSA) within the Department of Transportation.[4] The head of TSA was the Under Secretary of Transportation for Security. Under the Homeland Security Act of 2002, Public Law 107-296, TSA transferred to DHS. The head of TSA is now referred to as the Assistant Secretary of Homeland Security for the Transportation Security Administration.[5]

The TSA is responsible for security in all modes of transportation, including civil aviation security, and related research and development activities; and security responsibilities over other modes of transportation, in times of emergency, that are exercised by the Department of Transportation.

The TSA is responsible for day-to-day Federal security screening operations for passenger air transportation and intrastate air transportation. The TSA develops standards for hiring and retaining security screening personnel; training and testing security screening personnel; and hiring and training personnel to provide security screening at all airports in the United States.

The TSA conducts the following activities to secure the nation's transportation networks:

*   Receives, assesses, and distributes intelligence information related to transportation security;

*   Assesses threats to transportation;

*   Develops policies, strategies, and plans for dealing with threats to transportation security;

*   Makes other plans related to transportation security, including coordinating countermeasures with appropriate departments, agencies, and instrumentalities of the United States Government;

*   Serves as the primary liaison for transportation security to the intelli-

The Border and Transportation Security (BTS) Directorate is organized into three major subcomponents:
1. *Transportation Security Administration (TSA)*
2. *Customs and Border Protection (CBP)*
3. *Immigration and Customs Enforcement (ICE)*

gence and law enforcement communities;

- Manages and provides operational guidance to the field security resources of the Administration;

- Enforces security-related regulations and requirements;

- Identifies and undertakes research and development activities necessary to enhance transportation security;

- Inspects, maintains, and tests security facilities, equipment, and systems;

- Ensures the adequacy of security measures for the transportation of cargo;

- Oversees the implementation and ensures the adequacy of security measures at airports and other transportation facilities;

- Conducts background checks for airport security screening personnel, individuals with access to secure areas of airports, and other transportation security personnel;

- Works in conjunction with the Federal Aviation Administration with respect to any actions or activities that may affect aviation safety or air carrier operations;

- Works with the International Civil Aviation Organization and appropriate aeronautic authorities of foreign governments to address security concerns on passenger flights by foreign air carriers in foreign air transportation;

- Carries out such other duties, and exercise such other powers, relating to transportation security as the TSA considers appropriate.

In times of national emergency, the TSA is granted additional authority to coordinate domestic transportation, including aviation, rail, and other surface transportation, and maritime transportation (including port security), except for that belonging to the Department of Defense and the military departments. TSA also coordinates security alerts and provides threat notices to other departments and agencies of the Federal Government, and appropriate agencies of State and local governments, including departments and agencies for transportation, law enforcement, and border control.[6]

U.S. Customs and Border Protection

U.S. Customs and Border Protection (CBP) is the unified border agency within the Department of Homeland Security (DHS). CBP combined the inspectional workforces and broad border authorities of U.S. Customs, U.S. Immigration, Animal and Plant Health Inspection Service and the entire U.S. Border Patrol.

CBP includes more than 41,000 employees to manage, control and protect the Nation's borders, at and between official ports of entry. CBP's priority mission is preventing terrorists and terrorist weapons from entering the United States, while also facilitating the flow of legitimate trade and travel. CBP uses multiple strategies and employs the latest in technology to accomplish its dual goals. CBP's initiatives are designed to protect the homeland from acts of terrorism, and reduce vulnerability to terrorists through a multi-level inspection process.

U.S. Customs and Border Protection assess all passengers flying into the U.S. from abroad for terrorist risk using the Advance Passenger Information System (APIS), United States Visitor and Immigrant Status Indication Technology (US-VISIT), and the Student and Exchange Visitor System (SEVIS). CBP regularly refuses entry to people who may pose a threat to the security of our country.

In addition, CBP uses advance information from the Automated Targeting System (ATS), Automated Export System (AES), and the Trade Act of 2002 Advance Electronic Information Regulations to identify cargo that may pose a threat. CBP's Office of Intelligence and the National Targeting Center (NTC) enhance these initiatives by synthesizing information to provide tactical targeting. Using risk management techniques, they evaluate people and goods to identify a suspicious individual or container before it can reach our shores.

The Automated Commercial Environment (ACE) has made electronic risk management far more effective. The ACE Secure Data Portal provides a single, centralized on-line access point to connect CBP and the trade community. CBP's modernization efforts enhance border security while optimizing the flow of legitimate trade.

CBP also screens high-risk imported food shipments in order to prevent bio-terrorism/agro-terrorism. U.S. Food and Drug Administration (FDA) and CBP personnel work side by side at the NTC to protect the U.S. food supply by taking action, implementing provisions of the Bioterrorism Act of 2002. CBP and FDA are able to react quickly to threats of bio-terrorist attacks on the U.S. food supply or to other food related emergencies.

International Cooperation

U.S. Customs and Border Protection created smarter borders by extending a zone of security beyond our physical borders. CBP established working groups with its foreign counterparts to establish ties, improve security and facilitate the flow of legitimate trade and travel.

CBP established the Container Security Initiative (CSI). Under CSI, CBP pushes the border outward by working jointly with host nation counterparts to identify and pre-screen containers that pose a risk at the foreign port of departure before they are loaded on board vessels bound for the U.S. CSI is now implemented in 20 of the largest ports in terms of container shipments to the U.S.

CBP also implemented joint initiatives with Canada and Mexico: The Smart Border Declaration and associated 30-Point Action Plan with Canada and The Smart Border Accord with Mexico. The Secure Electronic Network for Travelers' Rapid Inspection (SENTRI) allows pre-screened, low-risk travelers from Mexico to be processed in an expeditious manner through dedicated lanes. Similarly, on our northern border with Canada, CBP is engaging in NEXUS to identify and facilitate low-risk travelers. Along both borders, CBP has implemented the Free and Secure Trade (FAST) program. The FAST program utilizes transponder technology and pre-arrival shipment information to process participating trucks as they arrive at the border, expediting trade while better securing our borders.

In addition, an agreement with Canada allows CBP to target, screen, and examine rail shipments headed to the U.S. CBP established attachés in Mexico and Canada to coordinate border security issues. CBP Border Patrol agents, the Royal Canadian Mounted Police, and the Drug Enforcement Administration, as well as state and local law enforcement agencies from Canada and the U.S. joined together to form fourteen Integrated Border Enforcement Teams (IBET). Covering our entire mutual border with Canada, these teams are used to target cross-border smuggling between Canada and the United States. The teams focus on criminal activity such as smuggling of drugs, humans, contraband and cross-border terrorist movements.

Partnering with Business

Processing the sheer volume of trade entering the U.S. each year requires help from the private sector. The Customs-Trade Partnership Against Terrorism (C-TPAT) is a joint government-business initiative designed to strengthen overall supply chain and border security while facilitating legitimate, compliant trade. To date, over 6,500 companies are partnering with CBP. C-TPAT is the largest, most successful government-private sector partnership to arise out of 9-11.

In addition, U.S. Customs and Border Protection is piloting the Advanced Trade Data Initiative. This program works with the trade community to obtain information on U.S. bound goods at the earliest possible point in the supply chain. Partnering with carriers, importers, shippers and terminal operators, we are gathering supply chain data and feeding it into our systems to validate container shipments during the supply process. This information increases CBP's existing ability to zero in on suspect movements and perform any necessary security inspections at the earliest point possible in the supply chain.

Advanced Screening

Given the magnitude of CBP's responsibility, the development and deployment of sophisticated detection technology is essential. Deployment of Non-Intrusive Inspection (NII) technology is increasing and viewed as "force multipliers" that enable CBP officers to screen or examine a larger portion of the stream of commercial traffic. CBP does not rely on any single technology or inspection process. Instead, officers and agents use various technologies in different combinations to substantially increase the likelihood that terrorist weapons including a nuclear or radiological weapon will be detected and interdicted.

Technologies deployed to our nation's land, sea, and airports of entry include large-scale x-ray and gamma-imaging systems. CBP has deployed radiation detection technology including Personal Radiation Detectors (PRDs), radiation isotope identifiers, and radiation portal monitors. CBP uses trained explosive and chemical detector dogs. CBP's Laboratories and Scientific Services Fast Response Team reacts to calls on suspicious containers. The Laboratories and Scientific Services also operates a 24x7x365 hotline at its Chemical, Biological, Radiation, and Nuclear Technical Data Assessment and Teleforensic Center.

U.S. Customs and Border Protection has the authority to search outbound, as well as inbound shipments, and uses targeting to carry out its mission in this area. Targeting of outbound shipments and people is a multi-dimensional effort that is enhanced by inter-agency cooperation. CBP in conjunction with the Department of State and the Bureau of the Census has put in place regulations that require submission of electronic export information on U.S. Munitions List and for technology for the Commerce Control List. This information flows via the Automated Export System (AES). CBP is also working with the Departments of State and Defense to improve procedures on exported shipments of foreign military sales commodities. CBP works with Immigration and Customs Enforcement (ICE) to seize outbound currency, particularly cash and monetary instruments going to the Middle East.

Border Surveillance

U.S. Customs and Border Protection's Border Patrol agents are better securing areas between the ports of entry by implementing a comprehensive border enforcement strategy, expanding, integrating, and coordinating the use of technology and communications through:

- Integrated Surveillance Intelligence System (ISIS) is a system that uses remotely monitored night-day camera and sensing systems to better detect, monitor, and respond to illegal crossings.

- Unmanned Aerial Vehicles (UAVs) are equipped with sophisticated on-board sensors. UAVs provide long-range surveillance and are useful for monitoring remote land border areas where patrols cannot easily travel and infrastructure is difficult or impossible to build.

- Remote Video Surveillance Systems (RVSS) provide coverage 24x7 to detect illegal crossings on both our northern and southern borders.

- Geographic Information System (GIS)—a CBP Border Patrol southwest border initiative to track illegal migration patterns.[7]

CBP's Air and Marine Operations Division is responsible for protecting the nation's borders and the American people from the smuggling of people, narcotics, and other contraband and for detecting and deterring terrorist activity with an integrated and coordinated air and marine interdiction force. The Air and Marine Operations Division also supports ICE investigations.[8]

Immigration and Customs Enforcement

Another important function of BTS's border management mission is enforcing the nation's immigration laws—both in deterring illegal immigration and pursuing investigations when laws are broken.[9] The U.S. Immigration and Customs Enforcement (ICE) was established on March 1, 2003, as part of the Department of Homeland Security. The 20,000 employees of ICE represent the largest investigative force within DHS. ICE enforces the nation's immigration and customs laws, provides commercial air security and protects federal facilities. ICE seeks to prevent acts of terrorism by targeting the people, money and materials that support terrorist and criminal activities. ICE is comprised of five offices:

1. Office of Investigations

2. Office of Detention and Removal Operations

3. Office of Federal Air Marshal Service

4. Office of Federal Protective Service

5. Office of Intelligence

Office of Investigations

The Office of Investigations is responsible for investigating a wide range of domestic and international activities arising from the movement of people and goods that violate immigration and custom laws and threaten national security.[10] The Office of Investigations focuses on a broad array of national security, financial and smuggling violations including illegal arms exports, financial crimes, commercial fraud, human trafficking, narcotics smuggling, child pornography/exploitation and immigration fraud. ICE special agents also conduct investigations aimed at protecting critical infrastructure industries that are vulnerable to sabotage, attack or exploitation. The Office of Investigations is comprised of five divisions:

1. The National Security Investigations Division oversees investigative programs designed to protect our national security by preventing the illegal importation, exportation and transfer of Weapons of Mass Destruction, arms and munitions and critical technology.

2. The Financial Investigations Division oversees ICE's efforts to eliminate potential vulnerabilities in the nation's financial infrastructure, and protect America's financial service systems from illegal money laundering, insurance schemes, bulk cash smuggling, intellectual property rights and counterfeit goods trafficking and other financial crimes.

3. The Smuggling/Public Safety Division oversees programs designed to identify, disrupt and dismantle significant organizations that smuggle contraband and humans into the United States, pose a threat to the health, safety and rights of our people, threaten our critical infrastructure or defraud the United States.

4. The Investigative Services Division assists and supports investigative programs and special agents.[11]

Immigration and Customs Enforcement is comprised of five offices:
1. *Office of Investigations*
2. *Office of Detention and Removal Operations*
3. *Office of Federal Air Marshal Service*
4. *Office of Federal Protective Service*
5. *Office of Intelligence*

Office of Detention and Removal Operations

The Office of Detention and Removal Operations (DRO) is responsible for public safety and national security by ensuring the departure from the United States of all removable aliens and by enforcing the nation's immigration laws.[12] The DRO provides adequate and appropriate custody management to support removals, to facilitate the processing of illegal aliens through the immigration court, and to enforce their departure from the United States. Key elements in exercising those responsibilities include: identifying and removing all high-risk illegal alien fugitives and absconders; ensuring that those aliens who have already been identified as criminals are expeditiously removed; and to develop and maintain a robust removals program with the capacity to remove all final order cases—thus precluding growth in the illegal alien absconder population.

The Immigration and Nationality Act (INA) grants aliens the right to a removal proceeding before an immigration judge to decide both inadmissibility and deportability. Aliens can be removed for reasons of health, criminal status, economic well-being, national security risks and others that are specifically defined in the Act. An immigration judge weighs evidence presented by both the alien and DHS, assesses the facts and renders a decision that can be appealed to the Board of Immigration Appeals. When the decision rendered is to depart the country, DRO takes over the responsibility to facilitate the process and ensure the alien does, in fact, depart.

The deportation process includes coordination with foreign government and embassies to obtain travel documents and country clearances, coordinating all the logistics and transportation necessary to repatriate the alien and, when required, escort the alien to his or her home of record.

The removal of criminal aliens from the United States is a national priority. To address this priority, DRO designed the National Fugitive Operations Program (NFOP). Its mission is to apprehend, process and remove from the United States aliens who have failed to surrender for removal or to comply with a removal order. NFOP teams work exclusively on fugitive cases, giving priority to the cases of criminal aliens.

The "Absconder Apprehension Initiative" uses the data available from National Crime Information Center databases as a virtual force multiplier. As part of the Alien Absconder Initiative, DRO developed and coordinated the "ICE Most Wanted" program. This program publicizes the names, faces and other identifying features of the 10 most wanted fugitive criminals by ICE. Aliens who are apprehended and not released from custody are placed in detention facilities. Those that cannot be legally released from secure custody constitute DRO's "nondetained" docket.

Every case, whether "detained" or "nondetained," remains part of DRO's caseload, actively managed until and unless it is formally closed. DRO processes and monitors detained and nondetained cases as they move through immigration court proceedings to conclusion. At that point, DRO executes the judge's order. DRO secures bed space in detention facilities, and monitors these facilities for compliance with national Detention Standards. The standards specify the living conditions appropriate for detainees. These standards have been collated and published in the Detention Operations Manual. This Manual provides uniform policies and procedures concerning the treatment of individuals detained by ICE.

ICE operates eight secure detention facilities called Service Processing Centers (SPCs). They are located in Aguadilla, Puerto Rico; Batavia, New York; El Centro, California; El Paso, Texas; Florence, Arizona; Miami, Florida; Los Fresnos, Texas; and San Pedro, California. The newest SPC, the Buffalo Federal Detention Facility, is unique because in addition to its 300 beds for detained aliens, it has 150 beds for use by the U.S. Marshals Service. ICE augments its SPC's with seven contract detention facilities located in Aurora, Colorado; Houston, Texas; Laredo, Texas; Seattle, Washington; Elizabeth, New Jersey; Queens, New York; and San Diego, California. ICE also uses state and local jails on a reimbursable detention day basis and has joint federal facilities with the Bureau of Prisons, the Federal Detention Center in Oakdale, Louisiana, and the contractor owned and operated (with the Bureau of Prisons) criminal alien facility in Eloy, Arizona. In addition, major expansion initiatives are underway at several SPCs'.[13]

Federal Air Marshal Service

The Federal Air Marshal Service (FAMs) is responsible for ensuring confidence in our nation's civil aviation system through the deployment of Federal Air Marshals to detect, deter, and defeat hostile acts targeting U.S. air carriers, airports, passengers, and crews.[14]

The Federal Air Marshal Service began in 1968 as the Federal Aviation Administration's (FAA) Sky Marshal Program. In 1985, President Ronald Reagan requested the expansion of the program, and Congress enacted the International Security and Development Cooperation Act, which provided the statutes behind today's Federal Air Marshal Service. On September 11, 2001, the Federal Air Marshal Service consisted of 33 FAMs. President George W. Bush quickly authorized an increase in the number of Federal Air Marshals, and almost overnight the Service received over 200,000 applications. A classified number of these applicants were screened, hired, trained, certified and deployed on flights around the world.

As one of the five divisions of ICE, the Federal Air Marshal Service continues its mission to promote confidence in the nation's civil aviation system through the effective deployment of Federal Air Marshals to detect, deter and defeat hostile acts targeting U.S. air carriers, airports, passengers and crews. The transfer of FAMs to ICE offers the Air Marshal Service multiple law enforcement resources, such as additional access to intelligence, better coordination with other enforcement agencies, and broader training opportunities. Federal Air Marshals receive training at the William J. Hughes Technical Center in Atlantic City, New Jersey. The stringent training program includes behavioral observation, intimidation tactics and close quarters self-defense. In addition, Federal Air Marshals are held to a higher standard for handgun accuracy than officers of any other federal law enforcement agency.[15]

Federal Protective Service

The Federal Protective Service (FPS) is responsible for policing, securing, and ensuring a safe environment in which federal agencies can conduct their business by reducing threats posed against more than 8,800 federal government facilities nationwide.[16]

In 1971, Congress created the FPS to be under the control of the GSA's Public Buildings Service. Congress directed "special police officers" be hired who would have the authority of "Sheriffs or Constables" on property under the charge and control of GSA. Title 40, United States Code, Sections 318a - 318d provided for the establishment of the service and defined the Authority and Jurisdiction of these officers. FPS Police Officers hired under this authority are responsible for the protection of public buildings and other areas under the charge and control of GSA. They are also responsible for the enforcement of laws enacted for the protection of persons and property, the prevention of breaches of peace, suppression of affrays or unlawful assemblies, and enforcement of any rules and regulations made and promulgated by the GSA Administrator. This authority can also be extended, by agreement, to any area with a significant federal interest.

On March 1, 2003, (in accordance with the Homeland Security Act of 2002) the FPS was transferred from the GSA to the Directorate of Border and Transportation Security within the Department of Homeland Security. The head of the FPS was re-titled Director of the Federal Protective Service in lieu of the previous designation under GSA of FPS Assistant Commissioner.[17]

The mission of the Federal Protective Service (FPS) is to provide law enforcement and security services to over one million tenants and daily visitors to all federally owned and leased facilities nationwide. FPS focuses directly on the interior security of the nation and the reduction of crimes and potential threats to federal facilities throughout the nation by:

- Providing a visible uniformed police presence.

- Managing and overseeing 10,000 armed contract security guards.

- Responding to criminal incidents and emergencies with full law enforcement authority.

- Exercising authority to detain and arrest individuals and seize goods or vehicles.

- Conducting comprehensive intelligence sharing at the federal, state and local levels.

- Participating in national and local Federal Anti-terrorism Task Forces.

- Developing specialized response capabilities—Canine and Weapons of Mass Destruction Teams.

- Providing protection during demonstrations, protests and acts of civil unrest.

- Investigating criminal incidents.

- Continuously monitoring building alarms/emergencies through four FPS MegaCenters.

- Conducting building vulnerability and security assessments.

- Implementing appropriate security threat countermeasures.

- Purchasing/installing/monitoring security equipment and enhancements to designated buildings.

- Providing police emergency services in natural disasters, civil disturbances and terrorist actions.

- Offering protection support for special events: Olympics, Kentucky Derby and Presidential Inaugurals.

- Chairing the Interagency Security Committee to establish government-wide security policy.

- Presenting formal crime prevention/security awareness presentations to the federal population.

- Conducting background suitability determinations and adjudications for contract security guards and GSA daycare workers.

- Providing Federal Emergency Management Agency (FEMA) support.[18]

The Department of Homeland Security has authority over the United States Coast Guard, which maintains its independent identity as a military organization under the leadership of the Commandant of the Coast Guard.

Office of Intelligence

The Office of Intelligence is responsible for the collection, analysis, and dissemination of strategic and tactical intelligence data for use by the operational elements of ICE and DHS.[19] The Office of Intelligence collects, analyzes, and shares information on critical homeland security vulnerabilities that could be exploited by terrorist and criminal organizations. The Office of Intelligence focuses data and information related to the movement of people, money and materials into, within and out of the United States to provide accurate and timely reporting to ICE leadership and field agents in support of enforcement operations.

ICE's intelligence functions are managed by a highly trained team of professionals with expertise in data and threat analysis, languages, financial investigations, counterterrorism and a number of other areas. The Office of Intelligence staffs the 24-hour ICE Operations Center (IOC) to handle significant incoming incident reports and facilitate the ongoing exchange of intelligence between ICE and other agencies. ICE intelligence professionals process information from a variety of sources to provide assessments of patterns, trends and new developments in a wide range of law enforcement areas including:

- Human Smuggling and Trafficking

- Money Laundering and Financial Crime

- Drug Smuggling

- Terrorism

- Criminal Aliens

- Air and Marine Smuggling

- Cyber Crimes

- Identity Fraud and Document Fraud

- Arms Trafficking and Technology Transfers

- Commercial Fraud

- Mass Migration and Conditions Affecting Immigration

- Security at Federal Facilities and Other Critical Infrastructure Sites

- Airspace Security[20]

The U.S. Coast Guard

In order to secure our nation's territorial waters, including our ports and waterways, the Department of Homeland Security has authority over the United States Coast Guard, which maintains its independent identity as a military organization under the leadership of the Commandant of the Coast Guard. Upon declaration of war or when the President so directs, the Coast Guard operates as an element of the Department of Defense, consistent with existing law. The BTS works closely with the Coast Guard to fulfill its border protection responsibilities.

The U.S. Coast Guard is charged with regulatory, law enforcement, humanitarian, and emergency response duties. It is responsible for the safety and security of America's inland waterways, ports, and harbors; more than 95,000 miles of U.S. coastlines; U.S. territorial seas; 3.4 million square miles of ocean defining our Exclusive Economic Zones; as well as other maritime regions of importance to the United States. The Coast Guard has command responsibilities for countering potential threats to America's coasts, ports, and inland waterways through numerous port security, harbor defense, and coastal warfare operations and exercises. In the name of port security specifically, the Coast Guard has broad authority in the nation's ports as "Captain of the Port." Recently the Coast Guard has worked to establish near shore and port domain awareness, and to provide an offshore force gathering intelligence and interdicting suspicious vessels prior to reaching U.S. shores.

The Department of Homeland Security separates immigration services from immigration law enforcement.

United States Citizenship and Immigration Services

The Department of Homeland Security separates immigration services from immigration law enforcement. BTS is responsible for immigration law enforcement acting through Immigration and Customs Enforcement (ICE). Immigration services, including citizenship and visas, are provided separately through the Bureau of Citizenship and Immigrations Services (USCIS). The BTS and USCIS work closely together to perform their respective immigration duties. Through the USCIS, the Department has legal authority to issue visas to foreign nationals and admit them into the country. The State Department, working through the United States embassies and consulates abroad, continues to administer the visa application and issuance process. The Department of Homeland Security makes certain that America continues to welcome visitors and those who seek opportunity within our shores while excluding terrorists and their supporters.[21]

Conclusion

Consolidating disparate federal agencies under the singular authority of the Department of Homeland Security has led to a marked improvement in efficiently securing our nation's borders. Prior to establishing the Department, when a ship entered a U.S. port, Customs, INS, the Coast Guard, the U.S. Department of Agriculture, and others had overlapping jurisdictions over pieces of the arriving vessel:

- Customs had jurisdiction over the goods aboard the ship;

- INS had jurisdiction over the people on the ship;

- The Coast Guard had jurisdiction over the ship while it was at sea;

- And the Department of Agriculture had jurisdiction over certain cargoes.

Consolidating disparate federal agencies under the singular authority of the Department of Homeland Security has led to a marked improvement in efficiently securing our nation's borders.

Although the Coast Guard had authority to act as an agent for these other organizations and assert jurisdiction over the entire vessel, in practice the system didn't work as well as it could to prevent the illegal entry of potential terrorists and instruments of terror. For example, if the Coast Guard stopped a ship at sea for inspection and found illegal immigrants aboard, the Coast Guard relied on the INS to enforce U.S. immigration law and prevent their entry. If the Coast Guard found potentially dangerous cargo, it relied on Customs to seize it. Unfortunately, those organizations did not always share information with each other as rapidly as necessary.

So, instead of arresting potential terrorists and seizing dangerous cargo at sea, the previous structure could allow terrorists to enter U.S. ports and infiltrate our society. The system could also allow dangerous cargo to enter our ports and threaten American lives.

Now, under the Directorate of Border and Transportation Security, the ship, potential terrorists, and dangerous cargo may be seized at sea by one Department that has no question about either its mission or its authority to prevent them from reaching our shores.[22]

Questions

1. What are the three subcomponents of the Border and Transportation Security directorate?

2. List the five offices of the Immigration and Customs Enforcement agency.

3. Explain the U.S. Coast Guard's relationship to the Department of Homeland Security.

4. What is the difference between ICE and USCIS?

5. How has BTS improved border security for the United States?

Chapter 15

U.S. Coast Guard

Objectives

- Describe the organization of the United States Coast Guard.

- Explain the five major missions of the United States Coast Guard.

- Explain how the Coast Guard is unique among the uniform services.

Recapitalize the U.S. Coast Guard. The Budget for Fiscal Year 2003 requested the largest increase in the history of the U.S. Coast Guard. The Budget for Fiscal Year 2004 will continue to support the recapitalization of the U.S. Coast Guard's aging fleet, as well as targeted improvements in the areas of maritime domain awareness, command and control systems, and shore-side facilities. The United States asks much of its U.S. Coast Guard and we will ensure the service has the resources needed to accomplish its multiple missions. We saw the dedication and the versatility of the U.S. Coast Guard in the aftermath of September 11, a performance that vividly demonstrated the U.S. Coast Guard's vital contribution to homeland security. Nevertheless, the U.S. Coast Guard is also responsible for national defense, maritime safety, maritime mobility, and protection of natural resources, and would continue to fulfill these functions in the Department of Homeland Security.

- National Strategy for Homeland Security, July 2002

Introduction

The mission of the United States Coast Guard is the safety of lives and property at sea.

In order to secure our nation's territorial waters, including our ports and waterways, the Department of Homeland Security has authority over the United States Coast Guard, which maintains its independent identity as a military organization under the leadership of the Commandant of the Coast Guard.[1]

Since its inception as the Revenue Cutter Service in 1790, the Coast Guard has provided unique benefits to America through its distinctive blend of humanitarian, law enforcement, diplomatic, and military capabilities. Whether equipped with 19th century wooden lifeboats or 20th century high endurance cutters, the Coast Guard has continuously served as America's Shield of Freedom.

Origins

On August 4, 1790, Congress created the Revenue Cutter Service under the Treasury Department to enforce customs laws. In January 1915, Congress combined the Lifesaving Service and Revenue Cutter Service to form the United States Coast Guard.

Mission

The mission of the United States Coast Guard is the safety of lives and property at sea. The Coast Guard's five operating goals include Maritime Security, Maritime Safety, Protection of Natural Resources, Maritime Mobility, and National Defense.

Organization

Located within the Department of Homeland Security, the Coast Guard is also one of the nation's five Armed Services. The Coast Guard is Headquartered in Washington, DC. The Coast Guard's field operating units are divided into two regions, the Atlantic Area, based in Portsmouth, VA, and the Pacific Area, in Alameda, CA. Each of these Areas is further broken down into Districts, with District headquarters located in nine key cities around the country.

1st District	Boston MA	11th District	Alameda CA
5th District	Portsmouth VA	13th District	Seattle WA
7th District	Miami FL	14th District	Honolulu HI
8th District	New Orleans LA	17th District	Juneau AK
9th District	Cleveland OH		

Table 15.1: Coast Guard Districts.

Each District, in turn, includes a wide range of facilities, including Marine Safety Offices, Groups, Air Stations, boat stations and cutters. With 38,000 active duty personnel, supported by 9,000 reservists and 34,000 auxiliaries, the Coast Guard is well positioned to be the first on scene — bringing the right people, equipment, skills, and partnerships — to respond to any local, regional, national, or international crisis. The Coast Guard commissions officers through the Coast Guard Academy in New London Connecticut.

Coast Guard missions are categorized into five core roles:
1. *Maritime Security*
2. *Maritime Safety*
3. *Protection of Natural Resources*
4. *Maritime Mobility*
5. *National Defense*

Operations

For more than two centuries the Coast Guard has protected the American public, the environment, and economic and security interests in U.S. waterways and any maritime region in which U.S. interests may be at risk. This wide range of Coast Guard missions can be categorized into five core roles:

1. Maritime Security

2. Maritime Safety

3. Protection of Natural Resources

4. Maritime Mobility

5. National Defense

Maritime security

Maritime law enforcement is the oldest of the Coast Guard's numerous responsibilities. As a member of the Department of Homeland Security, the Coast Guard is not subject to Posse Comitatus and may conduct law enforcement activities. The Coast Guard's Maritime Security role consists of seven primary missions:

1. Homeland Security

2. Drug Interdiction

3. Alien Migrant Interdiction

4. Mass Migration Interdiction

5. Treaty Enforcement

6. Domestic Fisheries Enforcement

7. General Maritime Law Enforcement

Homeland Security

The tragic events of September 11, 2001, highlighted the fact that the Coast Guard is also ideally positioned and equipped for the critical mission area of ports, waterways and coastal security. When America was attacked, Coast Guard National Strike Teams participated in rescue and recovery operations in New York City and Washington, DC. Additionally, Coast Guard boats, cutters, planes, port security units and reservists were mobilized to protect America's vital ports and waterways. This response signaled the largest homeland port security operation since World War II. Homeland Security now stands alongside Search and Rescue as Mission 1 for the Coast Guard.

Drug Interdiction

As the designated lead agency for maritime drug interdiction under the National Drug Control Strategy, the Coast Guard maintains round-the-clock patrols of cutters and aircraft at sea working closely with U.S. and foreign law enforcement agencies and militaries to deny drug traffickers key maritime smuggling routes.

Alien Migrant Interdiction

Alien migrant interdiction operations are an increasingly important area of U.S. national security concern particularly in the post 9-11 environment where control of America's borders is critical. During the past 20 years, the Coast Guard has interdicted more than 140,000 illegal migrants, primarily from Cuba, Haiti, the Dominican Republic, the Peoples Republic of China and Ecuador. Far too often, these migration attempts pose safety risks to the undocumented migrants themselves. Smugglers of human cargoes often use ships that are unseaworthy and even ship migrants in sealed cargo containers. Under these conditions, many interdiction missions rapidly evolve to search and rescue and humanitarian aid missions.

Mass Migrations

The Coast Guard is always poised to conduct "surge operations" as crises erupt. In 1994, for example, mass migrations brought migrant interdiction into the national spotlight, when more than 21,000 Haitians and 30,000 Cu-

The Coast Guard is unique among the uniform services, in as much that as a member of the Department of Homeland Security, the Coast Guard is not subject to Posse Comitatus and may conduct law enforcement activities.

bans were recovered in four months.

Treaty Enforcement

The Coast Guard faces the daunting challenge of protecting over 3.4 million square miles of Exclusive Economic Zones and 95,000 miles of coastlines.

Domestic Fisheries Enforcement

The objective of Coast Guard's fisheries law enforcement program is to provide the on-scene presence necessary to protect America's $52 billion commercial and recreational fishing industry. The Coast Guard's priorities are to eliminate illegal encroachment by foreign fishing vessels in our Exclusive Economic Zones and to enforce domestic fisheries laws on the 110,000 U.S. commercial vessels harvesting our critical fish stocks.

General Maritime Law Enforcement

The Coast Guard is also the primary federal agency responsible for enforcing all maritime laws and treaties. The Coast Guard possess the unique authority to board any vessel subject to U.S. jurisdiction to make inspections, searches, inquiries, and arrests.

Maritime Safety

One of the basic responsibilities of the U.S. government is to protect the lives and safety of Americans. On the nation's waterways, the Coast Guard strives to preserve safety at sea through a focused program of prevention, response, and investigation. The Coast Guard's Maritime Safety role consists of four primary missions:

1. Search and Rescue

2. Licensing and Inspection

3. Recreational Boating Safety

4. International Ice Patrol

Search & Rescue

Ocean Rescue. The sea can be unforgiving and even the most professional mariners can easily find themselves in peril. From its origins as the U.S. Life-Saving Service, the Coast Guard has a long and proud tradition of responding immediately to save lives in peril. The Coast Guard currently respond to more than 40,000 calls for help each year.

Flood Response. Coast Guard search and rescue operations are not limited to the high seas. In coastal and inland areas, it often assists in areas of flooding, as when North Dakota's Red River flooded in 1997 and Hurricane Floyd made landfall along the East Coast in 1999.

Licensing & Inspection

Commercial Fishing Vessel Safety. In some areas, such as the Gulf of Alaska, commercial fishing is 10 times more deadly than any other occupation in the country. Through a combination of regulatory, inspection, and education efforts, the Coast Guard strives to prevent tragedies before they occur.

Vessel Inspection & Prevention through People. As part of the Coast Guard's inspection efforts, it enforces a wide range of regulations to ensure U.S. and foreign vessels operating in U.S. waters are structurally sound, competently operated, and outfitted with adequate safety systems. Coast Guard safety inspectors track most U.S.-flagged vessels from shipyard construction to final voyage, and emphasize the Prevention through People initiative, which helps mariners to improve safety and decrease the number of accidents and casualties.

Global Merchant Fleet. In the past, the Coast Guard was primarily concerned with the safety of U.S. vessels. Today, however, the Coast Guard has increasingly shifted its focus to foreign commercial vessels, as 95 percent of passenger ships and 75 percent of cargo ships operating in U.S. waters are foreign-flagged. As the lead U.S. representative to the International Maritime Organization, an arm of the United Nations. In the wake of 9-11, the Coast Guard spearheaded the United States' efforts to increase international maritime security through IMO, resulting in sweeping changes to international security measures. Domestically, these changes were codified in the Maritime Transportation Security Act of 2002. the Coast Guard is a driving force behind the implementation of measures to improve the training and safety standards of all mariners and vessels plying U.S. waters.

Port State Control. Unfortunately, not every country enforces international standards. To address this reality, the Coast Guard has effective Captain of the Port and Port State Control mechanisms in place that are designed to bring substandard ships into compliance with international standards, or exclude or remove them from U.S. waters.

Recreational Boating Safety

In addition to commercial vessels, nearly 13 million recreational boats cruise American waterways each year. Consequently, recreational boating is second only to highway travel in the number of transportation fatalities. As the National Recreational Boating Safety Coordinator, the Coast Guard works to minimize loss of life, personal injury, and property damage through a variety of prevention, education, and enforcement efforts. The all-volunteer Coast Guard Auxiliary plays a central role in this effort.

International Ice Patrol

The Coast Guard is also responsible for the International Ice Patrol. This effort, which primarily takes place in the North Atlantic, is focused on monitoring shipping lanes to warn transiting ships of dangers posed by icebergs.

Protection of Natural Resources

America's marine waters and their ecosystems are vital to the health, well being, and economy of the nation. The Coast Guard's Protection of Natural Resources role focuses on two main mission areas:

1. Marine Environmental Protection

2. Marine Protected Species Law and Treaty Enforcement

Over fishing & By catch	Invasive Species & Pathogens
High Seas Drift Nets	Hazardous Materials Dumping
Habitat Destruction	Oil Spills
U.S. Coastal Population Growth	Garbage & Debris
Global Population Growth	Chemical Spills

Table 15.2: Marine Environmental Challenges.

Threats & Challenges

There are many diverse and harmful threats and challenges to our environment. These include: oil and chemical spills, hazardous materials dumping, and marine habitat destruction, among others. To address these challenges, the Coast Guard closely regulates the shipping industry to prevent or minimize the environmental damage caused by oil and chemical spills and the dumping of wastes at sea. The Coast Guard's mandate to do so was significantly strengthened by the Oil Pollution Act of 1990, which was passed in response to the devastating Exxon Valdez oil spill the year before. As a result of these efforts, oil spills have decreased by two-thirds during the past five years.

Marine Protected Species Law Treaty Enforcement

Along with the marine environment, the Coast Guard also protect sensitive marine habitats, marine mammals, and endangered marine species. For example, the Coast Guard is currently working with the marine industry to safeguard the endangered Right whales as they transit the Atlantic shipping lanes, as well as endangered sea turtles in the Gulf of Mexico.

Marine Mobility

The United States Coast Guard works to ensure an efficient and effective U.S. Marine Transportation System. The U.S. Marine Transportation System includes all of America's waterways and 361 ports, through which more than two billion tons of foreign and domestic freight and 3.3 billion barrels of oil move each year. The Coast Guard plays a key role in an ongoing initiative aimed at building the public and private partnerships necessary to support a world-class waterway system that improves our global competitiveness and national security.

In today's global economy, the United States remains dependent on ports and waterways for our economic survival. Excluding Mexico and Canada, 95 percent of the nation's foreign trade and 25 percent of its domestic trade depends upon maritime transportation. The Coast Guard conducts four maritime mobility-related missions that enhance the effectiveness and efficiency of the U.S. Marine Transportation System:

1. Aids to Navigation

2. Domestic Icebreaking

3. Bridge Administration

4. Waterways/Vessel Traffic Management

Aids to Navigation

To aid ships transiting congested and complex waterways, the Coast Guard maintains the world's largest system of long- and short-range aids-to-navigation, with more than 50,000 buoys, fixed markers, and lighthouses. The Coast Guard also maintains the differential global positioning system and Loran C radio navigation systems, enabling mariners to electronically determine their position.

Domestic Icebreaking

Coast Guard domestic icebreakers and buoy tenders ensure that ships carrying essential supplies are able to safely navigate U.S. waterways, especially on the Great Lakes, Chesapeake and Delaware Bays, and rivers of the Northeast, regardless of weather conditions.

Bridge Administration

The Coast Guard also is responsible for regulating, ensuring safety and proper operations for approximately 18,000 highway and railroad bridges that span navigable waterways. The Coast Guard routinely issue permits for new bridge construction, order obstructive bridges to be removed, and oversee drawbridge operations.

Waterways/Vessel Traffic Management

To facilitate the more than $1 trillion worth of domestic and foreign goods that move through U.S. ports and waterways each year, we operate a comprehensive network of precision electronic navigation systems and Vessel Traffic Services aimed at reducing the risk of collision and ensuring the safe, efficient passage of people, ships, and goods.

National Defense

Despite its many roles and missions, the Coast Guard is fully prepared to execute essential military tasks in support of joint and combined forces in peacetime, crisis, and war. The Coast Guard has five specific national defense missions in addition to its general defense operations and polar icebreaking duties. They are:

1. Maritime Interception Operations

2. Military Environmental Response Operations

3. Port Operations, Security, and Defense

4. Coastal Sea Control Operations

5. Peacetime Military Engagement.

General Defense Operations

Like the other U.S. armed services, warfare is one of the Coast Guard's core missions. It commands the U.S. Maritime Defense Zones around the nation and maintains a high state of readiness in order to perform as a specialized branch of the Navy in times of war. Coast Guard forces and capabilities are incorporated in the Unified Combatant Commanders' Operations Plans. As part of Operation Iraqi Freedom, the Coast Guard sent 11 cutters and 1250 personnel to secure ports and support coalition forces.

Maritime Interception Operations

Coast Guard maritime interception operations leverage its extensive training and expertise in stopping, boarding, searching, and seizing vessels to enforce international sanctions overseas, such as in the Arabian Gulf against Iraq.

Military Environmental Response Operations

Coast Guard military environmental response operations enable the Coast Guard to serve as the tip of the military's spear in responding to environmental disasters. Coast Guard experience with the containment and cleanup of environmental disasters has given its three National Strike Teams the specialized training necessary to respond wherever needed, whether in the burning oil fields of Kuwait or "ground zero" in New York City.

Port Operations, Security, and Defense

Coast Guard Port Operations, Security, and Defense mission leverages unique legal authorities, assets, and expertise to protect U.S. and overseas ports, facilities and vessels from hostilities. Port security Units, manned primarily by reservists, play a prominent role in this effort.

Coastal Sea Control Operations

Coast Guard coastal sea control operations mission, which was added to the Coast Guard's portfolio in July 2001, is designed to ensure the unimpeded use of designated coastal areas by friendly forces while denying the use of those areas by enemy forces. Specific duties include surveillance and reconnaissance, interdiction of enemy shipping, and protection of friendly forces.

Peacetime Military Engagement

The Coast Guard's peacetime engagement efforts include all activities involving other nations that are intended to shape the security environment in peacetime before military crises can arise. International engagement and training initiatives foster healthy relationships with other countries, thereby promoting peace and stability, democracy, and the rule of law.

Polar Icebreaking

Finally, the Coast Guard is also responsible for polar icebreaking operations. This is essential to ensure U.S. scientists in the Arctic and Antarctic have the access, equipment, and supplies they need, while providing them with a floating laboratory from which to conduct vital scientific research.[2]

Conclusion

The United States Coast Guard operates as part of the Department of Homeland Security to fulfill peacetime missions in Maritime Security, Maritime Safety, Protection of National Resources, and Maritime Mobility. The Coast Guard also fulfills roles vital to National Defense throughout peacetime, crisis, and war: General Defense Operations, Maritime Interception Operations, Military Environmental Response Operations, Port Operations/Security/Defense, Coastal Sea Control Operations, Peacetime Military Engagement, and Polar Icebreaking. In times of crisis and war, the Coast Guard will be given over to the Department of Navy.[3]

Questions

1. How is the Coast Guard organized?

2. What are the five major missions of the United States Coast Guard?

3. What makes the Coast Guard unique among the uniform services?

## Chapter 16

Planning Scenarios

Objectives

- Understand the purpose of the planning scenarios.
- Describe some probable methods of terrorist attack.
- Assess the impact of different types of attack.

Under the President's proposal, the Department of Homeland Security would establish a national exercise program designed to educate and evaluate civilian response personnel at all levels of government. It would require individuals and government bodies to complete successfully at least one exercise every year. The Department would use these exercises to measure performance and allocate future resources.

– National Strategy for Homeland Security, July 2002

Introduction

In early March 2005, a draft document called National Planning Scenarios was inadvertently posted on a Web site managed by the State of Hawaii. The document, reprinted by The New York Times on March 16, outlines 15 scenarios. They include three natural disasters and 12 terrorist attacks.

The scenarios for terrorist attacks include the detonation of a 10-kiloton nuclear bomb in a major city; a chemical weapons attack at a college football game; a release of sarin gas into the ventilation systems of three large office buildings; attacks with radiological bombs and improvised conventional bombs; and bioweapons attacks on the food supply. Each scenario includes an estimate of casualties and economic costs.

While the intelligence picture developed as part of each scenario generally reflects suspected terrorist capabilities and known tradecraft, the FBI is unaware of any credible intelligence that indicates that such attacks are being planned.

While DHS won't comment on the scenarios, Times' reporter Eric Lipton speculated that by identifying possible attacks and outlining how government might act to prevent, respond to, and recover from each, DHS is attempting to define preparedness for the war on terror.[1]

Background

The Homeland Security Council (HSC) – in partnership with the Department of Homeland Security (DHS), the federal interagency, and state and local homeland security agencies – developed fifteen all-hazards planning scenarios for use in national, federal, state, and local homeland security preparedness activities. These scenarios are designed to be the foundational structure for the development of national preparedness standards from which homeland security capabilities can be measured. While these scenarios reflect a rigorous analytical effort by federal, state, and local homeland security experts, it is recognized that refinement and revision over time may be necessary to ensure the scenarios remain accurate, represent the evolving all-hazards threat picture, and embody the capabilities necessary to respond to domestic incidents.

The scenarios were developed in a way that allows them to be adapted to local conditions throughout the country. Although certain areas have special concerns – continuity of government in Washington, D.C.; viability of financial markets in New York; and trade and commerce in other major cities – every part of the country is vulnerable to one or more major hazards.

Because the attacks could be caused by foreign terrorists; domestic radical groups; state sponsored adversaries; or in some cases, disgruntled employees, the perpetrator has been named, the Universal Adversary (UA). The focus of the scenarios is on response capabilities and needs, not threat-based prevention activities.

Since these scenarios were compiled to be the minimum number necessary to test the range of response capabilities and resources, other hazards were inevitably omitted. Examples of other potentially high-impact scenarios include nuclear power plant incidents, industrial and transportation accidents, and frequently occurring natural disasters. These either have well developed and tested response plans, and/or the response would be a subset of the requirements for scenarios contained in this set.

While the intelligence picture developed as part of each scenario generally reflects suspected terrorist capabilities and known tradecraft, the Federal Bureau of Investigation (FBI) is unaware of any credible intelligence that indicates that such an attack is being planned, or that the agents or devices in question are in possession of any known terrorist group.

There is a high probability that multiple incidents will occur simultaneously. When scoping resource requirements, organizations should always consider the need to respond to multiple incidents of the same type and multiple incidents of different types, at either the same or other geographic locations. These incidents will invariably require the coordination and cooperation of homeland security response organizations across multiple regional, state, and local jurisdictions.

There is a high probability that multiple incidents will occur simultaneously.

In most incidents, citizens will seek medical treatment even though they may not be injured by the incident. For example, in the World Trade Center incident on 9/11/01, the uninjured who sought medical treatment was approximately fifteen times the number of people who presented for medical treatment due to smoke inhalation; and in the Tokyo subway attack it was five times the number of victims experiencing chemical poisoning. For planning purposes, most experts calculate a ratio of ten-to-one.

The effect of disasters on national, state, and local transportation, communication, medical, and utility infrastructure will have a considerable effect on response strategies. As on 9/11, when the entire civilian air transportation system and much of the national telecommunications system were shut down or disabled, a terrorist incident may have repercussions that affect critical infrastructures necessary for coherent emergency response. These critical networks must be layered and properly coordinated across both civilian and military sectors to ensure the continuity of critical infrastructure support for responding jurisdictions.

Catastrophic disasters, depending upon the type, scope, and magnitude of the disaster incident, could threaten the economic sustainability of the communities affected and may cause severe disruption and long-term economic damage. Extreme disaster incidents can generate cascading economic situations extending outside the immediate community. Even in moderate disasters, of all businesses that close following a disaster, more than 43% never reopen, and an additional 29% close permanently within 2 years. The American Planning Association notes, "Economic recovery is quite likely the most serious issue facing most communities in the post-disaster period, and almost certainly the central issue in every major disaster."

Catastrophic natural and manmade disasters and terrorist attacks can result in extreme environmental impacts that challenge government and community recovery time. Long after the emergency phase subsides, contamination from disasters may remain, consisting of chemical, biological, or radiological materials. While decontamination technologies may be well established for some types of contamination, others are only moderately effective – some contaminants, especially radionuclides, are very difficult and costly to remediate. While some decontamination techniques may be effective in small sites, these techniques may not be suited for decontaminating expansive areas of varying physical characteristics. Evacuation and relocation during cleanup and restoration activities can result in significant business loss and failure, leading to local and regional economic downturn. In addition, agricultural and industrial products from an area contaminated, or thought to be contaminated, can generate impacts that extend within a region and beyond.

It is important to underline the significant international dimensions that arise in connection with some of the more damaging and devastating scenarios in which significant loss of life and property, together with the possibility of foreign-directed terrorism, are involved. First, there is the hemispheric dimension of effects on U.S. relations with Canada and Mexico in terms of cross-border trade, transit, law enforcement coordination, and other key issues. Second, there is the immediate treaty connection the United States has with other North Atlantic Treaty Organization (NATO) allies if the United States comes under attack. Third, there is the significant lobbying the United States will undertake at the United Nations (UN) to articulate American needs and interests. In addition to humanitarian and law enforcement assistance from NATO allies, other nations may contribute special equipment in order to meet other necessities. Instances where a disaster or terrorist attack has disrupted major urban centers and international transit/trade routes through U.S. cities will typically require significant coordination with the State Department to ensure all economic, trade, commercial, consular, military cooperative, and humanitarian assistance is rendered as needed.

The State Department plays several key roles in post-disaster situations. It assists foreign citizens affected by the incident. It identifies the specific needs of affected U.S. areas where foreign offers of assistance can be mediated and arranged. Moreover, in cases where explicit terrorist activities may have occurred, the State Department is a leader in facilitating the investigations abroad needed to determine the origins of the attack, in pursuing diplomatic and follow-up policies related to finding the guilty parties abroad, and in rendering coordinated international assistance to U.S. recovery efforts.

Scenario 1: Nuclear Detonation

– 10-Kiloton Improvised Nuclear Device

Casualties	Can vary widely
Infrastructure Damage	Total within radius of 0.5 to 1.0 mile
Evacuations/Displaced Persons	450,000 or more
Contamination	Approximately 3,000 square miles
Economic Impact	Hundreds of billions of dollars
Potential for Multiple Events	No
Recovery Timeline	Years

General Description

In this scenario, terrorist members of the Universal Adversary (UA) group assemble a gun-type nuclear device using highly enriched uranium (HEU) – used here to mean weapons-grade uranium – stolen from a nuclear facility located in the former Soviet Union. The nuclear device components are smuggled into the United States. The 10-kiloton nuclear device is assembled near a major metropolitan center. Using a delivery van, terrorists transport the device to the central business district of a large city and detonate it. Most buildings within 1,000 meters (~ 3,200 feet) of the detonation are severely damaged. Injuries from flying debris (missiles) may occur out to 6 kilometers (~ 3.7 miles). An Electromagnetic Pulse (EMP) damages many electronic devices within about 5 kilometers (~ 3 miles). A mushroom cloud rises above the city and begins to drift east-northeast.

Geographical Considerations/Description

This scenario postulates a 10-kiloton nuclear detonation in a large metropolitan area. The effects of the damage from the blast, thermal radiation, prompt radiation, and the subsequent radioactive fallout have been calculated, based on a detonation in Washington, D.C.. However, the calculation is general enough that most major cities in the United States can be substituted in a relatively straightforward manner. If the incident happened near the U.S. border, there would be a need for cooperation between the two border governments. Additionally, the IND (improvised nuclear device) attack may warrant the closure of U.S. borders for some period of time. If the detonation occurs in a coastal city, the fallout plume may be carried out over the water, causing a subsequent reduction in casualties. On the other hand, the surrounding water will likely restrict the zones that are suitable for evacuation. Bridges and tunnels that generally accompany coastal cities will restrict the evacuation, causing delay and an increase in the radioactive dose that evacuees receive. This delay may be substantial and the resulting dose increase may drive a decision to shelter-in-place or evacuate-in-stages.

Timeline/Event Dynamics

The response timeline will begin the instant the detonation occurs. Initially, only survivors in the immediate area will conduct rescue and lifesaving activities. Later (minutes to hours), rescue teams will begin to arrive and provide assistance. With the current state of education, training, and equipment, it is likely that many of these responders will subject themselves to very large (perhaps incapacitating or fatal) doses of radiation. As various command posts are setup (which may take hours to days), the response will become more coordinated. For a nuclear detonation, the actual occurrence of injuries does not stop when the immediate blast effects have subsided. The most critical components of the post-detonation response may not be the lifesaving efforts that assist the victims directly injured by the detonation. Instead, it is likely that the most effective lifesaving activities will be those that address the evacuation or sheltering-in-place decisions for the potential victims in the immediate fallout path, the effective communication of instructions to the affected population, and the efficient decontamination of the evacuated population.

Secondary Hazards/Events

The detonation will cause many secondary hazards. The intense heat of the nuclear explosion and other subsequent causes will produce numerous fires located throughout the immediate blast zone. Damaged buildings, downed power and phone lines, leaking gas lines, broken water mains, and weakened bridges and tunnels are just some of the hazardous conditions that will need to be assessed. Depending on the type of industries present (such as chemical or petroleum production, industrial storage facilities, and manufacturing operations), there could be significant releases of hazardous materials. Another secondary effect of a nuclear explosion is the Electromagnetic Pulse (EMP) that will be produced by the ionization and subsequent acceleration of electrons from the air and other materials by the intense radiation of the detonation. This EMP is a sharp, high-voltage spike that radiates out from the detonation site. It has the potential to disrupt the communication network, other electronic equipment, and associated systems within approximately a 5-kilometer (~ 3-mile) range from the 10-kiloton ground blast. There likely will be significant damage to the general public support infrastructure with potentially cascading effects. These systems include transportation lines and nodes (e.g., air, water, rail, highway); power generation and distribution systems; communications systems; food distribution; and fuel storage and distribution. There will be concerns about the safety and reliability of many structures (e.g., dams, levees, nuclear power plants, hazardous material storage facilities). Structures may be damaged that are used to provide essential services (e.g., hospitals, schools).

Key Implications

A full description of the fatalities and injuries for a nuclear detonation is difficult and complicated. There will be casualties directly associated with the blast, which will cause "translation/tumbling" (the human body being thrown) and subsequent impacts of people and other objects. A nuclear detonation will also produce a great deal of thermal (heat) energy that will cause burns to exposed skin (and eyes). There are two general "categories" of nuclear radiation produced in a detonation. First is the so-called "prompt" nuclear radiation, arbitrarily defined as being emitted within the first minute – it is actually produced as the device detonates or shortly thereafter. For a 10-kiloton blast, this radiation may expose unprotected people within a distance of a few kilometers (a couple of miles) to extremely large gamma ray and/or neutron doses. In addition, a detonation of a nuclear device near the surface of the ground will result in a great deal of fallout (in the form of dirt particles) that is radioactively contaminated. This fallout will settle out of the radioactive cloud over a period of minutes to weeks. By far, the most dangerously radioactive fallout will be deposited near the detonation site and will happen within the first couple of hours after detonation. Radioactive fallout will exponentially decay with time, but may expose many people to large doses and will certainly contaminate large areas of land for years. Many fatalities and injuries will result from a combination of these various effects.

The largest radiation concerns following an IND incident will be the "prompt" radiation (gamma ray and neutron) and the gamma dose received from the "ground shine" (radioactive particles deposited on the ground) as people are evacuated from the fallout areas. These effects are likely to have significantly larger impacts on the population than internal doses. Internal doses tend to expose the body to relatively small radiation doses over a long period of time, which produces different effects than large radiation doses received during a short period of time.

As the distance from ground zero increases past 20 kilometers (~ 12 miles), the injuries due to acute radiation exposure (from prompt radiation and the subsequent fallout) will decrease, and lower level contamination, evacuation, and sheltering issues will become the major concern. In general, at distances greater than 250 kilometers (~ 150 miles) from ground zero of a 10 kiloton nuclear detonation, acute health concerns will not be a significant issue. However, contamination of people and the environment will still be a concern.

Years later, there will still be health consequences in the form of increased probabilities of cancers in the exposed population. The number of these cancers will likely run into the thousands and will extract a large human, social, and financial cost. It is likely that the blast and subsequent fires will destroy all buildings in the immediate area of the detonation. Historically, decontamination of sites involves the removal of all affected material, so most buildings in the immediate downwind fallout path will likely have to be destroyed in the decontamination effort. As the distance from the detonation site increases, the contamination level will decrease. At some distance, the buildings will not have to be destroyed and removed but will still require decontamination of all affected surfaces. This decontamination process will take years and will be extremely expensive. The decontamination will produce a far greater challenge and cost much more than the actual rebuilding of the destroyed structures. Approximately 8,000 square kilometers (~ 3,000 square miles) of land will have to undergo varying degrees of decontamination. This effort will last for many years and will cost many billions of dollars to complete.

Service disruption will be extensive in the area near ground zero and in the fallout path for several miles downwind. Services in these areas will not be restored for years because the land affected will not be returned to use until the decontamination is complete and the structures rebuilt. Service disruption will be much less dramatic in areas that are less severely contaminated or not contaminated at all.

The electrical power grid is likely to be damaged by transients produced by the destruction of substations, as well as other power production and distribution installations, and perhaps by the EMP of the detonation. It is likely that the grid damage may cause power outages over wide areas, perhaps over several states, but these outages should be repaired within several days to a couple of weeks. The communication systems in the area will suffer similar damage and will likely be repaired within similar timeframes.

City water mains will likely survive without major damage. The city water supply is unlikely to become substantially contaminated with radiation via water main breaks, but it is possible that some small amount of radioactive and non-radioactive contamination may enter the lines.

To varying degrees, all government services will be impacted over some geographical area. The national economy will be significantly impacted. Decontamination, disposal, and replacement of lost infrastructure will cost many billions of dollars. Replacement of lost private property and goods could add billions more to the cost. Additionally, an overall national economic downturn, if not recession, is probable in the wake of the attack.

Scenario 2: Biological Attack

– Aerosol Anthrax

Casualties	13,000 fatalities and injuries
Infrastructure Damage	Minimal, other than contamination
Evacuations/Displaced Persons	Possibly
Contamination	Extensive
Economic Impact	Billions of dollars
Potential for Multiple Events	Yes
Recovery Timeline	Months

General Description

Anthrax spores delivered by aerosol delivery results in inhalation anthrax, which develops when the bacterial organism, Bacillus anthracis, is inhaled into the lungs. A progressive infection follows. This scenario describes a single aerosol anthrax attack in one city delivered by a truck using a concealed improvised spraying device in a densely populated urban city with a significant commuter workforce. It does not, however, exclude the possibility of multiple attacks in disparate cities or time-phased attacks (i.e., "reload"). For federal planning purposes, it will be assumed that the Universal Adversary (UA) will attack five separate metropolitan areas in a sequential manner. Three cities will be attacked initially, followed by two additional cities 2 weeks later.

Timeline/Event Dynamics

It is possible that a Bio-Watch signal would be received and processed, but this is not likely to occur until the day after the release. The first cases of anthrax would begin to present to Emergency Rooms (ERs) approximately 36 hours post-release, with rapid progression of symptoms and fatalities in untreated (or inappropriately treated) patients.

The situation in the hospitals will be complicated by the following facts: The release has occurred at the beginning of an unusually early influenza season and the prodromal symptoms of inhalation anthrax are relatively non-specific. Physician uncertainty will result in low thresholds for admission and administration of available countermeasures (e.g., antibiotics), producing severe strains on commercially available supplies of such medications as ciprofloxacin and doxycycline, and exacerbating the surge capacity problem.

Secondary Hazards/Events

Social order questions will arise. The public will want to know very quickly if it is safe to remain in the affected city and surrounding regions. Many persons will flee regardless of the public health guidance that is provided. Pressure may be placed directly on pharmacies to dispense medical countermeasures directly, and it will be necessary to provide public health guidance in more than a dozen languages.

Key Implications

This attack results in 328,484 exposures; 13,208 untreated fatalities; and 13,342 total casualties. Although property damage will be minimal, city services will be hampered by safety concerns.

There is the potential for a huge sell-off in the economic markets; moreover, the stock exchange and large businesses may be directly affected by the attack. There may also be a decline in consumer spending and a loss of revenue for the metropolitan area. An overall national economic downturn is possible in the wake of the attack due to loss of consumer confidence. The costs of the closure of a large section of the city and the decrease in revenue from tourism for an indeterminate period would be enormous, as would the costs of remediation and decontamination.

Scenario 3: Biological Disease Outbreak

– Pandemic Influenza

Casualties	At a 15% attack rate: 87,000 fatalities; 300,000 hospitalizations
Infrastructure Damage	None
Evacuations/Displaced Persons	Isolation of exposed persons
Contamination	None
Economic Impact	$70 to $160 billion
Potential for Multiple Events	Yes, would be worldwide nearly simultaneously
Recovery Timeline	Several months

General Description

Influenza pandemics have occurred every 10 to 60 years, with three occurring in the twentieth century (1918, 1957-1958, and 1967-1968). Influenza pandemics occur when there is a notable genetic change (termed genetic shift) in the circulating strain of influenza. Because of this genetic shift, a large portion of the human population is entirely vulnerable to infection from the new pandemic strain. This scenario hypothetically relates what could happen during the next influenza pandemic without an effective preplanned response. At least twenty-five cases occur first in a small village in south China. Over the next 2 months, outbreaks begin to appear in Hong Kong, Singapore, South Korea, and Japan. Although cases are reported in all age groups, young adults appear to be the most severely affected, and case-fatality rates approach 5%. Several weeks later, the virus appears in four major U.S. cities. By nature, pandemic influenza moves extremely rapidly, and the outbreaks continue.

Timeline/Event Dynamics

When planning and preparing for the next influenza pandemic, there are two equally important timelines. Due to the rapid spread of the influenza pandemic and the time required to develop, test, produce, and distribute an effective vaccine, the disease will likely arrive in the United States before a "significant" number of people can be vaccinated. The implication of this is that, as part of any pandemic influenza preparation and response plan, there must be a mechanism for allocating the vaccine among the population.

Secondary Hazards/Events

The greatest secondary hazard will be the problems caused by shortages of medical supplies (e.g., vaccines and antiviral drugs), equipment (e.g., mechanical ventilators), hospital beds, and health care workers. Having a detailed system for allocating resources potentially can reduce such difficulties. This system ideally should be in place well before an influenza pandemic actually occurs. Also of particular concern is the real likelihood that health care systems, particularly hospitals, will be overwhelmed. Another important secondary hazard is the disruption that might occur in society. Institutions, such as schools and workplaces, may close because a large proportion of students or employees are ill. A large array of essential services may be limited because workers are off work due to pandemic influenza. Travel between cities and countries may be sharply reduced.

Key Implications

Estimates of impact are provided in Table 16.1.

Health Outcomes	15% Gross Attack Rate* (5th, 95th percentiles)	15% Gross Attack Rate (5th, 95th percentiles)
Fatalities	87,000 (54,400; 122,200)	207,000 (127,200; 285,300)
Hospitalizations	314,400 (210,400; 417,200)	733,800 (491,000; 973,500)
Outpatient visits	18.1 million (17.5; 18.7)	42.2 million (40.8; 43.7)
Self-care ill	21.3 million (20.6; 21.9)	49.7 million (48.2; 51.2)
*Percent Gross Attack Rate refers to the percentage of the entire U.S. population that will have a clinical case of influenza.		

Table 16.1. Mean estimates (5th, 95th percentiles) of the impact of the next influenza pandemic in the United States without any large-scale and/or effective interventions.

Property damage is minimal. Service disruption, however, could be severe due to worker illness. Health care systems will be severely stressed, if not overwhelmed, and first responders are also likely to be severely strained.

Based on the estimates in Table 16.1, the economic impact, in 1995 U.S. dollars, will range from $71 billion (15% gross attack rate) to $166 billion (35% gross attack rate). These estimates include a value for time lost from work but do not include any estimate due to economic disruption or long-term health care costs.

Scenario 4: Biological Attack

– Plague

Casualties	2,500 fatalities; 7,000 injuries
Infrastructure Damage	None
Evacuations/Displaced Persons	Possibly
Contamination	Lasts for hours
Economic Impact	Millions of dollars
Potential for Multiple Events	Yes
Recovery Timeline	Weeks

General Description

Plague is a bacterium that causes high mortality in untreated cases and has epidemic potential. It is best known as the cause of Justinian's Plague (in the middle sixth century) and the Black Death (in the middle fourteenth century), two pandemics that killed millions. In this scenario, members of the Universal Adversary (UA) release pneumonic plague into three main areas of a major metropolitan city – in the bathrooms of the city's major airport, at the city's main sports arena, and at the city's major train station.

Timeline/Event Dynamics

Plague cases rapidly occur in the United States and Canada. As a result of foreign and domestic travel, rapid dissemination to distant locations occurs. By Day 3, the plague spreads across both the Pacific and Atlantic oceans and by Day 4, the plague is confirmed in eleven countries other than the United States and Canada.

Secondary Hazards/Events

As the financial world in Major City and elsewhere begins to realize the likelihood of an epidemic, a huge sell-off occurs in the markets. There is a high absentee rate at banks, other financial institutions, and major corporations. Adding to these complications is the fact that bank and other financial customers may be staying home. As a result, the phone systems at financial institutions may become completely tied up, with far fewer transactions than normal occurring. The fear of plague has raised memories of the anthrax incidents of 2001, which may cause many citizens to be afraid to open their mail.

Key Implications

Morbidity and mortality totals by the end of the fourth day are indicated in Table 4-1. Although the specific assumptions that underlie these totals are not generally available, nor can they be reliably recreated, the parameters affecting these figures include length of incubation period following primary exposure, rate of secondary transmission, incubation period following secondary exposure, and timing and effectiveness of the intervention.

Illnesses and Fatalities by Country		
	Illnesses	**Fatalities**
United States	7,348	2,287
Canada	787	246
Other Countries	33	10
Total	8,168	2,543

Table 16.2: Total illnesses and fatalities by country by the end of the fourth day (end of the exercise).

Although the actual physical damage to property will be negligible, there will be an associated negative impact of buildings and areas that were or could have been contaminated. Service disruption will be significant for call centers, pharmacies, and hospitals due to overwhelming casualty needs. It will be necessary to close or restrict certain transportation modes. The threat of reduced food supply will cause food prices to rise.

A huge sell-off in the economic markets is possible, and loss of life will result in a decline in consumer spending and subsequent loss of revenue in the metropolitan area. An overall national economic downturn is possible in the wake of the attack due to loss of consumer confidence.

Many people will be killed, permanently disabled, or sick as a result of the plague. The primary illness will be pneumonia, although the plague can also cause septicemia, circulatory complications, and other manifestations. The long-term effects of antimicrobial prophylaxis in large numbers will require follow-up study. The associated mental health issues relating to mass trauma and terrorism events will also require assessment.

Scenario 5: Chemical Attack

– Blister Agent

Casualties	150 fatalities; 70,000 hospitalized
Infrastructure Damage	Minimal
Evacuations/Displaced Persons	More than 100,000
Contamination	Structures affected
Economic Impact	$500 million
Potential for Multiple Events	Yes
Recovery Timeline	Weeks; many long-term health affects

General Description

Agent YELLOW, which is a mixture of the blister agents sulfur Mustard and Lewisite, is a liquid with a garlic-like odor. Individuals who breathe this mixture may experience damage to the respiratory system. Contact with the skin or eye can result in serious burns. Lewisite or Mustard- Lewisite also can cause damage to bone marrow and blood vessels. Exposure to high levels may be fatal.

In this scenario, the Universal Adversary (UA) uses a light aircraft to spray chemical agent YELLOW into a packed college football stadium. The agent directly contaminates the stadium and the immediate surrounding area, and generates a downwind vapor hazard. The attack causes a large number of casualties that require urgent and long-term medical treatment, but few immediate fatalities occur. Of the total stadium attendance, 70% is exposed to the liquid at the time of the attack. The remaining 30% (i.e., those in the covered areas of the stadium), plus 10% of the total population in the vapor hazard area, are exposed to vapor contamination.

Timeline/Event Dynamics

The total time of the attack, including the last mile of the plane's approach, is less than 5 minutes. The crowd will panic and immediately evacuate the stadium, which will require up to 30 minutes. First responders should begin arriving at the facility perimeter within 10 to 15 minutes of the attack. In order for the UA to succeed in this attack, certain meteorological conditions – wind speed, temperature, humidity, and precipitation – must be met.

Secondary Hazards/Events

Numerous injuries will occur as a result of crowd panic, including those that result from falling and crushing. Further injuries are likely to occur due to motor vehicle accidents in the parking lot and surrounding roadways.

Key Implications

In the case of a full, 100,000-seat stadium, 70,000 people (70%) may be contaminated in the attack. Of these, most will have only clothing and/or skin contamination, resulting in moderate to- severe skin blisters that will appear in 2 to 12 hours. Expedient decontamination (i.e., clothing removal and heavy water spray) will avoid half of these injuries. Systemic arsenic poisoning will occur in highly contaminated individuals. However, many will inhale sufficient agent vapor to cause severe lung damage, and many more will sustain permanent damage to the eyes. Fatalities and major injuries will occur due to falling and crushing during the evacuation, and to vehicle accidents.

There will be little direct property damage due to the attack. However, the stadium site and other contaminated property will be a total loss due to decontamination measures and/or psychological impacts of future usability.

Loss of use of the stadium and adjacent athletic facilities is expected. Additionally, some public transportation and other facilities may be lost due to contamination carried by fleeing victims. Overwhelming demand will disrupt communications (landline telephone and cellular) in the local area. Finally, some victims may self-transport to health care facilities and contaminate those facilities.

Decontamination, destruction, disposal, and replacement of a major stadium could cost up to $500 million. Enrollment at the college will be negatively affected, and the local community will experience significant losses resulting from the attack. Additionally, an overall national economic downturn is possible in the wake of the attack due to a loss of consumer confidence.

Many will be permanently blinded and many more will carry lifetime scars. Many may suffer significant damage to the lungs. In addition, Mustard is a known carcinogen, and systemic poisoning from the arsenic in Lewisite is also a concern.

Scenario 6: Chemical Attack

– Toxic Industrial Chemicals

Casualties	350 fatalities; 1,000 hospitalizations
Infrastructure Damage	50% of structures in area of explosion
Evacuations/Displaced Persons	Up to 700,000
Contamination	Yes
Economic Impact	Billions of dollars
Potential for Multiple Events	Yes
Recovery Timeline	Months

General Description

In this scenario, terrorists from the Universal Adversary (UA) land in several helicopters at fixed facility petroleum refineries. They quickly launch rocket-propelled grenades (RPGs) and plant improvised explosive devices (IEDs) before re-boarding and departing, resulting in major fires. At the same time, multiple cargo containers at a nearby port explode aboard or near several cargo ships with resulting fires. Two of the ships contain flammable liquids or solids. The wind is headed in the north-northeast direction, and there is a large, heavy plume of smoke drifting into heavily populated areas and releasing various metals into the air. One of the burning ships in the port contains resins and coatings including isocyanates, nitriles, and epoxy resins. Some IEDs are set for delayed detonation. Casualties occur onsite due to explosive blast and fragmentation, fire, and vapor/liquid exposure to the toxic industrial chemical (TIC). Downwind casualties occur due to vapor exposure.

Timeline/Event Dynamics

Total time to plan and prepare for the attack would be on the order of 2 years, including reconnaissance, pilot and weapons training, and accumulation of weapons. Time to execute the attack would be several weeks to coordinate the shipping and coincident arrival of the containers aboard separate ships at the port. Time to execute the airborne phase of the attack would be on the order of 1 to 2 hours from liftoff from the originating airport. Time over target for the helicopters would be about 10 minutes. Time on the ground would be 2 to 3 minutes at each site. Fires resulting from the attack would take many hours, possibly days, to extinguish. In order for the UA to succeed in this attack, certain meteorological conditions – wind speed, temperature, humidity, and precipitation – must be met.

Secondary Hazards/Events

Once they grasp the situation, authorities will evacuate or order shelter-in-place for a significant area downwind of the refineries and the port. Numerous injuries will occur as a result of population panic once downwind casualties begin to occur. Further injuries are likely to occur due to motor vehicle accidents in the surrounding roadways. (The rule of thumb is one fatality per 10,000 evacuated.) Significant contamination of the waterway may also result, including oil and cargo spills from sunk or burning ships.

Key Implications

Assuming a densely populated area, 7,000 people may be in the actual downwind area. Of these, 5% (350) will receive lethal exposures, and half of these will die before or during treatment. An additional 15% will require hospitalization, and the remainder will be treated and released at the scene by Emergency Medical Service (EMS) personnel. However, approximately 70,000 "worried well" may seek treatment at local medical facilities.

All three refineries sustain significant damage, with 50% of the equipment and facilities requiring significant repairs or replacement. Two ships in the port sink at their moorings; the port sustains heavy damage near the ships and at a dozen points where IEDs were dropped. Depending on which chemicals are released, there may be significant property damage in the downwind area.

Refinery capacity on the west coast is significantly diminished, resulting in fuel shortages and price increases. The port is temporarily closed due to damage and contamination. Contamination in the waterway may also result. Some public transportation and other facilities may be lost. Overwhelming demand will disrupt communications (landline telephone and cellular) in the local area. Significant disruptions in health care occur due to the overwhelming demand of the injured and the "worried well."

Decontamination, destruction, disposal, and replacement of major portions of the refineries could cost billions of dollars. Similar costs could be expected at the port. Loss of the port will have a significant impact on U.S. trade with the Pacific Rim. An overall national economic downturn is possible in the wake of the attack due to a loss of consumer confidence.

In addition to their toxic effects, many TICs are known carcinogens. Long-term damage to internal organs and eyes is possible, depending on which TICs are present.

Scenario 7: Chemical Attack

– Nerve Agent

Casualties	6,000 fatalities (95% of building occupants); 350 injuries
Infrastructure Damage	Minimal, other than contamination
Evacuations/Displaced Persons	Yes
Contamination	Extensive
Economic Impact	$300 million
Potential for Multiple Events	Extensive
Recovery Timeline	3 to 4 months

General Description

Sarin is a human-made chemical warfare agent classified as a nerve agent. Nerve agents are the most toxic and rapidly acting of the known chemical warfare agents. Sarin is a clear, colorless, and tasteless liquid that has no odor in its pure form. However, Sarin can evaporate into a vapor and spread into the environment. Sarin is also known as GB.

In this scenario, the Universal Adversary (UA) builds six spray dissemination devices and releases Sarin vapor into the ventilation systems of three large commercial office buildings in a metropolitan area. The agent kills 95% of the people in the buildings, and kills or sickens many of the first responders. In addition, some of the agent exits through rooftop ventilation stacks, creating a downwind hazard.

For purposes of estimating federal response requirements, each building is assumed to have an occupancy of 2,000 personnel (i.e., twenty-story buildings with 100 occupants per floor), and the outdoor/subway population density of the surrounding areas is 3,900 people per square mile (one-tenth of the total population density in the vicinity of Times Square, New York).

Timeline/Event Dynamics

The attack will require 6 months to plan, including putting faux janitors in place, shipping the agent, and fabricating the spray devices. The actual attack will take less than 10 minutes. First responders should arrive at the facility within 10 to 15 minutes of the attack. In order for the UA to succeed in this attack, certain meteorological conditions – wind speed, temperature, humidity, and precipitation – must be met.

Secondary Hazards/Events

Numerous injuries will occur as a result of panic on the street, including falling and crushing injuries. Further injuries are likely to occur due to motor vehicle accidents in the surrounding roadways.

Key Implications

Assuming 2,000 occupants per building, the initial fatality count will be 5,700 (95%) and 300 injured, including the initial Emergency Medical Service (EMS) and fire personnel at each building. Patients who experience prolonged seizures may sustain permanent damage to the central nervous system – assume 350 patients in this category (300 inside plus 50 outside). Fatalities and major injuries will occur due to falling and crushing during the panic on the street, and due to vehicle accidents.

Little direct damage due to the attack, except the building interiors and contents, will be highly contaminated by agent condensing on surfaces. The three buildings and their contents will be a total loss due to decontamination measures and/or psychological impacts of future usability. However, airing and washing should decontaminate adjacent structures adequately.

Overwhelming demand will disrupt communications (landline telephone and cellular) in the local area. There will be large numbers of "worried well" swamping the medical system. Loss of three fire crews and three EMS crews will impact readiness for other events in the short term.

Decontamination, destruction, disposal, and replacement of three large commercial office buildings could cost up to $300 million. Business in the buildings may never reopen, and an overall national economic downturn is possible in the wake of the attack due to loss of consumer confidence.

Those who survive usually recover within 4 to 6 weeks, with full cholinesterase level restoration within 3 to 4 months. Patients who experience prolonged seizures may sustain permanent damage to the central nervous system.

Scenario 8: Chemical Attack

– Chlorine Tank Explosion

Casualties	17,500 fatalities; 10,000 severe injuries; 100,000 hospitalizations
Infrastructure Damage	In immediate explosions areas, and metal corrosion in areas of heavy exposure
Evacuations/Displaced Persons	Up to 70,000 (self evacuate)
Contamination	Primarily at explosion site, and if waterways are impacted
Economic Impact	Millions of dollars
Potential for Multiple Events	Yes
Recovery Timeline	Weeks

General Description

Chlorine gas is poisonous and can be pressurized and cooled to change it into a liquid form so that it can be shipped and stored. When released, it quickly turns into a gas and stays close to the ground and spreads rapidly. Chlorine gas is yellow-green in color and although not flammable alone, it can react explosively or form explosive compounds with other chemicals such as turpentine or ammonia.

In this scenario, the Universal Adversary (UA) infiltrates an industrial facility and stores a large quantity of chlorine gas (liquefied under pressure). Using a low-order explosive, UA ruptures a storage tank man-way, releasing a large quantity of chlorine gas downwind of the site. Secondary devices are set to impact first responders.

Timeline/Event Dynamics

Total time to plan and prepare for the attack would be on the order of 2 years, including reconnaissance and weapons training, and accumulation of weapons. The actual infiltration, explosive charges setting, and ex-filtration would take less than 20 minutes. Except in very cold conditions, the release would be complete in less than an hour. The plume would travel downwind and be dispersed below the detection level in 6 hours. In order for the UA to succeed in this attack, certain meteorological conditions – wind speed, temperature, humidity, and precipitation – must be met.

Secondary Hazards/Events

Authorities will shelter-in-place a significant area downwind of the site. Numerous injuries will result from population panic once downwind casualties begin to occur, and as many as 10% of the people will self-evacuate. Additional injuries are likely, due to motor vehicle accidents in the surrounding roadways. The rule of thumb is one fatality per 10,000 evacuated. Any local waterways or wetlands will absorb the chlorine gas, creating hydrochloric acid and lowering the acidity (potential of hydrogen, or pH) of the water.

Key Implications

Assuming a high-density area, as many as 700,000 people may be in the actual downwind area, which could extend as far as 25 miles. Of these, 5% (35,000) will receive potentially lethal exposures, and half of these will die before or during treatment. An additional 15% will require hospitalization, and the remainder will be treated and released at the scene by Emergency Medical Service (EMS) personnel. However, approximately 450,000 "worried well" will seek treatment at local medical facilities.

The storage tank will be lost, along with some sensitive control systems damaged by the freezing liquefied gas. The secondary devices will cause damage to other plant facilities and equipment in a 20-meter radius of the blasts as well. There will be hundreds, if not thousands, of auto accidents during the evacuation. In areas of heavy chlorine exposure, there will also be heavy corrosion of metal objects.

The plant will be temporarily closed due to bomb damage. Overwhelming demand will disrupt communications (landline telephone and cellular) in the local area. Significant disruptions in health care occur due to the overwhelming demand of the injured and the "worried well."

Decontamination, destruction, disposal, and replacement of major portions of the plant could cost millions. The local economy will be impacted by a loss of jobs at the facility if it is unable to reopen. An overall national economic downturn is possible in the wake of the attack due to a loss of consumer confidence.

Most of the injured will recover in 7 to 14 days, except for those with severe lung damage. These individuals will require long-term monitoring and treatment.

Scenario 9: Natural Disaster

– Major Earthquake

Casualties	1,400 fatalities; 100,000 hospitalizations
Infrastructure Damage	150,000 buildings destroyed, 1 million buildings damaged
Evacuations/Displaced Persons	300,000 households
Contamination	From hazardous materials, in some areas
Economic Impact	Hundreds of billions
Potential for Multiple Events	Yes, aftershocks
Recovery Timeline	Months to years

General Description

Earthquakes occur when the plates that form under the Earth's surface suddenly shift, and most earthquakes occur at the boundaries where the plates meet. A fault is a fracture in the Earth's crust along which two blocks of the crust have slipped with respect to each other. The magnitude of an earthquake, usually expressed by the Richter Scale, is a measure of the amplitude of the seismic waves. The intensity, as expressed by the Modified Mercalli Scale, is a subjective measure that describes how strong a shock was felt at a particular location.

The Richter Scale is logarithmic so that a recording of 7, for example, indicates a disturbance with ground motion ten times as large as a recording of 6. A quake of magnitude 2 is the smallest quake normally felt by people. Earthquakes with a Richter value of 6 or more are commonly considered major; great earthquakes have magnitude of 8 or more. The Modified Mercalli (MM) Scale expresses the intensity of an earthquake's effects in a given locality in values ranging from I to XII. The most commonly used adaptation covers the range of intensity from the condition of "I – Not felt except by a very few under especially favorable conditions," to "XII – Damage total. Lines of sight and level are distorted. Objects thrown upward into the air."

In this scenario, a 7.2-magnitude earthquake occurs along a fault zone in a major metropolitan area (MMA) of a city. MM Scale VIII or greater intensity ground shaking extends throughout large sections of the metropolitan area, greatly impacting a six-county region with a population of approximately 10 million people. Subsurface faulting occurs along 45 miles of the fault zone, extending along a large portion of highly populated local jurisdictions, creating a large swath of destruction. Soil liquefaction occurs in some areas, creating quicksand-like conditions.

Timeline/Event Dynamics

While scientists have been predicting a moderate to catastrophic earthquake in the region sometime in the future, there were no specific indications that an earthquake was imminent in the days and weeks prior to this event.

Damage includes a large multi-state area of several hundred square miles. Rapid horizontal movements associated with the earthquake shift homes off their foundations and cause some tall buildings to collapse or "pancake" as floors collapse down onto one another. Shaking is exaggerated in areas where the underlying sediment is weak or saturated with water. (Note: In the central and eastern United States, earthquake waves travel more efficiently than in the western United States. An earthquake of a given size in the central and eastern United States may cause damage over a much broader area than the same size earthquake in California.)

Several hours later, an aftershock of magnitude 8.0 occurs. Based on past events, additional aftershocks are possible. Sizeable aftershocks (7.0 to 8.0 in magnitude) may occur for months after the original jolt.

Secondary Hazards/Events

As a result of the earthquake, hazardous contamination impacts of concern include natural gas compression stations and processing plants, oil refineries and major tank farms, and natural gas/crude oil pipelines. In addition, more than 2,000 spot fires occur and widespread debris results. Flooding may occur due to levee failures and breaks in water mains and sewage systems.

Transportation lines and nodes; power generation and distribution; communications lines; fuel storage and distribution; and various structures (ranging from dams to hospitals) may be damaged and will require damage assessment in order to continue operating. Reduced availability of services will be disruptive and costly.

Ground shaking from the earthquake has generated massive amounts of debris (more than 120 million tons) from collapsed structures. In addition, fuel pumps in several gas stations have sustained damages, leaking thousands of gallons of gasoline into the streets. There are numerous reports of toxic chemical fires, plumes with noxious fumes, and spills. Several other local waste treatment facilities have reported wastewater and sewage discharges. A large refining spill has contaminated the port facility and is spilling into the harbor. Significant concern for spilled hazardous materials from storage, overturned railcars, and chemical stockpiles make progress very slow as triage is conducted.

Key Implications

Approximately 1,400 fatalities occur as a direct result of the earthquake. More than 100,000 people are injured and continue to overwhelm area hospitals and medical facilities, most of which have sustained considerable damage. Approximately 18,000 of the injured require hospitalization. As many as 20,000 people are missing and may be trapped under collapsed buildings and underground commuter tunnels.

More than 1 million buildings were at least moderately damaged (40% of the buildings) and more than 150,000 buildings have been completely destroyed

Service disruptions are numerous to households, businesses, and military facilities. Medical services are overwhelmed and functioning hospitals are limited. Fire and Emergency Medical Services (EMS) stations and trucks were also damaged. Bridges and major highways are down or blocked and damaged runways have caused flight cancellations. There are widespread power outages and ruptures to underground fuel, oil, and natural gas lines. Water mains are broken. Wastewater primary receptors have broken, closing down systems and leaking raw sewage into the streets. As a result, public health is threatened.

More than 300,000 households have been displaced, and many businesses have lost employees and customers. The port has been adversely affected in its capacity to provide export/import and loading/unloading capabilities, and damage to vital parts of the communications infrastructure has resulted in limited communications capabilities.

The disruption to the nation's economy could be severe because the earthquake impacts major supply and transportation centers. Reconstruction, repairs, disposal, and replacement of lost infrastructure will cost billions of dollars. Replacement of lost private property and goods could also cost billions. An overall national economic downturn is probable in the wake of this event.

Scenario 10: Natural Disaster

– Major Hurricane

Casualties	1,000 fatalities, 5,000 hospitalizations
Infrastructure Damage	Buildings destroyed, large debris
Evacuations/Displaced Persons	1 million evacuated; 100,000 homes seriously damaged
Contamination	From hazardous materials, in some areas
Economic Impact	Millions of dollars
Potential for Multiple Events	Yes, seasonal
Recovery Timeline	Months

General Description

Hurricanes are intense tropical weather systems consisting of dangerous winds and torrential rains. Hurricanes often spawn tornadoes and can produce a storm surge of ocean water that can be up to 24 feet at its peak and 50 to 100 miles wide. The most destructive companion of hurricanes is the storm surge.

A typical hurricane is 400 miles in diameter and has an average forward speed of 15 miles per hour (mph) in a range of 0 to 60 mph. The average life span of a hurricane is 9 days in a range of less than 1 day to more than 12 days. Hurricanes' highest wind speeds are 20 to 30 miles from the center. Hurricane force winds cover almost 100 miles, and gale-force winds of 40 mph or more may cover 400 miles in diameter. A fully developed hurricane may tower 10 miles into the atmosphere.

A hurricane is categorized by its sustained wind intensity on a Saffir-Simpson Hurricane Scale that is used to estimate the potential for property damage and flooding. "Major" hurricanes are placed in Categories 3, 4, or 5 with sustained wind intensities between 111 mph to greater than 155 mph. The most dangerous potential storm would be a slow-moving Category 5 hurricane, making landfall in a highly populated area.

In this scenario, a Category 5 hurricane hits a Major Metropolitan Area (MMA). Sustained winds are at 160 mph with a storm surge greater than 20 feet above normal. As the storm moves closer to land, massive evacuations are required. Certain low-lying escape routes are inundated by water anywhere from 5 hours before the eye of the hurricane reaches land.

Timelines/Event Dynamics

A tropical storm develops in the Atlantic and is upgraded to a hurricane after 5 days in the open waters. After 4 days, the hurricane has steadied at dangerous Category 4 level on the Safir- Simson Hurricane Scale and models indicate a track that includes a possible landfall along the coast adjacent to the MMA within 2 more days. The hurricane reaches its peak as predicted and makes landfall with a direct hit on the MMA and coastal resort towns. The next day the hurricane moves out. The rain associated with the storm has caused rivers to overflow their banks, and several rivers systems are experiencing record flood levels.

Secondary Hazards/ Events

In addition to the massive destruction caused by the hurricane itself, there are also areas within the MMA and scattered inland areas that have sustained severe damage from tornadoes that were generated by the storm. Storm surges and heavy rains cause catastrophic flooding to low lying areas. Rainfall from the hurricane, in combination with earlier storms, causes significant flooding in multiple states along the coast.

Flooded and damaged petrochemical facilities, chemical plants, sewage treatment plants, and other facilities threaten the health of citizens, create a hazardous operating environment, and require cleanup and remediation. An oil tanker is blown off course during the storm and sustains serious damage and leaks oil into the waters adjacent to the MMA.

Key Implications

The hurricane results in more than 1,000 fatalities, and 5,000 thousand people have sustained injuries requiring professional treatment. Tourists and residents in low-lying areas were ordered to evacuate 48 hours prior to projected landfall. Twenty-four hours prior to predicted landfall massive evacuations were ordered, and evacuation routes have been overwhelmed.

Major portions of the MMA become flooded. Structures in the low-lying areas are inundated when storm surges reach their peak. Many older facilities suffer structural collapse due to the swift influx of water and degradation of the supporting structural base. Newer facilities and structures survive the influx of water, but sustain heavy damage to contents on the lower levels.

Most all shrubbery and trees within the storm's path are damaged or destroyed, generating massive amounts of debris. Debris is also generated from structures destroyed from tornadoes and structures that have been destroyed or damaged by the hurricane. Many structures will need to be demolished.

Service disruptions are numerous. Shelters throughout the region are also filled to capacity. Hundreds of people are trapped and require search and rescue. Until debris is cleared, rescue operations are difficult because much of the area is reachable only by helicopters and boats. Wind and downed trees have damaged nearly all of the electric transmission lines within the MMA. Most communications systems within the impacted area are not functioning due to damage and lack of power.

Thousands are homeless, and all areas are in serious need of drinking water, and food is in short supply and spoiling due to lack of refrigeration. Sewage treatment plants in the region have been flooded and sustained damaged from the storm. Factories, chemical plants, sewage treatment plants and other facilities in the MMA have suffered severe damage. Hundreds of thousands of gallons of extremely hazardous substances have spilled into the floodwaters. There is also gasoline, diesel fuel, and oil leaking from underground storage tanks. A 95,000-ton tanker struck a bridge, breaching the hull of the vessel, which then began to leak oil into waters adjacent to the MMA. All of these issues threaten public health.

Many businesses have experienced damage to buildings and infrastructure as well as lost employees and customers. Military facilities are damaged, and assistance is needed to provide for the military community and to reconstitute the facilities. The 20-foot storm surge has breached and overtopped flood control and hurricane protection works. All transportation routes are damaged to some degree, and the port facility has also been adversely affected. Many hospitals have sustained severe damage and those that are open are overwhelmed. Schools that are not severely damaged are being used as shelters for the disaster victims. Thousands of pets, domesticated animals, and wild animals have been killed or injured, and officials have been overwhelmed with requests for assistance in finding lost pets.

There are severe economic repercussions for the whole state and region. The impact of closing the port ripples through the country. The loss of the petrochemical supplies could raise prices and increase demand on foreign sources.

Scenario 11: Radiological Attack

– Radiological Dispersal Devices

Casualties	180 fatalities; 270 injuries; 20,000 detectible contaminations (at each site)
Infrastructure Damage	Near the explosion
Evacuations/Displaced Persons	Yes
Contamination	36 city blocks (at each site)
Economic Impact	Up to billions of dollars
Potential for Multiple Events	Yes
Recovery Timeline	Months to years

General Description

Cesium-137 (^{137}Cs) has a half-life of 33 years. It decays by both beta and gamma radiation. It is one of several known radioactive isotopes that stand out as being highly suitable for radiological terror. This isotope causes skin damage similar to burns, but the injury may be as deep within the body as on the skin. Cesium would be particularly dangerous if accidentally ingested or inhaled, even in small quantities. Cesium mimics potassium in the body. It binds to concrete and other masonry, making decontamination of such buildings extremely difficult and possibly economically infeasible. Use of ^{137}Cs in an urban setting would seriously raise the cost of cleanup.

^{137}Cs is mostly used in the form of cesium chloride (CsCl), because it is easy to precipitate. CsCl is a fairly fine, light powder with typical particle size median at about 300 microns. Fractions below 10 microns are typically less than 1%. In a Radiological Dispersal Device (RDD), most will fall out within approximately 1 to 2,000 feet (although many variables exist), but a small amount may be carried great distances, even hundreds of miles.

In this scenario, the Universal Adversary (UA) purchases stolen CsCl to make an RDD or "dirty bomb." The explosive and the shielded ^{137}Cs sources are smuggled into the country. Detonator cord is stolen from a mining operation, and all other materials are obtained legally in the United States. Devices are detonated in three separate, but regionally close, moderate-to-large cities. The cities are physically similar with geographic topography that is flat. The results in each city are essentially the same. The contaminated region covers approximately thirty-six blocks in each city and includes the business district (high-rise street canyons), residential row houses, crowded shopping areas, and a high school. Buildings in the affected areas are principally made of concrete and brick; some are stone faced.

The entire scene is contaminated with ^{137}Cs, though not at levels causing immediate concern to first responders. Due to the size of the explosion, the radioactive contamination is blown widely such that the ground zero area is not as radioactive as might have been expected. The detonation aerosol contains 90%

of the original 137^{Cs} source with radioactive particles whose sizes range from 1 micron (or micro-meter, μm) to 150 microns – the size of most of the particles is approximately 100 microns. Larger particles either penetrate building materials in the blast zone, or drop quickly to the ground as fall-out within about 500 feet.

Variable winds of 3 to 8 miles per hour carry the radioactively contaminated aerosol throughout an area of approximately thirty-six blocks (the primary deposition zone). Complex urban wind patterns carry the contamination in unpredictable directions, leaving highly variable contamination deposition with numerous hot spots created by wind eddies and vortices. Radioactivity concentrations in this zone are on the order of 5-50 microμi/m2, with hot spots measuring 100-500 microμi/m2; however, traces of the 137^{Cs} plume carry more than 3.5 kilometers (~2.2 miles) on prevailing winds. Air intakes contaminate interiors of larger buildings, and negative indoor building pressure draws contaminated aerosol into buildings via cracks around windows and doors. In city one, the subway air intakes contaminate the subway system.

Timeline/Event Dynamics

The attacks have no advance notice or intelligence that indicates their possibility. The explosions are instantaneous, but plume dispersion continues for 20 minutes while breezes navigate the complex environments before particles have fully settled. First responders do not recognize radioactive contamination for 15 minutes in city one. The explosions in cities two and three are promptly identified as "dirty bombs" – this provides some advantage to first responders and government officials in managing contamination on-scene, and in communicating with the public concerning topical contamination and spread of contamination.

Secondary Hazards/Events

Small fires from ruptured gas lines occur in the vicinity of the blasts. Unstable building facades, rubble, and broken glass create physical hazards for rescue workers. Small amounts of lead, asbestos, and Polychlorinated Biphenyls (PCBs) are present in the air and on surfaces. Human remains present a biohazard, and some of these are very radioactive.

Key Implications

At each site, the blast results in 180 fatalities and about 270 injured requiring medical care. In addition, up to 20,000 individuals in each primary deposition zone potentially have detectable superficial radioactive contamination. In each blast, one building and twenty vehicles are destroyed, and eight other buildings suffer varying degrees of damage, such as minor structural damage and broken windows. Radioactive contamination is found inside and outside of buildings over an area of approximately thirty-six blocks in each city. Minor contamination may be an issue further downwind as investigators perform more thorough surveys. Most of the subway system in city one is contaminated.

Over the long term, decontamination efforts are expected to be effective, but some property owners choose demolition and rebuilding. Many square blocks will be unavailable to businesses and residents for several years until remediation is completed.

Transportation is severely hampered in each city. Bus, rail, and air transport routes are altered, and officials build highway checkpoints to monitor incoming traffic for contamination. The subway system in city one is completely closed for an extended period. Hospitals in each region, already at maximum capacity with injuries from the blasts, are inundated with up 50,000 "worried well."

The sewage treatment plant is quickly contaminated. Seventy-five businesses are closed for an extended duration while radioactive contamination is remediated. Local tax revenues plummet, and people discover that insurance claims are rejected. The schools in the contamination zones are closed and students meet in alternate locations. Nearby towns and cities close their doors to residents of the impacted cities for fear of contamination spread.

Decontamination, destruction, disposal, and replacement of lost infrastructure will be costly (i.e., hundreds of millions of dollars per site). The entire contaminated area may be economically depressed for years. An overall national economic downturn may occur in the wake of the attack due to a loss of consumer confidence.

In the long term, no one will suffer acute radiation syndrome, but approximately 20,000 individuals are likely to become externally contaminated at each site. Low-level contamination may enter food and water supplies. The sum of the cumulative exposures results in an increased lifetime cancer risk proportionate to the dose. Mental health services will be required.

Scenario 12: Explosives Attack

– Bombing Using Improvised Explosive Device

Casualties	100 fatalities; 450 hospitalizations
Infrastructure Damage	Structures affected by blast and fire
Evacuations/Displaced Persons	Minimal
Contamination	None
Economic Impact	Local
Potential for Multiple Events	Yes
Recovery Timeline	Weeks to months

General Description

In this scenario, agents of the Universal Adversary (UA) use improvised explosive devices (IEDs) to detonate bombs inside a sports arena and create a large vehicle bomb (LVB). They also use suicide bombers in an underground public transportation concourse and detonate another bomb in a parking facility near the entertainment complex. An additional series of devices is detonated in the lobby of the nearest hospital emergency room (ER).

The event is primarily designed for an urban environment, but could be adapted for more rural area events such as county fairs and other large gatherings. Casualty estimates would be reduced as a function of a reduced target population and less population density at target points.

Timeline/Event Dynamics

The fire is ignited approximately 1 hour after the start of the entertainment event. The detonation of explosives is delayed approximately 10 to 15 minutes after the ignition of the fire in order to allow for detection, evacuation, and response of emergency services providers. The detonation of explosives at the hospital site will be the hardest to time for maximum effect and may need to be coordinated by some communication among cell members. In any case, the hospital device should be detonated before the arrival of casualties from the entertainment venue.

The timing of some of these events, with the exception of the evacuation stimulus, is not critical. The more people who evacuate the venue, the more potential explosives-related casualties are produced. If evacuation of the venue is delayed, the fire and detonation of the LVB near the venue can be expected to produce increased casualties inside the structure due to collapse, secondary and tertiary blast effects, increased exposure to products of combustion, thermal effects, and crowd surge.

Secondary Hazards/Events

Secondary hazards include the disruption of electric power, natural gas lines, and water mains – the disruption will cause undermining of streets and flooding of underground transit ways. There may be toxic smoke resulting from fires and explosions. There will be loss of traffic controls in the area, and fleeing citizens would likely cause traffic accidents. Media response to the area may affect responders. Since one of the bombs was disguised as an emergency response vehicle, other "legitimate" vehicles may be impeded in their response to the scene and hospitals.

Key Implications

Casualties will result at all five incident sites and will include civilians, emergency personnel, and the suicide bombers. The LVB detonation outside the venue can be expected to result in the largest number of fatalities and injuries due to the "population density" expected. Fatalities and injuries are summarized in Table 16.3.

Incident or Location	Fatalities	Serious Injuries
Fire	8	150
Large Vehicle Bomb	35	200
Car bomb	7	40
Transportation center (subway)	8	50
Hospital	8	40

Table 16.3: Summary of fatalities and serious injuries as a result of the bombings.

Property damage would include severe fire and blast damage to the entertainment venue, blast damage to buildings across from the entertainment venue, moderate damage to the transportation center, severe damage to vehicles and nearby buildings at the parking facility, and severe damage to the hospital ER.

Service disruption would be severe in the impacted city and would include traffic (especially the subway), public transportation, emergency services, and hospitals. The local economic impact includes loss of use of the entertainment venue for a period of 1 year during the repair of fire and blast damage.

Major health issues include severe burn treatment and therapy for the victims; permanent hearing loss; long-term tinnitus; vertigo for some exposed to the blast; and post-traumatic stress for victims, first responders, and nearby residents.

Scenario 13: Biological Attack

– Food Contamination

Casualties	300 fatalities; 400 hospitalizations
Infrastructure Damage	None
Evacuations/Displaced Persons	None
Contamination	Sites where contamination was dispersed
Economic Impact	Millions of dollars
Potential for Multiple Events	Yes
Recovery Timeline	Weeks

General Description

The U.S. food industry has significantly increased its physical and personnel security since 2001. A successful attack could only occur following the illegal acquisition of sensitive information revealing detailed vulnerabilities of a specific production site. However, in this scenario the Universal Adversary (UA) is able to acquire these restricted documents due to a security lapse. The UA uses these sensitive documents and a high degree of careful planning to avoid apprehension and conduct a serious attack.

The UA delivers liquid anthrax bacteria to pre-selected plant workers. At a beef plant in a west coast state, two batches of ground beef are contaminated with anthrax, with distribution to a city on the west coast, a southwest state, and a state in the northwest. At an orange juice plant in a southwestern state, three batches of orange juice are contaminated with anthrax, with distribution to a west coast city, a southwest city, and a northwest city.

Timeline/Event Dynamics

November: The biological agent is delivered to terrorists (plant workers).

December 3: The biological agent is inserted into ground beef and orange juice at production facilities, and the packages are shipped to affected cities.

December 5: The first signs of patients with unknown illness appear.

December 5-15: There is a significant influx of affected individuals into hospitals with 1,200 sick, 300 dead, and 400 hospitalized in ICU.

December 8: Health departments, the CDC, the FDA, and the USDA begin pursuing epidemiological investigations.

December 30: A contaminated product trace is made to ground beef and orange juice production plants. Decontamination of plants commences.

January 5: No new cases of illness are reported.

Secondary Hazards/Events

As a result of news of the contaminated food products, there is general public concern regarding food safety, and the "worried well" are taxing medical and laboratory facilities. The public floods into medical facilities seeking prescription drugs to prevent or recover from sickness. In addition, ground beef and orange juice sales plummet, and unemployment in these two industries rises dramatically.

Key Implications

The attack results in 300 fatalities, 400 hospitalizations, and 1,200 illnesses. Overall property damage is moderate, and due only to decontamination of affected facilities. However, property and facility disruption (downtime) are significant due to decontamination of affected facilities.

Service disruption is significant in ground beef and orange juice industries, and some moderate disruption occurs in other food industries due to the public's concern about food safety in general.

Although direct financial impact is significant, initial economic impact on the general economy is relatively low. However, the long-term financial impact on the beef and orange juice marketplace and associated businesses could be significant, and other food industries' income is likely to be negatively affected by the public's overall perception of unsafe food. The societal impact of attacks on the food supply generates demands for increased, costly, federally directed food security programs and other measures to reduce the possibility of future attacks. Anthrax may result in fatality and serious long-term illness.

Scenario 14: Biological Attack

– Foreign Animal Disease (Foot & Mouth Disease)

Casualties	None
Infrastructure Damage	Huge loss of livestock
Evacuations/Displaced Persons	None
Contamination	None
Economic Impact	Hundreds of millions of dollars
Potential for Multiple Events	Yes
Recovery Timeline	Months

General Description

Foot and mouth disease is an acute infectious viral disease that causes blisters, fever, and lameness in cloven-hoofed animals such as cattle and swine. Pregnant animals often abort and dairy cattle may dry up. It spreads rapidly among such animals and can be fatal in young animals. The disease is not considered a human threat.

In this scenario, members of the Universal Adversary (UA) enter the United States to survey large operations in the livestock industries. The UA targets several locations for a coordinated bioterrorism attack on the agricultural industry. Approximately two months later, UA teams enter the United States and infect farm animals at specific locations.

The U.S. livestock transportation system is highly efficient and movements are rapid and frequent. Although the initial event will be localized at transportation facilities in several states, as the biological agent matures and the livestock are transported, the geographical area will widen to include surrounding states where the livestock are delivered.

Timelines/Event Dynamics

The foreign animal disease (FAD) is initially detected using clinical signs and veterinary medical detection and identification. Over a period of approximately 2 weeks, federal, state, and local animal health professionals put in place surveillance, detection, containment, remediation, and disposal protocols. This is followed by surveillance, detection, containment, remediation, and disposal protocols continue until testing confirms the FAD is eradicated.

Secondary Hazards/Events

Environmental issues regarding contaminated land and equipment must be seriously considered and addressed. Disposal of carcasses of culled animals must be done in an environmentally conscious and expeditious manner.

Key Implications

There are no human fatalities or injuries. However, massive numbers of affected livestock are disposed of because the United States has a national policy not to vaccinate. Property damage will be limited to land mass required for disposal of euthanized livestock (burial).

All transportation into and out of the affected areas will be severely limited to prevent further dispersion of the FAD to unaffected areas. Both commercial and private/personal travel will be limited.

The extent of economic impact will depend on the ability to limit the geographical spread of the outbreak. A great economic impact will be realized in many sectors of the economy, including but not limited to agriculture. Long-term issues will be centered mostly on foreign trade.

Economic factors will include the value of the affected livestock that must be disposed of; the cost of federal, state, and local governments to identify, contain, and eradicate the FAD; the cost of disposal and remediation; the loss of revenue suffered by the commercial transportation industry; the loss of revenue suffered by the retail industry due to public perception that the FAD poses a disease risk; the loss of export markets immediately upon confirmation that the FAD exists; and the cost to renew the livestock lost to euthanasia.

The inevitable development and utilization of new technologies to include rapid detection, improved traditional vaccines/advanced molecular vaccines, and new therapeutics (including antiviral agents and other novel biomedical approaches) will lead to a physiological "hardening" of the U.S. farm animal population against FADs, thereby making them unattractive targets of bioterrorism. Although psychological impacts will be realized, human health issues will not be a consideration if a farm animal disease-causing agent is used.

Scenario 15: Cyber Attack

Casualties	None directly
Infrastructure Damage	Cyber
Evacuations/Displaced Persons	None
Contamination	None
Economic Impact	Millions of dollars
Potential for Multiple Events	Yes
Recovery Timeline	Weeks

General Description

In this scenario, the Universal Adversary conducts cyber attacks that affect several parts of the nation's financial infrastructure over the course of several weeks. Specifically, credit-card processing facilities are hacked and numbers are released to the Internet, causing 20 million cards to be cancelled; automated teller machines (ATMs) fail nearly simultaneously across the nation; major companies report payroll checks are not being received by workers; and several large pension and mutual fund companies have computer malfunctions so severe that they are unable to operate for more than a week. Individually, these attacks are not dangerous – but combined, they shatter faith in the stability of the system. Citizens no longer trust any part of the U.S. financial system and foreign speculators make a run on the dollar.

Timelines/Event Dynamics

Several years are needed for preparation. The attack is executed over a few weeks to ensure extended press coverage and undermine confidence in the financial system. However, there are no secondary hazards/events.

Key Implications

No fatalities, significant injuries, or property damage are expected. However, significant disruptions across many or most sectors of the financial industry do occur. The greatest impact of this event will be on the economy.[2]

Questions

1. What is the purpose of DHS planning scenarios?

2. List some of the anticipated methods of attack.

3. Which types of attack inflict the greatest number of casualties?

4. Which types of attack inflict the greatest economic damage?

5. What type of attack do you consider most probable?

6. What type of attack do you consider most dangerous?

Chapter 17

Emergency Preparedness

Objectives

- Know the four phases of emergency management.

- Describe FEMA's mission and organization.

- Explain the significance of the "all-hazards" emergency management model.

- Understand the role of the National Response Plan and Emergency Support Functions.

Emergency Preparedness and Response. We must prepare to minimize the damage and recover from any future terrorist attacks that may occur despite our best efforts at prevention. An effective response to a major terrorist incident—as well as a natural disaster—depends on being prepared. Therefore, we need a comprehensive national system to bring together and coordinate all necessary response assets quickly and effectively. We must plan, equip, train, and exercise many different response units to mobilize without warning for any emergency.

- Critical Mission Area #6, National Strategy for Homeland Security, July 2002

Introduction

The Homeland Security Act of 2002 established the Under Secretary for Emergency Preparedness and Response responsible for:

1. Helping to ensure the effectiveness of emergency response providers to terrorist attacks, major disasters, and other emergencies;

2. Maintaining the readiness of the Nuclear Incident Response Team;

3. Providing the Federal Government's response to terrorist attacks and major disasters, including—

    • managing such response;

    • directing the Domestic Emergency Support Team, the Strategic National Stockpile, the National Disaster Medical System, and the Nuclear Incident Response Team;

    • overseeing the Metropolitan Medical Response System; and

    • coordinating other Federal response resources in the event of a terrorist attack or major disaster;

4. Aiding the recovery from terrorist attacks and major disasters;

5. Building a comprehensive national incident management system with Federal, State, and local government personnel, agencies, and authorities, to respond to such attacks and disasters;

6. Consolidating existing Federal Government emergency response plans into a single, coordinated national response plan; and

7. Developing comprehensive programs for developing interoperative communications technology, and helping to ensure that emergency response providers acquire such technology.[1]

To fulfill these missions, the Department of Homeland Security built upon the Federal Emergency Management Agency (FEMA) as one of its key components. It continues FEMA's efforts to reduce the loss of life and property and to protect the nation's institutions from all types of hazards through a comprehensive, risk-based, all-hazards emergency management program of preparedness, mitigation, response, and recovery. It changes the emergency management culture from one that reacts to terrorism and other disasters, to one that proactively helps communities and citizens avoid becoming victims.[2]

History

The Federal Emergency Management Agency is tasked with responding to, planning for, recovering from and mitigating against disasters. FEMA can trace its beginnings to the Congressional Act of 1803. This act, generally considered the first piece of disaster legislation, provided assistance to a New Hampshire town following an extensive fire. In the century that followed, ad hoc legislation was passed more than 100 times in response to hurricanes, earthquakes, floods and other natural disasters.

By the 1930s, when the federal approach to problems became popular, the Reconstruction Finance Corporation was given authority to make disaster loans for repair and reconstruction of certain public facilities following an earthquake, and later, other types of disasters. In 1934, the Bureau of Public Roads was given authority to provide funding for highways and bridges damaged by natural disasters. The Flood Control Act, which gave the U.S. Army Corps of Engineers greater authority to implement flood control projects, was also passed. This piecemeal approach to disaster assistance was problematic and it prompted legislation that required greater cooperation between federal agencies and authorized the President to coordinate these activities.

The Federal Emergency Management Agency is tasked with responding to, planning for, recovering from and mitigating against disasters.

The 1960s and early 1970s brought massive disasters requiring major federal response and recovery operations by the Federal Disaster Assistance Administration, established within the Department of Housing and Urban Development (HUD). Hurricane Carla struck in 1962, Hurricane Betsy in 1965, Hurricane Camille in 1969 and Hurricane Agnes in 1972. The Alaskan Earthquake hit in 1964 and the San Fernando Earthquake rocked Southern California in 1971. These events served to focus attention on the issue of natural disasters and brought about increased legislation. In 1968, the National Flood Insurance Act offered new flood protection to homeowners, and in 1974 the Disaster Relief Act firmly established the process of Presidential disaster declarations.

However, emergency and disaster activities were still fragmented. When hazards associated with nuclear power plants and the transportation of hazardous substances were added to natural disasters, more than 100 federal agencies were involved in some aspect of disasters, hazards and emergencies. Many parallel programs and policies existed at the state and local level, compounding the complexity of federal disaster relief efforts. The National Governor's Association sought to decrease the many agencies with whom state and local governments were forced work. They asked President Jimmy Carter to centralize federal emergency functions.

President Carter's 1979 executive order merged many of the separate disaster-related responsibilities into a new Federal Emergency Management Agency (FEMA). Among other agencies, FEMA absorbed: the Federal Insurance Administration, the National Fire Prevention and Control Administration, the National Weather Service Community Preparedness Program, the Federal Preparedness Agency of the General Services Administration and the Federal

Disaster Assistance Administration activities from HUD. Civil defense responsibilities were also transferred to the new agency from the Defense Department's Defense Civil Preparedness Agency.

John Macy was named as FEMA's first director. Macy emphasized the similarities between natural hazards preparedness and the civil defense activities. FEMA began development of an Integrated Emergency Management System with an all-hazards approach that included "direction, control and warning systems which are common to the full range of emergencies from small isolated events to the ultimate emergency - war."

The new agency was faced with many unusual challenges in its first few years that emphasized how complex emergency management can be. Early disasters and emergencies included the contamination of Love Canal, the Cuban refugee crisis and the accident at the Three Mile Island nuclear power plant. Later, the Loma Prieta Earthquake in 1989 and Hurricane Andrew in 1992 focused major national attention on FEMA. In 1993, President Clinton nominated James L. Witt as the new FEMA director. Witt became the first agency director with experience as a state emergency manager. He initiated sweeping reforms that streamlined disaster relief and recovery operations, insisted on a new emphasis regarding preparedness and mitigation, and focused agency employees on customer service. The end of the Cold War also allowed Witt to redirect more of FEMA's limited resources from civil defense into disaster relief, recovery and mitigation programs.

In 2001, President George W. Bush appointed Joe M. Allbaugh as the director of FEMA. Within months, the terrorist attacks of Sept. 11th focused the agency on issues of national preparedness and homeland security, and tested the agency in unprecedented ways. The agency coordinated its activities with the newly formed Office of Homeland Security, and FEMA's Office of National Preparedness was given responsibility for helping to ensure that the nation's first responders were trained and equipped to deal with weapons of mass destruction.

In March 2003, FEMA joined 22 other federal agencies, programs and offices in becoming the Department of Homeland Security. The new department, brought a coordinated approach to national security from emergencies and disasters--both natural and man-made. Today, FEMA is one of four major branches of DHS. About 2,500 full-time employees in the Emergency Preparedness and Response Directorate are supplemented by more than 5,000 stand-by disaster reservists.[3]

Under the Department of Homeland Security, FEMA is authorized by the Robert T. Stafford Disaster Relief and Emergency Assistance Act (42 U.S.C. 5121 et seq.) to reduce the loss of life and property and protect the Nation from all hazards by leading and supporting the Nation in a comprehensive, risk-based emergency management program—

1. of mitigation, by taking sustained actions to reduce or eliminate long-term risk to people and property from hazards and their effects;

2. of planning for building the emergency management profession to prepare effectively for, mitigate against, respond to, and recover from any hazard;

3. of response, by conducting emergency operations to save lives and property through positioning emergency equipment and supplies, through evacuating potential victims, through providing food, water, shelter, and medical care to those in need, and through restoring critical public services;

4. of recovery, by rebuilding communities so individuals, businesses, and governments can function on their own, return to normal life, and protect against future hazards; and

5. of increased efficiencies, by coordinating efforts relating to mitigation, planning, response, and recovery.

FEMA also remains the lead agency for the National Response Plan established under Executive Order No. 12148 (44 Fed. Reg. 43239) and Executive Order No. 12656 (53 Fed. Reg. 47491).[4]

Emergency Management

Emergency management is the discipline and profession of applying science, technology, planning, and management to the extreme events that can injure or kill large numbers of people, do extensive property damage, and disrupt community life. The four phases of emergency management encompass:

The four phases of emergency management encompass:
1. *Mitigation*
2. *Preparedness*
3. *Response*
4. *Recovery*

Mitigation: Deciding what to do where a risk to the health, safety and welfare of a society has been determined to exist; and implementing a risk reduction program. It involves minimizing the potential adverse effects of hazard agents. It may also be any cost-effective measure that will reduce the potential for damage to a facility from a disaster event.

Preparedness: Developing a response plan and training first responders to save lives and reduce disaster damage, including the identification of critical resources and the development of necessary agreements among responding agencies, both within the jurisdiction and with other jurisdictions.

Response: Providing emergency aid and assistance, reducing the probability of secondary damage, and minimizing problems for recovery operations.

Recovery: Providing immediate support during the early recovery period necessary to return vital life support systems to minimum operational levels, and continuing to provide support until the community returns to normal.

The United States has an ongoing system intended to guide the governmental response to all natural disasters. Under the American system, the process works from the bottom up. It begins at the local level and follows a series of pre-specified steps up through the State and, ultimately, to the National Government. Local, State, and National governments are supposed to share their emergency management responsibilities. The higher levels of government are not intended to supersede or replace the activities of the lower levels. All three levels of government are supposed to develop coordinated, integrated emergency management procedures, and they should all participate in the process of implementing disaster-relief policies.[5]

Integrated Emergency Management System

The "all-hazards" emergency management model created under the auspices of the National Governors' Association in the 1970s was adopted to ensure that programs developed for national security-related disasters, such as nuclear wars, would be adaptable to natural and technological disasters.

In general, mitigation is the initial phase of "all hazards" emergency management, although it may be a component in the other phases, as well, and should be considered long before an emergency occurs to eliminate or reduce the probability of the occurrence of an emergency or disaster. Examples:

- Regulating the transportation of hazardous cargoes through congested urban areas.

- Requiring protective construction to reinforce a roof (thereby reducing damage from the high winds of a hurricane).

- Encouraging or requiring changes in construction standards and land-use to reduce the likelihood of future damage.

Mitigation also includes activities designed to postpone, dissipate, or lessen the effects of a disaster or emergency. Preventing the development of hazardous areas like floodplains or adjusting the use of such areas by elevating structures can reduce the chance of flooded buildings.

The "all-hazards" emergency management model was adopted to ensure that programs developed for national security-related disasters, such as nuclear wars, would be adaptable to natural and technological disasters.

Preparedness is planning how to respond in case of an emergency or disaster, and developing capabilities and programs that contribute to a more effective response. Preparedness is "insurance" against emergencies, because mitigation activities cannot prevent all emergencies from happening. Examples:

- Planning to ensure the most effective, efficient response.

- Efforts to minimize damages, such as forecasting and warning systems.

- Training emergency responders.

- Public education and preparedness programs to assure that residents know how to minimize risk to themselves and their property.

- Laying the groundwork for response operations, such as stockpiling emergency supplies and developing mutual aid agreements.

Response is the first phase and occurs when the disaster is imminent or soon after its onset. Response activities are intended to minimize the risks created in an emergency by protecting the people, the environment, and property and to provide emergency assistance for disaster victims. Examples:

- Pre-disaster activities:

  - Evacuation of people at risk

  - Securing property that may be damaged by winds

  - Buying food and water

  - Covering windows and doors

- Activities during disasters:

  - Emergency medical assistance for casualties

  - Search and rescue operations

  - Firefighting

Response also includes efforts to reduce the probability or extent of secondary damage through such measures as security patrols to prevent looting, and to reduce damage with efforts such as sandbagging against impending floodwaters or remedial movement of shelterees in heavily contaminated fallout areas, or other measures that will enhance future recovery operations, such as damage assessment.

Recovery activities continue beyond the emergency period immediately following a disaster. Their purpose is to return all systems, informal and formal, to as near their normal state as possible. They can be broken down into short-term and long-term activities.

Short-term activities attempt to return vital human systems to minimum operating standards and usually encompass approximately a two-week period. For example:

- Crisis counseling to help victims of catastrophic loss

- Temporary shelter

- Emergency power generators

Long-term activities stabilize all systems and can last as long as years after a disaster ends. For example:

- Redevelopment loans

- Legal assistance

- Community planning

- Radiation exposure control

- Public works rehabilitation—repair of infrastructure

FEMA used the "all hazards" model to develop the Integrated Emergency Management System (IEMS).[6]

Organization

For the most part, FEMA is organized functionally on the four phases of emergency management: mitigation, preparedness, response and recovery. Specifically, FEMA comprises five Directorates: mitigation; preparedness, training and exercises; response and recovery; operations support; and information technology services. It also includes the U.S. Fire Administration and the Federal Insurance Administration.

FEMA is geographically divided into ten standard Federal Regions and each Regional Office of FEMA is directed by a politically appointed Regional Director. FEMA's jurisdiction covers all 50 States and the District of Columbia. Other jurisdictions eligible to request Presidential Declarations of major disaster and emergency are: the trust territories of American Samoa, Guam, and the Virgin Islands; and, the commonwealths of Northern Mariana Islands and Puerto Rico.

State officials count on the FEMA Regional Office in their area to support ongoing Federal-State emergency management projects, and FEMA regional personnel are made available to help in damage assessment after a disaster. Ordinarily, States and localities are expected to perform a pre-assessment of damage before the State asks FEMA's Regional Director to undertake with them a Preliminary Damage Assessment (PDA). PDAs are comprised of Federal, State, and local officials with a designated Federal leader. Once all parties come to an agreement on the PDA, it is submitted to the FEMA regional office.

Thus, the Regional Offices play a crucial role in Federal and State emergency management relations. In addition to engaging in routine operations, FEMA Regional Directors, upon receipt of a Governor's request and upon completion of a damage assessment, prepare a regional summary and, regional analysis and recommendation. The regional summary contains only factual information while the regional analysis and recommendation contains opinions and recommendations for the President.

FEMA also operates the National Emergency Training Center (NETC), which is composed of the National Fire Academy and the Emergency Management Institute. The former deals directly and specifically with fire-fighting professionals, including hazardous materials training. The latter serves other emergency personnel through developing, monitoring, and delivering training in all categories of emergency and disaster threats to communities, including radiological emergency training.[7]

FEMA is organized functionally on the four phases of emergency management. Specifically, FEMA comprises five Directorates:
1. *Mitigation*
2. *Preparedness, Training and Exercises*
3. *Response and Recovery*
4. *Operations Support*
5. *Information Technology Services*

Coordinating Role

An examination of FEMA's missions and organization reveal that a significant amount of coordination is required for effective emergency management. FEMA'S coordinating role refers to its relations with different levels of government and various agencies in conducting emergency management. FEMA's primary purpose is to provide assistance to State and local governments in saving lives and protecting property and public health and safety for all types of emergencies. It also, however, directs or coordinates the Federal Agency disaster response.

Currently, FEMA provides funding, guidance, and training to State and local emergency management organizations through its regional structure. Its central relationship with States and localities is primarily through the medium of Performance Partnership Agreements (PPA) and Cooperative Agreements (CA) with State Offices of Emergency Management. The PPA and CA provide a means to pass funds through to State Offices of Emergency Management and from them funds go to local Offices of Emergency Management. PPAs and CAs are analogous to contracts. The PPA is a partnership document of both FEMA and the States regarding goals and objectives. States use the partnership to

Region I: Boston MA
    Maine
    Massachusetts
    New Hampshire
    Vermont

Region II: New York NY
    New York
    Puerto Rico
    Rhode Island
    US Virgin Islands

Region III: Philadelphia PA
    Delaware
    Maryland
    Pennsylvania
    Virginia
    West Virginia
    Washington DC

Region IV: Atlanta GA
    Alabama
    Florida
    Georgia
    Kentucky
    Mississippi
    North Carolina
    South Carolina
    Tennessee

Region V: Chicago IL
    Illinois
    Indiana
    Ohio
    Michigan
    Minnesota
    Wisconsin

Region VI: Denton TX
    Arkansas
    Louisiana
    New Mexico
    Oklahoma
    Texas

Region VII: Kansas City MO
    Iowa
    Kansas
    Missouri
    Nebraska

Region VIII: Denver CO
    Colorado
    Montana
    North Dakota
    South Dakota
    Wyoming

Region 1X: Oakland CA
    Arizona
    California
    Hawaii
    Guam
    Nevada

Region X: Seattle WA
    Alaska
    Idaho
    Oregon
    Washington

Table 17.1: FEMA Regions.

develop their own objectives and, in turn, many of these objectives may come to shape FEMA's own goals and objectives. For example, PPA and CAs can emphasize mitigation efforts. State and FEMA officials come to mutual agreement regarding expected State level outcomes given FEMA funding support.

FEMA's success or failure in meeting its duties rests largely and directly on its ability to coordinate and harmonize the disaster-related work of other Federal agencies. Although FEMA possesses the authority, funding, and limited assets to enable it to do some work independently, it must depend on other Federal departments and agencies to provide additional resources to ensure a complete Federal response. In the event of a Presidentially-declared disaster, a mission assignment may be issued to a Federal agency by the FEMA Director, Associate Director, or Regional Director.

A mission assignment is a work order given to a particular agency that directs completion by that agency of a specified task and cites funding, other managerial controls, and guidance. In effect, these assignments represent FEMA's role in coordinating a complete Federal response to a disaster. This term is also significant because it denotes how other Federal agencies, besides FEMA, engage in disaster recovery work through drawing from the President's Disaster Relief Fund.

As both the PPAs, CAs, and mission assignments indicate, a web of well-maintained political and administrative relations with customers, State and local emergency managers, and Federal agency partners is essential to the attainment of FEMA's goals and objectives. An excellent example of this is FEMA's governmental and interagency coordination work through the National Response Plan.[8]

National Response Plan

The National Response Plan (NRP) demonstrates much about the political and administrative environment of American disaster management. It manifests the framework for planning and conducting interagency response, recovery, and mitigation activities in Presidentially-declared disasters. The NRP's purpose is to integrate the capabilities of Federal departments and agencies for a coordinated Federal response to disasters, so as to provide emergency assistance to save lives, and protect property, public health, and safety for all types of emergencies.

The National Response Plan takes effect when States and local governments are overwhelmed by a disaster and the State Governor requests, and the President determines, that "an emergency exists for which the primary responsibility for response rests with the United States."

Hurricane Hugo in 1989 revealed the need for such a comprehensive Federal response program. Criticism of disaster relief efforts in response to Hurricane Hugo gave impetus to the creation of the Federal Response Plan of 1992, which is now the basis of Federal mobilization aimed at helping States and localities respond to all types of disasters. The Federal Response Plan of 1992 represented a cooperative agreement between 26 Federal agencies and the American Red Cross. The Federal Response Plan:

- Served as a blueprint to coordinate and mobilize resources in disaster and emergency circumstances;

- Provided greater detail concerning the roles and activities of different Federal agencies during large-scale natural disasters;

- Grouped together the different types of emergency assistance available to public organization and private citizens and identifies a lead agency for each of these types of assistance;

- Specified a process in which the resources of the Federal Government can be deployed more quickly and efficiently.

The Federal Response Plan was superceded in December 2004 by the National Response Plan (NRP). The NRP takes effect when States and local governments are overwhelmed by a disaster and the State Governor requests, and the President determines, that "an emergency exists for which the primary responsibility for response rests with the United States."

In presumed disaster or emergency circumstances, the Governor of the affected State must determine whether the magnitude of devastation warrants the request of a Presidential Disaster Declaration. The President, advised by FEMA, must be convinced by evidence that the event warrants Federal assistance. This help supplements the efforts and available resources of the affected State(s), local governments, and disaster relief organizations in alleviating the damage, loss, hardship, or suffering. The National Response Plan establishes the basis by which Federal resources will be organized and employed to support affected State and local jurisdictions.

Currently, the NRP includes 28 departments and agencies, and the American Red Cross, each of which are assigned primary and support roles to provide Federal resources to augment the efforts of local and State governments in responding to a disaster or emergency. The NRP incorporates the Incident Command Structure (ICS) approach to organizing the Federal interagency response teams. The NRP can be viewed as an action plan to support this organizational structure.

The NRP also is linked to other major Federal emergency plans to ensure a consistent and coordinated response to any event which necessitates Federal disaster or emergency assistance. A single Federal Coordinating Officer (FCO) is assigned to direct Federal response to the disaster. The FEMA Regional Office dispatches an Emergency Response Team (ERT) and establishes a Federal Disaster Office.

The NRP is organized into 15 Emergency Support Functions (ESFs) with a lead agency responsible for each:

1.	Transportation	DOT
2.	Communications	DHS/IAIP/NCS
3.	Public Works and Engineering	DOD/USACE
4.	Firefighting	USDA/FS
5.	Emergency Management	DHS/EPR/FEMA
6.	Mass Care, Housing, Human Services	DHS/EPR/FEMA
7.	Resource Support	
8.	Public Health and Medical Services	HHS
9.	Urban Search and Rescue	DHS/EPR/FEMA
10.	Oil and Hazardous Materials Response	DHS/USCG
11.	Agriculture and Natural Resources	DOI
12.	Energy	DOE
13.	Public Safety and Security	DHS/DOJ
14.	Long-Term Community Recovery and Mitigation	USDA/DOC/HHS/FEMA/HUD
15.	External Affairs	DHS/EPR/FEMA

The Emergency Support Functions in the National Response Plan describe essential resources which the departments and agencies can provide to augment local and State emergency response.

The Emergency Support Functions in the National Response Plan describe essential resources which the departments and agencies can provide to augment local and State emergency response. These resources are provided under the statutory authority of or by mission assignment from FEMA.

To facilitate obtaining resources through an Emergency Support Function, FEMA coordinates with the primary agency to validate the requirement and to provide the needed resource. Support agencies may also provide resources under the mission assignment. FEMA may also assign a mission to any agency to provide a unique or specialized resource.

When is the Response Plan implemented?

1. In anticipation of a significant event (e.g., hurricane) judged likely to result in a need for Federal assistance,

2. In response to an actual event (e.g., earthquake) which requires Federal disaster or emergency assistance,

3. In response to a request by a Governor to the President for Federal assistance to the State and/or

4. As the result of a major disaster or emergency declaration by the President.

What types of assistance can be provided?

1. Immediate response for life-saving and life-protecting needs,

2. Help in recovering from the disaster,

3. Assistance in restoration, repair, or replacement of critical public services and facilities,

4. Assistance to support disaster operations, and

5. Mitigation assistance to lessen the effects of a future disaster.

What resources can be provided?

1. Emergency Response and Support Teams

2. Specialized Teams for:

    • rapid assessment

    • emergency communication

    • medical assistance and support

    • urban search and rescue

    • emergency power restoration

    • incident management

    • community relations

3. Communications capabilities and equipment.

4. Facilities to support disaster operations.

5. Management and coordination expertise.

6. Supplies, including:

   - food

   - bulk and bottles water, and ice

   - tents, cots, blankets, and sleeping bags

   - diapers and bathroom supplies

   - tarps and plastic sheeting

   - portable radios, flashlights and tools

7. Equipment, such as:

   - mobile kitchens

   - water purification units

   - portable toilets and showers

   - emergency generators[9]

The Disaster Process and Disaster Aid Programs

First response to a disaster is the job of local government's emergency services with help from nearby municipalities, the state and volunteer agencies. In a catastrophic disaster, and if the governor requests, federal resources can be mobilized through FEMA for search and rescue, electrical power, food, water, shelter and other basic human needs.

A governor's request for a major disaster declaration could mean an infusion of federal funds, but the governor must also commit significant state funds and resources for recovery efforts.

A Major Disaster could result from a hurricane, earthquake, flood, tornado or major fire which the President determines warrants supplemental federal aid. The event must be clearly more than state or local governments can handle alone. If declared, funding comes from the President's Disaster Relief Fund, which is managed by FEMA, and disaster aid programs of other participating federal agencies.

A Presidential Major Disaster Declaration puts into motion long-term federal recovery programs, some of which are matched by state programs, and designed to help disaster victims, businesses and public entities.

An Emergency Declaration is more limited in scope and without the long-term federal recovery programs of a Major Disaster Declaration. Generally, federal assistance and funding are provided to meet a specific emergency need or to help prevent a major disaster from occurring.

A Presidential Major Disaster Declaration puts into motion long-term federal recovery programs, some of which are matched by state programs, and designed to help disaster victims, businesses and public entities. An Emergency Declaration is more limited in scope and without the long-term federal recovery programs of a Major Disaster Declaration.

A Major Disaster Declaration usually follows these steps:

1. Local Government Responds, supplemented by neighboring communities and volunteer agencies. If overwhelmed, turn to the state for assistance;

2. The State Responds with state resources, such as the National Guard and state agencies;

3. Damage Assessment by local, state, federal, and volunteer organizations determines losses and recovery needs;

4. A Major Disaster Declaration is requested by the governor, based on the damage assessment, and an agreement to commit state funds and resources to the long-term recovery;

5. FEMA Evaluates the request and recommends action to the White House based on the disaster, the local community and the state's ability to recover;

6. The President approves the request or FEMA informs the governor it has been denied. This decision process could take a few hours or several weeks depending on the nature of the disaster.

1. Individual Assistance - for damage to residences and businesses or personal property losses, and

2. Public Assistance - for repair of infrastructure, public facilities and debris removal.

Disaster Aid Programs

There are two major categories of disaster aid:

1. Individual Assistance - for damage to residences and businesses or personal property losses, and

2. Public Assistance - for repair of infrastructure, public facilities and debris removal.

Immediately after the declaration, disaster workers arrive and set up a central field office to coordinate the recovery effort. A toll-free telephone number is published for use by affected residents and business owners in registering for assistance. Disaster Recovery Centers also are opened where disaster victims can meet with program representatives and obtain information about available aid and the recovery process.

Disaster aid to individuals generally falls into the following categories:

- Disaster Housing may be available for up to 18 months, using local resources, for displaced persons whose residences were heavily damaged or destroyed. Funding also can be provided for housing repairs and replacement of damaged items to make homes habitable.

- Disaster Grants, are available to help meet other serious disaster related needs and necessary expenses not covered by insurance and other aid programs. These may include replacement of personal property, and transportation, medical, dental and funeral expenses.

- Low-Interest Disaster Loans are available after a disaster for homeowners and renters from the U.S. Small Business Administration (SBA) to cover uninsured property losses. Loans may be for repair or replacement of homes, automobiles, clothing or other damaged personal property. Loans are also available to businesses for property loss and economic injury.

Other Disaster Aid Programs include crisis counseling, disaster-related unemployment assistance, legal aid and assistance with income tax, Social Security and Veteran's benefits. Other state or local help may also be available.

Assistance Process—After the application is taken, the damaged property is inspected to verify the loss. If approved, an applicant will soon receive a check for rental assistance or a grant. Loan applications require more information and approval may take several weeks after application. The deadline for most individual assistance programs is 60 days following the President's major disaster declaration.

Audits are done later to ensure that aid went to only those who were eligible and that disaster aid funds were used only for their intended purposes. These federal program funds cannot duplicate assistance provided by other sources such as insurance.

After a major disaster, FEMA tries to notify all disaster victims about the available aid programs and urge them to apply. The news media are encouraged to visit a Disaster Recovery Center, meet with disaster officials, and help publicize the disaster aid programs and the toll-free teleregistration number.

Public Assistance is aid to state or local governments to pay part of the costs of rebuilding a community's damaged infrastructure. Generally, public assistance programs pay for 75 per cent of the approved project costs. Public Assistance may include debris removal, emergency protective measures and public services, repair of damaged public property, loans needed by communities for essential government functions and grants for public schools.

Disaster victims and public entities are encouraged to avoid the life and property risks of future disasters. Examples include the elevation or relocation of chronically flood-damaged homes away from flood hazard areas, retrofitting buildings to make them resistant to earthquakes or strong winds, and adoption and enforcement of adequate codes and standards by local, state and federal government. FEMA helps fund damage mitigation measures when repairing disaster-damaged structures and through the Hazard Mitigation.[10]

Audits are done later to ensure that aid went to only those who were eligible and that disaster aid funds were used only for their intended purposes. These federal program funds cannot duplicate assistance provided by other sources such as insurance.

Conclusion

In a serious emergency, the federal government augments state and local response efforts. FEMA, as a key component of the Department of Homeland Security, provides funding and command and control support. A number of important specialized federal emergency response assets that are housed in various departments also fall under the Secretary of Homeland Security's authority for responding to a major terrorist attack. Because response efforts to all major incidents entail the same basic elements, federal response capabilities for both terrorist attacks and natural disasters are located in the same organization. The resulting emergency response system is adaptable enough to deal with any terrorist attack, no matter how unlikely or catastrophic, as well as all manner of natural disasters. [11]

Questions

1. List the four phases of emergency management.

2. What is FEMA's role in preparing and responding to disasters?

3. How is FEMA activated?

4. What is the significance of the "all-hazards" emergency management model?

5. What is the purpose of the National Response Plan and Emergency Support Functions?

## Chapter 18

Emergency Response

Objectives

- Describe the purpose of the National Response Plan (NRP).

- Explain the relationship between the NRP and National Incident Management System (NIMS).

- Describe the NIMS framework.

- Explain the relationship between NIMS and the Department of Homeland Security.

- Describe the flow of initial national-level incident management actions.

- Understand the role of the FBI in terrorist incidents.

"An effective response to a major terrorist incident—as well as a natural disaster—depends on being prepared. Therefore, we need a comprehensive national system to bring together and coordinate all necessary response assets quickly and effectively. We must plan, equip, train, and exercise many different response units to mobilize without warning for any emergency."

- Critical Mission Area #6, National Strategy for Homeland Security

Introduction

The Nation's domestic incident management landscape changed dramatically following the terrorist attacks of September 11, 2001. Today's threat environment includes not only the traditional spectrum of manmade and natural hazards—wildland and urban fires, floods, oil spills, hazardous materials releases, transportation accidents, earthquakes, hurricanes, tornadoes, pandemics, and disruptions to the Nation's energy and information technology infrastructure—but also the deadly and devastating terrorist arsenal of chemical, biological, radiological, nuclear, and high-yield explosive weapons.

The National Response Plan, using the National Incident Management System, is an all-hazards plan that provides the structure and mechanisms for national level policy and operational coordination for domestic incident management.

These complex and emerging 21st century threats and hazards demand a unified and coordinated national approach to domestic incident management. The National Strategy for Homeland Security; Homeland Security Act of 2002; and Homeland Security Presidential Directive-5 (HSPD-5), Management of Domestic Incidents, establish clear objectives for a concerted national effort to prevent terrorist attacks within the United States; reduce America's vulnerability to terrorism, major disasters, and other emergencies; and minimize the damage and recover from attacks, major disasters, and other emergencies that occur.

An important initiative called for in the above documents is the development and implementation of a National Response Plan (NRP), predicated on a new National Incident Management System (NIMS), that aligns the patchwork of Federal special-purpose incident management and emergency response plans into an effective and efficient structure. Together, the NRP (December 2004) and the NIMS (March 2004) integrate the capabilities and resources of various governmental jurisdictions, incident management and emergency response disciplines, nongovernmental organizations (NGOs), and the private sector into a cohesive, coordinated, and seamless national framework for domestic incident management:

- The NIMS Provides a nationwide template enabling Federal, State, local, and tribal governments and private-sector and nongovernmental organizations to work together effectively and efficiently to prevent, prepare for, respond to, and recover from domestic incidents regardless of cause, size, or complexity.

- The NRP, using the NIMS, is an all-hazards plan that provides the structure and mechanisms for national level policy and operational coordination for domestic incident management. The NRP is a concerted national effort to prevent terrorist attacks within the United States; reduce America's vulnerability to terrorism, major disasters, and other emergencies;

and minimize the damage and recover from attacks, major disasters, and other emergencies that occur.

Incidents of National Significance

Pursuant to HSPD-5, the Secretary of Homeland Security is responsible for coordinating Federal operations within the United States to prepare for, respond to, and recover from terrorist attacks, major disasters, and other emergencies. HSPD-5 further designates the Secretary of Homeland Security as the "principal Federal official" for domestic incident management. In this role, the Secretary is also responsible for coordinating Federal resources utilized in response to or recovery from terrorist attacks, major disasters, or other Incidents of National Significance when:

1. A Federal department or agency acting under its own authority has requested DHS assistance;

2. The resources of State and local authorities are overwhelmed and Federal assistance has been requested;

3. More than one Federal department or agency has become substantially involved in responding to the incident; or

4. The Secretary has been directed to assume incident management responsibilities by the President.

Incident Response

> *Incident: An occurrence or event, natural or human caused, that requires an emergency response to protect life or property. Incidents can, for example, include major disasters, emergencies, terrorist attacks, terrorist threats, wildland and urban fires, floods, hazardous materials spills, nuclear accidents, aircraft accidents, earthquakes, hurricanes, tornadoes, tropical storms, war-related disasters, public health and medical emergencies, and other occurrences requiring an emergency response.*
>
> *—National Response Plan, December 2004*

A basic premise of the NRP is that incidents are generally handled at the lowest jurisdictional level possible. Police, fire, public health and medical, emergency management, and other personnel are responsible for incident management at the local level. In some instances, a Federal agency in the local area may act as a first responder and may provide direction or assistance consistent with its specific statutory authorities and responsibilities. In the vast majority of incidents, State and local resources and interstate mutual aid normally provide the first line of emergency response and incident management support.

The National Incident Management System (NIMS) establishes a clear progression of coordination and communication from the local level to regional to national headquarters level. Local incident command structures, namely Incident Command Posts (ICPs) and/or Area Commands (if needed), are responsi-

The National Incident Management System (NIMS) establishes a clear progression of coordination and communication from the local level to regional to national headquarters level.

ble for directing on-scene emergency management and maintaining command and control of the on-scene incident operations. The ICPs and Area Commands may be supported by local, state, tribal, and private-sector Emergency Operations Centers (EOCs) and multiagency coordination centers. Both provide central locations for operational information-sharing and resource coordination in support of on-scene efforts. Multiagency coordination entities aid in establishing priorities among the incidents and associated resource allocations, resolving agency policy conflicts, and providing strategic guidance to support incident management activities.

When an incident or potential incident is of such severity, magnitude, and/or complexity that it is considered an Incident of National Significance according to the criteria established in the NRP, the Secretary of Homeland Security, in coordination with other Federal departments and agencies, initiates actions to prevent, prepare for, respond to, and recover from the incident. These actions are taken in conjunction with State, local, tribal, nongovernmental, and private-sector entities as appropriate to the threat or incident. In the context of Stafford Act disasters or emergencies, DHS coordinates supplemental Federal assistance when the consequences of the incident exceed State, local, or tribal capabilities. When State resources and capabilities are overwhelmed, Governors may request Federal assistance under a Presidential disaster or emergency declaration.

During actual or potential Incidents of National Significance, the overall coordination of Federal incident management activities is executed through the Secretary of Homeland Security. Other Federal departments and agencies carry out their incident management and emergency response authorities and responsibilities within this overarching coordinating framework.

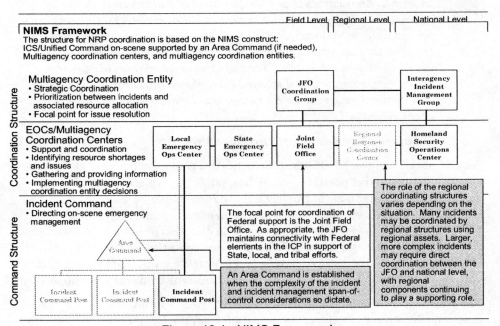

Figure 18.1: NIMS Framework.

The Secretary of Homeland Security utilizes multiagency structures at the headquarters, regional, and field levels to coordinate efforts and provide appropriate support to the incident command structure. At the Federal headquarters level, incident information-sharing, operational planning, and deployment of Federal resources are coordinated by the Homeland Security Operations Center (HSOC), and its component element, the National Response Coordination Center (NRCC).

The HSOC integrates representatives from DHS and other Federal departments and agencies to support steady-state threat-monitoring requirements and situational awareness, as well as operational incident management coordination. The organizational structure of the HSOC is designed to integrate a full spectrum of interagency subject-matter expertise and reach-back capability to meet the demands of a wide range of potential incident scenarios.

The NRCC is a multiagency center that provides overall Federal response coordination for Incidents of National Significance and emergency management program implementation. DHS/EPR/FEMA maintains the NRCC as a functional component of the HSOC in support of incident management operations.

Strategic-level interagency incident management coordination and course of action development are facilitated by the Interagency Incident Management Group (IIMG), which also serves as an advisory body to the Secretary of Homeland Security. The IIMG is comprised of senior representatives from DHS components, other Federal departments and agencies, and NGOs, as required. The Secretary of Homeland Security activates the IIMG based on the nature, severity, magnitude, and complexity of the threat or incident. The Secretary of Homeland Security may activate the IIMG for high-profile, large-scale events that present high-probability targets, such as National Special Security Events (NSSEs), and in heightened threat situations. An NSSE is a designated event that, by virtue of its political, economic, social, or religious significance, may be the target of terrorism or other criminal activity. Issues beyond the Secretary's authority to resolve are referred to the appropriate White House entity for resolution.

In the field, the Secretary of Homeland Security is represented by the Principal Federal Official (PFO) and/or the Federal Coordinating Officer (FCO)/Federal Resource Coordinator (FRC) as appropriate.

At the regional level, interagency resource coordination and multiagency incident support are provided by the RRCC. The RRCC is a standing facility operated by DHS/EPR/FEMA that is activated to coordinate regional response efforts, establish Federal priorities, and implement local Federal program support until authority can be transferred according to the NRP. The RRCC establishes communications with the affected State emergency management agency and the NRCC, coordinates deployment of the Emergency Response Team—Advance Element (ERT-A) to field locations, assesses damage information, develops situation reports, and issues initial mission assignments.

In the field, the Secretary of Homeland Security is represented by the Principal Federal Official (PFO) and/or the Federal Coordinating Officer (FCO)/Federal Resource Coordinator (FRC) as appropriate.

The Principal Federal Official (PFO) is personally designated by the Secretary of Homeland Security to facilitate Federal support to the established Incident Command System (ICS) Unified Command structure and to coordinate overall Federal incident management and assistance activities across the spectrum of prevention, preparedness, response, and recovery. The PFO ensures that incident management efforts are maximized through effective and efficient coordination. The PFO provides a primary point of contact and situational awareness locally for the Secretary of Homeland Security. The Secretary is not restricted to DHS officials when selecting a PFO.

The Federal Coordinating Officer (FCO) manages and coordinates Federal resource support activities related to Stafford Act disasters where a PFO has not been assigned. The FCO assists the Unified Command and/or the Area Command, and provides overall coordination for the Federal components of the Joint Field Office (JFO). The FCO works in partnership with the State Coordinating Officer (SCO) to determine and satisfy State and local assistance requirements.

The Robert T. Stafford Disaster Relief and Emergency Assistance Act, Public Law 93-288, as amended (the Stafford Act) was enacted to support State and local governments and their citizens when disasters overwhelm them. This law establishes a process for requesting and obtaining a Presidential disaster declaration, defines the type and scope of assistance available under the Stafford Act, and sets the conditions for obtaining that assistance.[1]

In non-Stafford Act situations, when a Federal department or agency acting under its own authority has requested the assistance of the Secretary of Homeland Security to obtain support from other Federal departments and agencies, DHS designates a Federal Resource Coordinator (FRC). In these situations, the FRC coordinates support through interagency agreements and memorandums of understanding (MOUs). Relying on the same skill set, DHS may select the FRC from the FCO cadre or other personnel with equivalent knowledge, skills, and abilities. The FRC is responsible for coordinating the timely delivery of resources to the requesting agency.

Joint Field Office

Overall Federal support to the incident command structure on-scene is coordinated through a Joint Field Office (JFO). The JFO is a multiagency coordination center and temporary Federal facility established locally to coordinate operational Federal assistance activities to the affected jurisdiction(s) during Incidents of National Significance. It provides a central location for coordination of Federal, State, local, tribal, nongovernmental, and private-sector organizations with primary responsibility for threat response and incident support. The JFO enables the effective and efficient coordination of Federal incident-related prevention, preparedness, response, and recovery actions.

The JFO utilizes the scalable organizational structure of the NIMS Incident Command System (ICS) in the context of both pre-incident and post-incident management activities. The JFO organization adapts to the magnitude and complexity of the situation at hand, and incorporates the NIMS principles regarding span of control and organizational structure: management, operations, planning, logistics, and finance/administration. Although the JFO uses an ICS structure, the JFO does not manage on-scene operations. Instead, the JFO focuses on providing support to on-scene efforts and conducting broader sup-

Overall Federal support to the incident command structure on-scene is coordinated through a Joint Field Office.

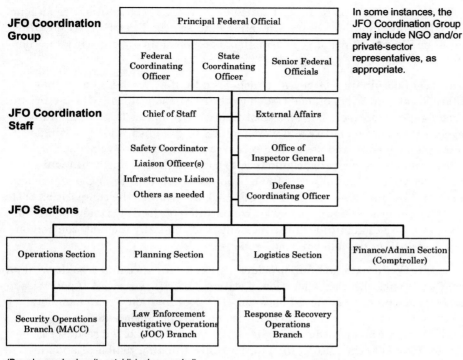

JFO Coordination Group

Principal Federal Official

In some instances, the JFO Coordination Group may include NGO and/or private-sector representatives, as appropriate.

Federal Coordinating Officer | State Coordinating Officer | Senior Federal Officials

JFO Coordination Staff

Chief of Staff

External Affairs

Safety Coordinator
Liaison Officer(s)
Infrastructure Liaison
Others as needed

Office of Inspector General

Defense Coordinating Officer

JFO Sections

Operations Section | Planning Section | Logistics Section | Finance/Admin Section (Comptroller)

Security Operations Branch (MACC) | Law Enforcement Investigative Operations (JOC) Branch | Response & Recovery Operations Branch

(Branches and sub-units established as needed)

Figure 18.2: Joint Field Office.

port operations that may extend beyond the incident site.

The JFO fully replaces the DHS/EPR/FEMA Disaster Field Office (DFO), and accommodates all entities (or their designated representatives) essential to incident management, information-sharing, and the delivery of disaster assistance and other support.

When activated to support an national special security event (NSSE) or other security coordination function, the DHS/U.S. Secret Service (USSS) Multiagency Command Center (MACC) and the FBI Joint Operations Center (JOC) are collocated at the JFO when possible. Other Federal operations centers collocate at the JFO whenever possible. In the event that collocation is not practical, Federal agencies are connected virtually to the JFO and assign liaisons to the JFO to facilitate the coordination of Federal incident management and assistance efforts. State, local, tribal, private-sector, and nongovernmental organizations are encouraged to assign liaisons to the JFO to facilitate interaction, communication, and coordination. Law enforcement activities are managed through the JOC, which becomes an operational branch of the JFO during terrorist-related Incidents of National Significance when required.

Threat situations or incidents that impact multiple States or localities may require separate JFOs. In these situations, one of the JFOs may be identified (typically in the most heavily impacted area) to provide strategic leadership and coordination for the overall incident management effort.

Utilizing the NIMS principle of Unified Command, JFO activities are directed by a JFO Coordination Group, which may include the PFO, SFLEO, FCO/FRC, or other SFOs with primary jurisdictional responsibility or functional authority for the incident.

The JFO Coordination Group also includes a limited number of principal State, local, and tribal officials (such as the SCO), as well as NGO and private-sector representatives. The JFO Coordination Group functions as a multi-agency coordination entity and works jointly to establish priorities (single or multiple incidents) and associated resource allocation, resolve agency policy issues, and provide strategic guidance to support Federal incident management activities. Generally, the PFO, in consultation with the FCO and Senior Federal Law Enforcement Official (SFLEO), determines the composition of the JFO Coordination Group. The exact composition of the JFO is dependent on the nature and magnitude of the incident, and generally includes the personnel described in the following subsections.

The JFO Coordination Group provides strategic guidance and resolution of any conflicts in priorities for allocation of critical Federal resources. If policy issue resolution cannot be achieved between JFO Coordination Group members, issues can be raised to the IIMG or through the appropriate agency chain of command for consideration by higher authorities. Unresolved resource issues are forwarded to the NRCC, then to the IIMG if further deliberation is required.

For terrorist incidents, the primary responsibilities for coordinating and conducting all Federal law enforcement and criminal investigation activities are executed by the Attorney General acting through the FBI.

For terrorist incidents, the primary responsibilities for coordinating and conducting all Federal law enforcement and criminal investigation activities are executed by the Attorney General acting through the FBI. During a terrorist incident, the local FBI Special Agent-in-Charge (SAC) coordinates these activities with other members of the law enforcement community, and works in conjunction with the PFO, who coordinates overall Federal incident management activities. Notwithstanding any other provision of the NRP, when a terrorist threat or actual incident falls within the criminal jurisdiction of the United States, any incident management activity by any other Federal department or agency that could adversely affect the Attorney General's ability to prevent, preempt, disrupt, and respond to such a threat or incident must be coordinated with the Attorney General through the SFLEO (i.e., the FBI SAC).

The framework created by these coordinating structures is designed to accommodate the various roles the Federal Government plays during an incident, whether it is Federal support to (and in coordination with) State, local, or tribal authorities; Federal-to-Federal support; or direct implementation of Federal incident management authorities and responsibilities when appropriate under Federal law. This structure also encompasses the dual roles and responsibilities of the Secretary of Homeland Security for operational and resource coordination in the context of domestic incident management.

Incident Management Actions

Federal, State, local, tribal, private-sector, and nongovernmental organizations report threats, incidents, and potential incidents using established communications and reporting channels. The HSOC receives threat and operational information regarding incidents or potential incidents and makes an initial determination to initiate the coordination of Federal information-sharing and incident management activities.

Federal, State, tribal, private-sector, and NGO EOCs are either required or encouraged to report incident information to the HSOC. In most situations, incident information is reported using existing mechanisms to State or Federal operations centers, which will in turn report the information to the HSOC. Suspicious activity, terrorist threats, and actual incidents with a potential or actual terrorist nexus are reported immediately to a local or regional Joint Terrorism Task Force (JTTF), or the National Joint Terrorism Task Force (NJTTF) in the case of Federal departments/agencies. Subsequently, the FBI Strategic Information and Operations Center (SIOC) immediately reports the terrorist threat, if the FBI deems the threat to be credible, or the actual incident to the HSOC and the National Counterterrorism Center (NCTC). Additionally, actual incidents, regardless of whether or not there is a terrorist nexus, are reported immediately to the HSOC by appropriate governmental and nongovernmental entities.

The FBI Strategic Information and Operations Center (SIOC) is the focal point and operational control center for all Federal intelligence, law enforcement, and investigative law enforcement activities related to domestic terrorist incidents or credible threats, including leading attribution investigations.

The SIOC houses the National Joint Terrorism Task Force (NJTTF). The mission of the NJTTF is to enhance communications, coordination, and cooperation among Federal, State, local, and tribal agencies representing the intelligence, law enforcement, defense, diplomatic, public safety, and homeland security communities by providing a point of fusion for terrorism intelligence and by supporting Joint Terrorism Task Forces (JTTFs) throughout the United States.

The National Counterterrorism Center (NCTC) serves as the primary Federal organization for analyzing and integrating all intelligence possessed or acquired by the U.S. Government pertaining to terrorism and counterterrorism, excepting purely domestic counterterrorism information. The Director of the Center is appointed by the Director of Central Intelligence who has authority, direction, and control over the Center and the Director of the Center.[2] The NCTC may, consistent with applicable law, receive, retain, and disseminate information from any Federal, State, or local government or other source necessary to fulfill its responsibilities.

The Homeland Security Operations Center (HSOC) maintains daily situational awareness to identify and monitor threats or potential threats inside, on, or approaching the borders of the United States. Upon receipt, the HSOC passes such information to appropriate Federal, State, local, and tribal intelligence and law enforcement agencies as expeditiously as possible, according to

The HSOC receives threat and operational information regarding incidents or potential incidents and makes an initial determination to initiate the coordination of Federal information-sharing and incident management activities.

established security protocols and in coordination with the FBI and NCTC.

The HSOC also monitors nonterrorist hazards and accidents, and receives reports from various operations centers, such as the FEMA Operations Center (FOC) regarding natural hazards (severe storms, floods, etc.) and the National Response Center (NRC) regarding oil spills and hazardous materials releases. When notified of a hazard or an incident with possible national-level implications, the HSOC assesses the situation and notifies the Secretary of Homeland Security accordingly. Based on the information, the Secretary of Homeland Security determines the need for activation of NRP elements. The HSOC coordinates with other departments and agencies regarding further field investigation, as required.

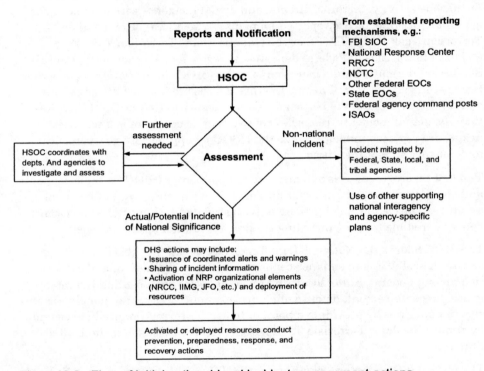

Figure 18.3: Flow of initial national-level incident management actions.

The HSOC coordinates with the NCTC, Terrorist Screening Center (TSC), FBI, Department of Health and Human Services (HHS), and similar programs for terrorism-related threat analysis and warning, and disseminates homeland security threat warnings and advisory bulletins. The HSOC performs this task consistent with normal steady-state threat monitoring, assessment, research, and reporting functions. The HSOC follows Executive orders, directives, MOUs/MOAs, and procedures in place between the NCTC, TSC, and DHS/IAIP.

Note: The Terrorist Screening Center was (TSC) established within the FBI, September 16, 2003, to consolidate terrorist watchlists and provide 24/7 operational support for Federal screeners across the country and around the world.

The TSC was created to ensure that government screeners are working from the same unified set of anti-terrorist information and comprehensive anti-terrorist list when a suspected terrorist is screened or stopped anywhere in the Federal system.[3]

The FBI disseminates terrorism law enforcement bulletins and warnings to ensure that vital information regarding terrorism reaches appropriate officials within the U.S. counterterrorism and law enforcement communities. This information is transmitted via secure teletype. Each message transmitted under this system is an alert, an advisory, or an assessment—an alert if the terrorist threat is credible and specific, an advisory if the threat is credible but general in both timing and target, or an assessment to impart facts and/or threat analysis concerning terrorism. These products are fully coordinated with DHS prior to release.

The FEMA Operations Center (FOC), in coordination with the HSOC, facilitates distribution of warnings, alerts, and bulletins to the emergency management community using a variety of communications systems such as:

- National Warning System (NAWAS): NAWAS is the primary system for emergency communications from the Federal Government to both State and county warning points.

- Washington Area Warning System (WAWAS): Although not directly tied to the NAWAS circuits, WAWAS is a mechanism for providing emergency communications to Washington, DC, area officials in the event of an emergency.

- National Emergency Alert System (National EAS): Formerly known as the Emergency Broadcast System, the National EAS is a nationwide network of broadcast stations and cable systems that provide a readily available and reliable means to communicate emergency information to the American people.

- State and Local Emergency Alert Systems (EAS): State and local authorities have their own EAS which may be used to broadcast information on major disasters or emergencies.

The ongoing fusion of intelligence at the national level may result in the detection of a potential terrorist threat of a specific and credible nature. Unlike incidents reported from the field, this process results in the initiation of initial incident management actions at the headquarters level and generates a "top-down" response to deter, prevent, and otherwise respond to the terrorist threat.

The HSOC, NCTC, and FBI SIOC coordinate information regarding terrorist threats. When the FBI or DHS/IAIP determines that a credible threat exists, it notifies and coordinates with the HSOC, which immediately notifies the FBI SIOC.

The HSOC, NCTC, and FBI SIOC coordinate information regarding terrorist threats. When the FBI or DHS/IAIP determines that a credible threat exists, it notifies and coordinates with the HSOC, which immediately notifies the FBI SIOC, if it has not been already informed. The HSOC then notifies the Secretary of Homeland Security, who may elect to activate any or all of the NRP organizational elements, as well as initiate the coordination of interagency policy issues and operational courses of action through the White House, as appropriate. The Secretary may also elect to activate and prepare to deploy various special teams to conduct prevention, preparedness, response, and recovery activities.

For actual or potential Incidents of National Significance, the HSOC reports the situation to the Secretary of Homeland Security and/or senior staff as delegated by the Secretary, who then determines the need to activate components of the NRP to conduct further assessment of the situation, initiate interagency coordination, share information with affected jurisdictions and the private sector, and/or initiate deployment of resources. Concurrently, the Secretary also makes a determination of whether an event meets the criteria established for a potential or actual Incident of National Significance as defined in this plan.

When the Secretary declares an Incident of National Significance, Federal departments and agencies are notified by the HSOC (as operational security considerations permit), and may be called upon to staff the IIMG and NRCC. The affected State(s) and tribes also are notified by the HSOC using appropriate operational security protocols. In the pre-incident mode, such notification may be conducted discreetly, on a need-to-know basis, so as to preserve the operational security and confidentiality of certain law enforcement and investigative operations.

NRP resources, such as a PFO, may be designated and activated in the context of a general threat, prior to a formal Incident of National Significance determination by the Secretary of Homeland Security, to facilitate pre-incident interagency and multijurisdictional coordination and threat assessment activities. For acts of terrorism, information-sharing, deployment of resources, and incident management actions during actual or potential terrorist incidents are coordinated with DOJ. The NRCC and RRCC deploy, track, and provide incident-related information until the JFO is established.

At the national level, the HSOC facilitates interagency information-sharing activities to enable the assessment, prevention, or resolution of a potential incident. Based upon guidance from the HSC/NSC (Principals, Deputies, or PCC), DHS coordinates with appropriate agencies as required during developing situations to utilize agency resources and authorities to prevent an incident, as well as to initiate appropriate preparatory and mitigating measures to reduce vulnerabilities. If warranted, the IIMG may recommend the activation of additional NRP organizational elements to provide appropriate resources to enable more robust prevention and/or preparedness activities.

Pre-Incident Actions

> *Prevention: Actions taken to avoid an incident or to intervene to stop an incident from occurring. Prevention involves actions taken to protect lives and property.*
>
> *—National Response Plan, December 2004*

Prevention actions related to terrorism threats and incidents include law enforcement activities and protective activities. All Federal law enforcement activities are coordinated by the Attorney General, generally acting through the FBI. Initial prevention efforts include, but are not limited to, actions to:

- Collect, analyze, and apply intelligence and other information;

- Conduct investigations to determine the full nature and source of the threat;

- Implement countermeasures such as surveillance and counterintelligence;

- Conduct security operations, including vulnerability assessments, site security, and infrastructure protection;

- Conduct tactical operations to prevent, interdict, preempt, or disrupt illegal activity;

- Conduct attribution investigations, including an assessment of the potential for future related incidents; and

- Conduct activities to prevent terrorists, terrorist weapons, and associated materials from entering or moving within the United States.

The majority of initial actions in the threat or hazard area are taken by first responders and local government authorities, and include efforts to protect the public and minimize damage to property and the environment, as follows:

- Public Health and Safety: Initial safety efforts focus on actions to detect, prevent, or reduce the impact to public health and safety. Such actions can include environmental analysis, plume modeling, evacuations, emergency sheltering, air monitoring, decontamination, emerging infectious disease tracking, emergency broadcasts, etc. These efforts may also include public health education; site and public health surveillance and testing procedures; and immunizations, prophylaxis, and isolation or quarantine for biological threats coordinated by HHS and State and local public health officials.

- Responder Health and Safety: The safety and health of responders is also a priority. Actions essential to limit their risks include full integration of deployed health and safety assets and expertise; risk assessments based upon timely and accurate data; and situational awareness that considers responder and recovery worker safety.

A comprehensive location and/or operational response safety and health plan is key to mitigating the hazards faced by responders. These efforts include incident hazard identification and characterization; implementation and monitoring of personal protective equipment selection, use, and decontamination; exposure sampling and analysis; worker health and safety risk analysis; health and safety monitoring; and development/ongoing evolution of the site-specific safety and health plan.

Responders may also take incident mitigation actions to protect public and private property and the environment. Such actions may include sandbagging in anticipation of a flood, or booming of environmentally sensitive areas in response to a potential oil spill.

Response Actions

Response: Activities that address the short-term, direct effects of an incident. These activities include immediate actions to preserve life, property, and the environment; meet basic human needs; and maintain the social, economic, and political structure of the affected community.

—National Response Plan, December 2004

Once an incident occurs, the priorities shift from prevention, preparedness, and incident mitigation to immediate and short-term response activities to preserve life, property, the environment, and the social, economic, and political structure of the community. In the context of a terrorist threat, simultaneous activities are initiated to assess regional and national-level impacts, as well as to assess and take appropriate action to prevent and protect against other potential threats.

Reinforcing the initial response to an incident, some Federal agencies may operate in the ICP as Federal first responders and participate in the Unified Command structure. Once the JFO is established, the JFO Coordination Group sets Federal operational priorities. The JFO provides resources in support of the Unified Command and incident management teams conducting on-scene operations through the State and local EOCs. Depending upon the scope and magnitude of the incident, the NRCC and/or the RRCCs activate the appropriate Emergency Support Functions (ESFs), as needed, to mobilize assets and the deployment of resources to support the incident. The NRCC and/or the RRCCs facilitate the deployment and transportation of the Emergency Response Team (ERT) and other teams and specialized capabilities such as, but not limited to, teams under the National Disaster Medical System (NDMS), the HHS Secretary's Emergency Response Team, the Epidemic Intelligence Service, HHS behavioral health response teams, the U.S. Public Health Service Commissioned Corps, and Urban Search and Rescue teams. Other response actions include the establishment of the JFO and other field facilities and providing a wide range of support for incident management, public health, and other community needs.

Response actions also include immediate law enforcement, fire, ambulance, and emergency medical service actions; emergency flood fighting; evacuations; transportation system detours; emergency public information; actions taken to minimize additional damage; urban search and rescue; the establishment of facilities for mass care; the provision of public health and medical services, food, ice, water, and other emergency essentials; debris clearance; the emergency restoration of critical infrastructure; control, containment, and removal of environmental contamination; and protection of responder health and safety.

During the response to a terrorist event, law enforcement actions to collect and preserve evidence and to apprehend perpetrators are critical. These actions take place simultaneously with response operations necessary to save lives and protect property, and are closely coordinated with the law enforcement effort to facilitate the collection of evidence without impacting ongoing life-saving operations.

In the context of a single incident, once immediate response missions and life-saving activities conclude, the emphasis shifts from response to recovery operations and, if applicable, hazard mitigation. The JFO Planning Section develops a demobilization plan for the release of appropriate components.

Emergency Support Functions

The ESF structure provides a modular structure to energize the precise components that can best address the requirements of the incident. For example, a large-scale natural disaster or massive terrorist event may require the activation of all ESFs. A localized flood or tornado might only require activation of a select number of ESFs. Based on the requirements of the incident, ESFs provide the interagency staff to support operations of the NRCC, the RRCC, and the JFO. Depending on the incident, deployed assets of the ESFs may also participate in the staffing of the ICP.

Under the NRP, each ESF is structured to provide optimal support of evolving incident management requirements. ESFs may be activated for Stafford Act and non-Stafford Act implementation of the NRP (although some Incidents of National Significance may not require ESF activations). ESF funding for non-Stafford Act situations will be accomplished using NRP Federal-to-Federal support mechanisms and will vary based on the incident. ESF activities and involvement vary throughout an incident from high-visibility, high-intensity activities during the early response, to program implementation and management during recovery, to a stage of declining requirements and deactivation as ESFs or ESF components complete their missions.

The ESF structure provides a modular structure to energize the precise components that can best address the requirements of the incident.

The National Response Coordination Center (NRCC), a component of the Homeland Security Operations Center (HSOC), develops and issues operation orders to activate individual ESFs based on the scope and magnitude of the threat or incident.

ESF primary agencies are notified of the operations orders and time to report to the NRCC by the Department of Homeland Security/Emergency Preparedness and Response/Federal Emergency Management Agency (DHS/EPR/FEMA) Operations Center. At the regional level, ESFs are notified by the Regional Response Coordination Center (RRCC) per established protocols.

ESF primary agencies notify and activate support agencies as required for the threat or incident, to include support to specialized teams. Each ESF is required to develop standard operating procedures (SOPs) and notification protocols and to maintain current rosters and contact information.

A Federal agency designated as an ESF primary agency serves as a Federal executive agent under the Federal Coordinating Officer (or Federal Resource Coordinator for non-Stafford Act incidents) to accomplish the ESF mission. When an ESF is activated in response to an Incident of National Significance, the primary agency is responsible for:

- Orchestrating Federal support within their functional area for an affected State;

ESF	Scope
ESF #1 – Transportation	• Federal and civil transportation support • Transportation safety • Restoration/recovery of transportation infrastructure • Movement restrictions • Damage and impact assessment
ESF #2 – Communications	• Coordination with telecommunications industry • Restoration/repair of telecommunications infrastructure • Protection, restoration, and sustainment of national cyber and information technology resources
ESF #3 – Public Works & Engineering	• Infrastructure protection and emergency repair • Infrastructure restoration • Engineering services, construction management • Critical infrastructure liaison
ESF #4 – Firefighting	• Firefighting activities on Federal lands • Resource support to rural and urban firefighting operations
ESF #5 – Emergency Management	• Coordination of incident management efforts • Issuance of mission assignments • Resource and human capital • Incident action planning • Financial management
ESF #6 – Mass Care, Housing, & Human Services	• Mass care • Disaster housing • Human services
ESF #7 – Resource Support	• Resource support (facility space, office equipment and supplies, contracting services, etc.)
ESF #8 – Public Health and Medical Services	• Public health • Medical • Mental health services • Mortuary services
ESF #9 – Urban Search & Rescue	• Life-saving assistance • Urban search and rescue
ESF #10 – Oil & Hazardous Materials Response	• Oil and hazardous materials (chemical, biological, radiological, etc.) response • Environmental safety and short- and long-term cleanup
ESF #11 – Agriculture & Natural Resources	• Nutrition assistance • Animal and plant disease/pest response • Food safety and security • Natural and cultural resources and historic properties protection and restoration
ESF #12 – Energy	• Energy infrastructure assessment, repair, and restoration • Energy industry utilities coordination • Energy forecast
ESF #13 – Public Safety & Security	• Facility and resource security • Security planning and technical and resource assistance • Public safety/security support • Support to access, traffic, and crowd control
ESF #14 – Long-Term Community Recovery & Mitigation	• Social and economic community impact assessment • Long-term community recovery assistance to States, local governments, and the private sector • Mitigation analysis and program implementation
ESF #15 – External Affairs	• Emergency public information and protective action guidance • Media and community relations • Congressional and international affairs • Tribal and insular affairs

- Providing staff for the operations functions at fixed and field facilities;

- Notifying and requesting assistance from support agencies;

- Managing mission assignments and coordinating with support agencies, as well as appropriate State agencies;

- Working with appropriate private-sector organizations to maximize use of all available resources;

- Supporting and keeping other ESFs and organizational elements informed of ESF operational priorities and activities;

- Executing contracts and procuring goods and services as needed;

- Ensuring financial and property accountability for ESF activities;

- Planning for short-term and long-term incident management and recovery operations; and

- Maintaining trained personnel to support interagency emergency response and support teams.

The ESF coordinator has ongoing responsibilities throughout the prevention, preparedness, response, recovery, and mitigation phases of incident management. The role of the ESF coordinator is carried out through a "unified command" approach as agreed upon collectively by the designated primary agencies. Responsibilities of the ESF coordinator include:

- Pre-incident planning and coordination;

- Maintaining ongoing contact with ESF primary and support agencies;

- Conducting periodic ESF meetings and conference calls;

- Coordinating efforts with corresponding private-sector organizations; and

- Coordinating ESF activities relating to catastrophic incident planning and critical infrastructure preparedness as appropriate.

When an ESF is activated in response to an Incident of National Significance, support agencies are responsible for:

- Conducting operations, when requested by DHS or the designated ESF primary agency, using their own authorities, subject-matter experts, capabilities, or resources;

- Participating in planning for short-term and long-term incident management and recovery operations and the development of supporting operational plans, SOPs, checklists, or other job aids, in concert with existing first-responder standards;

- Assisting in the conduct of situational assessments;

- Furnishing available personnel, equipment, or other resource support as requested by DHS or the ESF primary agency;

- Providing input to periodic readiness assessments;

- Participating in training and exercises aimed at continuous improvement of prevention, response, and recovery capabilities;

- Identifying new equipment or capabilities required to prevent or respond to new or emerging threats and hazards, or to improve the ability to address existing threats;

- Nominating new technologies to DHS for review and evaluation that have the potential to improve performance within or across functional areas; and

- Providing information or intelligence regarding their agency's area of expertise.

When requested, and upon approval of the Secretary of Defense, the Department of Defense (DOD) provides Defense Support of Civil Authorities (DSCA) during domestic incidents. Accordingly, DOD is considered a support agency to all ESFs. For additional information on DSCA, refer to the NRP Base Plan.

Agency	#1 - Transportation	#2 - Communications	#3 – Public Works and Engineering	#4 - Firefighting	#5 – Emergency Management	#6 – Mass Care, Housing And Human Services	#7 – Resource Support	#8 – Public Health and Medical Services	#9 – Urban Search and Rescue	#10 – Oil and Hazardous Materials Response	#11 – Agriculture and Natural Resources	#12 - Energy	#13 – Public Safety and Security	#14 – Long-term Community Recovery and Mitigation	#15 – External Affairs
USDA			S		S	S		S		S	C/P	S		P	S
USDA/FS	S	S	S	C/P	S	S	S	S	S	S			S		
DOC	S	S	S	S	S		S		S	S	S	S	S	P/S	S
DOD	S	S	S	S	S	S	S	S	S	S	S	S	S	S	S
DOD/USACE			C/P	S	S	S		S	S	S	S	S	S	S	
ED					S										S
DOE	S		S		S			S		S	S	C/P	S	S	S
HHS			S		S	S		C/P	S	S	S			P/S	S
DHS	S	S	S		S	S	S	S	S	S	S	S	C/P/S	S	C
DHS/EPR/FEMA		S	P	S	C/P	C/P			C/P	S				C/P	P
DHS/IAIP/NCS		C/P											S		
DHS/USCG	S		S	S				S	S	P			S		
HUD						S	S							P	S
DOI	S	S	S	S	S	S					S	P	S	S	S
DOJ	S				S		S		S	S	S		C/P/S		S
DOL			S		S	S	S	S	S	S	S	S		S	S

C = ESF Coordinator
P = Primary Agency
S = Support Agency

Figure 18.4: ESF Coordinator and primary and support agencies.

Recovery Actions

> *Recovery: The development, coordination, and execution of service- and site-restoration plans and the reconstitution of government operations and services through individual, private-sector, nongovernmental, and public assistance programs.*

> —*National Response Plan, December 2004*

Recovery involves actions needed to help individuals and communities return to normal when feasible. The JFO is the central coordination point among Federal, State, local, and tribal agencies and voluntary organizations for delivering recovery assistance programs.

The JFO Operations Section includes the Human Services Branch, the Infrastructure Support Branch, and the Community Recovery and Mitigation Branch. The Human Services and Infrastructure Support Branches of the JFO Operations Section assess State and local recovery needs at the outset of an incident and develop relevant timeframes for program delivery. These branches ensure Federal agencies that have relevant recovery assistance programs are notified of an incident and share relevant applicant and damage information with all involved agencies as appropriate, ensuring that the privacy of individuals is protected.

The Human Services Branch coordinates assistance programs to help individuals, families, and businesses meet basic needs and return to self-sufficiency. This branch also coordinates with volunteer organizations and is involved in donations management, and coordinates the need for and location of Disaster Recovery Centers (DRCs) with local and tribal governments. Federal, State, local, tribal, voluntary, and nongovernmental organizations staff the DRCs, as needed, with knowledgeable personnel to provide recovery and mitigation program information, advice, counseling, and related technical assistance.

The Infrastructure Support Branch of the JFO coordinates "public assistance programs" authorized by the Stafford Act to aid State and local governments and eligible private nonprofit organizations with the cost of emergency protective services and the repair or replacement of disaster-damaged public facilities and associated environmental restoration.

The Community Recovery and Mitigation Branch works with the other Operations branches and State and local officials to assess the long-term impacts of an Incident of National Significance, define available resources, and facilitate the development of a course of action to most efficiently apply available resources to restore and revitalize the community as well as reduce the impacts from future disasters.

The above branches coordinate with one another to identify appropriate agency assistance programs to meet applicant needs, synchronizing assistance delivery and encouraging incorporation of hazard mitigation measures where possible. Hazard mitigation measures are identified in concert with congressionally mandated, locally developed plans. Hazard mitigation risk analysis; technical assistance to State, local, and tribal governments, citizens, and business; and grant assistance are included within the mitigation framework. Additionally, these branches work in tandem to track overall progress of the recovery effort, particularly noting potential program deficiencies and problem areas.

Long-term environmental recovery may include cleanup and restoration of public facilities, businesses, and residences; re-establishment of habitats and prevention of subsequent damage to natural resources; protection of cultural or archeological sites; and protection of natural, cultural, and historical resources from intentional damage during other recovery operations.

Mitigation Actions

Mitigation: Activities designed to reduce or eliminate risks to persons or property or to lessen the actual or potential effects or consequences of an incident. Mitigation measures may be implemented prior to, during, or after an incident.

—*National Response Plan, December 2004*

Hazard mitigation involves reducing or eliminating long-term risk to people and property from hazards and their side effects. The JFO is the central coordination point among Federal, State, local, and tribal agencies and NGOs for beginning the process that leads to the delivery of mitigation assistance programs. The JFO's Community Recovery and Mitigation Branch is responsible for coordinating the delivery of all mitigation programs within the affected area, including hazard mitigation for:

- Grant programs for loss reduction measures (if available);

- Delivery of loss reduction building-science expertise;

- Coordination of Federal flood insurance operations and integration of mitigation with other program efforts;

- Conducting flood recovery mapping to permit expedited and accurate implementation of both recovery and mitigation programs;

- Predictive modeling to protect critical assets;

- Early documentation of losses avoided due to previous hazard mitigation measures; and

- Community education and outreach necessary to foster loss reduction.

The Community Recovery and Mitigation Branch works with the Infrastructure and Human Services Branches and with State, local, and tribal officials to facilitate the development of a long-term recovery strategy for the impacted area(s).

Demobilization

When a centralized Federal coordination presence is no longer required in the affected area, the JFO Coordination Group implements the demobilization plan to transfer responsibilities and close out the JFO. After the closing of the JFO, long-term recovery program management and monitoring transitions to individual agencies' regional offices and/or headquarters, as appropriate.

Remedial Actions

DHS formally convenes interagency meetings called "hotwashes" to identify critical issues requiring headquarters-level attention, lessons learned, and best practices associated with the Federal response to Incidents of National Significance. Hotwashes typically are conducted at major transition points over the course of incident management operations, and include State, local, and tribal participation as appropriate.

Identified issues are validated and promptly assigned to appropriate organizations for remediation, in accordance with DHS/EPR/FEMA's Remedial Action Management Program (RAMP). DHS/EPR/FEMA manages the RAMP and coordinates, monitors, and reports the status of Federal remediation actions for issues arising from Incidents of National Significance.

After Action Report

Following an incident, the JFO Coordination Group submits an after-action report to DHS Headquarters detailing operational successes, problems, and key issues affecting incident management. The report includes appropriate feedback from all Federal, State, local, tribal, nongovernmental, and private-sector partners participating in the incident. The Emergency Support Function Leaders Group (ESFLG) and the Regional Interagency Steering Committees (RISCs)— the headquarters-level and regional-level interagency NRP preparedness organizations—use information from these reports to update plans and procedures as required.

The DHS Office of State and Local Government Coordination and Preparedness (OSLGCP) has established and maintains the Lessons Learned Information Sharing system (formerly Ready-Net) as the national repository for reports and lessons learned. The NIMS Integration Center supports and contributes to this national system.[4]

Conclusion

The purpose of the NRP is to establish a comprehensive, national, all-hazards approach to domestic incident management across a spectrum of activities including prevention, preparedness, response, and recovery.

The NRP incorporates best practices and procedures from various incident management disciplines—homeland security, emergency management, law enforcement, firefighting, hazardous materials response, public works, public health, emergency medical services, and responder and recovery worker health and safety—and integrates them into a unified coordinating structure.

The NRP provides the framework for Federal interaction with State, local, and tribal governments; the private sector; and NGOs in the context of domestic incident prevention, preparedness, response, and recovery activities. It describes capabilities and resources and establishes responsibilities, operational processes, and protocols to help protect the Nation from terrorist attacks and other natural and manmade hazards; save lives; protect public health, safety, property, and the environment; and reduce adverse psychological consequences and disruptions. Finally, the NRP serves as the foundation for the development of detailed supplemental plans and procedures to effectively and efficiently implement Federal incident management activities and assistance in the context of specific types of incidents.

The NRP, using the NIMS, establishes mechanisms to:

- Maximize the integration of incident-related prevention, preparedness, response, and recovery activities;

- Improve coordination and integration of Federal, State, local, tribal, regional, private-sector, and nongovernmental organization partners;

- Maximize efficient utilization of resources needed for effective incident management and Critical Infrastructure/Key Resources (CI/KR) protection and restoration;

- Improve incident management communications and increase situational awareness across jurisdictions and between the public and private sectors;

- Facilitate emergency mutual aid and Federal emergency support to State, local, and tribal governments;

- Facilitate Federal-to-Federal interaction and emergency support;

- Provide a proactive and integrated Federal response to catastrophic events; and

- Address linkages to other Federal incident management and emergency response plans developed for specific types of incidents or hazards.[5]

Questions

1. What is the purpose of the NRP?

2. What is the relationship between the NRP and NIMS?

3. What is the purpose of the Joint Field Office?

4. What is the role of the Homeland Security Operations Center in relation to NIMS?

5. What is the role of the FBI in terrorist incidents?

## Chapter 19

First Responders

Objectives

- Understand the critical role of first responders.

- Describe how the Office of Domestic Preparedness supports first responders.

- Explain the purpose of the homeland security exercise program.

- Describe how the Citizen Corps program was designed to assist first responders.

Minimize the damage. The United States will prepare to manage the conse-quences of any future terrorist attacks that may occur despite our best efforts at prevention. Therefore, homeland security seeks to improve the systems and pre-pare the individuals that will respond to acts of terror. The National Strategy for Homeland Security recognizes that after an attack occurs, our greatest chance to minimize loss of life and property lies with our local first respond-ers—police officers, firefighters, emergency medical providers, public works per-sonnel, and emergency management officials. Many of our efforts to minimize the damage focus on these brave and dedicated public servants.

- National Strategy for Homeland Security, July 2002

Introduction

America's first line of defense in any terrorist attack is the "first responder" community—local police, firefighters, and emergency medical professionals. Properly trained and equipped first responders have the greatest potential to save lives and limit casualties after a terrorist attack. Currently, our capabili-ties for responding to a terrorist attack vary widely across the country. Many areas have little or no capability to respond to terrorist attack using weapons of mass destruction. Even the best prepared States and localities do not pos-sess adequate resources to respond to the full range of terrorist threats we face.

America's first line of defense in any terrorist attack is the "first re-sponder" community— local police, firefight-ers, and emergency medical professionals.

- There are over 1 million firefighters in the United States, of which ap-proximately 750,000 are volunteers.

- Local police departments have an estimated 556,000 full-time employees including about 436,000 sworn enforcement personnel.

- Sheriffs' offices reported about 291,000 full-time employees, including about 186,000 sworn personnel.

- There are over 155,000 nationally registered emergency medical techni-cians (EMTs).[1]

The terrorist attacks of September 11, 2001, placed enormous demands upon the capacities of state and local police and fire departments, emergency medi-cal and public health services, and other first responders. After the attacks, Congress, federal agencies, state and local governments, and a range of inde-pendent research organizations acknowledged that additional resources and intergovernmental coordination were needed to ensure that state and local first responders would be better prepared to respond to future domestic terror-ist threats or attacks.[2]

In January 2002, President Bush proposed the First Responder Initiative as part of his Fiscal Year 2003 Budget proposal. The purpose of this initiative was to improve dramatically first responder preparedness for terrorist inci-dents and disasters. This program increased federal funding levels more than tenfold (from $272 million in the pre-supplemental Fiscal Year 2002 Budget to $3.5 billion in Fiscal Year 2003). Under the President's Department of Home-land Security proposal, the new Department would consolidate all grant pro-grams that distribute federal funds to state and local first responders.

The new Department of Homeland Security ensures the readiness of first responders to work safely in areas where chemical, biological, radiological, or nuclear weapons are used. The Department requires annual certification of first responder preparedness to handle and decontaminate any hazard. This certification process also verifies the ability of state and local first responders to work effectively with related federal support assets. The Department of Homeland Security helps state and local agencies meet these certification standards by providing grant money (based on performance) for planning and equipping, training, and exercising first responders for chemical, biological, radiological and nuclear attacks.

The Department of Homeland Security establishes national standards for emergency response training and preparedness. These standards provide guidelines for the vaccination of civilian response personnel against certain biological agents. These standards also require certain coursework for individuals to receive and maintain certification as first responders and for state and local governments to receive federal grants. The Department established a national exercise program designed to educate and evaluate civilian response personnel at all levels of government. It requires individuals and government bodies to complete successfully at least one exercise every year. The Department uses these exercises to measure performance and allocate future resources.

The growing threat of terrorist attacks on American soil, including the potential use of weapons of mass destruction, strained the Nation's system for training emergency response personnel. The Department of Homeland Security launched a consolidated and expanded training and evaluation system to meet the increasing demand. This system is predicated on a four phased approach: requirements, plans, training (and exercises), and assessments (comprising of evaluations and corrective action plans). The Department serves as the central coordinating body responsible for overseeing curriculum standards and, through regional centers of excellence such as the Emergency Management Institute in Maryland, the Center for Domestic Preparedness in Alabama, and the National Domestic Preparedness Consortium, for training the instructors who train first responders. These instructors teach courses at thousands of facilities such as public safety academies, community colleges, and state and private universities.

The Department of Homeland Security launched a steady and long-term effort to provide first responders with technical capabilities for dealing with the effects of catastrophic threats—capabilities that aid both first responders and victims of the attack. These capabilities include protective gear and masks, prophylactic treatments, and decontamination equipment. The Department has undertaken sustained efforts to develop treatments and decontamination methodologies for radiological and nuclear events. The Department is also focusing on developing new methods to merge disparate databases and provide first responders with accurate and usable pictures of building layouts and other key information about the site of a terrorist incident. In all these efforts, the Department pays great attention to ensuring that these technologies are easy to use under the extreme conditions in which first responders operate.

The growing threat of terrorist attacks on American soil, including the potential use of weapons of mass destruction, strained the Nation's system for training emergency response personnel. The Department of Homeland Security launched a consolidated and expanded training and evaluation system to meet the increasing demand. This system is predicated on a four phased approach: requirements, plans, training (and exercises), and assessments.

The Department of Homeland Security is working to develop comprehensive emergency communications systems; most state and local first responders do not use compatible communications equipment. The National Communications System has been incorporated into the Department of Homeland Security to facilitate the effort. These systems will disseminate information about vulnerabilities and protective measures, as well as allow first responders to better manage incidents and minimize damage. The Department is pursuing technologies such as Project SAFECOM to address the Nation's critical public safety wireless shortcomings and create a tactical wireless infrastructure for first responders and federal, state, and local law enforcement and public safety entities.

Americans in their private capacities have joined in supporting emergency personnel as well. The President created the Citizen Corps initiative to offer Americans the opportunity to volunteer to protect their communities through emergency response and preparation. More than 100 communities, ranging from major metropolitan areas to small suburban and rural communities, have formed Citizen Corps Councils to coordinate local volunteer activities to support first responders. More than 38,000 individuals from all 50 states have signed up online to participate in one or more of the federally supported Citizen Corps programs, including Volunteers in Police Service, Neighborhood Watch and Operation TIPS, sponsored by the Department of Justice; the Medical Reserve Corps, sponsored by the Department of Health and Human Services; and the Federal Emergency Management Agency's Community Emergency Response Team training.[3]

Office for Domestic Preparedness

The Office for Domestic Preparedness (ODP) is the principal component of the U.S. Department of Homeland Security (DHS) that provides training, funds for the purchase of equipment, support for the planning and execution of exercises, technical assistance, and other support to all U.S. States and territories and the District of Columbia, tribal governments, and local jurisdictions to prevent, plan for, and respond to acts of terrorism.

The Office for Domestic Preparedness (ODP) is the principal component of the U.S. Department of Homeland Security (DHS) responsible for preparing the United States for acts of terrorism. In carrying out its mission, DHS/ODP is the primary office that provides training, funds for the purchase of equipment, support for the planning and execution of exercises, technical assistance, and other support to all U.S. States and territories and the District of Columbia, tribal governments, and local jurisdictions to prevent, plan for, and respond to acts of terrorism.[4]

The Department of Justice established the Office for Domestic Preparedness (ODP) in 1998 within the Office of Justice Programs (OJP) to assist state and local first responders in acquiring specialized training and equipment needed to respond to and manage terrorist incidents involving weapons of mass destruction. When DHS was created in March 2003, ODP was transferred from the Justice Department's OJP to DHS's Directorate of Border and Transportation Security. In March 2004, the Secretary of Homeland Security consolidated ODP with the Office of State and Local Government Coordination to form the Office of State and Local Government Coordination and Preparedness (SLGCP). In addition, other preparedness grant programs from agencies within DHS were transferred to SLGCP. SLGCP, which reports directly to the Secretary, was created to provide a "one-stop shop" for the numerous federal preparedness initiatives applicable to state and local first responders. While

SLGCP/ODP has program management and monitoring responsibility for domestic preparedness grants, it still relies upon the Justice Department's Office of the Comptroller (OC) for grant fund distribution and assistance with financial management support, which includes financial monitoring.

Within ODP, the Preparedness Programs Division (formerly the State and Local Program Management Division) is specifically tasked with enhancing the capability of state and local emergency responders to prevent, deter, respond to, and recover from terrorist attacks involving the use of chemical, biological, radiological, nuclear, or explosive (CBRNE) weapons. For these purposes, ODP provides grant funds to the 50 states, the District of Columbia, the Commonwealths of Puerto Rico and the Northern Mariana Islands, American Samoa, the Virgin Islands, Guam, and selected urban areas. In addition to this grant funding for specialized equipment and other purposes, ODP provides direct training, exercises, technical assistance, and other counterterrorism expertise.[5]

DHS/ODP programs are designed to equip, train, and exercise homeland security professionals who may be called on to prevent or respond to disaster situations. These programs consist of a State formula grant program, direct assistance to local jurisdictions, and activities of regional and national scope. DHS/ODP staff members are dedicated to the development and delivery of the four main components of assistance available to State and local governments: 1) grants management and planning, 2) equipment acquisition, 3) training support, and 4) exercise support. The DHS/ODP program management function encompasses monetary assistance as well as support of statewide risk and needs assessments; strategy development; management of DHS/ODP resources in planning, equipment, training, and exercises; and Federal agency coordination. Each State's preparedness program management is the responsibility of a State Administrative Agency (SAA) designated by the Governor.

A DHS/ODP Preparedness Officer has been assigned to each State to serve as the primary contact for ODP assistance. The Preparedness Officer's role is to:

- Conduct a formal strategy review and assist each State in preparing and identifying the resources to implement a State Homeland Security Strategy.

- Review grant applications, prepare award documents, and administer grant programs.

- Assist States and designated urban areas with strategy implementation, including working with other Federal agencies to coordinate assistance (e.g., Homeland Defense Equipment Reuse [HDER] Program, which provides surplus U.S. Department of Energy (DOE) radiological detection equipment and support to State and local homeland security agencies).

- Coordinate DHS/ODP resources for equipment funding, training courses, and exercise programs.

Grants Management and Planning

DHS/ODP provides State formula grant funds to assist with implementation of State Homeland Security Strategies. Eighty percent of funds must be obligated to local units of government, and all funds must be allocated in support of State and/or Urban Areas Security Initiative (UASI) homeland strategic goals and objectives. Additionally, funds for specific urban areas provided through the UASI are coordinated by the SAA.

All funds provided to the State are awarded to an SAA. The SAA is appointed by the Governor to apply and administer the various DHS/ODP grant funds. The SAA in turn subawards to State agencies and local governments for implementation. States use State Homeland Security Strategies to more effectively fill the gaps between needs and existing capabilities, and to determine how they will allocate their funding. The funds may be used for planning, purchasing equipment, supporting terrorism exercises, training, and/or management and administration.

Specific funding has been allocated for use in high-threat, high-density urban areas. The UASI program was developed to address the unique needs of urban areas; it will significantly enhance the ability of urban areas to prevent, deter, respond to, and recover from threats and incidents of terrorism. These cities were determined by a formula using a combination of current threat estimates, critical assets within an urban area, and population density. Urban areas selected for funding must approach the development and implementation of the UASI program regionally by involving core cities, core counties, contiguous jurisdictions, mutual aid partners, and State agencies in an Urban Area Working Group (UAWG). Funding is guided by UASI homeland security strategies drafted by the UAWGs.

State Homeland Security Strategy

To implement a program that addresses State and local needs, States are required to conduct vulnerability, risk, and needs assessments and to develop a State Homeland Security Strategy. The assessments are conducted at the State and local levels using an Assessment and Strategy Development Toolkit developed by DHS/ODP in cooperation with the Federal Bureau of Investigation (FBI) and the Centers for Disease Control and Prevention (CDC), and are used to guide the development of State Homeland Security Strategies by the State and local agencies responsible for responding to a terrorism incident. The assessment is prepared by the State's planning team; it outlines the State's goals for enhancing prevention, response, and recovery capabilities, and lists specific objectives and implementation steps for the use of planning, training, equipment, and exercise resources in attaining these objectives. The enhanced assessment tool includes an agricultural vulnerability assessment process developed in conjunction with the U.S. Department of Agriculture (USDA). Many States have adopted a regional approach to the distribution and sharing of resources. Numerous mutual aid agreements and emergency management assistance compacts have been executed, and coordination and cooperation have been enhanced among homeland security professionals at different levels of government and across disciplines. Strategy analysis has also provided DHS/ODP with a comprehensive picture of planning, equipment, training, exercise, and technical assistance needs across the Nation.[6]

During fiscal years 2002 and 2003, ODP managed 25 grant programs totaling approximately $3.5 billion. About $2.98 billion (85 percent) of the total ODP grant funds for both years was for statewide grants—the State Domestic Preparedness Program (SDPP), which is a predecessor grant program to the State Homeland Security Grant Programs (SHSGP I and II)—and grants targeted at selected urban areas, including the Urban Areas Security Initiative (UASI I and II). The SDPP/SHSGP grant funds accounted for about 68 percent ($2.38 billion) and the UASI I and II grant funds about 17 percent ($596 million).[7]

Scheduling

The DHS/ODP Centralized Scheduling and Information Desk (CSID) is a comprehensive coordination, management, information, and scheduling tool developed by DHS/ODP for homeland security preparedness activities. CSID is a "one-stop shop" for information on homeland security preparedness events for the Federal, State, and local communities. In addition, CSID schedules DHS/ODP training for the emergency responder community and maintains interagency exercise schedules. CSID helps Federal agencies coordinate, consolidate, and monitor Federal homeland security terrorism preparedness events in the United States.

CSID provides custom reports on a multitude of homeland security events to identified Federal, State, local, and private partners. CSID also creates informational reports (including comprehensive city and State reports) on the status of homeland security terrorism preparedness training, exercises, and grants. These reports are used for auditing and archiving purposes as well as for congressional hearings.

CSID comprises three components: a master calendar, a database, and an onsite call desk/help line. These components facilitate information sharing and allow CSID to respond to inquiries in a timely manner. The CSID toll-free number is (800) 368–6498. The onsite call desk is staffed weekdays from 8 a.m. to 7 p.m., eastern time. On weekends, holidays, and after business hours, callers can leave a voice mail message.

The DHS/ODP Homeland Security Preparedness Technical Assistance (TA) Program provides direct assistance to State and local jurisdictions to improve their ability to prevent, respond to, and recover from threats or acts of weapons of mass destruction (WMD) terrorism.

Technical Assistance Program

The DHS/ODP Homeland Security Preparedness Technical Assistance (TA) Program provides direct assistance to State and local jurisdictions to improve their ability to prevent, respond to, and recover from threats or acts of weapons of mass destruction (WMD) terrorism. Specifically, TA provides a process to help resolve a problem and/or create innovative approaches. All TA services are available to eligible recipients at no charge.

TA programs in place or currently under development within DHS/ODP include:

- Homeland Security Assessment and Strategy Technical Assistance: This program helps States and local jurisdictions with the assessment process, the ability to conduct assessments, and the development of a comprehensive homeland security strategy.

- Domestic Preparedness Equipment Technical Assistance Program (DPETAP): DPETAP provides equipment-specific training on WMD detection, decontamination, and personal protective equipment (PPE).

- Terrorism Early Warning Group Replication: This project replicates programs that enhance capabilities for analyzing the strategic and operational information needed to respond to terrorism and protect critical infrastructure.

- Interoperable Communication Technical Assistance Program (ICTAP): ICTAP enhances the interoperability of public safety communications with regard to WMD terrorism threats.

- Port and Mass Transit Planning Technical Assistance: This program assesses the needs of port/mass transit agencies in preparing for and countering post-9/11 terrorist threats.

- Rapid Assistance Team (RAT) Technical Assistance: This project deploys teams on short notice to support targeted projects such as identifying equipment needs or equipment procurement plans.

- General Technical Assistance: This program provides specialized assistance to enhance State and local strategies to prevent, respond to, and recover from WMD terrorism.

- Prevention Technical Assistance: This new initiative facilitates terrorism prevention efforts such as collaboration, information sharing, risk management, threat recognition, and intervention.

- Plans and Planning Synchronization Technical Assistance: This program offers planning support for multijurisdictional terrorism response using innovative software tools.

Equipment Acquisition

DHS/ODP provides assistance to State and local agencies with specialized response equipment programs. Applicant assistance services include the following:

- DPETAP: DPETAP is a comprehensive national technical assistance program operated in partnership with the U.S. Army's Pine Bluff Arsenal. DPETAP personnel provide training on the use and maintenance of specialized equipment that can be procured through the Homeland Security Grant Program (HSGP). This training is provided onsite at no cost through the use of mobile training teams.

- Prepositioned Equipment Program (PEP): PEP consists of standardized equipment pods that are prepositioned in selected geographic areas to allow rapid deployment to States and localities that are coping with a major chemical, biological, radiological, nuclear, or explosive (CBRNE) event. Eleven operational PEP sites will be phased in by the end of fiscal year (FY) 2004.

- HDER: HDER gives responder agencies across the Nation access to a substantial inventory of radiological detection instrumentation and other equipment that is no longer needed by the Federal Government. This equipment is rehabilitated and provided at no cost to the recipient.

- RAT: RAT provides telephone and onsite assistance to SAAs to identify statewide and/or local equipment needs, develop State and/or local equipment procurement plans, prepare grant application documents (e.g., program narratives, budgets), and offer other related support.

- Equipment Purchase Assistance Program: This program provides HSGP recipients with access to Federal purchasing programs through agreements with the Defense Logistics Agency and the Marine Corps Systems Command. Advantages include streamlined procurement as well as guaranteed product warranties and delivery timelines.

- Grant Assistance Program (GAP): GAP provides jurisdictions with training and technical assistance to expedite grant expenditures and ensure compliance with DHS/ODP grant programs.

- ICTAP: ICTAP brings Space and Naval Warfare Systems Center–San Diego (SSC San Diego) expertise and experience to State and local jurisdictions throughout the country to address interoperable communications needs regarding terrorism prevention, response, and recovery by helping State and local agencies develop engineering solutions to achieve communications interoperability.[8]

Authorized Equipment List for Grants

The Authorized Equipment List (AEL) for ODP grants was derived from the Standard Equipment List (SEL), which was developed by the Interagency Board (IAB) for Equipment Standardization and Interoperability. Changes and additions to the AEL reflect input received by DHS-ODP from State and local responders and reflect a continued commitment to better serve the nation. The new AEL also comports closely with the SEL, but has additional categories and equipment. A cross-section of officials representing the U.S. Department of Homeland Security, the U.S. Department of Justice, the Public Health Service, the U.S. Department of Energy, and State and local CBRNE response experts assisted in the development of this authorized equipment purchase list and in identifying allowable items.

The Authorized Equipment List has expanded beyond the initial focus on personal protective equipment, detection equipment, and communication equipment and is often updated for new grant solicitations. The FY 2004 Authorized Equipment List included the following eighteen categories:

1. Personal Protective Equipment

2. Explosive Device Mitigation and Remediation Equipment

3. CBRNE Search and Rescue Equipment

4. Interoperable Communications Equipment

5. Detection Equipment

6. Decontamination Equipment

7. Physical Security Enhancement Equipment

8. Terrorism Incident Prevention Equipment

9. CBRNE Logistical Support Equipment

10. CBRNE Incident Response Vehicles

11. Medical Supplies and Limited Types of Pharmaceuticals

12. CBRNE Reference Materials

13. Agricultural Terrorism Prevention, Response and Mitigation

14. CBRNE Response Watercraft

15. CBRNE Aviation Equipment

16. Cyber Security Enhancement Equipment

17. Intervention Equipment

18. Other Authorized Equipment[9]

Equipment Standards

On February 26, 2004, the Department of Homeland Security's Science and Technology directorate issued its first standards regarding personal protective equipment developed to protect first responders against chemical, biological, radiological and nuclear incidents (Appendix A).

Homeland Security adopted the standards, developed in partnership with the National Fire Protection Association (NFPA) and the National Institute for Occupational Safety and Health (NIOSH). The guidelines, which have also been adopted by the Interagency Board for Equipment Standardization and Interoperability, include NIOSH standards for CBRN three main categories of respiratory protection equipment and five current NFPA standards for protective suits and clothing to be used in responding to chemical, biological and radiological attacks.

Homeland Security's standards are designed to assist state and local officials in procurement decisions related to first responder equipment. In addition, guidelines will assist manufacturers by providing performance standards and test methods. This provides the manufacturing community with minimum performance requirements for equipment, and the test methods to confirm that the required performance levels are achieved.

Homeland Security's standards are designed to assist state and local officials in procurement decisions related to first responder equipment.

The U.S. Department of Homeland Security's Science and Technology division serves as the primary research and development arm of the Department. The Science and Technology division, managed by the National Institute of Standards and Technology (NIST), was given the task to develop chemical, biological, radiological and nuclear and explosive protective equipment standards. This program, which transitioned from the Department's Office of Domestic Preparedness in 2003, continues to facilitate the development of performance standards and test methods for first responder protective and operational equipment.[10]

Training Support

State-Level Training DHS/ODP offers more than 40 specialized courses ranging from basic awareness-level and operations training to advanced, hands-on technical and command courses. Courses are delivered to first responders nationwide, both onsite via mobile training teams and at state-of-the-art training facilities. All DHS/ODP-sponsored training delivered under the State Homeland Security Strategy is scheduled through the SAA's training point of contact (POC).

In addition to accessing specialized and advanced training from DHS/ODP-sponsored training centers and providers, States may use grant funds to support CBRNE training activities within existing training academies, universities, or junior colleges, or attendance at approved CBRNE classes. The goal of affording States the opportunity to deliver training locally is to enhance the capabilities of State and local homeland security professionals through the development of State homeland security training programs that institutionalize awareness-level training within the State.

Training Preparedness Officers are available to assist States in understanding and prioritizing their training resources. The role of a Training Preparedness Officer is to:

- Develop new training courses and conduct periodic reviews and enhancement of existing courses, with input by subject matter experts and practitioners

- Incorporate lessons learned and best practices from analysis of exercise findings into existing training and/or develop new courses to address gaps in training, and develop and maintain a compendium of homeland security lessons learned

- Review State Homeland Security Strategies and, based on identified needs, allocate training resources to the States through the SAAs

- Respond to requests for technical assistance from State and local agencies for help with conducting assessments and developing strategies, using and maintaining equipment, and other site-specific needs.

Annual Training and Exercise Conference

DHS/ODP hosts an annual conference for State training and exercise POCs, DHS/ODP regional training and exercise staff, and DHS/ ODP national training and exercise staff. Conferences include Federal partner agencies that either have direct or indirect involvement in DHS/ODP training or exercises, or that maintain training or exercise programs of their own. The typical agenda for the multiday event addresses State and local concerns, issues, and accomplishments, and provide overviews and updates of DHS/ODP programs. The environment fosters the sharing and showcasing of best practices in training, exercises, evaluations, and Improvement Plans (IPs). Special events, regional and breakout sessions, and guest speakers will round out the conference agenda. Costs associated with conference attendance are allowable expenses under HSGP.

Exercise Support

DHS/ODP-funded exercises are supported by two programs, the National Exercise Program (NEP) and the Homeland Security Exercise and Evaluation Program (HSEEP).

DHS/ODP-funded exercises are supported by two programs, the National Exercise Program (NEP) and the Homeland Security Exercise and Evaluation Program (HSEEP). NEP trains national leaders and departmental and agency staff, and facilitates collaboration among partners at all levels of government for assigned homeland security missions. HSEEP provides the overall doctrine and policy according to which all DHS/ ODP-funded exercises will be designed, developed, conducted, and evaluated.[11]

In addition to full scale, integrated National level exercises - the NEP provides for tailored exercise activities that serve as the Department's primary vehicle for training national leaders and staff. The NEP enhances the collaboration among partners at all levels of government for assigned homeland security missions. National-level exercises provide the means to conduct "full-scale, full system tests" of collective preparedness, interoperability, and collaboration across all levels of government and the private sector. The program also incorporates elements to allow DHS to identify the implications of changes to homeland security strategies, plans, technologies, policies, and procedures.

The cornerstone of national performance-based exercises is the Top Officials (TOPOFF), biennial exercise series. TOPOFF included a functional exercise in 2000 (TOPOFF 1) and a full-scale exercise in 2003 (TOPOFF 2). TOPOFF 3 is the most comprehensive terrorism exercise ever conducted in the United States. Sponsored by the U.S. Department of Homeland Security's (DHS) Office of State and Local Government Coordination and Preparedness (SLGCP), TOPOFF 3 will exercise the nation's capacity to prevent, protect against, respond to, and recover from terrorist attacks involving weapons of mass destruction (WMDs). Joining DHS and other federal agencies in this important effort are the States of Connecticut and New Jersey, as well as two international partners, the United Kingdom and Canada. These countries will conduct simultaneous, related exercises.

Mutual Aid Agreements

Terrorists can strike anytime, anywhere. Crop dusters, power generating plants, dams and reservoirs, crops, livestock, trains and highways are among the resources that could be targets. Homeland security in the heartland is just as important as homeland security in America's largest cities.

First responders from communities outside major metropolitan areas who must protect large geographic areas with small populations face many response challenges. In fact, over half of our firefighters protect small or rural communities of fewer than 5,000 people. Many of these communities rely upon volunteer departments with scarce resources. Fewer than 10% of counties surveyed by the National Association of Counties said they are prepared to respond to a bioterrorist attack.

One of the best strategies to build capability in communities outside major metropolitan areas is to develop mutual aid agreements to share resources. First responders from smaller communities need assistance in organizing and developing the unified command and control procedures and protocols necessary for operationally sound mutual aid. These agreements will enable neighboring jurisdictions to share specialized resources, rather than duplicate them in every jurisdiction.

As an established mechanism for sharing or pooling limited resources to augment existing capabilities and supplementing jurisdictions that have exhausted existing resources due to disaster, mutual aid processes will help ensure that jurisdictions across the United States can benefit from each other's efforts to enhance their first response capabilities. Jurisdictions can use the funding provided under this initiative to create or improve their response capabilities, without duplicating their efforts. Many areas have little or no capability to respond to terrorist attack using weapons of mass destruction. Even the best prepared States and localities do not possess adequate resources to respond to the full range of terrorist threats we face.[12]

The cornerstone of national performance-based exercises is the Top Officials (TOPOFF), biennial exercise series.

Citizen Corps

In the wake of the terrorist attacks of September 11, 2001, Americans have looked for and found many opportunities to help in their communities. President Bush created the USA Freedom Corps in an effort to capture those opportunities and foster an American culture of service, citizenship and responsibility. These volunteers are especially important in smaller communities where resources may be limited.

Citizen Corps is the arm of USA Freedom Corps that provides opportunities for citizens that want to help make their communities more secure. Since the President made his call to two years of volunteer service during his State of the Union address, there have been more than 1.6 million hits to the new www.citizencorps.gov web site. Almost 24,000 Americans from all 50 states and U.S. territories have volunteered to work with one or more of the Citizen Corps programs. These include:

- More than 15,000 volunteers are looking to be trained in emergency response skills through FEMA's Community Emergency Response Team program;

- Almost 7,000 volunteers have signed up to get involved in Neighborhood Watch activities in their communities

- More than 15,000 potential volunteers have expressed interest in the new Volunteers in Police Service and Operation TIPS programs being developed by the Department of Justice presently; and,

- More than 5,000 potential volunteers have expressed an interest in joining a Medical Reserve Corps in their community as part of a program being developed by the Department of Health and Human Services to tap the skills of doctors, nurses and other health care professionals in times of community crisis.[13]

Conclusion

America's first line of defense in the aftermath of any terrorist attack is its first responder community—police officers, firefighters, emergency medical providers, public works personnel, and emergency management officials. Nearly three million state and local first responders regularly put their lives on the line to save the lives of others and make our country safer. The Department of Homeland Security is working to improve the technical capabilities of first responders, and ensure their readiness to work safely in areas where chemical, biological, radiological, or nuclear weapons have been used.

The Department of Homeland Security is establishing national standards for emergency response training and preparedness. These standards provide guidelines for the vaccination of civilian response personnel against certain biological agents. These standards also require certain coursework for individuals to receive and maintain certification as first responders and for state and local governments to receive federal grants. The Department has established a national exercise program to educate and evaluate civilian response personnel at all levels of government. The Department uses these exercises to measure performance and allocate future resources. The Department helps state and local agencies meet certification standards by providing grant money (based on performance) for planning and equipping, training, and exercising first responders for chemical, biological, radiological and nuclear attacks. In addition, the Department has launched a national research and development effort to create new technologies for detection and clean-up of such attacks. The Department consolidates all grant programs that distribute federal funds to state and local first responders.

The Department of Homeland Security has commenced a steady and long-term effort to provide first responders with technical capabilities for dealing with the effects of catastrophic threats—capabilities that would aid both first responders and victims of the attack. These capabilities include protective gear and masks, prophylactic treatments, and decontamination equipment. The Department has undertaken sustained efforts to develop treatments and decontamination methodologies for radiological and nuclear events. The Department is also focusing on developing new methods to merge disparate databases and provide first responders with accurate and usable pictures of building layouts and other key information about the site of a terrorist incident.

The President launched Citizen Corps in January 2002 to train volunteers to support our first responders by providing immediate help to victims and by organizing volunteers at disaster sites.

The National Strategy for Homeland Security recognizes that after an attack occurs, our greatest chance to minimize loss of life and property lies with our local first responders. Many of our efforts to minimize the damage focus on these brave and dedicated public servants.[14]

The National Strategy for Homeland Security recognizes that after an attack occurs, our greatest chance to minimize loss of life and property lies with our local first responders. Many of our efforts to minimize the damage focus on these brave and dedicated public servants.

Text

Questions

1. What is the critical role performed by first responders?

2. Describe some of the ways the Office of Domestic Preparedness supports first responders.

3. How does the Citizen Corps assist first responders?

Chapter 20

Exercise Programs

Objectives

- Describe the purpose of the National Exercise Program (NEP).

- Explain the relationship between the NEP and the Homeland Security Exercise Evaluation Program (HSEEP).

- Describe some of the different types of exercises and their purpose.

Past experience has shown that preparedness efforts are key to providing an effective response to major terrorist incidents and natural disasters. Therefore, we need a comprehensive national system to bring together and command all necessary response assets quickly and effectively. We must equip, train, and exercise many different response units to mobilize for any emergency without warning.

- National Strategy for Homeland Security, July 2002

Introduction

The Office for Domestic Preparedness (ODP) is the principal component of the U.S. Department of Homeland Security (DHS) responsible for preparing the United States for acts of terrorism. In carrying out its mission, DHS/ODP is the primary office that provides training, funds for the purchase of equipment, support for the planning and execution of exercises, technical assistance, and other support to all U.S. States and territories and the District of Columbia (hereafter referred to as "the States"), tribal governments, and local jurisdictions to prevent, plan for, and respond to acts of terrorism.

The DHS/ODP program management function encompasses monetary assistance as well as support of statewide risk and needs assessments; strategy development; management of DHS/ODP resources in planning, equipment, training, and exercises; and Federal agency coordination. Each State's preparedness program management is the responsibility of a State Administrative Agency (SAA) designated by the Governor.

- A DHS/ODP Preparedness Officer has been assigned to each State to serve as the primary contact for ODP assistance. The Preparedness Officer's role is to:

- Conduct a formal strategy review and assist each State in preparing and identifying the resources to implement a State Homeland Security Strategy.

- Review grant applications, prepare award documents, and administer grant programs.

- Assist States and designated urban areas with strategy implementation, including working with other Federal agencies to coordinate assistance (e.g., Homeland Defense Equipment Reuse [HDER] Program, which provides surplus U.S. Department of Energy (DOE) radiological detection equipment and support to State and local homeland security agencies).

- Coordinate DHS/ODP resources for equipment funding, training courses, and exercise programs.

Exercise Support

DHS/ODP-funded exercises are supported by two programs, the National Exercise Program (NEP) and the Homeland Security Exercise and Evaluation Program (HSEEP). NEP trains national leaders and departmental and agency staff, and facilitates collaboration among partners at all levels of government for assigned homeland security missions. HSEEP provides the overall doctrine and policy according to which all DHS/ ODP-funded exercises will be designed, developed, conducted, and evaluated.

National Exercise Program

The National Strategy for Homeland Security directed DHS to establish a National Exercise Program (NEP). The Secretary of Homeland Security tasked the Office of Domestic Preparedness (DHS/ODP) with developing this program and ensuring that it serves the broadest community of learning. All NEP exercises are conducted in accordance with Homeland Security Exercise and Evaluation Program (HSEEP) doctrine. NEP serves as the Department's primary vehicle for training national leaders and Department and agency staff members, and for promoting collaboration among partners at all levels of government for assigned homeland security missions. National-level exercises provide the means to conduct full-scale, full-system tests of collective preparedness, improve interoperability, build strong teams across all levels of government and the private sector, and develop and strengthen international partnerships. The program also incorporates experiments, test beds, and concept development initiatives to identify the implications of changes to homeland security strategies, plans, technologies, policies, and procedures.

Exercises designated as national are managed at the national level to effectively and efficiently use the limited resources and funding available for such efforts. These exercises generally involve national leaders and staffs, entities of two or more Federal agencies, and interaction with multiple regions and States. Such exercises may be congressionally mandated and may have particular political significance, or may be likely to receive national media attention. Efforts are made to include international and/or private-sector participation. The cornerstone of national performance-based exercises will be the Top Officials (TOPOFF) National Exercise Series, a biennial program that included a functional exercise (FE) in year one and a full-scale exercise (FSE) in year two, with continuity provided by a series of seminars.

National-level exercises provide the means to conduct full-scale, full-system tests of collective preparedness, improve interoperability, build strong teams across all levels of government and the private sector, and develop and strengthen international partnerships.

The strategic goals of NEP are:

- To meet the requirements of the National Strategy for Homeland Security, applicable Presidential Directives, the Homeland Security Act of 2002, and various legislative requirements.

- To provide periodic training and exercises for national leaders and their staffs, and the organizations and systems they lead.

- To provide the processes and systems for collaboration among homeland security partners at all levels of government by training and exercising their leaders and department and agency components and staffs with assigned homeland security missions.

- To achieve and sustain national preparedness by ensuring that proficiency can be measured against consensus performance standards, and performance-based assessments can be made across all levels of government, against a range of hazards and threats that pose the greatest risk to homeland security.

- To ensure that programs at all levels of government are synchronized and to administer the programs within the established framework of the National Incident Management System (NIMS).

The establishment of NEP includes development of tools that will be useful to exercise planners at all levels of government. A Web-based system comprising a suite of applications and a centralized database will be developed to provide automated support for homeland security training and exercise programs. The system will provide the means to conduct collaborative management and scheduling and will support reuse of exercise scenarios, documentation, tools, and other exercise investments; it will support activities throughout the cycle of design, planning, preparation, execution, evaluation, reporting, and improvement actions. DHS/ODP's goal is to have this system available for use during FY 2005.

DHS/ODP also develops and manages several national-level programs that focus on the Federal Government's coordination of Federal, State, and local resources to prevent and respond to terrorist attacks. Most of these programs involve designing and conducting exercises that are broad in scope and simulate a coordinated response by participants from a range of disciplines and multiple levels of government, including international participants.

TOPOFF is a congressionally mandated, national, biennial exercise series designed to assess the Nation's capability to prevent, respond to, and recover from acts of terrorism.

TOPOFF National Exercise Series

TOPOFF is a congressionally mandated, national, biennial exercise series designed to assess the Nation's capability to prevent, respond to, and recover from acts of terrorism. It examines relationships among Federal, State, and local jurisdictions in response to a challenging series of integrated, geographically dispersed terrorist threats and acts. Participation in TOPOFF is by application and subsequent invitation. DHS/ ODP manages the design, planning, conduct, and evaluation of the exercises. This exercise series is typically codirected by DHS/ODP and other Federal agencies or departments. TOPOFF 2000 was codirected by DHS/ODP and the Federal Emergency Management Agency (FEMA). TOPOFF 2, completed in May 2003, was co-directed by DHS/ODP and the U.S. Department of State.

National Special Security Event Exercises

The Federal Government designates certain events as requiring special security because of their high visibility and potential attractiveness to threat elements. DHS/ODP provides support for designing, planning, conducting, and evaluating exercises in preparation for designated National Special Security Events (NSSEs) such as the 2002 Winter Olympic Games in Salt Lake City. These exercises provide a forum to practice the coordination and response to specific challenges that could arise if a terrorist incident occurred during the event.

Senior Officials Exercises

A Senior Officials Exercise (SOE) is designed to validate policies or procedures, develop concepts or focus issues, or rehearse for specific events, at the policy level. (The policy level may include principals, deputies, senior department/ agency management, or combinations thereof.) DHS/ODP designs and logically execute SOEs as deemed necessary by senior leaders at DHS, the Homeland Security Council (HSC), or other agencies.

The focus for content development of an SOE is the agency whose mission is primarily affected by the events to be exercised. The exercise scenario are synchronized with ongoing events and preparedness activities that include sufficient, appropriate preparatory events to align staff efforts. The SOE evaluation process is structured around input from external subject matter experts. The resultant After Action Reports (AARs)/Improvement Plans (IPs) outline issues discovered during the exercise and recommendations for resolution. The agency responsible for each recommendation will provide periodic status updates on issue progress to HSC, the Homeland Security Deputies Committee, and the DHS Secretary's Office for input and approval.

Annual Evaluated Exercise and Exercise Credit

The National Strategy for Homeland Security delineates a requirement for conducting annual exercises: "The Department would establish a national exercise program designed to educate and evaluate civilian response personnel at all levels of government. It would require individuals and government bodies to complete successfully at least one exercise every year. The Department would use these exercises to measure performance and allocate future resources."

In accordance with this national strategy, NEP will require each State to perform an annual evaluated terrorism exercise, which may be conducted as either a local, regional, State, or multijurisdictional exercise. In the future, the program will identify the performance measures to be evaluated.

Beginning in FY 2006, the National Exercise Program (NEP) will require each State to perform an annual evaluated terrorism exercise, which may be conducted as either a local, regional, State, or multijurisdictional exercise.

Once operational, NEP will provide stipulations for exercise credit for certain prevention, response, and recovery actions during real-world incidents that fulfill the criteria of the appropriate performance measures. This will also include results from non-terrorism exercises.

This requirement will be effective beginning in FY 2006 and further guidelines will be provided at that time. Until the requirement takes effect, it is recommended that States conduct at least one annual full-scale evaluated terrorism exercise.

State and Local Exercises

State and local agencies and responders are at the core of preparedness efforts. DHS/ODP is one of several Federal agencies that make preparedness resources available to States and local jurisdictions. These resources include assistance with conducting counterterrorism exercises, which may range in scope from single-agency efforts to multijurisdictional conglomerations to the inclusion of Federal partners.

Exercises funded by DHS/ODP, possibly through a Homeland Security Grant Program (HSGP) or Urban Areas Security Initiative (UASI), must be conducted in accordance with the Homeland Security Exercise and Evaluation Program (HSEEP) doctrine. To ensure accordance with HSEEP, a DHS/ODP Exercise Manager is assigned to work with each State and its jurisdictions. As the HSGP grant application states, "State and local units of government should consider their DHS/ODP Exercise Manager as their point of contact for questions and concerns regarding implementation of HSEEP."

The role of the DHS/ODP Exercise Manager is to:

- Coordinate exercise activities for States and jurisdictions

- Review State Homeland Security Strategies and coordinate with DHS/ODP Preparedness Officers to allocate resources and identify needs based on each strategy

- Work in partnership with the State to conduct an Exercise Plan Workshop (EPW) designed to review and update the current Exercise Plan and schedule

- Assist each State with the development of a Multiyear Exercise Plan that defines exercise goals, establishes a cycle of exercises, and sets priorities for conducting exercises within the State

- Help each State implement a State Homeland Security Exercise and Evaluation Program (SHSEEP)

- Assist States and local jurisdictions with designing, developing, conducting, and evaluating exercises

- Aid States and local jurisdictions in obtaining exercise participation from Federal departments and agencies

- Coordinate and direct the delivery of direct exercise contractor support when requested and approved. Under the direction of DHS/ODP's Exercise Manager, contractor teams will assist States and jurisdictions with the following tasks:

    - Develop homeland security exercise programs

    - Develop specific exercise objectives

    - Prepare detailed exercise planning and execution timelines

    - Coordinate and conduct exercise planning conferences

    - Develop a full range of exercise documentation for each type of exercise

    - Prepare an exercise control and evaluation methodology and assist in actual exercise control and evaluation

- Prepare postexercise reports and conduct critiques

- Design and conduct national, special event, and regional exercises and share lessons learned and best practices with Federal, State, and local agencies

- Ensure accordance with HSEEP doctrine and policy by attending planning conferences, reviewing exercise documentation, and observing exercises.

Homeland Security Exercise and Evaluation Program

The Homeland Security Exercise and Evaluation Program (HSEEP) consists of both doctrine and policy for designing, developing, conducting, and evaluating exercises. HSEEP is a threat-and performance-based exercise program that includes a cycle, mix, and range of exercise activities of varying degrees of complexity and interaction. HSEEP is also a program of financial and direct support designed to assist State and local governments with the development and implementation of a State exercise and evaluation program to assess and enhance domestic preparedness.

Exercises are an instrument to train for and practice prevention, vulnerability reduction, response, and recovery capabilities in a risk-free environment. They also can be used to assess and improve performance. Exercises are also an excellent way to demonstrate community resolve to prepare for disastrous events. The U.S. Department of Homeland Security, Office for Domestic Preparedness (DHS/ODP), has a goal of helping jurisdictions gain an objective assessment of their capacity to prevent or respond to, and recover from, a disaster so that jurisdictions can make modifications or improvements prior to the occurrence of a real incident. Well-designed and executed exercises are the most effective means of:

The Homeland Security Exercise and Evaluation Program (HSEEP) consists of both doctrine and policy for designing, developing, conducting, and evaluating exercises.

- Testing and validating policies, plans, procedures, training, equipment, and interagency agreements

- Clarifying and training personnel in roles and responsibilities

- Improving interagency coordination and communications

- Identifying gaps in resources

- Improving individual performance

- Identifying opportunities for improvement

Doctrine

All entities conducting exercises using DHS/ODP funds are subject to the following HSEEP requirements:

- States will conduct an annual Exercise Plan Workshop (EPW) to examine the progress and effectiveness of the current exercise strategy and program.

- A Multiyear Exercise Plan will be produced from the EPW and submitted to DHS/ODP. This Exercise Plan will include guidelines for the establishment of a State Homeland Security Exercise and Evaluation Program (SHSEEP) and a multiyear exercise schedule (to be updated annually).

- The Exercise Plan will employ a cycle of activity that includes exercises of increasing levels of complexity.

- The scenarios used in exercises will be terrorism related and threat based.

- All tabletop exercises (TTXs), drills, functional exercises (FEs), and full-scale exercises (FSEs) will be evaluated and performance based.

- An After Action Report (AAR) will be prepared and submitted to DHS/ODP following every TTX, drill, FE, and FSE.

- An Improvement Plan (IP) will be developed, submitted to DHS/ODP, and implemented to address findings and recommendations identified in the AAR.

- Periodic exercise scheduling and improvement implementation data will be reported to DHS/ODP.

SHSEEP

The Multiyear Exercise Plan submitted to DHS/ODP includes guidelines for establishing a SHSEEP. The plan will address the State and local exercise requirements (consistent with the State Homeland Security Strategy) and should define exercise goals, establish a cycle of exercises, and set priorities for conducting exercises within the State.

Using this plan as a foundation, the State should build its own exercise and evaluation program by incorporating requirements and guidance consistent with the national HSEEP model. For a State program to be consistent with HSEEP, each State should ensure that the exercise program addresses the following elements:

- Obtains grants and funding (annually).

- Identifies roles and responsibilities (e.g., hire full- or part-time staff or consultants for exercise program development and management).

- Develops and maintains the State's Multiyear Exercise Plan and its schedule and timeline.

- Develops the State's own means of monitoring exercises conducted throughout the State's jurisdictions and ensures compliance with HSEEP requirements.

- Designates an agency or organization that will serve as a clearinghouse for all exercises occurring throughout the State.

- Establishes a means of monitoring and compliance to ensure exercise program requirements are being met (e.g., submitting receipts, applying for grants, submitting documentation, scheduling planning conferences and exercise conduct).

- Conducts annual activities to review the program, ensures that the State's objectives are being met, revises or updates existing Multiyear Exercise Plans, and conducts EPWs.

- Meets Federal reporting requirements.

- Meets internal State reporting and briefing requirements.

State Strategies

The State Homeland Security Strategy development process begins in the assessment phase when States and jurisdictions conduct vulnerability, risk, and needs assessments. Using the knowledge gained in this phase, the State proceeds to develop plans and procedures and analyze planning, equipment, training, and exercise requirements. The results of this analysis are used to form the State Homeland Security Strategy.

After the strategy is distributed and all agencies have familiarized themselves with it, local communities work with the State to conduct EPWs. An EPW translates strategic goals and priorities into specific objectives and exercise activities and develops a multiyear timeline for conducting realistic and threat-based scenario exercises. These exercises are evaluated to identify and validate State and community preparedness. AARs are written after each exercise to document results and are then used to develop a jurisdiction's IP, which uses lessons learned and best practices to revise and update the State Homeland Security Strategy. Lessons learned also may dictate immediate special attention to areas with deficiencies.

All exercises conducted with Homeland Security Grant Program (HSGP) or Urban Areas Security Initiative (UASI) grant funds must focus on terrorism threats.

Threat-Based Scenarios

Attacks by international and domestic terrorists have demonstrated that no location is immune to attack. All exercises conducted with Homeland Security Grant Program (HSGP) or Urban Areas Security Initiative (UASI) grant funds must focus on terrorism threats. The exercise scenario should be appropriate to national threat conditions and the assessed threat for the jurisdictions involved in the exercise. This will enhance the exercise's training value and provide an opportunity to assess the jurisdiction's vulnerability in light of likely prevention or response actions. Exercise planners should review the jurisdiction's threat assessment (conducted as part of the State strategy development process) and develop an exercise scenario that is credible in terms of the means of attack, the target, and the likely opposing force. To assist State and local agencies, an interagency team of subject matter experts has developed a suite of common scenarios that provide the necessary conditions and stimuli to perform essential tasks and cover a range of threat probabilities. These scenarios will be validated by intelligence and law enforcement and will be periodically reviewed and updated. Once finalized, these scenarios will be provided to State and local agencies as a component of strategic planning guidance that will help with operational planning, training, exercises, evaluations, and assessments.

Performance of Plans, Policies, and Procedures

Exercises conducted under HSEEP should be performance based and require demonstration, practical application, and evaluation of proficiency for the discrete, essential tasks that enable a homeland security mission or function to be successfully accomplished. Discussion-based exercises such as seminars, workshops, TTXs, and games provide a forum for reviewing the adequacy of plans, policies, functions, and interagency/interjurisdictional agreements, whereas operations-based exercises such as drills, FEs, and FSEs are designed to validate personnel and equipment performance in achieving critical tasks and homeland security missions.

The exercise evaluation methodology, defined in HSEEP Volume II: Exercise Evaluation and Improvement, is designed to analyze performance at three levels, depending on the complexity of the exercise. For discussion-based exercises, the evaluation focuses on the adequacy of and familiarity with the jurisdiction's plans, policies, procedures, resources, and interagency/interjurisdictional relationships. For operations-based exercises, evaluators observe and assess actual performance in preventing or responding to a simulated terrorist attack.

Prevention Exercises

The importance of prevention is made clear in the executive summary of the National Strategy for Homeland Security. The strategic objectives of homeland security in order of priority are to:

- Prevent terrorist attacks within the United States.

- Reduce U.S. vulnerability to terrorism.

- Minimize damage and facilitate recovery from attacks that may occur.

State and local jurisdictions should try to incorporate as many preventive exercises into their programs as possible. These exercises can be either discussion or operations based and may focus on issues pertaining to:

- Information and intelligence sharing

- Credible threats

- Surveillance

- Opposing/adversary force or "red team" activity

The National Strategy for Homeland Security identifies a requirement to employ red team techniques to practice detecting terrorist activity before it manifests itself in an attack, with a goal of allowing proper preemptive, preventive, and protective actions to be taken. The red team mission is to apply knowledge of terrorists' motivations, organization, targeting, tactics, techniques, procedures, weapons, and equipment and assess Federal, State, and local governments' ability to deter, detect, and defend against and defeat terrorist attacks.

DHS/ODP employs strategic and tactical red team techniques in the National Exercise Program (NEP) and has targeted resources available to provide such an enhancement to specific State and local exercises conducted in accordance with HSEEP. States will be able to request an opportunity to employ a red team and/or universal adversary force in their State and local exercises. Such requests will be considered and granted based both on the availability of resources and scheduling and on the State's level of demonstrated exercise competency.

Response and Recovery Exercises

Although the prevention and deterrence of attacks are paramount, it remains probable that incidents will occur. Therefore, exercises should also include the response and recovery aspects of an event in addition to prevention. Response and recovery issues in an exercise may include notification, communication, command and control, remediation, return to normalcy, and continuity of government and business.

Interagency/Interjurisdictional Exercises

Although the prevention and deterrence of attacks are paramount, it remains probable that incidents will occur. Therefore, exercises should also include the response and recovery aspects of an event in addition to prevention.

Because the prevention of and/or response to a crisis situation will require resources and expertise from various agencies and disciplines throughout the Federal, State, and local government structures, an exercise should assess the capacity of multiple organizations and the effectiveness of interagency cooperation and interoperable communication. The organizations involved in an exercise may be public or private, from any level of government, and from disciplines ranging from public health to fire, as long as they reflect the type of exercise and scenario. Jurisdictions that would rely heavily on mutual aid assistance for response should include participants from the agencies with which they have agreements and compacts. It is also beneficial to conduct regional exercises that include participants from multiple agencies and jurisdictions, because such a scenario would likely reflect actual response to an event.

Private-Sector Coordination

Exercise scenarios mimic actual response to the greatest extent possible; therefore, local and State government agencies are encouraged to incorporate the private sector. The range of terrorist targets is not limited to civilian populations or government facilities. The private sector can be a target of terrorism because it is often viewed as a symbol of American economic, social, and military power or as an extension of the U.S. Government. The private sector includes commercial, business, and industrial facilities, tourist attractions, and special events. It also includes the personnel, source material (if a production entity), and support systems (for example, transportation capabilities) of such entities.

Private-sector preparedness and response activities often mirror those of the surrounding communities. Recognizing this need, DHS/ODP supports States' efforts to incorporate major community businesses and facilities into their SHSEEPs. For example, in one realistic scenario, a California community held its chemical FSE at a major industrial plant and used plant employees as victim actors. Another example of private-sector involvement is the DHS/ODP initiative to exercise the evacuation plans of Major League Baseball stadiums.

Private response capabilities, such as fire brigades, security forces, and medical staff, can augment local response capabilities and remove a significant burden from limited local resources during critical situations. In a real incident, these resources and activities should be available for mutual aid, and they should be exercised as such. Other examples of exercise contributions available from private industry include railroad lines, factory and other facilities, personal protective equipment (PPE), hazardous materials (HazMat) control and other content expertise, and personnel to serve as controllers, evaluators, or logistical support. Furthermore, in a real incident, private industry would be included in the Incident Command System (ICS) structure in the form of public works, hospitals, and other response entities.

Regional/International Exercises

The private sector can be a target of terrorism because it is often viewed as a symbol of American economic, social, and military power or as an extension of the U.S. Government.

Participation in regional and international exercises is a crucial aspect of emergency preparedness for many communities across the country. From Seattle and Vancouver to San Diego and Tijuana, communities need to plan with their neighbors for emergencies that cross State or national borders. Terrorist incidents do not stop at political borders, and neither should preparedness activities. Interstate and international resources should be incorporated into plans and used as appropriate. In some locales, such as in the Pacific Islands, international assistance is the closest available mutual aid. Communities should familiarize themselves with the resources available from potential regional and international partners and share their response concepts and standard/emergency operating procedures (SOPs/EOPs) with these groups.

DHS/ODP supports regional planning and exercise efforts and has conducted exercises with numerous international partners. The Urban Areas Security Initiative (UASI) grant program requires the formation of an Urban Area Working Group (UAWG) to collaborate on assessment and planning for urban areas and their surrounding communities and stakeholders; thus, many related exercises will be conducted on the regional level. During the Top Officials (TOPOFF 2) National Exercise Series, Canadian agencies participated as if real-world incidents had occurred in Seattle or Chicago. Plans to involve international partners in future national exercises and bordering State-sponsored exercises are currently in review.

Resources To Implement HSEEP

DHS/ODP provides a range of assistance under HSEEP to aid State and local jurisdictions with implementation of effective exercises. Types of assistance are described below. Grant Funds States receive an annual allocation of grant funds from DHS/ODP and may use a portion of the funds to enhance the prevention and response capabilities of States and local jurisdictions through terrorism exercises.

Exercise Funding

As part of their formula grant awards, States and urban areas receive exercise funding from DHS/ODP. These funds may be used for the following purposes:

- Expenses related to convening a statewide Exercise Plan Workshop (EPW).

- Hiring of full- or part-time staff or contractors/consultants to support exercise activities.

- Overtime for first responder/exercise management personnel involved in planning and conducting exercises.

- Travel associated with planning and conducting exercises.

- Supplies consumed during the course of planning and conducting exercises.

- Costs related to HSEEP implementation, including reporting of scheduled exercises and tracking and reporting of AARs and IPs from exercises.

- Other costs related to planning and conducting exercise activities

Direct Exercise Support

DHS/ODP has engaged multiple contractors with significant experience in designing, conducting, and evaluating exercises to provide support to States and local jurisdictions in accordance with State Homeland Security Strategies and HSEEP. Contract support is available to help States develop a Multiyear Exercise Plan and build or enhance the capacity of States and local jurisdictions to design, develop, conduct, and evaluate effective exercises. If a State decides to hire a private contractor, the State must ensure the contractor will follow HSEEP requirements and guidance.

Secure Web-Based Portal

All HSEEP reference manuals and materials are available through DHS/ODP's secure Web-based portal, which provides an environment in which sensitive documents and materials can be posted and continually updated or enhanced. The exercise portion of the portal contains a library of sample exercise materials (e.g., HSEEP Volume IV) as well as the text of HSEEP Volumes I, II, and III. The portal also includes an exercise scheduler and reporting system that allows States and local jurisdictions to schedule exercises, submit AAR/IPs, and report exercise data.

Access to the portal will be granted through the State Administrative Agency (SAA) or its designated exercise or training coordinators. A jurisdiction that would like access to the portal should contact its respective State agency,

As part of their formula grant awards, States and urban areas receive exercise funding from DHS/ODP.

which will send out invitations through e-mail.

Exercise Toolkit

DHS/ODP is developing an Exercise Planning Toolkit that will provide exercise planners with an interactive computer-based tool to help design, develop, and execute viable and effective exercises. The toolkit will help standardize the methods used to plan and conduct exercises and evaluate results.

Lessons Learned and Best Practices

Exercises and the resultant AARs/IPs not only provide lessons for exercise participants, they also offer a valuable source of information that can be analyzed at the national level to identify lessons learned and best practices that can be shared to enhance preparedness across the country. Lessons learned should encompass knowledge and experience (positive and negative) derived from observations and historical study of actual operations, training, and exercises. Best practices should encompass peer-validated techniques, procedures, and solutions that work and are solidly grounded in actual experience in operations, training, and exercises. Exercise AARs should identify lessons and highlight exemplary practices, and should be submitted to DHS/ODP for inclusion in the lessons learned/best practices Web portal (www.llis.gov), which will serve as a national network for generating, validating, and disseminating lessons learned and best practices.

With support and oversight from DHS/ODP, the National Memorial Institute for the Prevention of Terrorism (MIPT) in Oklahoma City has developed this secure Web-based network of peer-validated best practices and lessons learned. This network, known as Lessons Learned Information Sharing (LLIS), is designed to help emergency responders, homeland security officials, and healthcare professionals learn from each other and share information. LLIS offers access to a wide variety of original best practices and lessons learned, developed in consultation with frontline emergency responders and validated by emergency response and homeland security professionals. In addition to providing original best practices and lessons learned, the system also serves as a clearinghouse for domestic preparedness

Lessons learned should encompass knowledge and experience (positive and negative) derived from observations and historical study of actual operations, training, and exercises. Best practices should encompass peer-validated techniques, procedures, and solutions that work and are solidly grounded in actual experience in operations, training, and exercises.

Exercise Types

The type of exercise that best meets a jurisdiction's requirements is identified through analysis of the stated exercise purpose, proposed objectives, experience, operations, historical precedence, and recommended levels of participation. A specified planning process from concept development through conduct and evaluation has been defined for each type of exercise.

Discussion-Based Exercises

Discussion-based exercises are normally used as a starting point in the building block approach to the cycle, mix, and range of exercises. Discussion-based exercises include seminars, workshops, tabletop exercises (TTXs), and games. These types of exercises typically highlight existing plans, policies, mutual aid agreements, and procedures. Thus, they are exceptional tools for familiarizing agencies and personnel with current or expected jurisdictional capabilities. Discussion-based exercises typically focus on strategic, policy-oriented issues, and operations-based exercises tend to focus more on tactical response-related issues. Facilitators and/or presenters usually lead the discussion, keeping participants on track while meeting the objectives of the exercise.

Seminars

Seminars are generally employed to orient participants to, or provide an overview of, authorities, strategies, plans, policies, procedures, protocols, response resources, or concepts and ideas. Seminars provide a good starting point for jurisdictions that are developing or making major changes to their plans and procedures. They offer the following attributes:

- Low-stress environment employing a number of instruction techniques such as lectures, multimedia presentations, panel discussions, case study discussions, expert testimony, and decision support tools.

- Informal discussions led by a seminar leader.

- Lack of time constraints caused by real-time portrayal of events.

- Effective with both small and large groups.

Workshops

Workshops represent the second tier of exercises in the HSEEP building block approach. Although similar to seminars, workshops differ in two important aspects: participant interaction is increased, and the focus is on achieving or building a product (such as a plan or a policy). Workshops provide an ideal forum for:

- Collecting or sharing information

- Obtaining new or different perspectives

- Testing new ideas, processes, or procedures

- Training groups in coordinated activities

- Problem solving of complex issues

- Obtaining consensus

- Team building

In conjunction with exercise development, workshops are most useful in achieving specific aspects of exercise design such as:

- Determining program or exercise objectives.

- Developing exercise scenario and key events listings.

- Determining evaluation elements and standards of performance.

A workshop may be used to produce new standard/emergency operating procedures (SOPs/EOPs), mutual aid agreements, Multiyear Exercise Plans, and Improvement Plans (IPs). To be effective, workshops must be highly focused on a specific issue and the desired outcome or goal must be clearly defined.

Potential relevant topics and goals are numerous, but all workshops share the following common attributes:

- Low-stress environment

- No-fault forum

- Information conveyed employing different instructional techniques

- Facilitated, working breakout sessions

- Plenum discussions led by a workshop leader

- Goals oriented toward an identifiable product

- Lack of time constraint from real-time portrayal of events

- Effective with both small and large groups

Tabletop Exercises

TTXs involve senior staff, elected or appointed officials, or other key personnel in an informal setting, discussing simulated situations. This type of exercise is intended to stimulate discussion of various issues regarding a hypothetical situation. It can be used to assess plans, policies, and procedures or to assess types of systems needed to guide the prevention of, response to, and recovery from a defined event. TTXs typically are aimed at facilitating understanding of concepts, identifying of strengths and shortfalls, and/or achieving a change in attitude. Participants are encouraged to discuss issues in depth and develop decisions through slow-paced problem solving rather than the rapid, spontaneous decision-making that occurs under actual or simulated emergency conditions. In contrast to the scale and cost of operations-based exercises and games, TTXs can be a cost-effective tool when used in conjunction with more complex exercises. The effectiveness of a TTX is derived from the energetic involvement of participants and their assessment of recommended revisions to current policies, procedures, and plans.

TTX methods are divided into two categories: basic and advanced. In a basic TTX, the scene set by the scenario materials remains constant. It describes an event or emergency incident and brings discussion participants up to the simulated present time. Players apply their knowledge and skills to a list of problems presented the leader/moderator, problems are discussed as a group, and resolution is generally agreed on and summarized by the leader. In an advanced TTX, play revolves around delivery of pre-scripted messages to players that alter the original scenario. The exercise controller (moderator) usually introduces problems one at a time in the form of a written message, simulated telephone call, videotape, or other means. Participants discuss the issues raised by the problem, using appropriate plans and procedures. TTX attributes may include:

- Practicing group problem solving.

- Familiarizing senior officials with a situation.

- Conducting a specific case study.

- Examining personnel contingencies.

- Testing group message interpretation.

- Participating in information sharing.

- Assessing interagency coordination.

- Achieving limited or specific objectives.

Games

A game is a simulation of operations that often involves two or more teams, usually in a competitive environment, using rules, data, and procedures designed to depict an actual or assumed real-life situation. It does not involve the use of actual resources, and the sequence of events affects, and is in turn affected by, the decisions made by the players.

Players are commonly presented with scenarios and asked to perform a task associated with the scenario episode. As each episode moves to the next level of detail or complexity, it takes into account players' earlier decisions; thus, the decisions made by participants determine the flow of the game. The goal is to explore decision-making processes and the consequences of those decisions. In a game, the same situation can be examined from various perspectives by changing the variables and parameters that guide player actions. Large-scale games can be multijurisdictional and include active participation from Federal, State, and local governments. Games stress the importance of planners' and players' understanding and comprehension of interrelated processes.

With the evolving complexity and sophistication of current simulations, opportunities to provide enhanced realism for game participants have increased. Computer-generated scenarios and simulations can provide a more realistic and time-sensitive method of introducing situations for analysis. Planner decisions can be input and models run to show the effect of decisions made during a game. Distributed games (available via the Internet) offer many additional benefits, such as saving participants' time and travel expenses, offering more frequent training opportunities, and taking less time away from primary functions. They also provide a collaborative environment that reflects realistic occurrences. Games are excellent vehicles for the following:

- Gaining policy or process consensus.

- Conducting "what-if" analyses of existing plans.

- Developing new plans.

DHS/ODP conducts ongoing analysis of commercial- and government-sector models, games, and simulations to identify those of value for exercise use. Although models, games, and simulations are not a substitute for full-scale exercises (FSEs), they are an increasingly more sophisticated and useful component of exercise programs. DHS/ODP has issued a list of government and commercially developed models, games, and simulations that have been evaluated against its training and exercise requirements for the enhancement of homeland security preparedness.

Operations-Based Exercises

Operations-based exercises represent the next iteration of the exercise cycle; they are used to validate the plans, policies, agreements, and procedures solidified in discussion-based exercises. Operations-based exercises include drills, functional exercises (FEs), and FSEs. They can clarify roles and responsibilities, identify gaps in resources needed to implement plans and procedures, and improve individual and team performance. Operations-based exercises are characterized by actual response, mobilization of apparatus and resources, and commitment of personnel, usually over an extended period of time.

Drills

A drill is a coordinated, supervised activity usually employed to test a single specific operation or function in a single agency. Drills are commonly used to provide training on new equipment, develop or test new policies or procedures, or practice and maintain current skills. Typical attributes include:

- A narrow focus, measured against established standards

- Instant feedback

- Realistic environment

- Performance in isolation

Functional Exercises

The FE, also known as a command post exercise (CPX), is designed to test and evaluate individual capabilities, multiple functions or activities within a function, or interdependent groups of functions. FEs are generally focused on exercising the plans, policies, procedures, and staffs of the direction and control nodes of Incident Command (IC) and Unified Command (UC). Generally, events are projected through an exercise scenario with event updates that drive activity at the management level. Movement of personnel and equipment is simulated. The objective of the FE is to execute specific plans and procedures and apply established policies, plans, and procedures under crisis conditions, within or by particular function teams. An FE simulates the reality of operations in a functional area by presenting complex and realistic problems that require rapid and effective responses by trained personnel in a highly stressful environment. Attributes of an FE include:

- Evaluating functions

- Evaluating Emergency Operations Centers (EOCs), headquarters, and staff

- Reinforcing established policies and procedures

- Measuring resource adequacy

- Examining interjurisdictional relationships

Full-Scale Exercises

The FSE is the most complex step in the exercise cycle. FSEs are multiagency, multijurisdictional exercises that test many facets of emergency response and recovery. They include many first responders operating under the Incident Command System (ICS) or Unified Command System (UCS) to effectively and efficiently respond to, and recover from, an incident. An FSE focuses on implementing and analyzing the plans, policies, and procedures developed in discussion-based exercises and honed in previous, smaller, operations-based exercises. The events are projected through a scripted exercise scenario with built-in flexibility to allow updates to drive activity. It is conducted in a real-time, stressful environment that closely mirrors a real event. First responders and resources are mobilized and deployed to the scene where they conduct their actions as if a real incident had occurred (with minor exceptions). The FSE simulates the reality of operations in multiple functional areas by presenting complex and realistic problems requiring critical thinking, rapid problem solving, and effective responses by trained personnel in a highly stressful environment. Other entities that are not involved in the exercise, but who would be involved in an actual event, should be instructed not to respond.

An FSE provides an opportunity to execute plans, procedures, and cooperative (mutual aid) agreements in response to a simulated live event in a highly stressful environment. Typical FSE attributes include:

- Assessing organizational and individual performance.

- Demonstrating interagency cooperation.

- Allocating resources and personnel.

- Assessing equipment capabilities.

- Activating personnel and equipment.

- Assessing interjurisdictional cooperation.

- Exercising public information systems.

- Testing communications systems and procedures.

- Analyzing memorandums of understanding (MOUs), SOPs, plans, policies, and procedures.

The level of support needed to conduct an FSE is greater than needed during other types of exercises. The exercise site is usually extensive with complex site logistics. Food and water must be supplied to participants and volunteers. Safety issues, including those surrounding the use of props and special effects, must be monitored.

FSE controllers ensure that participants' behavior remains within predefined boundaries. Simulation Cell (SIMCELL) controllers continuously inject scenario elements to simulate real events. Evaluators observe behaviors and compare them against established plans, policies, procedures, and standard practices (if applicable). Safety controllers ensure all activity is executed within a safe environment.

Transportation Security Administration Exercises

The Aviation and Transportation Security Act, Pub. L. 107–71, gave the Transportation Security Administration (TSA) the responsibility for security across all modes of transportation. TSA is responsible for intermodal transportation security planning, prevention/protection measures, and preparedness initiatives. TSA, through regulatory development, intends to implement a National Intermodal Transportation Security Exercise and Evaluation Program (NITSEEP) as a mechanism to evaluate the effectiveness of the transportation industry's security plans and to ensure the national transportation system's preparedness to withstand or respond to a terrorist attack. TSA recognizes the U.S. Department of Homeland Security, Office for Domestic Preparedness (DHS/ODP) HSEEP program as an effective tool for the transportation industry to use to meet the intent of TSA regulations. Therefore, TSA recommends that an owner or operator subject to its regulations follow the guidelines set forth in HSEEP to fulfill the requirements. Currently, there is no direct HSEEP-related funding for owners and operators subject to TSA exercise requirements; however, those owners and operators who participate in a DHS/ODP-sponsored exercise will receive credit for a TSA-mandated exercise.

Emergency Preparedness and Response Exercises

The Chemical Stockpile Emergency Preparedness Program (CSEPP) is a partnership between the Federal Emergency Management Agency (FEMA) and the U.S. Army that intends to help communities surrounding the eight U.S. chemical stockpile sites enhance their abilities to respond in the unlikely event of a chemical agent emergency. CSEPP exercises focus on partnerships among Federal, State, and local jurisdictions involved in the program, which is administered through the States. CSEPP communities have been recognized nationally for their abilities to respond to emergencies of all kinds. Many of the lessons learned in CSEPP are used in industry and CSEPP employs partnerships with other public safety organizations to ensure that the knowledge gained has the greatest benefit for the most people. CSEPP activities include:

- Improving public warning capabilities.

- Building and upgrading state-of-the-art Emergency Operations Centers (EOCs).

- Training emergency managers and first responders.

- Including functional exercises (FEs) that improve readiness.

- Increasing public knowledge and understanding of protective actions.

- Overpressurizing schools to ensure children's safety.

- Studying emergency response options to determine the best way to protect communities.

- Training doctors and nurses to treat victims of chemical agent exposure.

Radiological Emergency Preparedness Program

The mission of the Radiological Emergency Preparedness (REP) program is to enhance planning, preparedness, and response for all types of peacetime radiological emergencies among all Federal, State, and local governments and the private sector, and to ensure that adequate offsite emergency plans and preparedness are in place and can be implemented by State and local governments. Emergency plans must protect the health and safety of the public living in the vicinity of commercial nuclear power plants and must be evaluated through biennial exercises.

Master Exercise Practitioner Program

The FEMA Emergency Management Institute (EMI) Master Exercise Practitioner Program (MEPP) is a performance-based curriculum focusing on the competencies required to plan, develop, design, conduct, and evaluate jurisdiction-specific exercises. The Resident MEPP consists of three resident courses and eight proficiency demonstration activities and the Nonresident MEPP requires the completion of several independent study courses and several additional courses administered by the appropriate State Emergency Management Agency. A Nonresident MEPP candidate may complete the training and proficiency demonstration requirements by enrolling in the exercise practicum, a unique self-directed and -negotiated series of 11 proficiency demonstrations. The MEPP candidate is challenged to apply the knowledge, skills, and abilities acquired through participation in Comprehensive Exercise Curriculum (CEC) courses to emergency management exercises. Additional information is available at http:// training.fema.gov/EMIWeb.

Metropolitan Medical Response System

The primary focus of the Metropolitan Medical Response System (MMRS) program is to develop or enhance existing emergency preparedness systems to effectively respond to a public health crisis, especially a weapons of mass destruction (WMD) event. Through preparation and coordination, local law enforcement, fire, hazardous materials (HazMat), emergency medical services (EMS), hospital, public health, and other first-responder personnel plan how to more effectively respond in the first 48 hours of a public health crisis.

Strategic National Stockpile Exercises

An act of terrorism (or a large-scale natural disaster) targeting the U.S. civilian population will require rapid access to large quantities of pharmaceuticals and medical supplies; such quantities may not be readily available unless special stockpiles are created. No one can anticipate exactly where a terrorist will strike and few State or local governments have the resources to create sufficient stockpiles on their own. Therefore, a national stockpile has been created as a resource for all.

The Homeland Security Act of 2002 tasked DHS with defining the goals and performance requirements of the Strategic National Stockpile (SNS) program (formerly the National Pharmaceutical Stockpile) as well as managing the actual deployment of its assets. The SNS program is managed jointly by DHS and the U.S. Department of Health and Human Services (HHS) and works with governmental and nongovernmental partners to upgrade the Nation's response capacity. Ensuring capacity is developed at the Federal, State, and local levels to receive, stage, and dispense SNS assets is critical to the success of this initiative.

The SNS program is committed to participating in one external (defined as involving an actual deployment of personnel and material) exercise each month. The SNS Exercise Life Cycle formalizes the process the SNS program uses to receive, process, and approve requests for exercise participation. The SNS Exercise Life Cycle spans more than 10 months, 9 prior to and 1 after the date of the exercise. Requests for SNS exercise support should be submitted a minimum of 9 months prior to an exercise; SNS exercise support is in high demand and may exceed the program's current capability. The SNS program also needs recovery time to refit specialized cargo containers and prepare them for shipment to the next exercise. The program prioritizes requests based on the order of receipt, the educational value of the request, previous opportunities provided to the requesting agency, resource requirements, and the exercise's proposed goals, objectives, and plans. Only the office of the director has the authority to commit SNS program participation in an exercise.

Coast Guard PREP

The U.S. Coast Guard (USCG) National Preparedness for Response Exercise Program (PREP) establishes an exercise program that meets the intent of section 4202(a) of the Oil Pollution Act of 1990 (OPA 90), amending section 311(j) of the Federal Water Pollution Control Act (FWPCA).

As described in the National Oil and Hazardous Substances Pollution Contingency plan (NCP 40 CFR 300), PREP focuses on exercise and evaluation government area contingency plans and industry spill response plans (oil and hazardous substance). PREP is a coordinated effort of the four Federal agencies with responsibility for oversight of private-sector oil and hazardous substance pollution response preparedness: USCG, the U.S. Environmental Protection Agency (EPA), the U.S. Department of Transportation's Research and Special Programs Administration (RSPA), and the U.S. Department of the Interior's Minerals Management Service (MMS). These agencies worked with Federal, State, and local governments, the oil and marine transportation industry, cleanup contractors, and the general public to develop the program. PREP meets the OPA mandate for exercises and represents minimum guidelines for ensuring overall preparedness within the response community. It also recognizes the economic and operational constraints faced by those affected by the exercise requirements. The guidelines, which are reviewed periodically through a public workshop process, outline an exercise program that satisfies the exercise requirements of the four Federal regulatory agencies.

PREP requires each industry response plan holder and government area contingency plan holder to engage in a series of exercises aimed at assessing the entire plan over the course of a 3-year cycle. Most of these exercises are conducted wholly within the plan holder's organization each year, including:

- Quarterly notification exercise to assess internal communications and coordination.

- Quarterly emergency procedures exercise to assess initial actions of facility or vessel personnel in the event of a spill emergency.

- Equipment deployment exercise to assess capability of response personnel and equipment in executing response strategies contained in the plan (semiannually if owned, annually if contracted).

- Annual spill management team exercise to assess plan holder's spill response management organization and its ability to implement and manage response plan strategies and resources.

- Unannounced exercise using one or more of the above exercise types to assess ongoing readiness to respond quickly in an emergency (at least annually).

- Government and industry plan holders also interact in external exercises:

  - The government initiated a maximum of four unannounced exercises in each contingency planning area, in which the government oversight agency requires an industry plan holder to initiate response to a small discharge, including equipment mobilization and deployment.

  - Once every 3 years each USCG and EPA contingency planning area holds an area exercise involving major joint government and industry plan holders to assess cooperation, compatibility, and adequacy of strategies. It must include both the spill management team and equipment deployment exercises.

Spill of National Significance Exercise Program

A Spill of National Significance (SONS) is a rare catastrophic oil or hazardous substance spill event that captures national attention and requires the coordinated response of multiple Federal and State agencies over an extended period of time.

The USCG SONS Exercise Program increases awareness of USCG response protocols in place for responding to a catastrophic spill event. The exercise allows senior administration officials at both the regional and national levels to practice emergency interaction with Congress, the States, and industry in a nonemergency environment. The program's major objectives are:

- Increase national preparedness for a SONS scenario by engaging all levels of spill management in a coordinated response.

- Improve, through practice, the ability of the National Incident Commander (NIC) organization to manage a SONS incident.

- Maintain awareness by agency heads and lawmakers in Washington, D.C., of their role during a SONS response.

A SONS exercise typically consists of field, regional, and headquarters components all connected by a common scenario. The field-level exercise is a full-scale exercise (FSE) that tests the area contingency plan for one or more port areas. The NIC-level exercise tests a regional contingency plan and internal USCG policy directives and their ability (as they relate to the NIC) to effectively manage a SONS, and supports the field and headquarters components. The headquarters-level exercise brings together senior agency officials and industry representatives to discuss interagency issues and responsibilities. It tests the national contingency plan and appropriate USCG policy as they relate to a SONS response.

SONS exercises are conducted approximately every 2 to 3 years, alternating among East Coast, Gulf Coast, West Coast, and Great Lakes scenarios.

Conclusion

The National Strategy for Homeland Security and the Homeland Security Act of 2002 identify the "prevention of terrorist attacks within the United States" and "the reduction of vulnerability of the United States to terrorism" as national priorities, and call on first responders to "minimize the damage and assist in the recovery from terrorist attacks that do occur within the United States." The Homeland Security Act also transferred the Office for Domestic Preparedness (ODP) from the U.S. Department of Justice (DOJ) to the U.S. Department of Homeland Security (DHS), and assigned ODP "the primary responsibility within the executive branch of government to build and sustain the preparedness of the United States to reduce vulnerabilities, prevent, respond to, and recover from acts of terrorism."

Although effective approaches to planning, training, and exercises have been developed to mitigate the effects of natural and manmade disasters, homeland security professionals at all levels of government and in all types of communities must prepare to prevent and respond to new threats to public safety from terrorism involving the use of chemical, biological, radiological, nuclear, or explosive (CBRNE) weapons or cyber or agricultural hostility.

DHS/ODP has designed a National Exercise Program (NEP) to address the delta between the "all hazards" emergency response requirements needed for natural disasters and the specialized requirements related to terrorism. Under the Homeland Security Grant Program (HSGP), U.S. States and territories and the District of Columbia have conducted risk and needs assessments and developed homeland security strategies. DHS/ODP provides grant funds and direct support to help address the equipment, training, and exercise needs identified in these strategies.

The Homeland Security Exercise and Evaluation Program (HSEEP) delivers an exercise program that helps address identified planning, training, and equipment needs and provides homeland security professionals with the tools to plan, conduct, and evaluate exercises to improve overall preparedness.[1]

Questions

1. What is the purpose of the National Exercise Program (NEP)?

2. What is the relationship between NEP and the Homeland Security Exercise Evaluation Program (HSEEP)?

3. List and describe some of the different types of exercises and their purposes.

Chapter 21

Homeland Defense

Objectives

- Know the DoD's two primary roles in homeland security.

- Explain the difference between homeland security and homeland defense.

- Describe the DoD organizational structure supporting homeland security.

- Understand the restrictions placed on the military by Posse Comitatus.

- Comprehend the unique roles performed by the U.S. Coast Guard and National Guard.

The Department of Defense contributes to homeland security through its military missions overseas, homeland defense, and support to civil authorities.

- National Strategy for Homeland Security, July 2002

Introduction

For over a century the U.S. military has focused on expeditionary warfare overseas. Its participation in domestic operations has been sporadic and generally in response to natural disasters. With the heightened concern about large-scale terrorism, have come efforts to involve DOD more closely with federal, state and local agencies in their homeland security activities. DOD resources are unique in the government, both in their size and capabilities, and can be applied to both deter and respond to terrorist acts. While the DOD leadership is ready and willing to play a supporting role in these efforts, it wishes to maintain overseas military operations as the Department's primary focus, and avoid an inadvertent drain of fiscal, materiel, and personnel resources to the homeland security mission. In addition, longstanding reservations about the use of military forces domestically, and the consequent statutory limitations on their use, remain strong considerations. Secretary Rumsfeld stated before the House Select Committee on Homeland Security, there are three types of situations when DOD resources are called upon to assist civilian authorities:

1. *Extraordinary* circumstances that require traditional military missions, such as combat air patrols;

2. *Emergency* circumstances of catastrophic nature resulting from terrorist attack or natural disaster; and

3. Provision of *security assistance* at National Security Special Events, such as the Olympics.[1]

> The National Strategy for Homeland Security envisions that the Armed Forces should focus on defense of the homeland from external threats and play a limited, supporting role to civilian responders, primarily when these authorities are overwhelmed by catastrophic attacks or require application of expertise uniquely resident in the Armed Forces.

The National Strategy for Homeland Security envisions that the Armed Forces should focus on defense of the homeland from external threats and play a limited, supporting role to civilian responders, primarily when these authorities are overwhelmed by catastrophic attacks or require application of expertise uniquely resident in the Armed Forces. The new combatant command, U.S. Northern Command, has the lead in this aspect of civil support, as well as defense of the United States and its immediate periphery. Expanding the Armed Forces' role in law enforcement raises legal and constitutional questions in civil/military relations. Some believe that the military has unique planning and operational capabilities that should give the Armed Forces, particularly the National Guard and the Coast Guard, more of a leading role in homeland security efforts. Most National Guard leaders and military planners want the Guard to remain available for the full spectrum of possible duties, and fear that specialization on homeland security would be detrimental to overall military readiness.[2]

The Department of Defense makes a distinction between "homeland security" and "homeland defense" in defining its mission responsibilities. Homeland security is defined as:

> *"A concerted national effort to prevent terrorist attacks within the United States, reduce the vulnerability of the United States to terrorism, and minimize the damage and assist in the recovery from terrorist attacks."*

Homeland defense is defined as:

> *"The military protection of United States territory, domestic population, and critical defense infrastructure against external threats and aggression. It also includes routine, steady state activities designed to deter aggressors and to prepare U.S. military forces for action if deterrence fails."*[3]

Homeland Defense

The National Strategy for Homeland Security has three main thrusts: prevent terrorist attacks in the U.S., reduce U.S. vulnerability to terrorism, and minimize damage and recover from attack. The Strategy identifies the Department of Defense (DoD) as contributing to homeland security and supporting it by homeland defense operations, its military missions overseas, and support to civil authorities. DoD further defines homeland defense as the protection of U.S. sovereignty, territory, domestic population, and critical defense infrastructure against external threats and aggression. DoD is not a first responder; rather, it is prepared to provide support to U.S. civil authorities for domestic emergencies and for designated law enforcement and other activities. DoD has implemented significant organizational changes to enhance conduct of all three missions, establishing an Office of Homeland Defense within the Office of the Secretary of Defense and creating a new combatant command for homeland defense, U.S. Northern Command (NORTHCOM).[4]

The focus of DoD's efforts to combat terrorism is on bringing the fight to the terrorists abroad through the prosecution of the global war on terrorism.

The focus of DoD's efforts to combat terrorism is on bringing the fight to the terrorists abroad through the prosecution of the global war on terrorism. The first line of defense is abroad—to confront the enemy where he lives, trains, plans, and recruits, as is being done in Afghanistan and Iraq. The second line of defense also lies beyond the borders of the nation—the air and maritime avenues of approach – where the military will engage terrorists before they reach our borders. Inside our borders, the domestic law enforcement community is responsible for countering terrorist threats; and the Department of Defense stands ready to provide assets and capabilities in support of civil authorities, consistent with U.S. law.

Securing the Nation

Following the tragic events of 9/11, at the direction of the President and with Congressional support, DoD moved to establish new organizations focused on homeland defense and civil support: U.S. Northern Command (NORTHCOM) and the Office of the Assistant Secretary of Defense for Homeland Defense (ASD(HD)).

At the request of the Secretary of Defense, the Office of the Assistant Secretary of Defense for Homeland Defense was established by Congress in the Bob Stump National Defense Authorization Act for Fiscal Year 2003. The office was established in recognition of the need to have a focal point to assist the Secretary in improving policy and providing guidance to combatant commanders regarding air, ground, and maritime defense of U.S. territory and the conduct of support to civilian authorities. As provided in the establishing statutory language, the DoD Office of Homeland Defense is responsible for overall supervision of the homeland defense activities of DoD.

On October 1, 2002, DoD activated NORTHCOM, headquartered in Colorado Springs, Colorado. This is the first combatant command with a primary mission to defend the land, sea, and air approaches to the United States. NORTHCOM conducts operations within its assigned area of responsibility to deter, prevent, and defeat threats and aggression aimed at the United States, its territories, and interests. Accordingly, as directed by the President or Secretary of Defense, NORTHCOM would direct military operations within its area of responsibility, including combat operations. In addition, when directed by the President or Secretary of Defense, NORTHCOM would also provide military assistance to civil authorities to mitigate the results of disasters and catastrophes, including those resulting from a WMD attack.

The Office of the Assistant Secretary of Defense for Homeland Defense was established to assist the Secretary in improving policy and providing guidance to combatant commanders regarding air, ground, and maritime defense of U.S. territory and the conduct of support to civilian authorities.

NORTHCOM's area of responsibility includes the continental United States, Alaska, Canada, Mexico, and the surrounding water out to approximately 500 nautical miles. The defense of Hawaii and U.S. territories and possessions in the Pacific remains the responsibility of U.S. Pacific Command. The commander of NORTHCOM is also the commander of the bi-national U.S.-Canada North American Aerospace Defense Command (NORAD). NORTHCOM achieved full operational capability on September 11, 2003 and is able to conduct missions assigned in the Unified Command Plan.

Air domain. NORAD guards, patrols, and monitors the skies over Canada and the United States. Each and every day the men and women of the United States Air Force, United States Air Force Reserve, and the Air National Guard secure the skies over major metropolitan areas, historic monuments, and the nation's critical infrastructure. Since September 11, 2001, these dedicated professionals have executed over 30,000 air defense sorties and responded to over 1700 requests from the Federal Aviation Administration to intercept potential air threats.

Maritime domain. Similarly, the U.S. Navy mans the sea approaches to the United States and works with the U.S. Coast Guard to patrol international waters and our territorial seas. On a daily basis, the U.S. Navy monitors the blue water approaches to our nation's territorial seas, operating under new and expanded authority to interdict vessels potentially bearing terrorists or their weapons before they reach our shores. Further, under Operation NOBLE EAGLE, naval maritime surveillance and engagement forces are designated for transfer to NORTHCOM command and control when directed by the Secretary of Defense.

Land domain. The Homeland Security Act of 2002 assigns the Secretary of Homeland Security the responsibility for the security of the nation's borders. That responsibility includes preventing terrorists and instruments of terrorism from penetrating our borders, protecting our ports of entry, immigration enforcement, and ensuring the speedy, orderly, and efficient flow of lawful traffic and commerce. DoD's role in that border security mission is to provide support to civil authorities, principally the Department of Homeland Security (DHS), when appropriate. To that end, DoD is prepared to respond swiftly when required. DoD has established and maintains Quick Reaction Forces and Rapid Reaction Forces, which, when deployed, will operate under NORTHCOM command and control. These highly-trained U.S. Army and Marine Corps personnel are postured to respond to the full range of potential threats to the United States. Additionally, when authorized by the Secretary of Defense, in the case of a WMD attack, Joint Task Force Civil Support (JTF-CS) headquartered in Norfolk, Virginia, Joint Task Force Consequence Management East headquartered at Fort Gillem, Georgia, or Joint Task Force Consequence Management West headquartered at Fort Sam Houston, Texas, under the command and control of NORTHCOM, would provide consequence management support to civil authorities.

Readiness

DoD maintains the readiness of military forces to execute the full spectrum of homeland defense operations and to support civil authorities, when needed. To this end, DoD has hosted or participated in exercises including: Unified Defense (February 2003); TOPOFF 2 (May 2003); Determined Promise (August 2003); Livewire (October 2003); Scarlet Cloud (November 2003); and Unified Defense (February 2004). These exercises addressed a range of potential threats to the United States, from cyber attacks to bioterror attacks, and from radiological attacks to a nuclear detonation. The exercises support the DHS National Exercise Program (NEP) established by the December 2003 Homeland Security Presidential Directive-8 (HSPD-8) on National Preparedness. Homeland security and homeland defense exercises are critical in identifying gaps and potential weaknesses within each agency and across agencies in responding to terrorist attacks, including multiple, simultaneous challenges.

Critical Infrastructure Protection

The Homeland Security Act of 2002 assigned DHS the responsibility to develop a comprehensive national plan to protect our nation's critical infrastructure and key assets. The National Strategy to Secure Cyberspace (February 2003) and the National Strategy for the Physical Protection of Critical Infrastructure and Key Assets (February 2003), as well as HSPD-7 on Critical Infrastructure Identification, Prioritization, and Protection (December 2003), designate DoD as the Sector Specific Agency for the Defense Industrial Base sector. This designation recognizes DoD's important role in the protection of the nation's critical infrastructure that sustain our capability to defend our

Accordingly, as directed by the President or Secretary of Defense, NORTHCOM would direct military operations within its area of responsibility, including combat operations. In addition, when directed by the President or Secretary of Defense, NORTHCOM would also provide military assistance to civil authorities to mitigate the results of disasters and catastrophes, including those resulting from a WMD attack.

nation and fight its wars. In this capacity, DoD must work closely with private sector owners of critical defense infrastructure to deter, mitigate, or neutralize terrorist attacks in order to sustain military operations.

In September 2003, the Office of Homeland Defense was assigned the responsibility for Defense Critical Infrastructure Protection by the Secretary of Defense. Since then, it has consolidated Critical Infrastructure Protection (CIP) funding within the Office of the Secretary of Defense into a single program, managed by the newly-established Defense Program Office for Mission Assurance. This office conducts focused research and development using a systems approach for CIP activities supporting DoD missions. The DoD has also taken steps to protect critical defense installations and facilities from chemical, biological, radiological, and nuclear threats. Pentagon efforts are helping to develop DoD-wide installation protection standards and requirements, which will be applied at 200 other key installations over the next few years.

Homeland Security

In simpler terms, the DoD provides the military defense of our nation from all attacks that originate from abroad, while DHS protects the nation against, and prepares for, acts of terrorism.

DoD focuses on and is responsible for homeland defense, which is the protection of United States territory, domestic population, and critical defense infrastructure against external threats and aggression. It also includes routine, steady-state activities designed to deter aggressors and to prepare U.S. military forces for action if deterrence fails. DHS, on the other hand, focuses on homeland security, which is defined in the 2002 National Strategy for Homeland Security as "a concerted national effort to prevent terrorist attacks within the United States, reduce the vulnerability of the United States to terrorism, and minimize the damage and assist in the recovery from terrorist attacks."

In simpler terms, the Defense Department provides the military defense of our nation from all attacks that originate from abroad, while DHS protects the nation against, and prepares for, acts of terrorism. DoD is organized and prepared, however, at the direction of the President and the Secretary of Defense, to play a vital role in support of the DHS mission.[5]

In the context of homeland security, DOD will operate only in support of a civilian lead federal agency when needed, while the larger area of homeland defense it views as its primary mission. Pursuant to the DOD FY2003 authorizing legislation (P.L. 107-314, Sec. 902), DOD created the Assistant Secretary of Defense for Homeland Defense (ASD(HD)) who is charged with leading the department's activities in homeland defense and security. This office also serves as Secretary of Defense's liaison with the Department of Homeland Security, the National Security Council, and the Homeland Security Council.[6]

DoD/DHS Coordination

The Assistant Secretary of Defense for Homeland Defense maintains working relationships throughout the Department of Homeland Security. The DoD provides on a detail basis some sixty-four personnel to DHS to fill critical specialties, principally in the areas of communications and intelligence. There is a 24/7 DoD presence in the DHS Homeland Security Operations Center

(HSOC) with direct connectivity back to DoD for rapid response. Additionally, planning teams assist the DHS Interagency Incident Management Group (IIMG) – a group of senior interagency officials focused on incident response. In 2004, the DoD enhanced its partnership with DHS by establishing a DoD advisory and liaison office—called the Homeland Defense Coordination Office—within DHS headquarters.

In accordance with Section 1401 of Public Law 107-314, The ASD(HD) serves as the "senior official of the Department of Defense to coordinate all Department of Defense efforts to identify, evaluate, deploy, and transfer to Federal, State, and local first responders technology items and equipment in support of homeland security." In that capacity, the ASD(HD) works closely with the DHS Under Secretary for Science and Technology.

Examples of technology transfer initiatives include: information-sharing systems, such as the Disaster Management Interoperability Services; biometrics identification technologies; ground sensors and their application in border security; and unmanned aerial vehicle experimentation. Additionally, new Advanced Concept Technology Demonstration (ACTD) efforts are underway that have the potential to deliver capabilities supporting both DoD missions abroad and DHS missions at home. These include the High Altitude Airship, a prototype untethered platform that could provide wide area surveillance and communications capabilities, and the Air Transportable Cargo screening ACTD, designed to detect explosive threats in pallet cargo loads moving through military transportation systems.

DoD invests nearly $100 million yearly in the Technical Support Working Group (TSWG), a U.S. national forum that brings together over 85 federal agencies to identify, prioritize, and coordinate interagency and international research and development requirements for combating terrorism. The TSWG rapidly develops technologies and equipment to meet the high-priority needs of the combating terrorism community. These technologies typically are also applicable to first responders and other homeland security missions. DHS is now a partner in the TSWG.

The President established the Homeland Security Council (HSC) on October 8, 2001 to develop and implement a comprehensive national strategy to secure the United States from terrorist threats. The Secretary of Defense is, along with the President, Vice President, Secretary of Homeland Security, the Attorney General, and other Cabinet officials, a member of the HSC. DoD works closely with the HSC staff.

The Assistant Secretary of Defense for Homeland Defense is DoD's principal representative to the HSC staff and normally represents DoD at HSC principals and deputies committee meetings. ASD(HD) represents DoD on the HSC's inter-agency policy coordination committees (PCCs) and subordinate working groups, with the participation of other DoD offices as appropriate. The HSC is an effective forum for interagency communication on homeland security and homeland defense matters, including evaluation of terrorist threats and the development of responses in a crisis environment. As one example, the HSC functioned effectively throughout the tense weeks of Code Orange alert during the December 2003 holiday season.[7]

DoD Contributions to Homeland Security

In general, DOD's contributions to homeland security can be divided into two general areas: deterrence, and response. Under these categories are a variety of activities and capabilities that can contribute directly or indirectly to improved homeland security.

Deterrence

The Department of Defense's deterrent efforts seek to prevent attack against the United States by eliminating the threat before it can materialize.

Intelligence Sharing

The intelligence collection and analysis capabilities within the Department of Defense are a substantial portion of the United States' national intelligence assets. They include the National Security Agency (NSA), the National Reconnaissance Office (NRO), the National Geospatial-intelligence Agency (NGA), the Defense Intelligence Agency (DIA), and the intelligence and security branches of the individual armed services. These assets provide communication intercepts, satellite reconnaissance, and human intelligence worldwide. Consequently, the means and extent of cooperation/coordination between DOD and DHS is of great importance to the success of DHS's efforts to provide comprehensive intelligence analysis.

In general, DOD's contributions to homeland security can be divided into two general areas: deterrence, and response

The DHS legislation does not address DOD's intelligence assets specifically. but in establishing the DHS Under-Secretary for Information and Infrastructure Protection, grants the new department

> " *...access to all reports, assessments, and analytical information relating to threats or terrorism in the United States, and to all information concerning infrastructure vulnerabilities....*"

The DHS legislation does not grant any administrative or tasking authority over DOD intelligence assets, and both specifically states that no provision of the legislation shall be construed as affecting the intelligence authorities of the Secretary of Defense under the National Security Act of 1947. It does, however, create a DHS Intelligence Center, and directs the Secretary of Defense to enter into cooperative agreements with DHS to detail to this center "an appropriate number of individuals" from the NSA, NGA, and DIA.

Reflecting an increasing interest in the organization of DOD's intelligence elements, the FY2003 Defense Authorization Act (P.L. 107-314) created an Under Secretary of Defense for Intelligence (USD(I)).[8] The Assistant Secretary for Homeland Defense engages actively with the USD(I) on all homeland defense intelligence matters. The USD(I) is charged with ensuring that the senior DoD leadership receives the warning, actionable intelligence, and counter-intelligence support needed to pursue all of the objectives of the updated defense strategy, including defense of the homeland. USD(I) also provides a single point of contact for coordination of national and military intelligence activities with the Community Management Staff under the Director of Central Intelligence (DCI) and strengthens the relationship between the Secretary of Defense and the DCI.

Furthermore, the Office of the Under Secretary of Defense for Intelligence is working with DHS and other federal departments and agencies to fulfill the tasking set forth by Executive Order 13311, "Homeland Security Information Sharing," (July 2003) to establish procedures for the horizontal sharing of information between federal agencies and the vertical sharing of information with authorities at the state and local levels.[9]

Additionally, DoD is a full partner in the Terrorist Threat Integration Center (TTIC), a multi-agency joint venture announced by the President in the January 2003 State of the Union address and launched in May 2003. Under the direction of the Director of Central Intelligence (DCI)[10], the TTIC integrates terrorist-threat related information, minimizing any seams between analysis of terrorism intelligence collected overseas and inside the United States, to form a comprehensive threat picture. On a daily basis, TTIC coordinates terrorist threat assessments with partner agencies, including DoD, DHS, the Federal Bureau of Investigation, the Central Intelligence Agency, and the Department of State.[11]

One area of concern involving intelligence which the Secretary of Homeland Security still has to resolve is how to fulfill its information-sharing responsibilities to state and local law enforcement and first responders without compromising classified national security information or sources. Providing meaningful and actionable warnings to state and local officials has proven a challenge. Lack of specificity and recommended actions have been the primary criticisms.

The Posse Comitatus Act outlaws willful use of any part of the Army or Air Force to execute the law unless expressly authorized by the Constitution or an Act of Congress.

Personnel Augmentation

The Department of Defense, with its active duty and reserve forces, and the option of federalizing National Guard units, has the largest and most diversified personnel assets in the Federal Government. As was demonstrated in the months after the September 2001 terrorist attacks, they can be used in a variety of security roles. The National Guard augmented the border patrol, customs agencies, and airport security personnel, flew air patrols, and provided site security in Washington, DC and New York City. A major concern when armed forces personnel are deployed in these roles under federal command is their remaining within the provisions of the Posse Comitatus Act, which generally prohibits their conducting law enforcement activities such as arrests or search and seizures. Other subjects of controversy have been whether these detailed military personnel shculd be armed and whether they have had sufficient training in civilian law enforcement procedures.[12]

The Posse Comitatus Act outlaws willful use of any part of the Army or Air Force to execute the law unless expressly authorized by the Constitution or an Act of Congress. The language of the Act mentions only the Army and Air Force, but it is applicable to the Navy and Marines by virtue of administrative action and commands of other laws. The express statutory exceptions include legislation which allows the President to use military force to suppress an insurrection, 10 U.S.C. 331- 335, and sections which permit the Department of Defense to provide federal, state and local police with information and equipment, 10 U.S.C. 371-381.

Existing case law indicates that "execution of the law" in violation of the Posse Comitatus Act occurs (a) when the armed forces perform tasks which are assigned not to them but to an organ of civil government, or (b) when the armed forces perform tasks assigned to them solely for purposes of civilian government. Questions arise most often in the context of assistance to civilian police. At least in this context, the courts have held that, absent a recognized exception, the Posse Comitatus Act is violated, (1) when civilian law enforcement officials make "direct active use" of military investigators; or (2) when the use of the military "pervades the activities" of the civilian officials; or (3) when the military is used so as to subject "citizens to the exercise of military power which was regulatory, prescriptive, or compulsory in nature." The Act is not violated when the armed forces conduct activities for a military purpose which have incidental benefits for civilian law enforcement officials. The Act is a criminal statute under which there has never been a prosecution. Although violations will on rare occasions result in the exclusion of evidence, the dismissal of criminal charges, or a civil cause of action, as a practical matter compliance is ordinarily the result of military self-restraint.

The Posse Comitatus Act says nothing about the Coast Guard. The Coast Guard was formed by merging two civilian agencies, the revenue cutter service and the lifesaving service. Although created and used for law enforcement purposes, the cutter service had already been used as part of the military forces of the United States by the time the Posse Comitatus Act was enacted.

The Coast Guard is now a branch of the armed forces, located within the Department of Homeland Security, 14 U.S.C. 1, but relocated within the Navy in time of war or upon the order of the President, 14 U.S.C. 3. The Act does not apply to the Coast Guard while it remains part of the Department of Homeland Security. While part of the Navy, it is subject to the orders of the Secretary of the Navy, 14 U.S.C. 3, and consequently to any generally applicable directives or instructions issued under the Department of Defense or the Navy.

As a practical matter, however, the Coast Guard is statutorily authorized to perform law enforcement functions, 14 U.S.C. 2. Even while part of the Navy its law enforcement activities would come within the statutory exception to the Posse Comitatus restrictions, and the restrictions applicable to components of the Department of Defense would only apply to activities beyond those authorized.[13]

The U.S. Coast Guard (USCG) plays several critical roles in homeland security. Its assets include the unique attribute of being a militia with legal authority for certain law enforcement actions.

The U.S. Coast Guard (USCG) plays several critical roles in homeland security. Its assets include the unique attribute of being a militia with legal authority for certain law enforcement actions. The USCG is charged with waterside port security and can detain or expulse ships in ports and has the authority to board vessels at sea. It also has authority for enforcing drug trafficking laws outside of 200 nautical miles, pollution response capabilities, and an Incident Command System established to allow different agencies to communicate and work together. The USCG has long balanced the flow of commerce and security. Since 9/11, it has expanded its efforts in maritime domain awareness, which include: maritime layered defense, increased level of security operations in general and in ports, search and rescue, and organizing and sustaining a lasting relationship between the public and private sector. Development of a national vessel tracking system similar to the Air Traffic Control system, i.e., speed, location, and direction, is a critical USCG priority. There needs to be a shipboard identification system of friend or foe. Some participants voiced concern that the USCG's other missions of search and rescue, fisheries protection, and counterdrug trafficking operations will be eclipsed by the demands of homeland security and counterterrorism functions, particularly since it was absorbed by the DHS. However, resources are limited. While some Coast Guard operations support multiple missions, resource limitations mean some tradeoffs will be necessary.

The Posse Comitatus Act is also silent as to what constitutes "part" of the Army or Air Force for purposes of proscription. There is little commentary or case law to resolve questions concerning the coverage of the National Guard, the Civil Air Patrol, civilian employees of the armed forces, or regular members of the armed forces while off duty.

Strictly speaking, the Posse Comitatus Act predates the National Guard only in name, for the Guard "is the modern Militia reserved to the States by Art.I, §8, cls.15, 16, of the Constitution" which has become "an organized force, capable of being assimilated with ease into the regular military establishment of the United States," Maryland v. United States, 381 U.S. 41, 46 (1965). There seems every reason to consider the National Guard part of the Army or Air Force, for purposes of the Posse Comitatus Act, when in federal service.

On the other hand, the National Guard is creature of both state and federal law, a condition which as the militia it has enjoyed since the days of the Articles of Confederation. And the courts have said that members of the National Guard when not in federal service are not covered by the Posse Comitatus Act. Similarly, the DoD directive is only applicable to members of the National Guard when they are in federal service.[14]

Courts have said that members of the National Guard when not in federal service are not covered by the Posse Comitatus Act. Similarly, the DoD directive is only applicable to members of the National Guard when they are in federal service.

Consequently it appears that the National Guard will continue to play the major role in homeland security personnel augmentation when needed. Some National Guard officials have expressed concern about increased homeland security responsibilities detracting from its current primary mission of supporting active duty forces in overseas military operations (e.g. peacekeeping in Bosnia). Today's U.S. armed forces organization and war-fighting doctrine rely significantly upon the participation of National Guard and reserve personnel, and it has been questioned whether these requirements could still be met if the homeland security mission predominates. It also must be remembered that National Guard and reserve personnel are primarily part-time "citizen soldiers", and that significantly increased operational activations may well have a negative effect on personnel retention. Reflecting this concern, some National Guard officials have called for an increase in full-time active duty personnel. The National Guard stands at about 57% of its full-time personnel requirement, and the Army has developed a plan to bring that level up to 71% before 2011.[15]

The National Guard's role in homeland security warrants further study and clarification. As part of this process, Title 10, United States Code (USC), "Armed Forces," and Title 32, "National Guard," should be subject to careful review in light of the new demands of homeland security. Army and Air National Guard units are located in 3300 locations around the country. Guard units function as a state militia under control of the relevant governor and become a federal support force when called up by the President. In recent years, the Guard has seen a significant growth in its operational deployments due to many overseas missions and new homeland security requirements. An increasing difficulty for the National Guard is the greater call-up time to serve, which impacts employment to include job security, families, and community welfare. Multiple or conflicting commitments will require prioritization and planning for various future contingencies. The Reserve Component, which includes the National Guard and service reserve forces, wants to be full partner with the active forces.

Posse Comitatus conflicts have not been a major concern for the Active or Reserve components of the Armed Forces thus far, since military units were directed to support civilian law enforcement agencies under Title 32 and various emergency exceptions to Title 10. Airport security is a significant example of initial homeland security duties. However, Posse Comitatus should also be reviewed in light of the new demands for military support to homeland security efforts. Such a review could head off future legal squabbles and enhance the responsiveness of military support to civil authorities.[16]

Response

Recognizing that no defense is invulnerable, the DoD is prepared to respond after attack, lending it's unique capabilities to support mitigation and recovery efforts.

Military Assistance to Civil Authority

DoD has a long tradition of support to civil authorities, while maintaining its primary mission of fighting and winning the nation's wars. DoD continues to lend necessary assistance to civil authorities when they are overwhelmed or faced with challenges necessitating the Department's unique capabilities.[17]

Support to civil authorities is United States Northern Command's (NORTHCOM's) key mission in homeland security. NORTHCOM responds in accordance with the National Response Plan (NRP) when "invited" in support of a lead federal agency or to support consequence management. Rules of engagement will change as the situations demand.

NORTHCOM does not have a large number of active duty personnel or units permanently assigned to it, but rather has units "earmarked" for potential assignment as events warrant. National Guard units, if federalized for homeland security operations, will come under NORTHCOM command. Formerly, the Joint Forces Command's Joint Force Headquarters-Homeland Security coordinated the land and maritime defense of the continental United States,

DoD continues to lend necessary assistance to civil authorities when they are overwhelmed or faced with challenges necessitating the Department's unique capabilities.

and all military assistance to civilian authorities. Subordinate to this headquarters is the Joint Task Force-Civil Support (JTF-CS) which provides command and control for DOD units deployed in response to any incident involving chemical, biological, nuclear, radiological, or high-yield conventional explosives. Generally, these units are deployed only upon the request of state or local officials to the President. The JTF-CS, and the units deployed under its command, remain under the direction of the lead federal civilian agency at the incident site. These Joint Forces Command headquarters units were transferred to NORTHCOM. It is also expected that NORTHCOM will expand upon the efforts of the JTF-CS to establish and maintain close coordination with state and local authorities.[18]

In 2003 the DoD acted on 75 requests for assistance from more than 20 civilian agencies, including DHS, the Department of Justice, the Department of Health and Human Services, the Department of Transportation, the Department of State, the National Air and Space Administration, the U.S. Marshals Service, and the National Interagency Fire Center.

DoD provided emergency support in natural disasters such as Hurricane Isabel in September 2003 and the October 2003 California wildfires. During the January 2004 ricin incident on Capitol Hill, NORTHCOM's Joint Force Headquarters-National Capitol Region, in its first operational use, provided command and control of U.S. Marine Corps Chemical-Biological Incident Response Force assistance to the U.S. Capitol Police.[19]

CBRN Incident Response

The Department of Defense remains the greatest federal repository of resources for responding to a chemical, biological, radiological, or nuclear (CBRN) incident. It is anticipated that civilian authorities will eventually develop better capabilities to deal with CBRN incidents, however for the foreseeable future there will be continued reliance upon DOD assets.

U.S. Army Soldier and Biological-Chemical Command. In 1996, Congress directed the Department of Defense to organize a joint service Chemical and Biological Rapid Response Team (CB-RRT) to support civilian authorities (P.L. 104-201, Sec. 1414). This team was established in 1997 under the U.S. Army Soldier and Biological-Chemical Command. CB-RRT's mission is to deploy and coordinate DOD's technical assistance in support of the federal lead agency (FBI or FEMA) in both crisis and consequence management of an incident involving chemical or biological agents. The CB-RRT may also deploy for designated National Security Special Events (e.g. the Olympics, presidential inaugurations, etc.). Headquartered at Aberdeen Proving Ground, MD, the CB-RTT would coordinate the CB incident response activities of the following DOD assets:

- U.S. Army Technical Escort Unit

- U.S. Army Edgewood Chemical and Biological Center

- U.S. Army Medical Command Special Medical Augmentation

- Response Teams and Regional Medical Commands

- U.S. Army Medical Research Institute for Infectious Diseases
- U.S. Navy Environmental Health Center
- U.S. Marine Corps Chemical-Biological Incident Response Force
- National Guard Weapons of Mass Destruction-Civil Support Teams
- U.S. Army 52nd Ordnance Group (explosive ordnance disposal)

Brief descriptions of the units most likely to be deployed to a chemical or biological incident are provided below.

National Guard WMD-Civil Support Teams

The National Guard Weapons of Mass Destruction Civil Support Teams (WMDCST) are full-time active duty personnel whose mission is to assess a suspected CBRN incident, advise civilian authorities, and expedite the arrival of additional military personnel. Each team consists of 22 personnel and is equipped with CBRN detection, analysis, and protective equipment. Congress has authorized 55 WMDCSTs to ensure that each state and territory has a team.

Of the 55 teams authorized, 27 have received certification of the requisite training and equipment. The remainder are still being staffed and equipped. The certified teams are located in : Colorado, Georgia, Illinois, California, Massachusetts, Missouri, New York, Pennsylvania, Texas, Washington, Alaska, Arizona, Arkansas, California, Florida, Hawaii, Idaho, Iowa, Kentucky, Louisiana, Maine, Minnesota, New Mexico, Ohio, Oklahoma, South Carolina, and Virginia.

U.S. Army Technical Escort Unit

Established in 1944, the Technical Escort Unit is the longest-standing chemical and biological weapons unit in DOD. Its mission is to conduct rapid deployment to provide chemical and biological advice, verification, detection, mitigation, decontamination, escort, and remediation of chemical and biological devices or hazards worldwide. In accomplishing this mission, it has provided support to, among others, the Federal Bureau of Investigation, the Federal Emergency Management Agency, the Environmental Protection Agency, and the United Nations. The Technical Escort unit has also deployed in the United States as part of security operations at national political conventions, NATO conferences, presidential inaugurations and State of the Union addresses, and the Olympics. Headquartered at Aberdeen Proving Ground, MD, it has subordinate units stationed at Dugway Proving Ground, UT, Fort Belvoir, VA, and Pine Bluff Arsenal, AR.

U.S. Marine Corps Chemical-Biological Incident Response Force

The Marines' Chemical-Biological Incident Response Force (CBIRF) was established in 1996, and is currently headquartered outside Washington, DC.

CBIRF's primary mission is to provide chemical-biological force protection and defensive training for the Marine Corps, however since its inception it has placed significant emphasis upon preparation to assist state and local authorities in the event of a domestic chemical-biological incident, participating in over 120 "table-top" and field exercises with first-responders around the country. The capabilities which CBIRF can bring to bear include: CBW agent detection and identification, decontamination, emergency medical treatment and triage, search and rescue, and casualty evacuation assistance.

U.S. Special Operations Command

Both the U.S. Army and the U.S. Navy have dedicated counterterrorist units whose primary focus is overseas operations. They could be called upon to advise/assist civilian law enforcement officials, although the FBI'S Hostage Rescue Team would normally be the first federal counterterrorist responders in domestic situations. Official open source information on the organization and mission of these DOD units is not available. Generally, even official acknowledgment of their existence is not forthcoming. From unofficial sources, a few details can be provided.

The Army's 1st Special Forces Operational Detachment-Delta, also known as Delta Force, is based at Ft. Bragg, NC and the Naval Special Warfare Development Group (formerly SEAL Team 6) is based at Dam Neck, VA. Both units number several hundred personnel, and undergo very rigorous and constant training in marksmanship, close combat, urban combat, SCUBA diving, and high-altitude parachuting, among other skills. Cross-training with other national counterterrorist units such as the British Special Air Services and the German Grenzschutz Polizei (GSG-9) is frequent. Both units have reportedly participated in every significant U.S. military operation over the last two decades.[20]

Conclusion

Throughout our history, U.S. military forces – active duty and reserves—have defended our nation against its enemies on land, at sea, and in the air, adapting continuously to engage threats to our nation.

Today we face a challenge that is equal to or greater than any we have ever faced before. We must cope not only with the threats produced by the proliferation of weapons of mass destruction and missile technology among nation-states, but also with threats posed by individual terrorists and terrorist organizations with global reach.

The DoD is transforming, increasing its capabilities for warfighting and homeland defense on a daily basis, while continuing a long tradition of support to civil authorities. Homeland defense and homeland security are featured on Secretary Rumsfeld's top priorities list. DoD intends to develop a comprehensive Homeland Defense Strategy for the 21st century. This strategy will support the National Security Strategy, the National Strategy for Homeland Security, and the updated Defense Strategy. It will also provide the framework for pursuing operational capabilities to prepare for tomorrow's challenges.[21]

Questions

1. What are the DoD's two primary roles related to homeland security?

2. What is the difference between homeland security and homeland defense?

3. List and describe the two DoD organizations dedicated to homeland security.

4. What restrictions do Posse Comitatus place on the military?

5. How are the U.S. Coast Guard and National Guard uniquely positioned to support homeland security?

## Chapter 22

Legislating Homeland Security

Objectives

- List and describe anti-terrorist legislation stemming from the events of 9-11.

- Describe the key provisions of the USA PATRIOT Act.

- Understand the challenge to legislating homeland security.

Throughout this Nation's history we have used our laws to promote and safeguard our security and our liberty. The law will both provide mechanisms for the government to act and define the appropriate limits of that action.

- National Strategy for Homeland Security, July 2002

Introduction

On June 18, 2002, the President provided Congress with proposed legislation to establish the Department of Homeland Security. The new Cabinet agency has a single, urgent mission: securing the homeland of America and protecting the American people from terrorism. Yet creating the Department of Homeland Security does not in and of itself constitute a sufficient response to the terrorist threat. Complementary legislation was needed to address innate deficiencies in the nation's overall ability to counter terrorism.

The USA PATRIOT Act, signed into law on October 26, 2001, improved government coordination in law enforcement, intelligence gathering, and information-sharing. The Aviation and Transportation Security Act, which established the Transportation Security Administration, strengthened civil aviation security. The Enhanced Border Security and Visa Entry Reform Act reinforced border security systems. Finally, the Public Health Security and Bioterrorism Preparedness and Response Act improved the nation's ability to prevent, prepare for, and respond to bioterrorism.

"They that can give up essential liberty to obtain a little temporary safety deserve neither liberty nor safety."

– Benjamin Franklin

The Department of Homeland Security is sensitive to the need to ensure that newly crafted federal laws do not preempt state law unnecessarily or overly federalize counterterrorism efforts. The Tenth Amendment makes clear that each state retains substantial independent power with respect to the general welfare of its populace. States are expected to avail themselves to the resources and expertise offered by their sister states and federal counterparts. Guided by these precepts, the National Strategy for Homeland Security outlines a number of legislative actions at the State and Federal level.[1]

Federal Initiatives

USA Patriot Act

Congress passed the USA PATRIOT Act (the Act) in response to the terrorists' attacks of September 11, 2001. The Act gives federal officials greater authority to track and intercept communications, both for law enforcement and foreign intelligence gathering purposes. It vests the Secretary of the Treasury with regulatory powers to combat corruption of U.S. financial institutions for foreign money laundering purposes. It seeks to further close our borders to foreign terrorists and to detain and remove those within our borders. It creates new crimes, new penalties, and new procedural efficiencies for use against domestic and international terrorists. Although it is not without safeguards, critics contend some of its provisions go too far. Although it grants many of the enhancements sought by the Department of Justice, others are concerned that it does not go far enough.

The Act originated as H.R.2975 (the PATRIOT Act) in the House and S.1510 in the Senate (the USA Act). S.1510 passed the Senate on October 11, 2001, 147 Cong. Rec. S10604 (daily ed.). The House Judiciary Committee reported out an amended version of H.R. 2975 on the same day, H.R.Rep.No. 107-236. The House passed H.R. 2975 the following day after substituting the text of H.R. 3108, 147 Cong.Rec. H6775- 776 (daily ed. Oct. 12, 2001). The House version incorporated most of the money laundering provisions found in an earlier House bill, H.R. 3004, many of which had counterparts in S.1510 as approved by the Senate. The House subsequently passed a clean bill, H.R. 3162 (under suspension of the rules), which resolved the differences between H.R. 2975 and S.1510, 147 Cong.Rec. H7224 (daily ed. Oct. 24, 2001). The Senate agreed to the changes, 147 Cong.Rec. S10969 (daily ed. Oct. 24, 2001), and H.R. 3162 was sent to the President who signed it on October 26, 2001.

The following paragraphs provide an abbreviated legal analysis of the Act conducted by Charles Doyle, Senior Specialist of the American Law Division on the Congressional Research Staff at the Library of Congress.

Criminal Investigations: Tracking and Gathering Communications

Federal communications privacy law features a three tiered system, erected for the dual purpose of protecting the confidentiality of private telephone, face-to-face, and computer communications while enabling authorities to identify and intercept criminal communications. Title III of the Omnibus Crime Control and Safe Streets Act of 1968 supplies the first level. It prohibits electronic eavesdropping on telephone conversations, face-to-face conversations, or computer and other forms of electronic communications in most instances. It does, however, give authorities a narrowly defined process for electronic surveillance to be used as a last resort in serious criminal cases. When approved by senior Justice Department officials, law enforcement officers may seek a court order authorizing them to secretly capture conversations concerning any of a statutory list of offenses (predicate offenses). Title III court orders come replete with instructions describing the permissible duration and scope of the surveillance as well as the conversations which may be seized and the efforts to be taken to minimize the seizure of innocent conversations. The court notifies the parties to any conversations seized under the order after the order expires.

Below Title III, the next tier of privacy protection covers telephone records, e-mail held in third party storage, and the like, 18 U.S.C. 2701-2709 (Chapter 121). Here, the law permits law enforcement access, ordinarily pursuant to a warrant or court order or under a subpoena in some cases, but in connection with any criminal investigation and without the extraordinary levels of approval or constraint that mark a Title III interception.

Least demanding and perhaps least intrusive of all is the procedure that governs court orders approving the government's use of trap and trace devices and pen registers, a kind of secret "caller id.", which identify the source and destination of calls made to and from a particular telephone, 18 U.S.C. 3121-3127 (Chapter 206). The orders are available based on the government's certification, rather than a finding of a court, that use of the device is likely to produce information relevant to the investigation of a crime, any crime. The devices record no more than

The USA PATRIOT Act gives federal officials greater authority to track and intercept communications, both for law enforcement and foreign intelligence gathering purposes.

identity of the participants in a telephone conversation, but neither the orders nor the results they produce need ever be revealed to the participants.

The PATRIOT Act modifies the procedures at each of the three levels. It:

- permits pen register and trap and trace orders for electronic communications (e.g., e-mail);

- authorizes nationwide execution of court orders for pen registers, trap and trace devices, and access to stored e-mail or communication records;

- treats stored voice mail like stored e-mail (rather than like telephone conversations);

- permits authorities to intercept communications to and from a trespasser within a computer system (with the permission of the system's owner);

- adds terrorist and computer crimes to Title III's predicate offense list;

- reinforces protection for those who help execute Title III, ch. 121, and ch. 206 orders;

- encourages cooperation between law enforcement and foreign intelligence investigators;

- establishes a claim against the U.S. for certain communications privacy violations by government personnel; and

- terminates the authority found in many of these provisions and several of the foreign intelligence amendments with a sunset provision (Dec. 31, 2005).

Foreign Intelligence Investigations

The PATRIOT Act eases some of the restrictions on foreign intelligence gathering within the United States, and affords the U.S. intelligence community greater access to information unearthed during a criminal investigation, but it also establishes and expands safeguards against official abuse. More specifically, it:

- permits "roving" surveillance (court orders omitting the identification of the particular instrument, facilities, or place where the surveillance is to occur when the court finds the target is likely to thwart identification with particularity);

- increases the number of judges on the Foreign Intelligence Surveillance Act (FISA) court from 7 to 11;

- allows application for a FISA surveillance or search order when gathering foreign intelligence is a significant reason for the application rather than the reason;

- authorizes pen register and trap & trace device orders for e-mail as well as telephone conversations;

- sanctions court ordered access to any tangible item rather than only business records held by lodging, car rental, and locker rental businesses;

- carries a sunset provision;

- establishes a claim against the U.S. for certain communications privacy violations by government personnel; and

- expands the prohibition against FISA orders based solely on an American's exercise of his or her First Amendment rights.

Money Laundering

In federal law, money laundering is the flow of cash or other valuables derived from, or intended to facilitate, the commission of a criminal offense. It is the movement of the fruits and instruments of crime. Federal authorities attack money laundering through regulations, criminal sanctions, and forfeiture. The Act bolsters federal efforts in each area.

Regulation: The PATRIOT Act expands the authority of the Secretary of the Treasury to regulate the activities of U.S. financial institutions, particularly their relations with foreign individuals and entities. He is to promulgate regulations:

- under which securities brokers and dealers as well as commodity merchants, advisors and pool operators must file suspicious activity reports (SARs);

- requiring businesses, which were only to report cash transactions involving more than $10,000 to the IRS, to file SARs as well;

- imposing additional "special measures" and "due diligence" requirements to combat foreign money laundering;

- prohibiting U.S. financial institutions from maintaining correspondent accounts for foreign shell banks;

- preventing financial institutions from allowing their customers to conceal their financial activities by taking advantage of the institutions' concentration account practices;

- establishing minimum new customer identification standards and record-keeping and recommending an effective means to verify the identity of foreign customers;

- encouraging financial institutions and law enforcement agencies to share information concerning suspected money laundering and terrorist activities; and

- requiring financial institutions to maintain anti-money laundering programs which must include at least a compliance officer; an employee training program; the development of internal policies, procedures and controls; and an independent audit feature.

Crimes: The PATRIOT Act contains a number of new money laundering crimes, as well as amendments and increased penalties for earlier crimes. It:

- outlaws laundering (in the U.S.) any of the proceeds from foreign crimes of violence or political corruption;

- prohibits laundering the proceeds from cybercrime or supporting a terrorist organization;

- increases the penalties for counterfeiting;

- seeks to overcome a Supreme Court decision finding that the confiscation of over $300,000 (for attempt to leave the country without reporting it to customs) constituted an unconstitutionally excessive fine;

- provides explicit authority to prosecute overseas fraud involving American credit cards; and

- endeavors to permit prosecution of money laundering in the place where the predicate offense occurs.

Forfeiture: The Act creates two types of forfeitures and modifies several confiscation related procedures. It allows confiscation of all of the property of any individual or entity that participates in or plans an act of domestic or international terrorism; it also permits confiscation of any property derived from or used to facilitate domestic or international terrorism. The Constitution's due process, double jeopardy, and ex post facto clauses may limit the anticipated breadth of these provisions. Procedurally, the Act:

- establishes a mechanism to acquire long arm jurisdiction, for purposes of forfeiture proceedings, over individuals and entities;

- allows confiscation of property located in this country for a wider range of crimes committed in violation of foreign law;

- permits U.S. enforcement of foreign forfeiture orders;

- calls for the seizure of correspondent accounts held in U.S. financial institutions for foreign banks who are in turn holding forfeitable assets overseas; and

- denies corporate entities the right to contest a confiscation if their principal shareholder is a fugitive.

Alien Terrorists and Victims

The Act contains a number of provisions designed to prevent alien terrorists from entering the United States, particularly from Canada; to enable authorities to detain and deport alien terrorists and those who support them; and to provide humanitarian immigration relief for foreign victims of the attacks on September 11.

Other Crimes, Penalties, & Procedures

New crimes: The Act creates new federal crimes for terrorist attacks on mass transportation facilities, for biological weapons offenses, for harboring terrorists, for affording terrorists material support, for misconduct associated with money laundering already mentioned, for conducting the affairs of an enterprise which affects interstate or foreign commerce through the patterned commission of terrorist offenses, and for fraudulent charitable solicitation. Although strictly speaking these are new federal crimes, they generally supplement existing law by filling gaps and increasing penalties.

New Penalties: The Act increases the penalties for acts of terrorism and for crimes which terrorists might commit. More specifically it establishes an alternative maximum penalty for acts of terrorism, raises the penalties for conspiracy to commit certain terrorist offenses, envisions sentencing some terrorists to life-long parole, and increases the penalties for counterfeiting, cybercrime, and charity fraud.

Other Procedural Adjustments: In other procedural adjustments designed to facilitate criminal investigations, the Act:

- increases the rewards for information in terrorism cases;

- expands the Posse Comitatus Act exceptions;

- authorizes "sneak and peek" search warrants;

- permits nationwide and perhaps worldwide execution of warrants in terrorism cases;

- eases government access to confidential information;

- allows the Attorney General to collect DNA samples from prisoners convicted of any federal crime of violence or terrorism;

- lengthens the statute of limitations applicable to crimes of terrorism;

- clarifies the application of federal criminal law on American installations and in residences of U.S. government personnel overseas; and

- adjusts federal victims' compensation and assistance programs.

A section, found in the Senate bill but ultimately dropped, would have changed the provision of federal law which requires Justice Department prosecutors to adhere to the ethical standards of the legal profession where they conduct their activities (the McDade- Murtha Amendment), 28 U.S.C. 530B.[2]

The Terrorist Bombings Convention Implementation Act of 2002 makes terrorist bombings and financing terrorism illegal.

Terrorist Bombings Convention Implementation Act of 2002

This Act brought the United States into compliance with two international anti-terrorist conventions that the United States had signed after the 1998 embassy bombings in Kenya and Tanzania. Title I makes it a crime to deliver, place, discharge or detonate, with the intent to cause death, serious bodily injury or extensive destruction where such destruction results in or is likely to result in major economic loss, an explosive or other lethal device in, among other things, a public transportation system. "Public transportation system" means all "facilities, conveyances and instrumentalities, whether publicly or privately owned, that are used in or for publicly available services for the transportation of persons or cargo."

Title I provides for jurisdiction over such an offense if, among other things, the offense takes place in the United States and is committed on board a vessel flying the flag of another state or the perpetrator is a national of another state. There is also jurisdiction if the offense occurs outside the United States and is committed on board a vessel flying the flag of the United States; if a victim is a United States national; if a perpetrator is found in the United States or if the act is committed in an attempt to compel the United States to do or abstain from doing any act.

Title II of this Act makes it a crime to finance terrorism. Specifically, it provides that whoever directly or indirectly unlawfully and willfully provides or collects funds with the intention that such funds be used, or with the knowledge that such funds are to be used, in full or in part, to carry out any terrorist act commits a crime. It includes as a covered act any act intended to cause death or serious bodily injury to a civilian when the purpose of such act is, by its nature or context, to intimidate a population or to compel a government or international organization to do or abstain from any act. It provides for jurisdiction over perpetrators who committed offenses abroad but are later found within the United States.[3]

Bioterrorism Response Act of 2002

On June 12, 2002, President George W. Bush signed into law the "Public Health Security and Bioterrorism Preparedness and Response Act of 2002." The ceremony, attended by Senate cosponsors Bill Frist (R-TN) and Ted Kennedy (D-MA) and House cosponsors W.J. "Billy" Tauzin (R-LA) and John Dingell (D-MI), highlighted the bipartisan Congressional support for this far-reaching legislation. The new law seeks to significantly increase America's ability to prepare for, prevent, detect and respond to bioterrorism in an efficient and coordinated manner.

Title I of the law primarily addresses issues of emergency preparedness and response. It directs the Department of Health and Human Services (HHS) to develop a national preparedness strategy designed to improve communications between state and local governments and federal agencies, and authorizes grant programs to that end. It also requires the development of a comprehensive plan to combat disease outbreak. The plan will ensure that health care facilities nationwide have adequate capacity, up-to-date equipment, and highly trained personnel capable of identifying possible bioterrorist attacks.

Legislators drafting the bill determined that the ability to identify and treat disease outbreaks was the best way to foil terrorist intentions. Therefore, the bill specifically provides funding to train and educate public health professionals with respect to recognition and identification of potential bioterrorist incidents. In total, the bill authorizes approximately $1.5 billion in grants to state and local governments to improve communications, community and hospital preparedness, laboratory capacity, and education of health care personnel. It authorizes nearly $1.2 billion to expand stockpiles of vaccines, drugs, and other treatment measures.

Title II of the law combats potential sub-state biological weapons proliferation more directly by restricting access to dangerous pathogens to individuals who can demonstrate genuine need. By enacting measures to track the possession, use, or transfer of 36 of the most dangerous biological agents, the law dramatically cuts the numbers of people with access to pathogens and enables the government to screen potential users for suspected terrorist activity or association with terrorist groups. It also requires individuals or groups working with any agent on the list of dangerous pathogens to register with a federal database, a significant change from existing law, which requires notification only in cases of biological agent transferal. It increases accountability standards by requir-

The Bioterrorism Response Act of 2002 seeks to significantly increase America's ability to prepare for, prevent, detect, and respond to bioterrorism in an efficient and coordinated manner.

ing HHS to review and republish the list of restricted agents every two years. Additionally, the act mandates the establishment of new standards of lab protection and security measures for facilities that handle select agents and procedures to deal with breaches in transfer or possession safeguards.

Finally, the bill addresses additional aspects of bioterrorism related to food and water supply safety. By improving the process by which imported food is inspected, this bill aims to decrease the likelihood that imported food can become a vehicle for bioterrorism through tampering. Similarly, the new law contains provisions to ensure safe drinking water by requiring community water suppliers to undertake an assessment of their facilities in order to identify and correct vulnerabilities. A last provision will reauthorize the Prescription Drug User Fee Act, which will provide funds to enable the Federal Drug Administration to more effectively monitor adverse events and publish market studies of newly approved drugs and biologics.[4]

Enhanced Border Security and Visa Entry Reform Act of 2002

On May 14, 2002, President Bush signed into Law the Enhanced Border Security and Visa Entry Reform Act of 2002. The law focuses on securing the borders of the United States and provides funding to that end. The law also calls for interagency cooperation. The bill provides for funding to increase the number of border patrol agents at the northern and southern borders, including pay incentives for those agents remaining in the position more than one year. Additional staff will be allocated for those airports that receive a significant number of individuals who arrive from countries that do not have preclearance checks and those airports that have high incidents of fraud. In an attempt to reduce fraud, the President has called for the adequate staffing and training of consular offices in detecting fraudulent visa applications.

The Enhanced Border Security and Visa Entry Reform Act of 2002 focuses on securing the borders of the United States and provides funding to that end. The law also calls for interagency cooperation.

The President has provided funding to enhance the technology at the border as well as to provide additional training for those agents at the border. The improvements will hopefully ease the flow of commerce and individuals across the borders and make it possible for preclearance for entry into the United States. The bill also calls for the federal law enforcement data bases to be linked to those of the INS and Department of State to aid in the issuance of visas to individuals wishing to enter the United States.

The President has stressed interagency cooperation to enhance border security. To that end, the bill requires the INS and the Department of State to submit the necessary information they need from other governmental agencies and the intelligence sectors that would allow them to effectively protect the borders and prevent the entry of those individuals who are inadmissible to the President and congressional committees. The collection of information raises many privacy concerns. As a result, the law provides limitations on the use and dissemination of the collected data. In addition, the bill provides guidance for incorrect and outdated information, including criminal penalties for the misuse of the data collected.

In an effort to safeguard and confirm the identity of individuals traveling, the bill requires that travel documents that contain biometric identifiers be issued.

Those countries participating in the Visa Waiver program will also be required to issue travel documents with biometric identifiers as a condition of remaining in the program. In addition, biometric scanners must be installed at all ports of entry in the United States. This mandate carries with it the necessary funding requirements.

The countries participating in the Visa Waiver program must also establish a reporting system to alert the United States of all the stolen blank passports. This will aid in the enhanced security at the borders given that individuals from visa waiver countries simply present their passports at the ports of entry and are not subject to security clearances at United States embassies and consulates prior to entry to the United States.

The enhanced border security bill calls for a great deal of interagency cooperation and increased effort by the INS and Department of State to take an active role in securing the United States borders against undocumented and falsely documented individuals.[5]

Aviation and Transportation Security Act

ATSA provides that, within one year, federal employees shall be hired to take over airport security screening services at all but five U.S. commercial airports. Two years later, however, airports may opt-out of the federal screener system and switch to contractor screeners.

On November 19, 2001, President Bush signed the Aviation and Transportation Security Act (ATSA) (P.L. 107-71; H. Rept. 107-296). ATSA provides that, within one year, federal employees shall be hired to take over airport security screening services at all but five U.S. commercial airports. Two years later, however, airports may opt-out of the federal screener system and switch to contractor screeners. The Act also establishes a new Transportation Security Administration (TSA) headed by an Under Secretary of Transportation for Security. Within three months of enactment, the responsibilities for aviation security would be transferred from the Federal Aviation Administration (FAA) to the TSA. Also included in the Act are provisions: requiring that, within 60 days, airports provide for the screening or bag-matching of all checked baggage; allowing pilots to carry firearms; requiring the electronic transmission of passenger manifests on international flights prior to landing in the U.S.; requiring background checks, including national security checks, of persons who have access to secure areas at airports; and requiring that all federal security screeners be U.S. citizens.[6]

Maritime Transportation Security Act of 2002

The U.S. maritime system consists of more than 300 sea and river ports with more than 3,700 cargo and passenger terminals. However, a large fraction of maritime cargo is concentrated at a few major ports. Most ships calling at U.S. ports are foreign owned with foreign crews. Container ships have been the focus of much of the attention on seaport security because they are seen as vulnerable to terrorist infiltration. More than 6 million marine containers enter U.S. ports each year. While the Bureau of Customs and Border Protection (CBP) analyzes cargo information to target specific shipments for closer inspection, it physically inspects only a small fraction of the containers.

The Coast Guard and CBP are the federal agencies with the strongest presence in seaports. In response to September 11, 2001, the Coast Guard created the largest port-security operation since World War II. The Coast Guard has advanced its 24-hour Notice of Arrival (NOA) for ships to a 96-hour NOA. The NOA allows Coast Guard officials to select high risk ships for boarding upon their arrival at the entrance to a harbor. CBP has also advanced the timing of cargo information it receives from ocean carriers. Through the Container Security Initiative (CSI) program, CBP inspectors pre-screen U.S.-bound marine containers at foreign ports of loading. To raise port security standards, Congress passed the Maritime Transportation Security Act of 2002 on November 14, 2002 and the President signed it into law as P.L. 107-295 on November 25, 2002.

The Act creates a U.S. maritime security system and requires federal agencies, ports, and vessel owners to take numerous steps to upgrade security. The Act requires the Coast Guard to develop national and regional area maritime transportation security plans. It requires ports, waterfront terminals, and certain types of vessels to develop security and incident response plans with approval from the Coast Guard. The Act authorizes CBP to require that cargo manifest information for inbound or outbound shipments be provided to the agency electronically prior to the arrival or departure of the cargo. This information may be shared with other appropriate federal agencies. The legislation calls on the Department of Transportation to determine the level of funding needed for a grant program that will finance security upgrades. The Act also authorizes $90 million in grants for research and development in improving cargo inspection, detecting nuclear materials, and improving the physical security of marine containers.[7]

President Bush signed the Maritime Transportation Security Act into law on November 14, 2002, to create a U.S. maritime security system and require federal agencies, ports, and vessel owners to take numerous steps to upgrade security.

Cyber Security Enhancement Act

In 2002, Congress passed the Cyber Security Enhancement Act (H .R . 3482) as part of the Homeland Security Act (P .L.107 29_6).   The Cyber Security Enhancement Act, section 225 of the Homeland Security Act (P.L. 107-296), amends section 212 of the USA PATRIOT Act.

Section 212 of the USA PATRIOT Act allows Internet Service Providers (ISPs) to divulge records or other information (but not the contents of communications) pertaining to a subscriber if they believe there is immediate danger of death or serious physical injury or as otherwise authorized, and requires them to divulge such records or information (excluding contents of communications) to a governmental entity under certain conditions . It also allows an ISP to divulge the contents of communications to a law enforcement agency if it reasonably believes that an emergency involving immediate danger of death or serious physical injury requires disclosure of the information without delay.

The Cyber Security Enhancement Act lowers the threshold for when ISPs may voluntarily divulge the content of communications. Now ISPs need only a "good faith" (instead of a "reasonable") belief that there is an emergency involving danger (instead of "immediate" danger) of death or serious physical injury. The contents can be disclosed to "a Federal, state, or local governmental entity" (instead of a "law enforcement agency").

Privacy advocates are especially concerned about the new language added by the Cyber Security Enhancement Act. The Electronic Privacy Information Center (EPIC) notes, for example, that allowing the contents of Internet communications to be disclosed voluntarily to any governmental entity not only poses increased risk to personal privacy, but also is a poor security strategy. Another concern is that the law does not provide for judicial oversight of the use of these procedures.

The SAFETY Act

The Department of Homeland Security (DHS), specifically the Under Secretary for Science and Technology (the Under Secretary), is responsible for review and approval of applications for Designation and Certification of Qualified Anti-Terrorism Technologies (QATTs) under the SAFETY Act, The Support Anti-terrorism by Fostering Effective Technologies Act of 2002 (Public Law 107-296).

The purpose of the SAFETY Act is to encourage the development and deployment of antiterrorism technologies that will substantially enhance the protection of the nation. The SAFETY Act reflects the intent of Congress to ensure that the threat of liability does not deter potential sellers from developing and commercializing technologies that could significantly reduce the risk of, or mitigate the effect of, acts of terrorism. Specifically, the SAFETY Act creates certain liability limitations for (claims arising out of, relating to, or resulting from an act of terrorism) when QATTs have been deployed. The SAFETY Act does not limit liability where an act of terrorism has not occurred. All forms of technology, including products, software, services, and various forms of intellectual property, may qualify for SAFETY Act protection. The two separate protections available to sellers of qualifying anti-terrorism technologies are (Designation) as a QATT (which enables the seller to invoke certain liability limitations) and (Certification) of a QATT (which enables the seller to invoke a rebuttable presumption that the government contractor defense applies and confers on the QATT status as an (Approved Product for Homeland Security).

In determining whether to grant a Designation, the Under Secretary exercises discretion and judgment in interpreting, weighing, and determining the overall significance of certain criteria, which include (but are not limited to) the following seven criteria stated in the Act:

- Prior United States Government use or demonstrated substantial utility and effectiveness.

- Availability of the technology for immediate deployment in public and private settings.

- Existence of extraordinarily large or unquantifiable potential third party liability risk exposure to seller (or another provider of the technology).

- Substantial likelihood that the technology will not be deployed unless SAFETY Act protections are extended.

- Magnitude of risk exposure to the public if the technology is not deployed.

The Cyber Security Enhancement Act lowers the threshold for when Internet Service Providers (ISPs) may voluntarily divulge the content of Internet communications.

- Evaluation of all scientific studies that can be feasibly conducted to assess the capability of the technology to substantially reduce risks of harm.

- Whether the technology would be effective in facilitating the defense against acts of terrorism.

A Designation is valid for five to eight years (as specified by the Under Secretary in individual cases) and automatically terminates if the QATT is significantly changed, unless an (Application for Modification of Designation) is filed and approved as provided in the implementing regulations. Sellers may transfer a Designation in connection with the sale of the related QATT if an (Application for Transfer of Designation) is filed with the Under Secretary. Sellers may also apply for renewal at any time commencing two years prior to the expiration of the Designation.

Receipt of a Designation is a prerequisite for receipt of a Certification. Accordingly, sellers may apply for a Certification either in conjunction with, or subsequent to an application for Designation. The seller is required to provide safety and hazard analysis in connection with the application. Certification establishes a rebuttable presumption of the applicability of the (Government Contractor Defense.) In determining whether a QATT qualifies for a Certification, there are three additional criteria against which the QATT is evaluated:

- It must perform as intended

- Conform to the seller's specifications

- Be safe for use as intended

SAFETY Caveats:

- Designation and Certification of an anti-terrorism technology has no bearing per se on the award of a contract from DHS or any other agency for these technologies.

- Designation and Certification under the SAFETY Act does not constitute designation under FAR 9.2 qualifications requirements (qualified products lists, qualified manufacturers lists, etc.).

- Designation and Certification do not limit liability for harm where no act of terrorism has occurred.

- The availability of indemnification under Public Law 85-804 is not necessarily affected by the issuance of a Designation or a Certification, but the approval of the Director of the Office of Management and Budget may be required before indemnification may be granted pursuant to Executive Order 10789 of November 14, 1958 (as amended in 2003).

- The DHS Applicant Help Desk (1-866-788-9318) assists sellers in administrative processes, but cannot provide advice on the content or substance of an application.

- All individuals involved in the processing and evaluation of applications, including DHS personnel, supporting administrative contractors, and gov-

The SAFETY Act reflects the intent of Congress to ensure that the threat of liability does not deter potential sellers from developing and commercializing technologies that could significantly reduce the risk of, or mitigate the effect of, acts of terrorism.

ernment and non-government evaluators, are bound by appropriate non-disclosure and conflict of interest agreements.

- Applications are provided secure handling and treated as proprietary information.

- Sellers must not, under any circumstances, submit or include U.S. Government classified information as part of an application. The submission of such information must be separately arranged with DHS.

DHS offers a simplified Pre-Application process that affords sellers an opportunity to obtain preliminary feedback from DHS on their prospects for obtaining SAFETY act protections without preparing and submitting the full SAFETY Act application. DHS also provides expedited review of SAFETY Act applications relating to technologies that are the subject of Federal, state, or local government procurements.

Terrorism Risk Insurance Act of 2002

Congress enacted the Terrorism Risk Insurance Act of 2002 (TRIA), Public Law 107-297, to create a temporary program to share future insured terrorism losses with the property-casualty insurance industry and policyholders.

After September 11, 2001, many businesses were no longer able to purchase insurance protecting against property losses that might occur in future terrorist attacks. Addressing this problem, Congress enacted the Terrorism Risk Insurance Act of 2002 (TRIA), Public Law 107-297, to create a temporary program to share future insured terrorism losses with the property-casualty insurance industry and policyholders. The act requires insurers to offer terrorism insurance to their commercial policyholders, preserves state regulation of this type of insurance, and directs the Secretary of the Treasury to administer a program for sharing terrorism losses. The three-year program that TRIA created backs up commercial property and casualty insurance, covering up to $100 billion each year after set insurer deductibles. The government pays 90% of insured losses over the deductible, with the insurer paying 10%.

Concern was expressed even before the enactment of TRIA that a three-year program would be too limited to allow the private sector to develop the capacity to insure terrorism risk. Three pieces of legislation were introduced in the 108th Congress to extend the program. One bill, H.R. 4634, was reported favorably from the House Financial Services Committee, but no floor action occurred. In the 109th, two bills have been introduced, S. 467 by Senator Christopher Dodd and H.R. 1153 by Representative Michael Capuano. In addition, a Senate hearing on TRIA is scheduled for April 14, 2005. This report provides an overview of the issues, including a summary of TRIA and the TRIA extension legislation. It will be updated as significant events occur.

State Legislation

The following summary is a synopsis of homeland security legislation that has either been introduced or enacted in each of the fifty states following the terrorist attacks against the United States on September 11, 2001. The topics that were researched include anti-terrorism legislation, bio-terrorism legislation, transportation legislation, hazardous material legislation, border security legislation, driver's licenses/national identification system legislation, electronic surveillance legislation, cyber-security legislation, first-responder legislation, and vaccination legislation.

Anti-terrorism legislation pertains to establishing homeland security and anti-terrorism legislative committees, defining terrorism, crimes of terrorism, penalties for crimes of terrorism, funding for anti-terrorism, necessary security measures, anti-terrorism training, offices of preparedness and security, building safety, compensation to innocent victims of terrorism, stimulation of economic activity and public safety in general. Key pieces of adopted legislation include: CA A.J.R. 31, CA E.O. 47, CO H.B. 1315, CO S.B. 113, DE E.O. 22, DE S.B. 288, DE H.B. 343, FL E.O. 300, KY H.B. 258, MD H.B. 1036, MI H.B. 5509, MI H.B. 995, MI H.B. 1036, MI H.B. 5509, MI H.B. 995, MI 946, MI S.B. 948, MI S.B. 949, NJ S.B. 2575, WV S.B. 6002.

Bio-terrorism legislation pertains to funds for response to biological threats, terrorism by crop dusters, protection against biological terrorism, public health emergency powers, maintaining registries of qualified physicians to be used in cases involving biological hazards, detecting/tracking/reporting public health emergencies, developments of emergency plans, criminal penalties for biological terrorism, creating working groups to evaluate existing bio-terrorism laws and statewide control of bio-terror. Key pieces of adopted legislation include: FL E.O. 300, IA E.O. 7, KS E.O. 10, KS E.O. 9, PA E.O. 6, TN S.B. 2392.

Hazardous material legislation pertains to the handling of hazardous waste of concern, criminal history information for hazardous material transporters, criminal penalties for hazardous material terrorism, designation of state training centers for domestic preparedness, establishment of a hazardous material incident response program, funds for the response of hazardous material terrorism, collaboration of statewide strategies, submission of annual reports on statewide strategies and environmental terrorism. Key pieces of adopted legislation include: CO H.B. 1046, KY H.B. 258, NY E.O. 39, NY E.O. 44, NY E.O. 17.

Cyber security legislation pertains to money laundering and racketeering by terrorist groups, computer crime law and computer-related crime, enhancement of privacy in cyberspace, online fraud, threat assessment and preparedness, introducing viruses and breach of computer security. Key pieces of adopted legislation include: RI H.B. 6528, TX S.B. 917.

Driver's License identification legislation pertains to proof of lawful residence in the United States in order to obtain a license from a state DMV, obtaining false identification, strengthening of requirements for issuance of driver's licenses, driver's license expiration coinciding with visa expiration, manufacturing of false documents, fingerprint encoding on driver's licenses, foreign nationals, criminal penalties for operating a motor vehicle without lawful presence in the United States, re-structuring of DMVs, digitized driver's licenses, exchange of information between states and agencies and biometric identifiers. Key pieces of adopted legislation include: AK H.B. 344, CO S.B. 112, IA S.S. 3122, MD H.B. 1036, NJ E.O. 19, VA H.B. 637.

Electronic surveillance legislation pertains to wiretapping, electronic surveillance, eavesdropping, investigations of money laundering by terrorist groups, making telecommunications terrorism an illegal act, computer security, investigative warrants, forfeiture of assets involved in terrorist activity, and any form of crime that deals with telecommunications terrorism. Key pieces of adopted legislation include: GA S.B. 459, MD H.B. 1036.

First responder legislation pertains to funds available for state first-responder preparedness, exposures to communicable diseases for first-responders, first-responder/terrorism awareness, consequence management training programs, first-responder equipment, designation of first-responder authority, administration of antidotes, terrorism prevention, and any form of emergency medical response. Key pieces of adopted legislation include: CO H.B. 1315, FL E.O. 300, LA E.O. 48.

Transportation legislation pertains to funding for transportation homeland security, public safety background checks, aviation screeners, airport security, funding for security projects at airports, criminal background checks for all civilian pilot training schools and aircraft maintenance training school applicants, seaport security, loan guarantees to seaports, National Guard at airports and prohibition of certain people working at certain airports. Key pieces of adopted legislation include: FL H.B. 811, GA S.B. 330, ID E.O. 7, IA E.O.6.

Vaccination legislation pertains to quarantines for disease prevention, screening of people that apply for medical assistance, response to public health emergencies, availability of drugs and medical personnel in the event of a public health emergency, provisions for physicians, regulations involving diseases, criminal penalties for spreading diseases and modifying state public health codes. Key pieces of adopted legislation include: MD H.B. 303.[8]

We are a nation built on the rule of law, and we must utilize our laws to win the war on terrorism while always protecting our civil liberties.

Conclusion

We are a nation built on the rule of law, and we must utilize our laws to win the war on terrorism while always protecting our civil liberties. It is necessary to use our federal immigration laws and customs regulations to protect our borders and ensure uninterrupted commerce; state codes must be strengthened to protect our public welfare; local, state, and federal criminal justice systems must be employed to prosecute terrorists; and the nation must engage its partners around the world in countering the global threat of terrorism through treaties and mutually supporting laws. Where our existing laws are inadequate in light of the terrorist threat, we must craft new laws carefully, never losing sight of our strategic purpose for waging this war—to provide security and liberty to our people. The challenge is to guard scrupulously against incursions on our freedoms, recognizing that liberty cannot exist in the absence of governmental restraint. As the country moves forward in the fight, it should refrain from instituting unnecessary laws, as the government remains true to its principles of federalism and individual freedom.[9]

Questions

1. Describe some of the legislation that has been enacted to reduce the threat of terrorism.

2. What are the key provisions of the USA PATRIOT Act?

3. Discuss whether you agree or disagree with the USA PATRIOT Act.

4. What is the basic challenge to legislating homeland security?

## Chapter 23

Science & Technology

Objectives

- Understand the mission of the Science and Technology Directorate.

- Explain the relationship between HSARPA and SED.

- Describe the mission of ORD.

- List and describe some of the portfolios managed by PPB.

- Compare the different missions of the HSSTAC and HSI.

Science and Technology. The Nation's advantage in science and technology is a key to securing the homeland. New technologies for analysis, information sharing, detection of attacks, and countering chemical, biological, radiological, and nuclear weapons will help prevent and minimize the damage from future terrorist attacks. Just as science has helped us defeat past enemies overseas, so too will it help us defeat the efforts of terrorists to attack our homeland and disrupt our way of life.

- National Strategy for Homeland Security, July 2002

Introduction

In the post-9/11 world, the challenges faced by the Department of Homeland Security (DHS) in detecting and preventing another attack on American soil are considerable. Our enemies use our open society to their full advantage. They are elusive, working quietly in the shadows, assessing our vulnerabilities, and waiting for the most opportune time to strike. Our challenge is to be several steps ahead of them so we are able to anticipate and thwart their threats against the American people.

Science and Technology (S&T) marshals the intellectual capital of the engineering and scientific communities to develop fresh and effective approaches to homeland protection.

To gain an appreciation for the scope of the DHS mission, consider that the United States has 95,000 miles of shoreline, including 7,000 miles of border that we share with Canada and Mexico. Each day, the U.S. monitors 621 border points of entry, including international airports. Approximately 1 million people, 360,000 vehicles, 5,100 trucks, 2,600 aircraft, 600 vessels and 10,000 shipping containers cross our borders, arrive at our airports and enter our ports each day. With this volume of activity, our risk exposure is immense. Our adversaries need only to land one strategically placed blow to cause major repercussions in our society. DHS and our other partners in homeland security need to be right over a million times each day, 365 days a year — never letting our guard down. The terrorists only need to get it right once to succeed in their mission of large-scale destruction.

President Bush envisioned the Department of Homeland Security as an organization that would engage entrepreneurs and tap America's inventive spirit and strengths in science and technology in the war on terror. DHS mobilizes the efforts of 22 federal agencies under a common mission and chain of command. It also has full access to the Coast Guard and Secret Service, further enhancing its ability to react swiftly to threats against our nation. Key areas within the department's responsibilities are border and transportation security, emergency preparedness and response, information analysis and infrastructure protection, and science and technology — the primary research and development arm of DHS. Science and Technology (S&T) marshals the intellectual capital of the engineering and scientific communities to develop fresh and effective approaches to homeland protection.[1]

Origins

The Department of Homeland Security, as proposed by President Bush, would lead the federal government's efforts in preparing for and responding to the full range of terrorist threats involving weapons of mass destruction. To do this, the Department would set national policy and establish guidelines for state and local governments. It would direct exercises and drills for federal, state, and local chemical, biological, radiological, and nuclear (CBRN) response teams and plans. The result of this effort would be to consolidate and synchronize the disparate efforts of multiple federal agencies previously scattered across several departments. This would create a single office whose primary mission was the critical task of protecting the United States from catastrophic terrorism.[2]

H.R. 5005, The Homeland Security Act as introduced by Rep. Richard Armey (R-TX) on June 24th 2002 contained provisions for an Under Secretary for Chemical, Biological, Radiological, and Nuclear Countermeasures who's responsibilities included:

1. Securing the people, infrastructures, property, resources, and systems in the United States from acts f terrorism involving chemical, biological, radiological, or nuclear weapons or other emerging threats;

2. Conducting a national scientific research and development program to support the mission of the Department, including developing national policy for and coordinating the Federal Government's civilian efforts to identify, devise and implement scientific, technological, and other countermeasures to chemical, biological, radiological, nuclear, and other emerging terrorist threats, including directing, funding, and conducting research and development relating to the same;

3. Establishing priorities for, directing, funding, and conducting national research, development, and procurement of technology and systems—

   - for preventing the importation of chemical, biological, radiological, nuclear, and related weapons and material; and

   - for detecting, preventing, protecting against, and responding to terrorist attacks that involve such weapons or material; and

4. Establishing guidelines for State and local government efforts to develop and implement countermeasures to threats of chemical, biological, radiological, and nuclear terrorism, and other emerging terrorist threats.[3]

On June 25th and 27th the House Science Committee, chaired by Rep. Sherwood Boehlert (R-NY), held two hearings focused on research and development (R&D) in homeland security. At the June 27th hearing the focus was on the structure of DHS. The witnesses included Presidential Science Adviser and Director of the Office of Science and Technology Policy (OSTP) John Marburger, Director of the Office of Science in the Department of Energy Raymond Orbach, and John Tritak, Director of the Critical Infrastructure Assurance Office at the National Institute of Standards and Technology.

In his prepared testimony, Marburger defended the President's proposed structure for DHS where the Department's science and technology (S&T) component was located in the office of the Under Secretary for Chemical, Biological, Radiological and Nuclear Countermeasures. The mandate with regard to S&T was: 1) to conduct homeland security-related R&D, as well as to develop national policy for, and to coordinate federal efforts related to countering terrorist threats; and 2) to establish priorities for directing, funding, and conducting national research and development and procurement of technology and systems related to countering these weapons of mass destruction.

Chairman Boehlert, after noting the President's proposal was hastily prepared, declared his determination to amend the legislation to create an Undersecretary for Science and Technology in DHS. A separate office for S&T was contained in S. 2452, the Senate bill sponsored by Sen. Joseph Lieberman (D-CT). Boehlert proclaimed that H.R. 5005 "simply does not give R&D a high enough profile to enable the Department of Homeland Security to accomplish its goals."[4]

At a July 10th markup of H.R. 5005, Rep. Boehlert (R-NY) and Rep. Ralph Hall (D-TX), the Ranking Democrat on the House Science Committee, called for the appointment of a DHS Under Secretary for Science and Technology responsible for coordinating and organizing all research and development pertaining to homeland security. The amendment was passed along with a proposal by Rep. Lynn Woolsey (D-CA) to establish a Homeland Security Institute, and a proposal by Rep. Steve Israel (D-NY) to establish a scientific advisory committee.[5]

H.R. 5005, The Homeland Security Act as signed by the President on November 25th, 2002, included the changes introduced by Rep. Boehlert replacing the Under Secretary for Chemical, Biological Radiological, and Nuclear Countermeasures with the Under Secretary for Science and Technology who's responsibilities included:

1. Advising the Secretary regarding research and development efforts and priorities in support of the Department's missions;

2. Developing, in consultation with other appropriate executive agencies, a national policy and strategic plan for, identifying priorities, goals, objectives and policies for, and coordinating the Federal Government's civilian efforts to identify and develop countermeasures to chemical, biological, radiological, nuclear, and other emerging terrorist threats, including the development of comprehensive, research-based definable goals for such efforts and development of annual measurable objectives and specific targets to accomplish and evaluate the goals for such efforts;

3. Supporting the Under Secretary for Information Analysis and Infrastructure Protection, by assessing and testing homeland security vulnerabilities and possible threats;

4. Conducting basic and applied research, development, demonstration, testing, and evaluation activities that are relevant to any or all elements of the Department, through both intramural and extramural programs, except that such responsibility does not extend to human health-related research and development activities;

5. Establishing priorities for, directing, funding, and conducting national

research, development, test and evaluation, and procurement of technology and systems for:

- preventing the importation of chemical, biological, radiological, nuclear, and related weapons and material; and

- detecting, preventing, protecting against, and responding to terrorist attacks;

6. Establishing a system for transferring homeland security developments or technologies to Federal, State, local government, and private sector entities;

7. Entering into work agreements, joint sponsorships, contracts, or any other agreements with the Department of Energy regarding the use of the national laboratories or sites and support of the science and technology base at those facilities;

8. Collaborating with the Secretary of Agriculture and the Attorney General as provided in section 212 of the Agricultural Bioterrorism Protection Act of 2002 (7 U.S.C. 8401), as amended by section 1709(b);

9. Collaborating with the Secretary of Health and Human Services and the Attorney General in determining any new biological agents and toxins that shall be listed as `select agents' in Appendix A of part 72 of title 42, Code of Federal Regulations, pursuant to section 351A of the Public Health Service Act (42 U.S.C. 262a);

10. Supporting United States leadership in science and technology;

11. Establishing and administering the primary research and development activities of the Department, including the long-term research and development needs and capabilities for all elements of the Department;

12. Coordinating and integrating all research, development, demonstration, testing, and evaluation activities of the Department;

13. Coordinating with other appropriate executive agencies in developing and carrying out the science and technology agenda of the Department to reduce duplication and identify unmet needs; and

14. Developing and overseeing the administration of guidelines for merit review of research and development projects throughout the Department, and for the dissemination of research conducted or sponsored by the Department.[6]

S&T is the primary research and development arm of the Department of Homeland Security.

Mission and Organization

S&T is the primary research and development arm of the Department of Homeland Security. S&T organizes the scientific and technological resources of the United States to prevent or mitigate the effects of catastrophic terrorism against the United States and its allies. S&T unifies and coordinates much of the federal government's efforts to develop and implement scientific and technological countermeasures, including channeling the intellectual energy and research capacity of national laboratories and scientific institutions.

In the war against terrorism, America's already existent science and technology base provides a key advantage. The Department presses this advantage with a national research and development enterprise for homeland security comparable in emphasis and scope to that which supported national security for more than fifty years.

This research and development emphasis is driven by a constant examination of the nation's vulnerabilities, constant testing of our security systems, and a thorough evaluation of the threats and its weaknesses. The emphasis within this enterprise is on catastrophic terrorism – threats to the security of our homeland that could result in large-scale loss of life and major economic impact. It is aimed at both evolutionary improvements to current capabilities as well as the development of revolutionary new capabilities.[7]

The mission of the Science and Technology Directorate (S&T) is to create enduring homeland security capabilities through research, development, testing, evaluation, and transitioning of revolutionary and existing technologies to:

- Detect, prevent, and mitigate chemical, biological, radiological, nuclear, and explosive threats;

- Assess and analyze threats and vulnerabilities;

- Provide technical solutions to Federal, State, and local emergency responders in accordance with operational requirements; and

- Secure the nation's borders and critical infrastructure.[8]

The S&T Directorate directs mission activities to address homeland security long-term strategic objectives to:

- Develop and deploy state-of-the art, high-performance, low-operating-cost systems to prevent, detect, and mitigate the consequences of chemical, biological, radiological, nuclear, and explosive attacks;

- Develop equipment, protocols, and training procedures for response to and recovery from chemical, biological, radiological, nuclear, and explosive attacks;

- Enhance the technical capabilities of the Department's operational elements and other Federal, State, local, and tribal agencies to fulfill their homeland security related missions;

- Develop methods and capabilities to test and assess threats and vulnerabilities, and prevent technology surprise and anticipate emerging threats;

- Develop technical standards and establish certified laboratories to evaluate homeland security and emergency responder technologies, and evaluate technologies for SAFETY Act certification; and

- Support U.S. leadership in science and technology.[9]

To accomplish its mission and achieve its long-term objectives, S&T is organized into four major divisions:

1. Programs, Plans, & Budgets (PPB)

2. Office of Research & Development (ORD)

3. Homeland Security Advanced Research Projects Agency (HSARPA)

4. Systems Engineering and Development (SED)

In addition, the Homeland Security Act authorized two consulting bodies to advise and assist S&T with its mission:

1. Homeland Security Science & Technology Advisory Committee

2. Homeland Security Institute[10]

S&T Operations

An important function of S&T is to engage businesses, federally funded research centers, universities and other government partners in identifying and developing viable concepts for advanced technologies to protect America.

The Homeland Security Advanced Research Projects Agency (HSARPA) strives to produce prototypes of homeland protection technologies for commercial application. Approximately 90 percent of HSARPA's efforts focus on improving existing technologies that can be developed and deployed quickly, while 10 percent address revolutionary, long-range research for breakthrough technologies. State and local first responders and federal agencies allied with homeland security are among the users that will benefit from technologies advanced by HSARPA.

After HSARPA identifies a promising technology, S&T's Office of Systems Engineering and Development (SED) conducts rigorous analysis and testing to determine its suitability and potential for commercial success. In some cases, military technologies are evaluated to see if they can be adapted successfully for use in proximity to civilian populations. SED's role is to identify and systematically eliminate the risks associated with these technologies. SED views each technology through the prism of affordability, performance and supportability—all critical to local responders.

The Homeland Security Act of 2002 gives DHS access to the resources of the Department of Energy's national laboratories to carry out its mission. Some labs have been designated as "intramural," meaning they are assigned projects that are uniquely federal responsibilities and involved in setting standards while the "extramural" labs have established relationship with the private sector and academia making them uniquely qualified to compete in open solicitations. All other DOE national labs, sites, and technology centers are eligible to participate in S&T extramural programs.

HSARPA's extramural programs engage the private sector through research, development, testing and evaluation programs to satisfy homeland security mission requirements. SED manages extramural homeland security project

The Homeland Security Advanced Research Projects Agency (HSARPA) strives to produce prototypes of homeland protection technologies for commercial application. Approximately 90 percent of HSARPA's efforts focus on improving existing technologies that can be developed and deployed quickly, while 10 percent address revolutionary, long-range research for breakthrough technologies.

offices for operational and pilot deployments, technology test beds and limited scale systems acquisition.

DHS also contributes to a government wide effort to help ensure a robust labor pool of technically skilled individuals in the future and build U.S. leadership in science and technology.

The Homeland Security Scholars and Fellows Program is open to U.S. students pursuing areas of study relating to scientific and technological innovations that are aligned with the Homeland Security mission.

S&T is also establishing a series of university-based Homeland Security Centers of Excellence, each with a different R&D focus, that are dedicated to preventing terror strikes and minimizing the consequences of an attack. The first center at the University of Southern California addresses the targets and means of terrorism with emphasis on protecting critical infrastructure. It also develops emergency response tools to minimize both the threat to human lives and the economic impact of an attack. Texas A&M University was selected to investigate defenses against plant and animal diseases. The University of Minnesota was selected to conduct R&D of agricultural terrorism and securing the safety of the nation's food supply.

In addition to these centers, the department's mission is supported by the more than 1,200 community colleges that provide training for more than 80 percent of our country's first responders.[11]

After HSARPA identifies a promising technology, S&T's Office of Systems Engineering and Development (SED) conducts rigorous analysis and testing to determine its suitability and potential for commercial success.

HSARPA

Can technology monitor security at a bustling seaport more effectively than people? Can hardware and software search out security threats at an airport or railroad terminal faster than people? Can technological systems perceive evolving threats at a premier event like the Super Bowl where the crush of activity overwhelms human eyes and ears?

The Department of Homeland Security wants to find out. Working with the U.S. Coast Guard, the DHS Science and Technology Directorate is exploring the concept through a prototype called Hawkeye in South Florida. A maritime surveillance system, Hawkeye will integrate a host of different imaging technologies into an intelligent system capable of automating the detection, tracking, and even the evaluation of vessel traffic around ports, between ports and over the horizon. The goal is to create reliable technology that can monitor activities, connect diverse events that suggest potential threats and alert security personnel when necessary.

The $8 million, 24-month program will scan Port Everglades, Miami, part of Biscayne Bay and offshore approaches to the South Florida coast.

The DHS Science and Technology Directorate manages the research and development programs that lead to new security technologies like Hawkeye.

The Directorate's numerous technology initiatives reflect DHS priorities for protecting critical infrastructure, such as the port facilities along the South Florida coast, improving transportation and border security, boosting emergency preparedness and response capabilities, anticipating emerging threats, speeding the development of prototypes and much more.

Setting technological research priorities begins with risk analysis. Since specific threats aren't always known, risk is evaluated in terms of potential vulnerabilities and consequences. S&T teams evaluate national guidance, vulnerabilities and gaps in our capabilities to come up with what they think will be the highest-payoff technology pursuits. The S&T Directorate also identifies research projects by studying the needs of its operating agencies, such as Customs and Border Protection (CPB). S&T looks at the technologies the agencies are currently using and asks what innovations and advancements would make those tools more effective. S&T also evaluates tasks agencies are performing without technology and asks how technology might help.

The S&T Directorate will spend approximately $1.2 billion of the $40 billion DHS budget in 2005. About $320 million will flow through the Homeland Security Advanced Research Projects Agency (HSARPA) to private-sector technology providers for fast-track research and development.[12] The purpose of HSARPA is to promote research and development in industry and academia. HSARPA's primary goals are:

1. Satisfy operational needs.

2. Conduct rapid prototyping and commercial adaptation.

3. Research revolutionary options.[13]

What kinds of attacks can technology help defend against? While DHS steadfastly refuses to provide details related to security challenges, the agency does appear to use specific and chilling scenarios to help define its security goals.

In early March 2005, a draft document called National Planning Scenarios was inadvertently posted on a Web site managed by the State of Hawaii. The document, reprinted by The New York Times on March 16, 2005, outlines 15 scenarios. They include three natural disasters and 12 terrorist attacks.

The scenarios for terrorist attacks include the detonation of a 10-kiloton nuclear bomb in a major city; a chemical weapons attack at a college football game; a release of sarin gas into the ventilation systems of three large office buildings; attacks with radiological bombs and improvised conventional bombs; and bioweapons attacks on the food supply. Each scenario includes an estimate of casualties and economic costs.

Times' reporter Eric Lipton speculated that by identifying possible attacks and outlining how government might act to prevent, respond to, and recover from each, DHS is attempting to define preparedness for the war on terror.

Currently, HSARPA is pursuing a number of new technology research initiatives that might be considered key components of preparedness. Matching the National Planning Scenarios with HSARPA initiatives provides some insight into the priorities DHS has set for technology.

One of the National Planning Scenarios describes an attack on a chemical plant, in which terrorists sneak into a facility and bomb a chlorine gas storage tank. The resulting release of chlorine gas could leave 17,500 people dead,

Setting technological research priorities begins with risk analysis. Since specific threats aren't always known, risk is evaluated in terms of potential vulnerabilities and consequences.

10,000 severely injured, and as many as 100,000 hospitalized. Recovery costs would range into the millions.

Can such an attack or others that are similar in nature be detected and prevented? Perhaps. An HSARPA initiative called Automated Scene Understanding (ASU) might produce technology capable of detecting unusual activities in and around facilities in the months and weeks preceding a terrorist attack. Early detection of a terrorist plan might make it possible to prevent an attack.

Right now, many secure installations deploy closed circuit television (CCTV), specialized video and infrared cameras, radars and other kinds of imaging sensors to security personnel with a general situational awareness. But the volume of data generated by these vast sensing networks far outstrips the ability of operators to monitor and interpret. Operators after a few minutes might not be able to focus the attention required to notice and connect events that might raise concern.

ASU aims to "fuse, correlate, and interpret" fragments of data from diverse sensing and imaging systems — video, radar, seismic, acoustic, and other sources. The goal is to notice events that might take place in different areas of a facility, to connect the dots and raise an alarm while a preventive response remains possible.

It's a complex area of science requiring sophisticated algorithms, computational resources, and numerous disciplines. While machines can't match the human ability of using the eyes and the brain to recognize things, HSARPA hopes to perhaps create subsets of those abilities.

ASU research contractors believe the analysis conducted by such an intelligent system will eventually be able to identify anomalous or explicitly specified scenarios, behaviors, events, patterns, tracks or objects. The intent is to reduce potentially thousands of sensor readings into a manageable, significant and interesting few.

In pursuing technology intelligent enough to think about what it sees, the ASU initiative focuses on three areas. First, research contractors are reviewing the conventional components of imaging systems, aiming to boost capabilities. Second, they have been asked to develop standardized components that will interoperate and help drive down the costs of expensive proprietary systems. Third, they will apply advanced techniques to the analysis of a test scene: i.e., the South Florida coastline.

Begun in 2003, the Hawkeye project in South Florida serves as the operational test platform for ASU. In 2004, Coast Guard centers in South Florida were equipped with new sensor systems including radar, video, infrared and Automatic Identification Systems.

The prototype's goal is to provide a coastal surveillance capability in a high priority area; offer the Coast Guard and its DHS and local and state partners the means to develop additional operational platforms; and test interoperability among Homeland Security and Department of Defense systems and networks.

Operated by a team of six watch-standers, Hawkeye aims to push the borders out and give the Coast Guard new ways to find mariners in distress, intercept drug smugglers and defend against terrorist attacks. If successful, Hawkeye technology would enhance the security of large potential targets across the country, from a marine terminal to a chemical plant.

HSARPA is managing more than a dozen fast-track technological research initiatives for the Department of Homeland Security. Profiles of the eight newest projects include:

1. The Automated Scene Understanding Program aims to develop intelligent surveillance systems capable of correlating and interpreting fragments of information derived from video, radar, seismic, acoustic and other monitoring technologies. The intent is to reduce thousands of objects, tracks, events, situations, behaviors and scenarios to the few that matter —so that security teams can respond before an attack occurs.

2. The Detection Systems For Radiological and Nuclear Countermeasure Program is designed to contribute to an overall system of countermeasures aimed at radiological or dirty bombs or nuclear weapons. In its solicitation, HSARPA asked research contractors for systems capable of detecting shielded nuclear materials, while reducing nuisance or false alarms. The technology must also be economical enough to be deployed liberally at points of entry and critical installations around the country.

3. The Prototypes and Technology for Improvised Explosive Device Detection Program calls for the rapid prototyping of improved and new systems capable of detecting explosive compounds in vehicles — car and truck bombs. In addition, this initiative provides funds for the research and development of next-generation bomb detection technology that will be capable of detecting not only bombs concealed in vehicles but also those carried by suicide bombers or hidden in leave-behind packages.

4. The Advanced Spectroscopic Portal Monitors Program asks for the fast track development of new detectors capable of identifying controlled nuclear materials. Designed to scan vehicles, cargo trucks and rail cars, the walls of the spectroscopic portal would contain sensors capable of detecting gamma rays and neutron emissions from bombs or plutonium and highly enriched uranium that could be used to make bombs. Acceptable designs must be able to discriminate between medical, industrial and other legitimate sources of radiation, exploit inexpensive commercial components, and offer pricing to facilitate widespread acquisition.

5. The Innovative New Materials for Personal Protective Equipment Program calls on research contractors to develop revolutionary new materials for first responders to wear when responding to an emergency. In its request, DHS urges researchers to develop a single revolutionary material that will protect against chemical, biological, radiological, thermal, and environmental hazards — without compromising freedom of movement.

6. The Low Vapor Pressure Chemicals Detection Systems Program requests technological enhancements for existing chemical detection systems as well as the development of next-generation detection systems. The program aims to equip first responders with handheld devices effective at a

standoff distance of three meters. It also aims at the development of chemical detection systems that will be permanently installed for continuous monitoring.

7. The Food Biological Agent Detection Sensor Program calls for the development of portable or laboratory-based detection methods that can be used at food manufacturing facilities. Sensors will offer low-level detection, low probabilities of both false positives and false negatives, automated operation for non-technical personnel, rapid analysis and low total cost of ownership.

8. The Instantaneous Bio-Aerosol Detector Systems Program aims to improve existing biological weapons detection systems, while extending detection to new forums. Under this program, HSARPA asks for new, low-cost systems that can speed the detection of very low levels of biological materials in the air inside enclosed spaces. The program also calls for sensors capable of monitoring large indoor and semi-enclosed outdoor spaces including auditoriums, arenas, airports, subways, atriums and shopping malls.

Three other Science and Technology units will spend the remaining $880 million in the 2005 Directorate budget. The Office of Research and Development deals with long-term technology research, working with a network of National Laboratories and research universities. The Systems Engineering and Development unit manages operational technical programs such as BioWatch, which monitors for biological threats. The Programs, Plans and Budgets office sets priorities, budgets and coordinates the needs of DHS agencies such as Customs and Border Protection with research and development activities.[14]

Office of Research & Development

The Office of Research and Development (ORD) executes the Directorate's Research, Development, Test and Evaluation (RDT&E) programs within the national and Federal laboratories. ORD establishes the University Centers of Excellence and maintains the nation's enduring research and development complex dedicated to homeland security.

The Office of Research and Development (ORD) executes the Directorate's Research, Development, Test and Evaluation (RDT&E) programs within the national and Federal laboratories. ORD establishes the University Centers of Excellence and maintains the nation's enduring research and development complex dedicated to homeland security.

ORD's primary goals are:

1. Provide the nation with an enduring RDT&E capability.

2. Coordinate homeland security research through the nation's science and technology complex.

3. Preserve and broaden U.S. leadership in science and technology.[15]

The National and Federal Lab system possesses significant expertise in the area of weapons of mass destruction in addition to massive computing power. The S&T Directorate has forged strategic partnering relationships marshaling these capabilities to address the problems of prevention, deterrence, detection, mitigation and identification of the use of weapons of mass destruction. These labs include:

•   DOE National Nuclear Security Administration Labs

- Lawrence Livermore Laboratory

- Los Alamos National Laboratory

- Sandia National Laboratory

- DOE Office of Science Labs

  - Argonne National Laboratory

  - Brookhaven National Laboratory

  - Oak Ridge National Laboratory

  - Pacific Northwest National Laboratory

  - Other DOE Laboratories

- Department of Homeland Security Labs

  - Environmental Measurements Laboratory

  - Plum Island Animal Disease Center

- Department of Health and Human Services Labs

  - HHS operates several laboratories focused on wide-ranging health and disease prevention issues

- U.S. Customs Laboratory and Scientific Services

  - The U.S. Customs Laboratory and Scientific Services does testing to determine the origin of agricultural and manufactured products[16]

The Department of Homeland Security is harnessing the nation's scientific knowledge and technological expertise to protect America and our way of life from terrorism. The Department's Science and Technology directorate, through its Office of University Programs, is furthering this mission by engaging the academic community to create learning and research environments in areas critical to Homeland Security.

Through the Homeland Security Centers of Excellence program, Homeland Security is investing in university-based partnerships to develop centers of multi-disciplinary research where important fields of inquiry can be analyzed and best practices developed, debated, and shared.

The Department's Homeland Security Centers of Excellence (HS-Centers) bring together the nation's best experts and focuses its most talented researchers on a variety of threats that include agricultural, chemical, biological, nuclear and radiological, explosive and cyber terrorism as well as the behavioral aspects of terrorism.

The Department selected the University of Southern California (partnering with the University of Wisconsin at Madison, New York University, North Carolina State University, Carnegie Mellon University, Cornell University, and others) to house the first HS-Center, known as the Homeland Security Center for Risk and Economic Analysis of Terrorism Events (CREATE). The

Department is providing the University of Southern California and its partners with $12 million over the course of the next three years for the study of risk analysis related to the economic consequences of terrorist threats and events. (Awarded November 2003.)

Texas A&M University and its partners have been awarded $18 million over the course of the next three years for the Homeland Security National Center for Foreign Animal and Zoonotic Disease Defense. Texas A&M University has assembled a team of experts from across the country, which includes partnerships with the University of Texas Medical Branch, University of California at Davis, University of Southern California and University of Maryland. Texas A&M University's HS-Center will work closely with partners in academia, industry and government to address potential threats to animal agriculture including foot and mouth disease, Rift Valley fever, Avian influenza and Brucellosis. Their research on foot and mouth disease will be carried out in close collaboration with Homeland Security's Plum Island Animal Disease Center. (Awarded April 2004.)

The University of Minnesota and its partners have been awarded $15 million over the course of the next three years for the Homeland Security Center for Food Protection and Defense, which will address agrosecurity issues related to post-harvest food protection. The University of Minnesota's team includes partnerships with major food companies as well as other universities including Michigan State University, University of Wisconsin at Madison, North Dakota State University, Georgia Institute of Technology, Rutgers University, Harvard University, University of Tennessee, Cornell University, Purdue University and North Carolina State University. (Awarded April 2004.)[17]

Systems Engineering and Development

The System Engineering and Development (SED) division oversees the transition of large-scale and pilot systems to the field through program offices, which bring mature technologies from the lab to the user through a rapid, efficient, and disciplined project management process.

SED's primary goals are:

1. Develop systems context for solutions.

2. Conduct rapid full-scale development.

3. Conduct acceptance testing.

4. Transition mature technologies to production.[18]

SED's responsibilities and initiatives include the following:

- Office of Interoperability and Compatibility (including the SAFECOM Program)

- Counter-MANPADS (Man-Portable Air Defense Systems)

- BioWatch

- Counter Measures Test Bed (CMTB)

Office of Interoperability and Compatibility

The Office of Interoperability and Compatibility (OIC) was launched October 1, 2004 to oversee the wide range of public safety interoperability programs and efforts previously spread across Homeland Security. These programs address critical interoperability issues relating to public safety and emergency response, including communications, equipment, training, and other areas as needs are identified. Specific responsibilities for the OIC include: supporting the creation of interoperability standards; establishing a comprehensive research, development, testing, and evaluation program for improving public safety interoperability; identifying and certifying all DHS programs that touch on interoperability; integrating coordinated grant guidance across all DHS grant making agencies that touch on public safety interoperability; overseeing the development and implementation of technical assistance for public safety interoperability; conducting pilot demonstrations; creating an interagency interoperability coordination council; and coordinating and working closely with the National Incident Management System (NIMS) Integration Center. The OIC will help leverage public safety community resources by promoting cooperation across all levels of government and coordination among federal programs and activities related to interoperability. As a central clearinghouse for information about and assistance with interoperability issues, the office reduces unnecessary duplication in public safety programs and spending, and identifies and promotes interoperability best practices in the public safety arena.[19]

SAFECOM Program

The tragic events of 9/11 clarified the critical importance of effective first responder communication systems. The lack of public safety interoperability is a long-standing, complex, and costly problem with many impediments to overcome. Interoperability is the ability of public safety agencies to talk to one another via radio communication systems—to exchange voice and/or data with one another on demand, in real time, when needed and when authorized. The mission of SAFECOM is to enable public safety nationwide (across local, tribal, state, and federal organizations) by improving public safety response through more effective and efficient interoperable communications. Specifically, SAFECOM functions as an umbrella program within the Federal Government, managed by the Department of Homeland Security's Science and Technology Directorate. SAFECOM is pursuing its mission on a variety of fronts and is consistently guided by the input of local and regional public safety officials. On July 22, 2004, President Bush formally announced the RapidCom initiative, a program designed to ensure that a minimum level of public safety interoperability would be in place in ten high-threat urban areas by September 30, 2004. SAFECOM partnered with the Commonwealth of Virginia to develop a strategic plan for improving statewide interoperable communications with support from the National Institute of Justice (NIJ). Based on lessons learned from the Virginia planning process, SAFECOM released the Statewide Communications Interoperability Planning (SCIP) Methodology for integrating practitioner input into a successful statewide strategic plan. SAFECOM released the first-ever Statement of Requirements (SoR) for public safety communications interoperability in April 2004. This statement defines future requirements for crucial voice and data communications in day-to-day, task force, and mutual aid operations. With the SoR, the nation's 50,000 public safety agencies – for the first time – have a document that serves as a first step toward establishing base-level communications and interoperability standards for all public safety agencies. The SoR helps the public safety community convey a shared and vetted vision that ultimately will help private industry better align research and development efforts with critical interoperable communication needs. The SoR, was submitted to a National Public Safety Telecommunications Council (NPSTC) working group for technical review and endorsement. It was finally provided to 55 regional planning committees for comment before final review and release.[20]

Counter-MANPADS

The Department of Homeland Security announced it is awarding contracts for the final engineering, prototype development, and deployment testing of a protective system for U.S. commercial aircraft against shoulder fired missiles, known as Man-Portable Air Defense Systems (MANPADS). Two teams, one led by BAE Systems and one led by Northrop Grumman, are receiving funding of approximately $45 million each for this 18-month final prototype phase of the program. While there is no credible, specific intelligence information about planned MANPADS attacks against U.S. commercial aircraft, Homeland Security has aggressively pursued countermeasures technology development as part of the administration's strategy to counter this potential threat. This significantly expedited pilot program is adapting existing technology already in use on military aircraft for commercial aviation use. This technology adaptation approach will speed the development of a deployable prototype, and will ensure that the resulting countermeasures are consistent with airport operations and commercial air carrier logistics and safety that include such activities as maintenance, support, and training. While this technology has been used by the U.S. military and some foreign commercial airlines, the challenges in adapting these technologies for use commercially in the United States are significant. In the military, there are a limited number of air bases from which these planes take-off and land, with personnel and replacement parts dedicated to the maintenance of these technologies at each base. The current military technologies must be serviced after a few flying hours, and there are significant questions about the safety on the ground in the event of a false alarm. In Israel, for example, El Al Airlines is able to use these technologies because they fly out of one airport where their maintenance personnel can all be centrally located. In the U.S., with more than 400 airports and more than 6,000 aircraft in the commercial fleet, the maintenance cost of Counter-MANPADS technology at current system costs would be staggering. These challenges are being addressed in this prototype development program.

BioWatch

Early detection and response to a bioterrorism event are crucial for saving lives and mitigating the consequences of an attack. The U.S. Department of

Homeland Security's BioWatch initiative has been successfully operating in many of the nation's urban centers since early 2003. It is one of the important tools used by public health agencies to warn citizens against the presence of biological agents. BioWatch is an early warning system that can rapidly detect trace amounts of biological materials in the air whether they are due to intentional release or due to minute quantities that may occur naturally in the environment. The system assists public health experts in determining the presence and geographic extent of a biological agent release, allowing federal, state, and local officials to more quickly determine emergency response, medical care and consequence management needs. BioWatch operates nationwide, focusing on major urban centers. Routine air samples are collected on a daily basis or more frequently if necessary. To date, BioWatch has analyzed well over half a million samples. Specialized sampling devices developed by the Department have been placed at key locations nationwide that include many of the EPA Air Quality Monitoring Network sites in partnership with state, local and tribal environmental agencies. The specific site locations and other system details are closely held to avoid compromising the system. BioWatch is a DHS initiative that funds, manages and provides policy oversight for this effort in partnership with federal, state and local agencies. Key partners are: Centers for Disease Control and Prevention, which provides technical expertise through its Laboratory Response Network on the laboratory analysis methods and serves as the liaison for laboratory analyses with state health departments; Environmental Protection Agency, which leads the field deployment of the network, and serves as primary liaison to state and local environmental monitoring agencies; laboratories associated with the Department of Homeland Security, especially Los Alamos and Lawrence Livermore National Laboratories, which provide technical expertise in biological sampling systems, and training assistance to state and local agencies. In the event of a positive detection by the BioWatch system, DHS can as appropriate, dispatch several federal response assets to support the public health infrastructure of an impacted area. These include: the Strategic National Stockpile, the nation's pharmaceutical reserve of millions of doses of life-saving and life-sustaining medicines to be administered to populations exposed to natural or man-made biological or chemical threats; and the National Disaster Medical System, composed of teams of professional medical personnel to be deployed to support local public health officials in the event of a national emergency.[21]

Countermeasures Test Bed

The S&T Countermeasures Test Bed (CMTB) is a program for field trials of technologies to detect, interdict, and prevent CBRNE threat materials and weapons. Facilities at the Port Authority of New York and New Jersey (PANYNJ) are used as test beds for technologies designed to detect weapons of mass destruction at critical elements of an intermodal transportation system. These technologies include commercial-off-the-shelf (COTS) radiation detection equipment as well as advanced sensor systems and prototypes being developed by the DOE national laboratories. Field trials play a key role in providing a link between the state and local users of technology and the developers of that technology, and in establishing a transferable technology for countering and addressing the radiological/nuclear threat across the entire nation.

The CMTB includes a pre-deployment testing phase at Brookhaven National Laboratory's Radiation Detector Testing and Evaluation Center (RADTEC) using a variety of radiation sources under a variety of operational conditions. BNL's RADTEC will produce normalized baseline data that can be used to compare the performance of the radiation detection system prior to the deployment at PANYNJ locations. The New York Project Office (NYPO) is located at EML and was established to lead the implementation of the project in the New York area as well as to coordinate, manage, and facilitate the CMTB field activities and project information and data.[22]

Programs, Plans, & Budgets

The Programs, Plans, & Budgets (PPB) Division provides the strategic technical vision for the S&T Directorate and its Research, Development, Technology, and Engineering process.

PPB's primary goals are:

1. Align research and development efforts with the mission and objectives of the Department.

2. Identify user needs and formulate technology investment plans to produce solutions.[23]

The PPB Division conducts and funds research in various areas, or portfolios, organized into three main categories:
1. Countermeasures
2. Support to Department Components
3. Cross-Cutting

The PPB Division conducts and funds research in various areas, or portfolios, organized into three main categories; (1) Countermeasures; (2) Support to Department Components; and (3) Cross-Cutting.[24]

Countermeasure Portfolios

Biological Countermeasures. The mission of the Biological Countermeasures portfolio is to provide the understanding, technologies, and systems needed to anticipate, deter, protect against, detect, mitigate, and recover from possible biological attacks on the nation's population, agriculture, or infrastructure.

Strategic Objectives:

- Develop an integrated national biodefense architecture against all biological threat with emphasis on high consequence events.

- Provide decision makers and responders with knowledge and decision support tools needed to anticipate, prevent, prepare for and respond to events.

- Develop and transition to deployment needed technologies and systems for threat assessment, protection, early detection, attack assessment, forensic analysis, agricultural security, and response and recovery.

- Support partnering agencies, with their leads in public health (Health & Human Services), agriculture (U.S. Department of Agriculture), food (HHS and USDA), water security (EPA), decontamination (EPA), and criminal investigations (Department of Justice).

- Coordinate with partnering agencies in the intelligence and defense fields.

- Where appropriate, incorporate bio-defense as part of an integrated CBRNE defense across civil and military sectors.

Homeland Security Impact:

- BioAssays and detection technologies.

- Biological threat assessment, characterization, forensics, and attribution.

- Food and water protection.

- National agro-bioterrorism strategy.

Chemical Countermeasures. The mission of the Chemical Countermeasures portfolio is to enhance and coordinate the nation's capability to anticipate, prevent, protect, respond to and recover from chemical threat attacks through innovative research, development, and transition capabilities.

Strategic Objectives:

- Develop a national chemical defense architecture.

- Enhance rapid recovery from chemical attacks.

- Develop pre-event assessment, discovery, and interdiction capabilities for chemical threats.

- Minimize loss of life and economic impact from chemical attack.

- Enhance the capability to identify chemical attack sources.

Homeland Security Impact:

- National chemical defense architecture.

- Chemical characterization, detection, and interdiction.

- Rapid recovery and decontamination.

- Chemical source attribution and forensics.

- Minimize effects of chemical attacks.

Radiological and Nuclear Countermeasures. The mission of the Radiological and Nuclear Countermeasures portfolio is to counter the threat of radiological and nuclear terrorism by developing and transitioning advanced, integrated systems and capabilities to operational end users.

Strategic Objectives:

- Understand and characterize nuclear and radiological threats and terrorist events.

- Prevent the importation, transport and delivery to target of illicit radiological and nuclear devices and materials without impeding commerce and the legitimate flow of people.

- Severely minimize the attractiveness and illicit use of nuclear and radiological materials and devices.

- Safeguard the public and critical infrastructure against the use of nuclear and radiological threats.

- Provide scalable and robust radiological and nuclear federal, state, and local incident response and recovery capabilities.

- Provide leadership in RDT&E efforts in radiological and nuclear countermeasures.

Homeland Security Impact:

- Assess and characterize radiological and nuclear threats.

- Response, recovery, and decontamination capabilities.

- Prevent import and use of illicit nuclear materials and devices.

- Advanced detectors (active and passive) and sensor architectures.

- Radiological forensics and attribution.

High Explosive Countermeasures. The mission of the High Explosives Countermeasures portfolio is to develop technical capabilities to detect, interdict, and mitigate the consequences of the use of explosives and other conventional means (non-CBRN) in terrorist attacks against the population, mass transit, civil aviation and critical infrastructure without impeding the flow of commerce.

Strategic Objectives:

- Reduce the risk of a successful attack on critical infrastructure, including all forms of transportation, from explosives and other conventional means.

- Reduce the risk to the population from explosive devices.

- Detect and interdict the illicit movement and use of explosives and explosive devices within or inbound to the United States.

Homeland Security Impact:

- Suicide bombers and leave-behind bombs.

- Truck and car bombs.

- Passenger screening.

- Transportation security.

- Facility blast mitigation.

- Stand-off explosive detection.

Support to DHS Component Portfolios

Border and Transportation Security Research and Development. The mission of the Border and Transportation Security R&D portfolio is to develop and transition capabilities to improve the security of the nation's borders and transportation systems without impeding the flow of commerce and travelers.

Strategic Objectives:

- Prevent entry of terrorists, criminals and illegal aliens.

- Interdict terrorist instruments and contraband at the earliest opportunity.

- Improve the security of U.S. transportation systems.

- Facilitate the flow of commerce and travelers while disrupting and dismantling entities that threaten the United States.

Homeland Security Impact:

- Illegal alien, criminal, and terrorist entry interdiction.

- Facilitate flow of safe commerce and travelers.

- U.S. transportation system security enhancement.

- Secure borders between major points of entry.

Emergency Preparedness and Response R&D. The mission of the Emergency Preparedness and Response R&D portfolio is to improve the ability of the nation to prepare for, respond to and recover from all-hazards emergencies through development and deployment of enabling technologies.

Strategic Objectives:

- Identify and develop relevant technology systems solutions through partnerships with operational end-users (Federal, state, and local).

- Integrate advanced "all hazard" technology into Federal, state, and local emergency response infrastructures.

- Provide scientific underpinnings for public and responder readiness through Federal, state, and local programs.

Homeland Security Impact:

- Personal protective equipment.

- Hazardous material dispersion modeling.

- Regional Technology Integration (RTI) initiative incident response development.

- Emergency responder location and health monitoring.

- Decontamination and restoration technologies.

- Training and education for the responder community.

Threat and Vulnerability, Testing and Assessment. The mission of this portfolio is to develop capabilities through science and technology that enable the creation, application, and dissemination of knowledge to prepare for, anticipate, detect, and prevent terrorist activities and restore the nation's operational capabilities.

Strategic Objectives:

- Tactical and Strategic Assessment of Terrorist uses of CBRNE.

- Capabilities to understand and exploit terrorist intentions, motives, and behaviors.

- Federal, state, local and international-level knowledge services capabilities for data and information sharing.

- Federal, state and local-level incident planning support through management of knowledge services.

Homeland Security Impact:

- Biometrics and determination of intent.

- Knowledge management for threat and capability assessments.

- Understand terrorist intentions, motives and behaviors.

- Federal, state and local knowledge sharing and collaboration.

- International data and information sharing.

Critical Infrastructure Protection. The mission of the Critical Infrastructure Protection portfolio is to protect the nation's critical infrastructure and key resources from acts of terrorism, natural disasters, or other emergencies by developing and deploying tools to anticipate, identify, and analyze risks, and systems to reduce those risks and the consequences of an event.

Strategic Objectives:

- Support the scientific prioritization of components of critical infrastructure and key resources/assets.

- Reduce critical infrastructure vulnerabilities and consequences of events.

- Anticipate the threat/event and predict the consequences.

- Meet Critical Infrastructure Protection (CIP) technical and operational requirements from DHS elements (including real-time support during an event).

- Partner with other portfolios, agencies, industry, and international entities to catalyze development of CIP technologies.

Homeland Security Impact:

- Prioritization of critical infrastructure and key assets.

- Anticipate threats and events and predict consequences.

- Reduce critical infrastructure vulnerabilities and consequences of events.

- Incident decision support system for attacks on infrastructure.

Cyber Security. The mission of the Cyber Security portfolio is to lead cyber security research, development, testing and evaluation endeavors to secure the nation's critical information infrastructure, through coordinated efforts that will improve the security of the existing cyber infrastructure, and provide a foundation for a more secure infrastructure.

Strategic Objectives:

- Conduct RDT&E of cyber security technology aimed at preventing, protecting against, detecting, responding to, and recovering from large-scale, high-impact cyber attacks.

- Enable the creation of and migration to more secure critical information infrastructure, through the development and use of more secure communication protocols.

- Address cyber security R&D needs that are unique to critical infrastructure sectors, particularly those that rely on the Internet to a great extent (Information and Telecommunications, Banking and finance), and in coordination with the CIP Portfolio, address the cross-cutting issue of securing process control systems.

- Provide a foundation for the long-term goal of economically-informed, risk-based cyber security decision making.

- Provide novel and next-generation secure information technology concepts and architectures through long-term research efforts.

Homeland Security Impact:

- Security for data networks and information.

- Security for data flow and communications.

- Security for software applications.

- Security for hardware components and machines.

- Insider access detection and prevention.

- Robust process control and SCADA systems.

U.S. Coast Guard Research & Development. The mission of the U.S. Coast Guard R&D portfolio is to develop technology and systems to provide the capability to safeguard lives, property and the environment from intentional and accidental maritime threats and protect maritime mobility through the free flow of goods and people while maximizing the recreational use of the nation's waterways.

Strategic Objectives:

- Identify maritime threats.

- Prevent the unauthorized entry of illegal aliens and contraband, including WMD, over maritime borders.

- Reduce critical maritime infrastructure vulnerability.

- Enhance maritime safety and mobility.

- Prevent and mitigate accidental and intentional maritime environmental incidents.

- Enforce maritime laws including fisheries and environmental regulations.

Homeland Security Impact:

- Maritime threat characterization.

- Safety and mobility enhancement for the nation's waterways.

- Illegal alien and contraband interdiction.

- Environmental threats and incident mitigation.

- Critical maritime infrastructure protection.

U.S. Secret Service Research and Development. The mission of the U.S. Secret Service R&D portfolio is to develop and deploy advanced technologies to enhance the protective and investigative abilities of the U.S. Secret Service.

Strategic Objectives:

- Protect our nation's leaders, visiting world leaders, and other protectees as well as reduce threats posed by global terrorists and other adversaries.

- Reduce crimes against our nation's financial infrastructure, to include currency and financial payment systems.

Homeland Security Impact:

- National Special Security Events (NSSEs)

- Protectees and facilities.

- Hardening targets.

- Investigation and apprehension.

Cross-Cutting Portfolios

Emerging Threats. The mission of the Emerging Threats portfolio is to anticipate and define potential threats and technological advances, terrorist use of existing capabilities in new or unexpected manners, and self assessments of S&T research activities and jump-start countermeasures capability development.

Strategic Objectives:

- Identify and prioritize emerging threats for S&T by evaluating the implications of the state of scientific advancement and S&T countermeasures.

- Identify and sponsor high risk, high pay-off basic technology research.

Homeland Security Impact:

- Advanced technology development to address long-term needs.

- Future potential threat implications and countermeasure development based on state-of-the-art and cutting edge technologies.

Rapid Prototyping. The mission of the Rapid Prototyping portfolio is to accelerate deployment of advanced technologies to address urgent user requirements.

Strategic Objectives:

- Define and apply a structured approach for rapid prototyping to adapt existing technologies for new homeland security applications or incorporate new technologies in homeland security applications.

- Implement a mechanism for selecting candidate prototyping projects.

- Ensure transition planning for technology prototypes.

- Provide coordination of prototype programs.

Homeland Security Impact:

- Accelerated development of mature technologies for rapid transition to the field.

- Re-engineering existing technologies to serve new functions.

- Deployment of prototypes to address immediate security needs.

Standards Portfolio. The mission of the Standards portfolio is to develop and coordinate the adoption of national standards and appropriate evaluation methods to meet homeland security mission needs.

Strategic Objectives:

- Identify requirements and prioritize needs for HLS standards.

- Develop, adopt and recommend standards and guidance necessary for homeland security mission needs.

- Develop metrics and protocols for component and system test and evaluation.

- Coordinate standards development with other U.S. government and international partners.

Homeland Security Impact:

- Requirements for homeland security standards.

- Standards and guidance for DHS mission areas.

- Metrics for testing and evaluation protocols.

- International standards compliance.

University and Fellowship Programs. the mission of the University and Fellowship Programs portfolio is to stimulate, coordinate, leverage, and utilize the unique intellectual capital in the academic community to address current and future homeland security challenges, and educate and inspire the next generation homeland security workforce.

The mission of the Homeland Security Science and Technology Advisory Committee (HSSTAC) is to be a source of independent, scientific and technical planning advice for the Under Secretary for Science and Technology

Strategic Objectives:

- Foster a homeland security culture within the academic community through research and educational programs.

- Strengthen U.S. scientific leadership in homeland security research; generate and disseminate knowledge and technical advances to advance the homeland security mission.

- Integrate homeland security activities across agencies engaged in relevant academic research.

- Create and leverage intellectual capital and nurture a homeland security science and engineering workforce.

Homeland Security Impact:

- University Centers of Excellence to study homeland security issues.

- Summer faculty.

- Scholars and fellows programs.

- Post-doctoral fellowships.[25]

HSSTAC

The Homeland Security Act of 2002 (Public Law 107- 296) established within the Department of Homeland Security the Homeland Security Science and Technology Advisory Committee (HSSTAC). The Committee operates in accordance with the provisions of the Federal Advisory Committee Act (FACA) (5 U.S.C. App. 2) to make recommendations with respect to the activities of the Under Secretary for Science and Technology. The mission of the HSSTAC is to be a source of independent, scientific and technical planning advice for the Under Secretary for Science and Technology. The duties of the HSSTAC are solely advisory and include the following:

- In keeping with its mission, the Committee's activities focus on the responsibilities of the Under Secretary for Science and Technology to organize the Nation's scientific and technological resources to prevent or mitigate the effects of catastrophic terrorism against the United States, including both sponsorship and coordination of research and development efforts for this purpose.

- The Committee makes recommendations with respect to the activities of the Under Secretary for Science and Technology, including identifying research areas of potential importance to the security of the Nation. The Committee is concerned with matters relating to science, technology, research, engineering, new product development (including demonstration and deployment), business processes, emergency response, and other matters of special interest to the Department of Homeland Security.

- The Committee assists the Under Secretary in establishing mission goals for the future; advises on whether the policies, actions, management processes, and organization constructs of the Science and Technology Directorate are focused on mission objectives; advises on whether the research, development, test, evaluation, and systems engineering activities are properly resourced (capital, financial, and human) to accomplish the objectives; identifies outreach activities (particularly in accessing and developing, where necessary, the industrial base of the Nation); and, reviews the technical quality and relevance of the Directorate's programs.

- Upon request, the Committee provides scientifically- and technically-based advice to the Homeland Security Advisory Council. Conversely, the Committee draws, when needed, on the expertise of outside advisory groups for independent advice on specific technical and policy matters.

The HSSTAC meets at least quarterly at the call of the Chair or whenever one-third of the members so request in writing. Subcommittees and ad hoc task forces meet as required to accomplish their particular tasks.

The HSSTAC consists of 20 members appointed by the Under Secretary for Science and Technology. The HSSTAC members are (1) eminent in fields such as emergency response, research, engineering, new product development, business, and management consulting; (2) selected solely on the basis of established records of distinguished service; (3) not employees of the Federal Government; and, (4) selected as to provide representation of a cross-section of the research, development, demonstration, and deployment activities supported by the Under Secretary for Science and Technology. These distinguished scientists, engineers, medical researchers, first responders, industrial and academic leaders, former government officials, and other citizens provide expertise and experience relevant to the full breadth of the Department's science and technology enterprise. Specific expertise includes: countermeasures to chemical, biological, radiological, nuclear, and high explosive threats; critical infrastructure protection; borders and transportation security; intelligence; vulnerability analysis; systems engineering; and, first response.

In general, the term of office of each member is 3 years. The Under Secretary for Science and Technology designates a Chair from among the appointed members of HSSTAC. The Chair is appointed for a two-year term and may be reappointed for additional terms. The Chair is the presiding officer of the Committee and guides its efforts to the effective completion of its assigned tasks.

The Under Secretary for Science and Technology establishes as needed any number of subcommittees to advise the HSSTAC. Each subcommittee is composed of HSSTAC members. The HSSTAC Chair designates a Chair for each of the subcommittees from among the HSSTAC members. The Chair of each subcommittee, in consultation with the HSSTAC, may establish ad hoc working groups or task forces to advise the subcommittees as needed.

While attending meetings or otherwise engaged in Committee business, Committee members are authorized travel and subsistence or per diem allowances (as appropriate) in accordance with Federal Government regulations.[26]

Homeland Security Institute

The Homeland Security Institute (HSI) provides a dedicated, high-quality technical and analytical support capability aimed at helping the [Department of] Homeland Security set priorities and guide investments.

In April 2004, the U.S. Department of Homeland Security's Science and Technology Directorate established the Homeland Security Institute (HSI), this is the Department's first government "think tank" or Federally Funded Research and Development Center (FFRDC). The Institute, managed by Analytic Services Incorporated (ANSER), provides independent analysis on a variety of issues related to defense of the homeland. The Homeland Security Institute will particularly focus on those matters involving policy and security where scientific, technical, and analytical expertise is required such as those in the extremely complex threat and vulnerability assessment areas.

The Homeland Security Act of 2002, Section 312, mandated the establishment of an FFRDC to provide Homeland Security, access to an independent resource that could analyze and assess homeland security issues as they relate to critical analysis and decision support; mitigating homeland security threats, vulnerabilities, and risks while continually enhancing operational effectiveness.

The Homeland Security Institute provides a dedicated, high-quality technical and analytical support capability aimed at helping Homeland Security set priorities and guide investments. The Institute maintains an integrated systems approach to its mission by engaging in the following activities:

- Systems Evaluations - Systems evaluations provide analyses that support homeland security program planning and execution. These analyses cover all stages of development and deployment: initiation and conduct of research; development of technology; testing, evaluating, building and/or acquiring, deploying and using systems. Included are systems analyses, risk analyses, vulnerability analyses and the creation of strategic technology development plans to reduce vulnerabilities in the nation's critical infrastructure and key resources.

- Operational Assessments - Operational assessments relate to systems development, operational performance, and homeland security strategy while providing a basis for revising operational concepts and mission needs. Included are evaluation of the effectiveness of measures deployed to enhance security of institutions and infrastructure; design and use of metrics to evaluate the effectiveness of Homeland Security programs; and, design and support for exercises and simulations.

- Technology Assessments - Technology assessments provide scientific, technical, and analytical support for the identification, evaluation, and use of advanced technologies for homeland security systems. Assistance is provided to Homeland Security as well as other agencies and departments by evaluating the effectiveness of technologies under development and assess their appropriateness for deployment.

- Resource and Support Analyses - Resource and support efforts develop methods, techniques, and tools (e.g., models) and conduct analyses that lead to improved means for addressing resource issues including investment decisions and cost implications of pending decisions. Included are the economic and policy analyses to assess the distributed costs and benefits of alternative approaches to enhancing security.

- Analyses Supporting the SAFETY Act - The SAFETY Act analyses will provide analytical and technical evaluations that can be used to support DHS determinations about candidate technologies.

- Field Operations Analyses - The Institute is sometimes required to provide small numbers of personnel to field activities to provide objective operations analyses, systems evaluations, and other technical and analytic support.[27]

Conclusion

The Nation's advantage in science and technology is a key to securing the homeland. New technologies for analysis, information sharing, detection of attacks, and countering chemical, biological, radiological, and nuclear weapons will help prevent and minimize the damage from future terrorist attacks. Just as science and technology have helped us defeat past enemies overseas, so too will they help us defeat the efforts of terrorists to attack our homeland and disrupt our way of life.

The Nation needs a systematic national effort to harness science and technology in support of homeland security. Our national research enterprise is vast and complex, with companies, universities, research institutes, and government laboratories of all sizes conducting research and development on a very broad range of issues. Guiding this enterprise to field important new capabilities and focus new efforts in support of homeland security is a major undertaking.

The Science and Technology Directorate of the Department of Homeland Security serves as the federal government's lead for this effort, to work with private and public entities to ensure that our homeland security research and development are of sufficient size and sophistication to counter the threat posed by modern terrorism.[28]

Questions

1. What is the mission of the Science and Technology Directorate?

2. How are HSARPA and SED related?

3. What is the mission of ORD?

4. List and describe some of the portfolios managed by PPB.

5. How do the HSSTAC and HSI missions differ?

Part IV:
Securing Our Future

## Chapter 24

America's New Normalcy

Objectives

- Understand the components to reducing terrorism.

- Explain the resource challenge in reducing terrorism.

- Describe "America's New Normalcy", a future vision offered by the Gilmore Commission.

One fact dominates all homeland security threat assessments: terrorists are strategic actors. They choose their targets deliberately based on the weaknesses they observe in our defenses and our preparations. They can balance the difficulty in successfully executing a particular attack against the magnitude of loss it might cause. They can monitor our media and listen to our policymakers as our Nation discusses how to protect itself—and adjust their plans accordingly. Where we insulate ourselves from one form of attack, they can shift and focus on another exposed vulnerability.

- National Strategy for Homeland Security

The Gilmore Commission Reports

The Advisory Panel to Assess Domestic Response for Terrorism Involving Weapons of Mass Destruction—chaired by former Virginia Governor James S. Gilmore III and known as the Gilmore Commission—was established by Section 1405 of the National Defense Authorization Act for 1999, Public Law 105-261 (H.R. 3616, 105th Congress, 2nd Session, October 17, 1998). The panel was directed to submit, beginning in December 1999, three annual reports to the President and Congress assessing how well the Federal government was supporting State and local efforts to combat catastrophic terrorism. The panel was also charged to recommend strategies for ensuring fully effective local response capabilities. As a result of the attacks on September 11, 2001, Congress extended the panel's charter with the requirement to submit two additional annual reports on December 15 2002 and 2003, respectively.

The [Gilmore] panel was guided by the recognition that the threat of terrorism can never be completely eliminated and that no level of resources can prevent the United States from being attacked in the future

The fifth and final report, submitted December 15, 2003, sought to develop a strategic vision of the future of homeland security—one that the panel chose to call "America's New Normalcy." The panel was guided by the recognition that the threat of terrorism can never be completely eliminated and that no level of resources can prevent the United States from being attacked in the future. At the same time, the panel believes that the Nation is achieving an important, critical understanding of the risks posed to America by terrorism, an understanding that derives from America's inherent strengths—the strength in our Constitutional form of government and particularly the strength of its people.

The Threat Assessment Dilemma

It is now well recognized that the nature of global and national affairs dictates that a wide variety of terrorism threats already exist, that others will assuredly emerge and develop, and that the United States homeland will be among the targets of such threats for the foreseeable future. While ameliorating the political, social, and economic conditions that give rise to terrorism is a challenging undertaking clearly worthy of the expenditure of national and international time and treasure, it is an effort not likely to pay major dividends in the short term—failing to meet the typical expectation of our citizens that we will immediately solve any problem. However, it is extremely difficult to assess the magnitude and character of the current threat, much less do a genuinely useful, specific, or actionable threat projection. This clearly will hamper any efforts to develop even crude metrics or measures of performance that reflect whether the threat is being reduced to a strategically meaningful degree. Fortunately, we have had to this point few attacks against which to measure certain performance. It is likely that future attacks will provide the meaningful measure of certain aspects of our preparedness. It can be argued, however, that the absence of attacks is one appropriate measure of how well we are doing in deterring and preventing attacks.

In casting a strategic vision for U.S. efforts to combat terrorism, inevitable issues of priorities in setting goals arise along with the debate about the allocation of scarce resources to achieve those goals. In an environment where you cannot do it all, where will the nation get the greatest return on investment in its efforts to reduce the risk of terrorism? In threat reduction efforts? In improved hardening or other methods of reducing traditional vulnerabilities? In improved warning and associated planning to permit adequate time to take (presumably temporary) measures to reduce vulnerabilities?

The dilemma is portrayed graphically in Figure 24.1, which emphasizes the three main areas of competition for resources in the effort to reduce the risk from terrorism:

- Threat reduction through direct action to destroy or dismantle terrorist groups ("draining the swamp") and deny such groups chemical, biological, radiological, and nuclear weapons and other instruments of terror;

- Vulnerability reduction through a wide variety of pre-attack terrorism-specific actions that would be effectively independent of near-term strategic or tactical warning (a "fortress against terrorism"); and

- Vulnerability reduction through terrorism-specific actions that would be implemented upon tactical warning of an imminent attack or that an attack is on the way but has not yet arrived.

In the simplest terms, any of the three main areas of risk reduction could dominate a strategic vision.

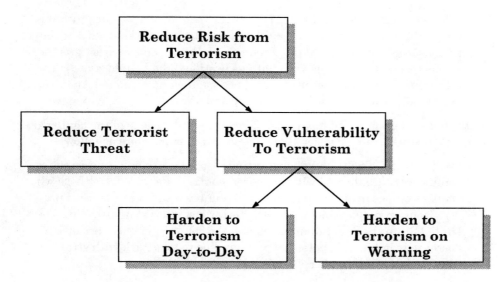

Figure 24.1: Terrorism Risk Reduction Components.

It can be inferred from Figure 24.1 that more than one legitimate strategic vision—i.e., a vision fully defensible in the light of terrorism-related uncertainties—is possible in this context through a mixing of priorities between the three main areas of competition for resources. In the simplest terms, any of the three main areas of risk reduction cited above could dominate a strategic vision. A fourth simple and extreme alternative would be not to take any counter-terrorism actions and rely wholly on existing plans and programs for natural disasters and other hazards.

Four Specific Alternative Visions

Terrorism is and will remain vague, ambiguous, unpredictable, and largely episodic. It will continue to require an approach unlike any other enemy with which we have had to deal. In considering alternative visions, the panel postulated three somewhat different threat scenarios over the next five years, recognizing that reality may prove to be some combination or permutation of them:

- Very Infrequent Attacks. This scenario is characterized by the absence of significant terrorist attacks in the United States. It assumes an eventual success in the Iraq war and a reduction in Israeli-Palestinian tensions over the next five years. In retrospect, September 11 is seen as a unique event, highly unlikely ever to be repeated particularly as time goes by. It is also characterized by the absence of successful terrorist attacks on U.S. assets and bases overseas (akin to the African Embassy bombings or the attack on the U.S.S. Cole.)

- A Continuation of Post-9/11 Threat Levels. The country continues on basically the course it is on today, anticipating a long-term slow-motion, highly episodic strategic threat. The episodic incidents of terrorism might include some major incidents, albeit most likely not with the impact of September 11.

- A Rise in Terrorist Attacks and Lethality. In spite of a U.S.-led international effort to combat terrorism, the overall terrorist threat stays ahead of national and international preparedness. Independent terrorist groups are increasingly in league with nations hostile to the United States. In this scenario, attacks continue to be successful worldwide, and Americans are killed or injured in attacks at home and abroad.

With that background and having considered the dimensions of the challenge, four illustrative strategic visions considered by the panel were as follows:

1. Complacence. The push for committing resources to combat terrorism is significantly diminished with increased political pressure from those who want resources in other areas, and the country returns to a state of pre-9/11 focus on preparedness. But the terrorists' interest in attacking the United States have not diminished and the country, in effect because of decreased vigilance, is potentially vulnerable to an attack with strategic impact akin to September 11.

2. Reactive. There would be steady funding but be no major increases in the level of assets (time, money, coordination, training, exercises, etc.) committed to homeland security and other dimensions of the terrorism problem. Organizational and other efforts that have been launched since September 11 would be continued with some consolidation. The country will react strongly in the short term, but not fundamentally change its resource allocation priorities over the longer term.

3. Fortress America. Most observers express skepticism about the prospects of significantly curtailing the terrorist threat without draconian measures. The prospect of unforeseen severe terrorism-related financial and personal losses is acknowledged and addressed through insurance and government programs that compensate victims under procedures akin to the aid provided to victims of natural disasters. An ever-increasing level of resources is committed to combating terrorism with a focus on improved prevention and response, as well as hardening and reducing vulnerabilities in critical infrastructures. Significant resources are devoted tot he "fortress" at the expense of other programs and initiatives, and civil liberties are actually or perceived to be eroded.

4. The New Normalcy. The country navigates toward a new normalcy in its posture and approach to terrorism. The threat of terrorism is not eliminated but the threat is viewed in light of an aggressive and coordinated international effort to combat the threat. The destructive risks associated with terrorism are normalized at the personal, State, and local level vis-à-vis other destructive acts against U.S. society and interests both natural and manmade ("take the terror out of terrorism"). Efforts to combat terrorism are substantial as compared to the period before September 11 but are prioritized, institutionalized, and sustained. Terrorism is essentially treated as criminal action of a hybrid intranational/international character, with attendant clear roles and responsibilities at the Federal, State, and local level and in the private sector, as well as among citizens. This approach provides duality of purpose so that we are better prepared for all emergencies and disasters, including terrorism. It is broad and considers not only the physical impact but economic and societal as well.

"America's New Normalcy" proffers a view of the future—five years out—that the panel believes offers a reasonable, measurable, and attainable benchmark.

Based on the panel's conception of what is both possible and desirable, the panel chose "The New Normalcy" as the strategic vision to guide U.S. decision-making and strategic planning for the foreseeable future.

America's New Normalcy

"America's New Normalcy" proffers a view of the future—five years out—that the panel believes offers a reasonable, measurable, and attainable benchmark. In the absence of longer-term measurable goals, this benchmark can provide government at all levels, the private sector, and citizens a future set of objectives for readiness and preparedness. The panel does not claim that the objectives presented in this future view are all encompassing nor necessarily reflect the full continuum of advances that America may accomplish or the successes that its enemies may realize in the next five years. It is, however, a snapshot in time for the purpose of guiding the actions of today and a roadmap for the future.

January 20, 2009—Washington DC

It is the morning of January 20, 2009. In a few hours the President will give his Inaugural Address which will cover, among other things, the significant progress that has been made in combating terrorism both worldwide and in the homeland. The President will describe major improvements across the entire spectrum of capabilities to combat terrorism from awareness activities (intelligence and information sharing), to prevention, to preparedness, through response and recovery.

The news has not all been good in the five years prior to New Year's Day 2009. American interests have continued to be attacked around the world by those who hate freedom and the country that most epitomizes liberty and equality. Overseas, scores of Americans have died and many more have been injured. At home, while nothing on the scale of September 11 has recurred, the remnants of al Qaeda and others trying to imitate it have attacked a few soft targets with "conventional" type devices, and killed 21 more Americans on our own soil.

Nevertheless, with vastly improved intelligence and cooperation from our allies—some very nontraditional—several attempts by terrorist groups to acquire a variety of chemical and biological weapons, and low-yield radiological devices, have all seemingly been thwarted.

On the home front, coordination at all levels of government and with the private sector has improved significantly and has been institutionalized and regularized. The public at large understands the nature of the terrorist threats, and has increasing confidence in government to deal with those threats appropriately. There is a stronger sense among our citizens of physical and economic security as well as societal stability, as a result of visible successes among governments and the private sector in developing and implementing strategies and plans that address the threats.

Future Vision 2009—State, Local, and Private Sector Empowerment

States, localities, and appropriate entities in the private sector are fully and consistently integrated into planning and decision-making processes. The DHS regional structure and an integrated communications and information network provides for real time, day-to-day coordination across a broad spectrum of prevention, preparedness, response and recovery issues at all levels. The Homeland Security Council is engaged in continuous, sustained, and well-organized dialogue with all levels of government, the private sector, and academia to develop a forward looking vision of readiness efforts.

The Federal government has developed and implemented a consistent program of financial support for State and local government efforts to combat terrorism, a program that has played a major role in sustaining State and local investment to combat terrorism and coordination in Federal, State, and local preparedness planning. Of particular significance has been the sustained funding to strengthen preparedness and coordination within the public health system. Information on Federal support is available through a central clearinghouse managed by DHS.

The Federal government, in coordination with the States, has developed grants and other forms of Federal assistance to fund programs that are based on continuing risk assessments where population is only one measure of vulnerability. Federal assistance is based on a fully developed system of priorities and requirements generation that flows up from the local level, is consolidated and coordinated at the State and territorial level, and then is rationalized against available Federal funding.

DHS, in cooperation with other Federal agencies and State and local governments, has coordinated the development and implementation of a comprehensive process for State and localities, and appropriate entities in the private sector, to assess and articulate potential requirements for all-hazards Federal support. That process has vastly improved the allocation of Federal resources based on a prioritization of capabilities for potential support.

Most important, the Federal government has incentivized through funding a nationwide system and has provided significant support to States for the implementation of a comprehensive, integrated, overlapping network of mutual aid for all-hazards response—a "matrix" of intrastate multijurisdictional and interstate supporting capabilities that has helped to ensure responsiveness anywhere in the country. Federal assistance in this system is based on various considerations, including localities and areas of higher threat, the efficiency of consolidating resources in highly trained and well equipped government response entities, and close coordination among all levels of government and the private sector.

State and local responders have been adequately funded, equipped and trained to meet nationally defined and accepted terrorism preparedness standards. Risk assessments have been developed and updated in line with national guidelines. There is a National Incident Management System (NIMS) adopted and used by all levels of government and the private sector. Significant progress has been made in communications interoperability for all response disciplines. Regular exercises are held to refine and practice in the effective response to potential terrorist attacks and other hazards.

Future Vision 2009—Intelligence

The relationship between DHS, the intelligence community, the Department of Justice and the FBI, and the other Federal agencies involved in collection, analysis, and dissemination of terrorist threat information is increasingly mature with strong and effective coordination responding to DHS leadership and DHS-levied intelligence requirements.

The Terrorist Threat Integration Center (TTIC) is seen as increasingly successful in integrating overseas and domestic intelligence, including information from State, local and private sector sources, to provide a well-reasoned comprehensive strategic terrorism threat assessment covering potential perpetrators, capabilities, and objectives. The overseas and domestic intelligence assessments that are emerging acknowledge continued uncertainties in the current and projected terrorism threat, while at the same time placing bounds in a manner useful for planning purposes on the magnitude and character of that threat. All appropriate elements of other Federal agencies have been fully integrated into the TTIC, and it has significant staff elements representing State and local government entities and the private sector. Executive Branch and Congressional oversight mechanisms have proven to be highly effective in preventing any abuses.

The emphasis on combating terrorism within the intelligence community over the years has led to an unprecedented level of expertise and cooperation, including matters related to health and medical factors.

The broad national commitment to combating terrorism has led to vastly improved vulnerability assessments across the different elements of society (including in particular in the area of critical infrastructures) and a commensurate ongoing effort to reduce existing vulnerabilities and limit the emergence of new vulnerability problems.

The improvements in both threat and vulnerability assessments have enabled DHS to produce overall national risk assessments for critical target sets (such as infrastructures and national icons) and to aid State and local governments in high-risk target areas in performing site- and community-specific risk assessments, including real-time risk assessments that respond to new actionable intelligence. These data are being used to guide the allocation of preparedness funding but not to the exclusion of those low threat areas. The national warning system has been refined to provide more geographic specific information based on the actual or potential threats.

While the availability of actionable warning cannot be guaranteed, there have been instances in which such warning has been available and has contributed substantially to reducing the impact of terrorist attacks. For planning purposes, however, it is still assumed that in many cases of terrorist attack, such warning will not be available.

Future Vision 2009—Information Sharing

In addition to the information sharing within the Federal government that has enabled improved threat assessments, terrorism-related cooperation on sharing information on every aspect of combating terrorism— from risk assessments to best practices for responding to specific threats—within the Federal government, between the Federal government and State and local entities, and between governments and the private sector, has vastly improved.

The Intelligence Community, in cooperation with other Federal agencies, with State and local governments, and with the private sector, has developed a new classification system and a series of products that are unclassified but limited in distribution to allow dissemination to those responsible for public and private sector preparedness. Specific products with actionable guidance are designed to meet the needs of and available daily to public health officials, State and local law enforcement, and other responders.

Most noteworthy is the improvement in information sharing between the government and among the owners and operators of critical infrastructures, made possible by major changes in previously existing laws and regulations regarding freedom of information and restraint of trade.

The Federal government has led the development of a comprehensive risk communications strategy for educating the public on the threats from and consequences of terrorist attacks. The strategy covers both prevent communications and protocols for communications when an event occurs and during recovery.

The Health Alert Network and other health-related secure communications systems that generate all-hazard surveillance, epidemiological, and laboratory information have been substantially improved and strengthened and are now being utilized with high reliability by all entities of the medical and health communities—public and private.

In the border control arena, there is now a well-established, comprehensive database and information technology systems internal to the border agencies under DHS and those of other Federal agencies, State and local entities, private sector operators, and cooperating foreign governments, who conduct activities related to people or things moving across U.S. borders or are involved in border-related intelligence collection, analysis, and dissemination.

Future Vision 2009 – Training, Exercising, Equipping, and Standards

Grant programs in DHS have been consolidated into a single entity that reports directly to the Secretary. In addition, the President has established a Federal interagency coordinating entity for homeland security grants, headed by the Secretary of Homeland Security. Allocation criteria have been developed for all Federal grants that considers risk/threat, capabilities, progress towards achieving national standards in various disciplines, population and regional cooperative efforts. That entity has also streamlined the grant application and decision process throughout the government, and has been instrumental in eliminating unnecessary redundancies in programs.

The insurance industry is basing rates on the level of preparedness of communities, States and businesses based on established nationwide standards, providing incentives for enhanced risk management.

DHS has implemented a program that has established training standards for first responders that outlines the tasks, conditions, and standards of performance for individuals and units.

In addition, a broad program of all-hazards exercises, with specific standards for conducting and evaluating them, and funded in part by DHS, continues to expand at the State and local level and with substantial private sector participation. Training specifically for responding to terrorist attacks is given a high priority.

A joint combating terrorism exercise program for potential major terrorists involving CBRN has been institutionalized and implemented nationwide for Federal, State, and local officials and the private sector participants. It has steadily improved the ability of government and private entities to work together effectively.

The sustained level of government funding for terrorism preparedness has facilitated the establishment of standards and proficiency tests associated.

A successful national effort to improve communications interoperability (particularly at the local level) through the promulgating of national equipment standards, facilitated by substantial Federal and private sector investment in RDT&E, has been a hallmark of progress in combating terrorism as a component of all hazards preparedness.

Best practices in all aspects of combating terrorism, informed by lessons learned from exercises and actual events, is available through a significantly improved national database. This best practices database is seen as particularly useful in assisting States in meeting surge capacity requirements and dealing with associated resource allocation issues.

Future Vision 2009 – Enhanced Critical Infrastructure Protection

There are major improvements in protective and defensive measures, especially for critical infrastructures. As appropriate, many programs have been implemented as old infrastructures and supporting systems are replaced.

Improvements in the aviation industry include measures mandating the screening of all baggage and cargo for passenger and commercial aircraft and the implementation of a new set of comprehensive security guidelines for general aviation. In the shipping industry, U.S. seaports and many international air and seaports are now equipped with extensive suites of detection and monitoring equipment. In the energy, chemical, and telecommunications sectors, there are now well-established models and metrics for evaluating the vulnerability existing systems and facilities and additional protective measures. In the process of reducing vulnerability to natural disasters and providing redundancy in response to lessons learned from the power outages of 2003, the vulnerability of the energy supply sector has been reduced.

For U.S. border crossings, there are stiff pre-entry identification requirements for people, and pre-shipping reporting requirements and other regulations for commercial shipments that have dramatically improved the prospects of detecting people or materials that terrorists might attempt to move into the United States. Technology has helped the private sector to adjust to new requirements at minimal economic impact.

The country has a vigorous, comprehensive public health system infrastructure, with the capacity to respond around the clock to acute threats, while maintaining the capability to simultaneously respond to chronic public health issues. Public health officials institutionalized relationships with the public and private medical community and other response entities to deal with the full range of potential challenges. Other major improvements include an emphasis on an all hazards/dual use capabilities, and well defined health care requirements for bioterrorism. The national system of special response teams for medical/health contingencies has been unified and modernized with a special emphasis on preparedness for a broad range of bioterrorism attacks, as well as chemical, radiological, and nuclear health effects. The Congress authorized several programs to encourage nursing, epidemiological, large animal veterinarian, environmental health, and pharmaceutical education and training; and workforce issues are fading. After the development of a strategic communications plan, a cooperative effort of Federal, State and local public health officials, the nation is in the middle a five-year campaign to improve the psychological readiness and resilience of the U.S. population.

Cyber and physical threats to critical infrastructures have been addressed through a strategy that recognizes interdependencies and potential cascading effects. Programs to ensure that the latest in protective tools and practices are implemented have been increasingly successful in building confidence throughout the networked systems that are vulnerable to attack.

The potential threat to the agriculture and food industries is continually being assessed in a cooperative effort between the intelligence community, DHS, DHHS, and the Department of Agriculture (USDA) that includes joint education and training programs. As a consequence of this continuing assessment, specific actions to protect the agriculture and food industries have been undertaken, to include specially designated laboratories to perform tests on foreign agricultural diseases. In addition, Federal support has substantially increased the level of research and funding for veterinary medicine education. USDA has an integrated network of Federal and State BSL-3 and BSL-4 laboratories for the detection and diagnosis for foreign animal and plant diseases. Through an integrated, voluntary effort, all food production, processing and transport and distribution facilities have achieved basic security guidelines described in Federal guidance. The inspection force is fully trained. Response to an outbreak is clearly defined within a national strategy and a fair system of indemnity to compensate those affected by agricultural losses is available along the spectrum of food production and dissemination (which has helped to encourage rather than discourage the rapid disclosure of outbreaks). Aggressive R&D has produced vaccines for high-risk pathogens such as Foot and Mouth and the USDA research portfolio has been prioritized according to a comprehensive risk assessment matrix for both deliberate and natural outbreaks. In addition, the Federal Government has continued to expand its cooperation and surveillance presence overseas to prevent introduction of pathogens into the United States.

Future Vision 2009 – Research & Development, and Related Standards

The Federal government is providing sustained funding for a wide-ranging R&D program that is seeking major improvements in the ability to detect and analyze terrorism-related materials or devices both at the borders and in transit within the country. The Federal R&D agenda is coordinated and prioritized through a comprehensive interagency and intergovernmental process led by the Secretary of Homeland Security.

The National Institute for Mental health has undertaken a long-term research program examining the most effective ways to both prepare people mentally for possible terrorist attacks and to treat people with mental and emotional problems following such attacks.

The Congress has expanded incentives under Bioshield to encourage industrial production and development of biological and chemical defense pharmaceuticals. NIAID, in collaboration with industry, has launched a major research effort in the area of vaccine development in anticipation of possibly facing threats from natural and genetically modified biological agents, and is building on its successes of rapid and reliable diagnostic tests for the full spectrum of biological agents.

New approaches in epidemiologic surveillance are yielding dramatic results, and State and local public health departments are implementing the findings to reduce time in detection of disease outbreaks.

The challenge of improving cybersecurity is being addressed through a comprehensive government industry R&D partnership that has developed not only improved defensive tools and procedures but also industry standards for ensuring that improved protective techniques and tools are implemented on a continual basis.

Future Vision 2009 – Role of the Military

Statutory authority and implementing regulations for use of the military inside the homeland—for both homeland defense and civil support missions—have been clarified. Extensive public education—for State and local governments, for the private sector (especially critical infrastructure operators) and for the populace at large, has greatly improved the understanding about legal authority for using the military as well as its capabilities and limitations. Specific attention has been focused on defining the parameters of homeland defense and its distinctions from civil support.

Clearly articulated Rules for the Use of Force exist to govern the military's actions inside the United States in situations where it is unclear if the foe is a combatant or a criminal

In recent years, the role of USNORTHCOM and USPACOM in enhanced civil-military integration for homeland security has been clarified and institutionalized within the Department of Defense. A critically important part of this process has been, as noted, the development of a comprehensive requirements identification process by DHS, and tested through extensive exercises involving USNORTHCOM and State and local emergency response officials.

The potential role and responsibilities of the military in supporting civilian authorities in the event of a terrorist attack has been refined largely through a continued program of training and exercises involving USNORTHCOM, other military entities, and State and local partners with preparedness responsibilities.

USNORTHCOM now maintains dedicated rapid-reaction units with a wide range of response capabilities relating to attack assessment, emergency medical support, isolation and quarantine, and communications support. Capabilities are intended for military homeland defense missions but have been implemented in a way to be applicable to civil support missions as well.

The National Guard has been given the new homeland security mission with a comparable increase in funds for civil support planning, training, exercises, and operations. Some Guard units are trained for and assigned homeland security missions as their primary or exclusive missions. With authorizing legislation, the Department of Defense has established a collaborative process for deploying National Guard units including authority to employ the Guard on a multi-state basis for homeland security missions. The National Guard remains a strong component of the military for the war-fighting mission, but enhanced resources are maintained for military assistance to States and communities for all types of emergencies. Use of Reserve Component forces for extended homeland security missions has been structured in a manner that does not detract from recruiting and retention efforts.

Military missions in the homeland are consistent with traditional military missions. Specialized State and local responder capabilities have been enhanced through a sharing of military technology and realignment of funding. State and local responders have more effectively funded, trained, and equipped to address the impacts of a terrorist attack and the military (including the National Guard) have funded and trained for missions distinctively different than those of State and local responders. With this substantial empowerment of State and local civilian response organizations, the potential reliance on any part of the military—active forces and the reserve components (including the National Guard in its non-Federal status)—for military support to civil authorities has diminished.

Analysis

America's new normalcy in January of 2009 reflects:

- Both the sustainment and further empowerment of individual freedoms in the context of measurable advances that secure the homeland.

- Consistent commitment of resources that improve the ability of all levels of government, the private sector and our citizens to prevent terrorist attacks and, if warranted, to respond and recover effectively to the full range of threats faced by the nation.

- A standardized and effective process for sharing information and intelligence among all stakeholders—one that is built on moving actionable information to the broadest possible audience rapidly, and that allows for heightened security with minimal undesirable economic and societal consequences.

- Strong preparedness and readiness across State and local government and the private sector with corresponding processes that provide an enterprise wide national capacity to plan, equip, train, and exercise against measurable standards.

- Clear definition about the roles, responsibilities, and acceptable uses of the military domestically—that strengthens the role of the National Guard and Federal Reserve Components for any domestic mission, and ensures that America's leaders will never be confronted with competing choices of using the military to respond to a domestic emergency versus the need to project our strength globally to defeat those who would seek to do us harm.

- Clear processes for engaging academia, business, all levels of government, and others in rapidly developing and implementing research, development and standards across technology, public policy, and other areas needed to secure the homeland—a process that focuses efforts on real versus perceived needs.

- Well-understood and shared process, plans, and incentives for protecting the nation's critical infrastructures of government and in the private sector—a unified approach to managing our risks.

A Roadmap to the Future

In developing its strategic vision for homeland security, the panel outlined an ambitious vision for the near future not only to counter the threat of terrorism but to advance America's ability to prepare more effectively for the full range of threats to our nation. The vision requires a firm commitment and sustained effort among all levels of government and in the private sector. Nor should it necessarily take five years to achieve its stated goals. Even with current programs and resources, the nation must achieve real and measurable improvements soon. Clearly, however, additional steps are needed to bring the United States from its current state of preparedness to the panel's view of America's New Normalcy. The panel identified key steps to achieving the vision. The panel does not suggest that these are the only actions required to achieve an acceptable future state of security, nor that implementing all of these steps exactly as recommended will ensure attainment of the future state. They are, nevertheless, the best judgment of individual panel members within their own discipline and the collective view of the full panel as an opportunity for translating resolve and policy into action and accomplishment.

The vision requires a firm commitment and sustained effort among all levels of government and in the private sector.

Civil Liberties

- Establish a civil liberties oversight board to provide advice on any statutory, regulatory, or procedural change that may have civil liberties implications.

State and Local Empowerment

- Combine all departmental grant making programs into a single entity (DHS).

- Establish an interagency mechanism for homeland security grants (President).

- Develop a comprehensive process for establishing training and exercise standards for responders (DHS).

- Revise the Homeland Security Advisory System to include (1) a regional alert system; (2) training to emergency responders about preventative actions; and (3) specific guidance to potentially affect regions (DHS).

- Establish sustained funding to enhance Emergency Medical Systems response capacity for acts of terrorism (Congress).

- Reestablish a Federal office specifically to support EMS operational and systems issues (Congress).

- Establish a "Matrix" of Mutual Aid in coordination with local, State, and other Federal agencies, for a nationwide system of mutually supporting capabilities (DHS).

Private Sector Engagement

- Adopt the Business Roundtable's Principle's of Corporate Governance security component (DHS and private sector).

Intelligence and Information Sharing

- Establish the Terrorist Threat Integration Center (TTIC) as an independent agency and require TTIC to have permanent staff from representative State and local entities (Congress).

- Develop and disseminate continuing comprehensive strategic threat assessments (Intelligence Community and DHS).

- Designate one or more security clearance-granting authorities, which can grant clearances Federal government wide that are recognized by all Federal agencies (President).

- Develop a new regime of clearances and classification of intelligence and other information for dissemination to States, localities, and the private sector (President).

- Develop a training program for State, local, and private sector for interpreting intelligence products (DHS).

- Establish comprehensive procedures for sharing information with relevant State and local officials (DHS).

Research and Development and Related Standards

- Implement the Institute of Medicine (IOM) Committee's recommendations on psychological preparedness (DHS and DHHS).

- Provide increased funding and DHS and DHHS monitor State and local compliance of incorporating in plans an appropriate focus on psychological and behavioral consequence preparedness and management (Congress, DHS, and DHHS).

- Create a Federal task force on psychological issues, jointly led by DHHS and DHS (President).

Agroterrorism

- Designate DHS as the lead and USDA as the technical advisor on food safety and agriculture and emergency preparedness (President).[1]

Conclusion

The national effort to enhance homeland security will yield tremendous benefits and entail substantial financial and other costs. The benefit will be a reduction in both the risk of future terrorist events and their consequences should an attack occur. The financial costs are the amount of money, manpower, equipment, and innovative potential that must be devoted to homeland security—resources which then cannot be used for goods, services, and other productive investments. Americans also incur substantial costs in longer delays at airport security checkpoints and restrictions on some individual freedoms. While these costs are often difficult to measure quantitatively, they are no less real and burdensome to Americans. We must measure and balance both benefits and costs to determine the correct level of homeland security efforts.

The United States spends roughly $100 billion per year on homeland security. This includes the services of federal, state, and local law enforcement and emergency services but excludes most spending for the armed forces. The cost is great, and we will strive to minimize the sacrifices asked of Americans, but as a Nation we will spend whatever is necessary to secure the homeland.[2]

Questions

1. Can we stop terrorism?

2. List and describe the components to reducing terrorism.

3. What is the challenge to devoting resources to reducing terrorism.

4. Explain why you agree or disagree with the Gilmore Panel's future vision: "America's New Normalcy".

Appendices

Equipment Standards

Standards for Personal Protective Gear
for First Responders

NIOSH Chemical, Biological, Radiological and Nuclear (CBRN) Standard for Open-Circuit Self-Contained Breathing Apparatus (December 2001)

This standard establishes performance and design requirements to certify Self-Contained Breathing Apparatus (SCBA) for use in chemical, biological, radiological, and nuclear (CBRN) exposures for use by emergency responders

NIOSH Standard for Chemical, Biological, Radiological, and Nuclear (CBRN) Full Facepiece Air Purifying Respirator (APR)

The purpose of this standard is to specify minimum requirements to determine the effectiveness of full facepiece air purifying respirators (APR), commonly referred to as gas masks, used during entry into chemical, biological, radiological, and nuclear (CBRN) atmospheres not immediately dangerous to life or health (IDLH)

NIOSH Standard for Chemical, Biological, Radiological, and Nuclear (CBRN) Air-Purifying Escape Respirator and CBRN Self-Contained Escape Respirator

The purpose of this standard is to specify minimum requirements to determine the effectiveness of escape respirators that address CBRN materials identified as inhalation hazards from possible terrorist events for use by the general working population.

NFPA 1951, Standard on Protective Ensemble for USAR Operations

Based on work begun in 1997, this standard answers the need for personal protective equipment for fire and emergency services personnel operating at technical rescue incidents involving building or structural collapse, vehicle accidents, confined spaces, trench cave-ins, scaffolding collapses, high angle climbing accidents, and similar incidents. The first edition of this standard was issued in July 2001.

NFPA 1981, Standard on Open-Circuit Self-Contained Breathing Apparatus for Fire and Emergency Services

Based on work begun in 1975, this standard specifies the minimum requirements for the design, performance, testing, and certification of open-circuit self-contained breathing apparatus (SCBA) and combination open-circuit self-contained breathing apparatus and supplied air respirators (SCBA/SAR) for the respiratory protection of fire and emergency responders where unknown, IDLH (immediately dangerous to life and health), or potentially IDLH atmospheres exist. The first edition was issued in July 1981 and the current edition, issued in July 2002, is the fifth edition.

NFPA 1991, Standard on Vapor-Protective Ensembles for Hazardous Materials Emergencies

Based on work begun in 1986, this standard specifies the minimum requirements for the design, performance, testing, and certification of vapor-protective ensembles and individual protective elements for chemical vapor protection for fire and emergency service personnel. Additional optional criteria are provided for ensembles and individual protective elements that provide protection for chemical flash fire escape, liquefied gas, chemical and biological warfare agents, and chemical and biological terrorism incidents. The first edition was issued in January 1990 and the current edition, issued in January 2000, is the third edition.

NFPA 1994, Standard on Protective Ensembles for Chemical/ Biological Terrorism Incidents

Based on work begun in 1998, this standard specifies the minimum requirements for the design, performance, testing, and certification of protective ensembles for fire and emergency services personnel operating at domestic terrorism incidents involving dual-use industrial chemicals, chemical terrorism agents, or biological terrorism agents. The intent is that the ensembles would be available in quantity, easily donned and used, and designed for single exposure use. The first edition of this standard was issued in July 2001.

NFPA 1999, Standard on Protective Clothing for Emergency Medical Operations

Based on work begun in 1990, this standard specifies the minimum requirements for the design, performance, testing, and certification of new single-use and multiple-use emergency medical protective clothing, including garments, gloves, footwear, and face protection devices, used by fire and emergency services personnel performing patient care during emergency medical operations for protection against exposure to blood and body fluid-borne pathogens. The first edition was issued in July 1992 and the current edition, issued in January 2003, is the third edition.

Standards for Radiation and Nuclear Detection Equipment

Copies of the complete standards are available from the Institute of Electrical and Electronics Engineers (IEEE).

ANSI N42.32: Performance Criteria for Alarming Personal Radiation Detectors for Homeland Security

This standard describes design and performance criteria along with testing methods for evaluating the performance of instruments for homeland security that are pocket sized and carried on the body for the purpose of detecting the presence and magnitude of radiation. This standard specifies the performance criteria for radiation detection and measurement instruments that may be used in a variety of environmental conditions. The performance criteria contained in this standard are meant to provide a means for verifying the capability of these instruments to reliably detect significant changes above background levels of radiation and alert the user to these changes.

ANSI N42.33: Radiation Detection Instrumentation for Homeland Security

This standard establishes design and performance criteria, test and calibration requirements, and operating instruction requirements for portable radiation detection instruments. These instruments are used for detection and measurement of photon emitting radioactive substances for the purposes of detection and interdiction and hazard assessment. The informative annexes of this standard provide reference information.

ANSI N42.34: Performance Criteria for Hand-Held Instruments for the Detection and Identification of Radionuclides

This standard addresses instruments that can be used for homeland security applications to detect and identify radionuclides, for gamma dose rate measurement, and for indication of neutron radiation. This standard specifies general requirements and test procedures, radiation response requirements, and electrical, mechanical, and environmental requirements. Successful completion of the tests described in this standard should not be construed as an ability to successfully identify all isotopes in all environments.

ANSI N42.35: Evaluation and Performance of Radiation Detection Portal Monitors for Use in Homeland Security

This standard provides the testing and evaluation criteria for Radiation Detection Portal Monitors to detect radioactive materials that could be used for nuclear weapons or radiological dispersal devices (RDDs). Portal monitors may be used in permanent installations, in temporary installations for short-duration detection needs, or as a transportable system. These systems are used to provide monitoring of people, packages and vehicles to detect illicit radioactive material transportation, or for emergency response to an event that releases radioactive material.

Appendix B

Glossary

AAR	After Action Report
ABA	American Banking Association
ACE	Automated Commercial Environment
ACTD	Advanced Concept Technology Demonstration
AEL	Authorized Equipment List
AES	Automated Export System
AFIS	Automated Fingerprint Identification System
APIS	Advance Passenger Information System
APR	Air Purifying Respirators
ASD(HD)	Assistant Secretary of Defense for Homeland Defense
ASU	Automated Scene Understanding
AT	Antiterrorism
ATC	Air Traffic Control Center
ATF	Bureau of Alcohol, Tobacco, and Firearms
ATM	Automatic Teller Machine
ATS	Automated Targeting System
ATSA	Aviation and Transportation Security Act
BTS	Border and Transportation Security
CA	Cooperative Agreement
CAPPS	Computer Assisted Passenger Prescreening System
CBIRF	Chemical-Biological Incident Response Force
CBP	U.S. Customs and Border Protection
CBRN	Chemical, Biological, Radiological, Nuclear, and Explosive
CB-RRT	Chemical and Biological Rapid Response Team
CBTB	Counter Measures Test Bed
CCTV	Closed Circuit Television
CDC	Centers for Disease Control and Prevention
CEC	Comprehensive Exercise Curriculum
CeCl	Cesium Chloride
CI/KR	Critical Infrastructure/Key Resources
CIA	Central Intelligence Agency
CII	Critical Infrastructure Information Act
COTS	Commercial-off-the-Shelf
CPX	Command Post Exercise

CREATE	Center for Risk and Economic Analysis of Terrorism Events
CSEPP	Chemical Stockpile Emergency Preparedness Program
CSG	Counterterrorism Security Group
CSI	Container Security Initiative
CSID	Centralized Scheduling and Information Desk
CSTARC	Cyber Security Tracking, Analysis, & Response Center
CT	Counterterrorism
CTC	Counterterrorist Center (CIA)
C-TPAT	Customs-Trade Partnership Against Terrorism
CWC	Chemical Weapons Convention
DC	Deputies Committee
DCI	Director of Central Intelligence
DFO	Disaster Field Office
DHHS	Department of Health and Human Services
DHS	Department of Homeland Security
DIA	Defense Intelligence Agency
DoD	Department of Defense
DoE	Department of Energy
DoI	Department of the Interior
DoJ	Department of Justice
DoS	Department of State
DoT	Department of Transportation
DPETAP	Domestic Preparedness Equipment Technical Assistance Program
DRO	Detention and Removal Operations
DSCA	Defense Support of Civil Authorities
EAS	Emergency Alert System
EBT	Electronic Benefits Transfer
ED	Education Department
EMP	Electromagnetic Pulse
EMS	Emergency Medical Service
EMT	Emergency Medical Team
EOC	Emergency Operations Center
EOP	Emergency Operating Procedure
EPA	Environmental Protection Agency

EPIC	Electronic Privacy Information Center
EPR	Emergency Preparedness and Response
EPW	Exercise Plan Workshop
ER	Emergency Room
ERT	Emergency Response Team
ERT-A	Emergency Response Team Advance Element
ESCAP	Electronic Crimes Special Agent Program
ESF	Emergency Support Function
ESFLG	Emergency Support Function Leaders Group
ESN	Electronic Serial Number
FAA	Federal Aviation Administration
FACA	Federal Advisory Committee Act
FAD	Foreign Animal Disease
FAMs	Federal Air Marshal Service
FAST	Free and Secure Trade
FBI	Federal Bureau of Investigation
FCD	Financial Crime Division (USSS)
FCO	Field Coordinating Officer
FDA	Food and Drug Administration
FE	Functional Exercise
FEMA	Federal Emergency Management Agency
FFRDC	Federally Funded Research and Development Center
FIF	Financial Institution Fraud
FISA	Foreign Intelligence Surveillance Act
FLETC	Federal Law Enforcement Training Center
FOC	FEMA Operations Center
FPS	Federal Protective Service
FRC	Federal Resource Coordinator
FSD	Forensic Services Division (USSS)
FSE	Full-Scale Exercise
FWPCA	Federal Water Pollution Control Act
FY	Fiscal Year
GAP	Grant Assistance Program
GIS	Geographic Information System

GSA	General Services Administration
HDER	Homeland Defense Equipment Reuse Program
HE	High Explosive
HEU	Highly Enriched Uranium
HR	House Resolution
HSARPA	Homeland Security Advanced Research Projects Agency
HSAS	Homeland Security Advisory System
HSC	Homeland Security Council
HSEEP	Homeland Security Exercise and Evaluation Program
HSGP	Homeland Security Grant Program
HSI	Homeland Security Institute
HSIN	Homeland Security Information Network
HSOC	Homeland Security Operations Center
HSPD	Homeland Security Presidential Directive
HSSTAC	Homeland Security Science and Technology Advisory Committee
HUD	Housing and Urban Development
IAB	Interagency Board
IAIP	Information Analysis and Infrastructure Protection
IBET	Integrated Border Enforcement Teams
ICE	U.S. Immigration and Customs Enforcement
ICP	Incident Command Post
ICS	Incident Command Structure
ICTAP	Interoperable Communication Technical Assistance Program
IDLH	Immediately Dangerous to Life or Health
IED	Improvised Explosive Device
IEEE	Institute of Electrical and Electronics Engineers
IEMS	Integrated Emergency Management System
IIMG	Interagency Incident Management Group
INA	Immigration and Nationality Act
IND	Improvised Nuclear Device
INS	Immigration and Naturalization Service
IOC	ICE Operations Center
IOM	Institute of Medicine
IP	Improvement Plan

ISIS	Integrated Surveillance Intelligence System
ISP	Internet Service Provider
JFO	Joint Field Office
JOC	Joint Operations Center
JTF	Joint Task Force
JTF-CS	Joint Task Force – Civil Support
JTTF	Joint Terrorism Task Force
LFA	Lead Federal Agent
LLIS	Lessons Learned Information Sharing
LNG	Liquefied Natural Gas
LVB	Large Vehicle Bomb
MACA	Military Assistance to Civil Authorities
MACC	Multiagency Command Center
MANPADS	Man-Portable Air Defense System
MEPP	Master Exercise Practitioner Program
MIN	Mobile Identification Number
MIPT	National Memorial Institute for Prevention of Terrorism
MMA	Major Metropolitan Area
MMRS	Metropolitan Medical Response System
MMS	Minerals Management Service (DOI)
MOU	Memorandum of Understanding
MSHA	Mine Safety & Health Administration
NAS	National Academy of Science
NATO	North Atlantic Treaty Organization
NAWAS	National Warning System
NCP	National Oil and Hazardous Substances Pollution Contingency Plan
NCSD	National Cyber Security Division
NDMS	National Disaster Medical System
NEADS	North East Air Defense Sector
NEP	National Exercise Program
NETC	National Emergency Training Center
NFOP	National Fugitive Operations Program
NFPA	National Fire Protection Association
NGA	National Geospatial-intelligence Agency

NGO	Nongovernmental Organization
NHSA	National Homeland Security Agency
NHSD	National Homeland Security Department
NIC	National Incident Commander
NII	Non-Intrusive Inspection
NIJ	National Institute of Justice
NIMS	National Incident Management System
NIMS ·	National Incident Management System
NIOSH	National Institute for Occupational Safety and Health
NIST	National Institute of Standards and Technology
NITSEEP	National Intermodal Transportation Security Exercise and Evaluation Program
NJTTF	National Joint Terrorism Task Force
NOA	Notice of Arrival
NORAD	North American Aerospace Defense Command
NORTHCOM	Northern Command
NPSTC	National Public Safety Telecommunications Council
NRC	National Response Center
NRCC	National Response Coordination Center
NRO	National Reconnaissance Office
NRP	National Response Plan
NSA	National Security Agency
NSC	National Security Council
NSDD	National Security Decision Directive
NSSE	National Special Security Event
NTC	National Training Center
NYPO	New York Project Office
OC	Office of the Comptroller
ODP	Office of Domestic Preparedness
OHS	Office of Homeland Security
OIG	Office of the Inspector General
OJP	Office of Justice Program
OMB	Office of Management and Budget
ONDCP	Office of National Drug Control Policy
OPM	Office of Personnel Management

ORD	Office of Research & Development
OSHA	Occupational Safety & Health Administration
OSLC	Office of State and Local Coordination
OSLGCP	Office of State and Local Government Coordination and Preparedness
OSTP	Office of Science and Technology Policy
PANYNJ	Port Authority of New York and New Jersey
PC	Principals Committee
PCB	Polychlorinated Biphenyl
PCC	Policy Coordinating Committee
PCII	Protected Critical Infrastructure Information
PDA	Preliminary Damage Assessment
PDD	Presidential Decision Directive
PEP	Propositioned Equipment Program
PFO	Principal Coordinating Officer
PIN	Personal Identification Number
PL	Public Law
PLO	Palestinian Liberation Organization
POC	Point of Contact
PPA	Performance Partnership Agreement
PPB	Programs, Plans, & Budgets
PPE	Personal Protective Equipment
PRD	Personal Radiation Detector
PREP	National Preparedness for Response Exercise (USCG)
QATT	Qualified Anti-Terrorism Technology
R&D	Research & Development
RADTEC	Radiation Detector Testing and Evaluation Center
RAMP	Remedial Action Management Program
RAT	Rapid Assistance Team
RDD	Radiological Dispersal Device
RDD	Radiological Dispersal Devices
RDT&E	Research, Development, Test, and Evaluation
REP	Radiological Emergency Preparedness
RICO	Racketeer Influenced and Corrupt Organizations Act
RISC	Regional Interagency Steering Committee

RPG	Rocket Propelled Grenade
RRCC	Regional Response Coordination Center
RSPA	Research and Special Programs Administration
RTI	Regional Technology Integration
RVSS	Remote Video Surveillance Systems (RVSS)
S&T	Science and Technology
SAA	State Administrative Agency
SAC	Special Agent-in-Charge
SAFETY	Support Anti-Terrorism by Fostering Effective Technologies Act
SAR	Suspicious Activity Report
SAR	Supplied Air Respirator
SB	Senate Bill
SBA	Small Business Administration
SBU	Sensitive-but-Unclassified
SCBA	Self-Contained Breathing Apparatus
SCIP	Statewide Communications Interoperability Planning
SCO	State Coordinating Officer
SCUBA	Self-Contained Underwater Breathing Apparatus
SDPP	State Domestic Preparedness Program
SEAL	Sea-Air-Land (Navy special forces)
SED	Systems Engineering and Development
SEL	Standard Equipment List
SENTRI	Secure Electronic Network for Travelers' Rapid Inspection
SEVIS	Student and Exchange Visitor System
SFLEO	Senior Federal Law Enforcement Official
SHSEEP	State Homeland Security Exercise and Evaluation Program
SHSGP	State Homeland Security Grant Programs
SIMCELL	Simulation Cell
SIOC	Strategic Information Operations Center (FBI)
SNS	Strategic National Stockpile
SOE	Senior Official Exercise
SONS	Spill of National Significance (USCG)
SOP	Standard Operating Procedure
SoR	Statement of Requirements

SPC	Special Processing Center
SUA	Special Unlawful Activities
TIC	Toxic Industrial Chemical
TOPOFF	Top Officials (exercise)
TRIA	Terrorism Risk Insurance Act
TSA	Transportation Security Administration
TSC	Terrorist Screening Center
TSWG	Technical Support Working Group
TTIC	Terrorist Threat Integration Center
TTX	Tabletop Exercise
UA	Universal Adversary
UASI	Urban Area Security Initiative
UAV	Unmanned Aerial Vehicle
UAWG	Urban Area Working Group
UC	Unified Command
UN	United Nations
USACE	United States Army Corps of Engineers
USC	United States Code
USCG	United States Coast Guard
USCIS	U.S. Citizenship and Immigration Services
USD(I)	Under Secretary of Defense for Intelligence
USDA	United States Department of Agriculture
USSS	United States Secret Service
US-VISIT	U.S. Visitor and Immigrant Status Indication Technology
WAWAS	Washington Area Warning System
WMD	Weapons of Mass Destruction

Bibliography

Chapter 1: 9-11 Survivors

1. Elsis, Mark R. (2005) "911 Timeline". Retrieved June 2, 2005 from http://www.911.timeline.net/.

2. Trevor, Greg. (2005) "A Race to Safety". Retrieved June 2, 2005 from http://www.coping.org/911/survivor/race.htm.

3. Mayblum, Adam. (2005) "The Price We Pay: A Survivor's Story". Retrieved June 2, 2005 from http://www.coping.org/911/survivor/price.htm.

4. Zoroya, Gregg. (2002) "The Griffiths". USATODAY.com. Retrieved June 2, 2005 from http://www.usatoday.com/lief/sept11/2002-09-10-survivor-griffiths_x.htm.

5. LaTorre, Cara. (2002) "Survivor: 'We didn't know what to do'". USATODAY.com. Retrieved June 2, 2005 from http://www.usatoday.com/news/sept11/2002-09-10-first-person-latorre_x.htm.

6. Barg, Jaede. (2002) "Survivor: 'The world has changed for us indeed'". USATODAY.com. Retrieved June 2, 2005 from http://www.usatoday.com/news/sept11/2002-09-09-first-person-barg_x.htm.

7. Borgo, Phyllis. (2002) "World Trade Center: First-person account". Retrieved June 2, 2005 from http://www.usatoday.com/news/sept11/2002-09-06-first-person-borgo_x.htm.

8. McLaughlin, Sean. (2002) "NY firefighters discuss 9/11 experience." *The Heights News*. September 10, 2002. Retrieved June 2, 2005 from http://www.bcheights.com/global_user_elements/printpage.cfm?storyid=268941.

9. Trevor, Greg. (2005) "A Race to Safety". Retrieved June 2, 2005 from http://www.coping.org/911/survivor/race.htm.

10. Mayblum, Adam. (2005) "The Price We Pay: A Survivor's Story". Retrieved June 2, 2005 from http://www.coping.org/911/survivor/price.htm.

11. Mayblum, Adam. (2005) "The Price We Pay: A Survivor's Story". Retrieved June 2, 2005 from http://www.coping.org/911/survivor/price.htm.

12. Trevor, Greg. (2005) "A Race to Safety". Retrieved June 2, 2005 from http://www.coping.org/911/survivor/race.htm.

13. Zoroya, Gregg. (2002) "The Griffiths". USATODAY.com. Retrieved June 2, 2005 from http://www.usatoday.com/lief/sept11/2002-09-10-survivor-griffiths_x.htm.

14. Borgo, Phyllis. (2002) "World Trade Center: First-person account". Retrieved June 2, 2005 from http://www.usatoday.com/news/sept11/2002-09-06-first-person-borgo_x.htm.

15. Barg, Jaede. (2002) "Survivor: 'The world has changed for us indeed'". USATODAY.com. Retrieved June 2, 2005 from http://www.usatoday.com/news/sept11/2002-09-09-first-person-barg_x.htm.

16. Barg, Jaede. (2002) "Survivor: 'The world has changed for us indeed'". USATODAY.com. Retrieved June 2, 2005 from http://www.usatoday.com/news/sept11/2002-09-09-first-person-barg_x.htm.

17. McLaughlin, Sean. (2002) "NY firefighters discuss 9/11 experience." *The Heights News*. September 10, 2002. Retrieved June 2, 2005 from http://www.bcheights.com/global_user_elements/printpage.cfm?storyid=268941.

18. Mayblum, Adam. (2005) "The Price We Pay: A Survivor's Story". Retrieved June 2, 2005 from http://www.coping.org/911/survivor/price.htm.

19. Barg, Jaede. (2002) "Survivor: 'The world has changed for us indeed'". USATODAY.com. Retrieved June 2, 2005 from http://www.usatoday.com/news/sept11/2002-09-09-first-person-barg_x.htm.

20. McLaughlin, Sean. (2002) "NY firefighters discuss 9/11 experience." *The Heights News*. September 10, 2002. Retrieved June 2, 2005 from http://www.bcheights.com/global_user_elements/printpage.cfm?storyid=268941.

21. Elsis, Mark R. (2005) "911 Timeline". Retrieved June 2, 2005 from http://www.911.timeline.net/.

22. LaTorre, Cara. (2002) "Survivor: 'We didn't know what to do'". USATODAY.com. Retrieved June 2, 2005 from http://www.usatoday.com/news/sept11/2002-09-10-first-person-latorre_x.htm.

23. Borgo, Phyllis. (2002) "World Trade Center: First-person account". Retrieved June 2, 2005 from http://www.usatoday.com/news/sept11/2002-09-06-first-person-borgo_x.htm.

24. Barg, Jaede. (2002) "Survivor: 'The world has changed for us indeed'". USATODAY.com. Retrieved June 2, 2005 from http://www.usatoday.com/news/sept11/2002-09-09-first-person-barg_x.htm.

25. LaTorre, Cara. (2002) "Survivor: 'We didn't know what to do'". USATODAY.com. Retrieved June 2, 2005 from http://www.usatoday.com/news/sept11/2002-09-10-first-person-latorre_x.htm.

26. McLaughlin, Sean. (2002) "NY firefighters discuss 9/11 experience." *The Heights News*. September 10, 2002. Retrieved June 2, 2005 from http://www.bcheights.com/global_user_elements/printpage.cfm?storyid=268941.

27. Trevor, Greg. (2005) "A Race to Safety". Retrieved June 2, 2005 from http://www.coping.org/911/survivor/race.htm.

28. Mayblum, Adam. (2005) "The Price We Pay: A

Survivor's Story". Retrieved June 2, 2005 from
http://www.coping.org/911/survivor/price.htm.

29. Borgo, Phyllis. (2002) "World Trade Center: First-
person account". Retrieved June 2, 2005 from http://
www.usatoday.com/news/sept11/2002-09-06-first-
person-borgo_x.htm.

30. Elsis, Mark R. (2005) "911 Timeline". Retrieved
June 2, 2005 from http://www.911.timeline.net/.

31. Morin, Terry. (2001) "Eyewitness Account of Pentagon Attack." Retrieved June 2, 2005 from http://
www.coping.org/911/survivor/pentagon.htm.

32. LaTorre, Cara. (2002) "Survivor: 'We didn't know
what to do'". USATODAY.com. Retrieved June 2,
2005 from http://www.usatoday.com/news/
sept11/2002-09-10-first-person-latorre_x.htm.

33. Barg, Jaede. (2002) "Survivor: 'The world has
changed for us indeed'". USATODAY.com. Retrieved June 2, 2005 from http://www.usatoday.com/
news/sept11/2002-09-09-first-person-barg_x.htm.

34. Ibid

35. Ibid

36. Elsis, Mark R. (2005) "911 Timeline". Retrieved
June 2, 2005 from http://www.911.timeline.net/.

37. McLaughlin, Sean. (2002) "NY firefighters discuss
9/11 experience." *The Heights News*. September 10,
2002. Retrieved June 2, 2005 from http://
www.bcheights.com/global_user_elements/
printpage.cfm?storyid=268941.

38. Borgo, Phyllis. (2002) "World Trade Center: First-
person account". Retrieved June 2, 2005 from http://
www.usatoday.com/news/sept11/2002-09-06-first-
person-borgo_x.htm.

39. Trevor, Greg. (2005) "A Race to Safety". Retrieved
June 2, 2005 from http://www.coping.org/911/
survivor/race.htm.

40. Ibid

41. Mayblum, Adam. (2005) "The Price We Pay: A
Survivor's Story". Retrieved June 2, 2005 from
http://www.coping.org/911/survivor/price.htm.

42. Ibid

43. McLaughlin, Sean. (2002) "NY firefighters discuss
9/11 experience." *The Heights News*. September 10,
2002. Retrieved June 2, 2005 from http://
www.bcheights.com/global_user_elements/
printpage.cfm?storyid=268941.

44. Ibid

45. Ibid

46. Ibid

47. Zoroya, Gregg. (2002) "The Griffiths". USATO-
DAY.com. Retrieved June 2, 2005 from http://
www.usatoday.com/lief/sept11/2002-09-10-survivor-
griffiths_x.htm.

48. Overberg, Paul. (2002) "Final Sept. 11 death toll
remains elusive". USATODAY.com. Retrieved June
2, 2005 from http://www.usatoday.com/news/
sept11/2002-08-22-death-toll_x.htm.

Chapter 2: 9-11 Attacks

1. The National Commission on Terrorist Attacks
Upon the United States (2004) "The 9/11 Commission Report", pp 1-14. July 22, 2004.

2. The National Commission on Terrorist Attacks
Upon the United States (2004) "The 9/11 Commission Report", pp 2. July 22, 2004.

Chapter 3: 9-11 Analysis

1. The 9/11 Commission Report. (2004) "Executive
Summary", pp 1-16.

Chapter 4: Terrorist Threat

1. Wikipedia.Org. (2004) "United States Department
of Homeland Security". Retrieved October 23, 2004
from http://en.wikipedia.org/wiki/
Department_of_Homeland_Security.

2. TerrorismFiles.Org. (2004) "Definition of Terrorism". Retrieved October 18, 2004, from http://
www.terrorismfiles.org/encyclopedia/terrorism.html.

3. Roberts, Adam (2004) "The Changing Face of Terrorism". Retrieved October 29, 2004, from http://
www.bbc.co.uk/history.

4. Federal Bureau of Investigation (1998) "Terrorism
in the United States." 1998.

5. Roberts, Adam (2004) "The Changing Face of Terrorism". Retrieved October 29, 2004, from http://
www.bbc.co.uk/history.

6. Brake, Jeffrey D. (2001) "Terrorism and the Military's Role in Domestic Crisis Management: Background and Issues for Congress". April 19, 2001.

7. United States Congress (1995) "Testimony of Acting
DCI William O. Studeman, Omnibus Counterterrorism Act of 1995". April 6, 1995.

8. Federal Bureau of Investigation (1998) "Terrorism
in the United States." 1998.

9. Wikipedia.Org. (2004) "Oklahoma City Bombing".
Retrieved October 23, 2004 from http://
en.wikipedia.org/wiki/Oklahoma_City_bombing.

10. Brake, Jeffrey D. (2001) "Terrorism and the Military's Role in Domestic Crisis Management: Background and Issues for Congress". April 19, 2001.

11. The National Commission on Terrorist Attacks Upon the United States (2004) "The 9/11 Commission Report". July 22, 2004.

12. Brake, Jeffrey D. (2001) "Terrorism and the Military's Role in Domestic Crisis Management: Background and Issues for Congress". April 19, 2001.

13. Brake, Jeffrey D. (2001) "Terrorism and the Military's Role in Domestic Crisis Management: Background and Issues for Congress". April 19, 2001.

14. Brake, Jeffrey D. (2001) "Terrorism and the Military's Role in Domestic Crisis Management: Background and Issues for Congress". April 19, 2001.

Chapter 5: Islamic Extremism

1. The National Commission on Terrorist Attacks Upon the United States (2004) "The 9/11 Commission Report", pp 47-54. July 22, 2004.

Chapter 6: CBRNE

1. Advisory Panel to Assess Domestic Response Capabilities For Terrorism Involving Weapons of Mass Destruction (1999) "Assessing the Threat". December 15, 1999.

2. Wikipedia.Org (2004) "Weapons of Mass Destruction". Retrieved November 6, 2004 from http://en.wikipedia.org/wiki/Weapons_of_mass_destruction.

3. NTI.Org (2004) "Definitions of WMD". Retrieved November 6, 2004 from http://www.nti.org/f_wmd411/flal.html.

4. Advisory Panel to Assess Domestic Response Capabilities For Terrorism Involving Weapons of Mass Destruction (1999) "Assessing the Threat". December 15, 1999.

5. Siegrist, David W. (2004) "The Threat of Biological Attack: Why Concern Now?". Retrieved November 6, 2004 from http://www.cdc.gov/ncidod/EID/vol5no4/siegrist.htm.

6. Porteus, Liza (2003) "Weapons of Mass Destruction Handbook". July 8, 2003.

7. Siegrist, David W. (2004) "The Threat of Biological Attack: Why Concern Now?". Retrieved November 6, 2004 from http://www.cdc.gov/ncidod/EID/vol5no4/siegrist.htm.

8. Wikipedia.Org (2004) "Chemical Warfare". Retrieved November 6, 2004 from http://en.wikipedia.org/wiki/Chemical_warfare.

9. Porteus, Liza (2003) "Weapons of Mass Destruction Handbook". July 8, 2003.

10. Porteus, Liza (2003) "Weapons of Mass Destruction Handbook". July 8, 2003.

11. Wikipedia.Org (2004) "Sarin Gas Attack on the Tokyo Subway". Retrieved November 7, 2004 from http://en.wikipedia.org/wiki/Sarin_gas_attack_on_the_Tokyo_subway.

12. Porteus, Liza (2003) "Weapons of Mass Destruction Handbook". July 8, 2003.

13. Carson Mark, Theodore Taylor, Eugene Eyster, William Maraman, Jacob Weschler (2004) "Can Terrorists Build Nuclear Weapons?". Retrieved November 1, 2004 from http://www.nci.org/k-m/makeab.htm.

14. Matthew Bunn, George Bunn (2001) "Reducing the Threat of Nuclear Theft and Sabotage", Conference Proceedings, Symposium on International Safeguards: Verification and Nuclear Material Security, Vienna, Austria, October 29—November 2, 2001.

15. Porteus, Liza (2003) "Weapons of Mass Destruction Handbook". July 8, 2003.

16. Senate Committee on Foregin Relations (2002) "Testimony of Dr. Henry Kelly, President of Federation of American Scientists". March 6, 2002.

17. Capricorn.Org (2004) "The Terrorist's Handbook". Retrieved November 8, 2004 from http://www.capricorn.org/~akira/home/terror.html.

18. International Society of Explosives Engineers (2003) "Securing Explosives, A Prime Responsibility of Industry". September 16, 2003.

19. Capricorn.Org (2004) "The Terrorist's Handbook". Retrieved November 8, 2004 from http://www.capricorn.org/~akira/home/terror.html.

20. Wikipedia.Org. (2004) "Oklahoma City Bombing". Retrieved October 23, 2004 from http://en.wikipedia.org/wiki/Oklahoma_City_bombing.

21. Bush, George W. (2002) "National Strategy for Homeland Security". July 2002.

Chapter 7: Combating Terrorism

1. The National Commission on Terrorist Attacks Upon the United States (2004) "The 9/11 Commission Report", July 22, 2004.

2. Perl, Raphael F. (2001) "Terrorism, the Future, and U.S. Foreign Policy", CRS Issue Brief for Congress, Congressional Research Service, The Library of Congress. September 13, 2001.

3. Brake, Jeffrey D. (2001) "Terrorism and the Mili-

tary's Role in Domestic Crisis Management: Background and Issues for Congress". April 19, 2001.

4. The United States Congress (2002) "The Homeland Security Act of 2002". November 25, 2002.

5. Perl, Raphael F. (2001) "Terrorism, the Future, and U.S. Foreign Policy", CRS Issue Brief for Congress, Congressional Research Service, The Library of Congress. September 13, 2001.

6. The White House (2001) Executive Order 13228 "Establishing the Office of Homeland Security and the Homeland Security Council". October 8, 2001.

7. Perro, Catherine M., Lt. Col., USAF (2004) "The Homeland Security Council—The Best Structure for the Presdient?". National Defense University, National War College. 2004.

8. The White House (2001) Executive Order 13228 "Establishing the Office of Homeland Security and the Homeland Security Council". October 8, 2001.

9. Bush, George W. (2003) "National Strategy for Combating Terrorism". February 2003.

10. Ibid

Chapter 8: DHS Origins

1. Wikipedia.Org. (2004) "United States Department of Homeland Security". Retrieved October 23, 2004 from http://en.wikipedia.org/wiki/ Department_of_Homeland_Security.

2. United States General Accounting Office (2001) "Combating Terrorism, Selected Challenges and Related Recommendations". September 20, 2001.

3. The White House (1982) "Managing Terrorist Incidents", National Security Decision Directive 30. April 10, 1982.

4. Brake, Jeffrey D. (2001) "Terrorism and the Military's Role in Domestic Crisis Management: Background and Issues for Congress". April 19, 2001.

5. United States General Accounting Office (2001) "Combating Terrorism, Selected Challenges and Related Recommendations". September 20, 2001.

6. National Commission on Terrorism (2000) "Countering the Changing Threat of International Terrorism". June 7, 2000.

7. Panel to Assess Domestic Response Capabilities for Terrorism Involving Weapons of Mass Destruction (2000) "II. Toward a National Strategy for Combating Terrorism". December 15, 2000.

8. The United States Commission on National Security/21st Century (2001) Phase III Report "Road Map for National Security: Imperative for Change".

February 15, 2001.

9. United States General Accounting Office (2001) "Combating Terrorism, Selected Challenges and Related Recommendations". September 20, 2001.

10. Scardaville, Michael (2002) "Principles for Creating an Effective U.S. Department of Homeland Security", The Heritage Foundation Backgrounder. June 12, 2002.

11. Kirk, Robert S. (2002) "Department of Homeland Security: Should the Transportation Security Administration be Included?" Congressional Research Staff Report to Congress. July 24, 2002.

12. Thomas.Loc.Gov (2004) "Bill Summary and Status", H.R. 5005. Retrieved December 4, 2004 from http:// Thomas.loc.gov/cgi-bin/bdquery/z?d107:HR05005.

13. Wikipedia.Org. (2004) "United States Department of Homeland Security". Retrieved October 23, 2004 from http://en.wikipedia.org/wiki/ Department_of_Homeland_Security.

14. ArmsControlCenter.Org (2004) "DoHS Countdown: Play-by-Play Archive". Retrieved December 4, 2004 from http://www.armscontrolcenter.org/terrorism/ playbyplay/archive.html.

Chapter 9: National Strategy for Homeland Security

1. Bush, George W. (2002) "National Strategy for Homeland Security". July 2002.

Chapter 10: DHS Organization

1. Department of Homeland Security (2004) "Performance and Accountability Report, Fiscal Year 2003. February 13, 2004.

2. Bush, George W. (2002). "The Department of Homeland Security". June 2002.

3. Relyea, Harold C. (2004) "Homeland Security: The Presidential Coordination Office", Congressional Research Staff Report for Congress. March 30, 2004.

4. Department of Homeland Security (2004) "Performance and Accountability Report, Fiscal Year 2003. February 13, 2004.

5. Department of Homeland Security (2004) "Who Will Be Part of the New Department?". Retrieved October 4, 2004 from http://www.dhs.gov/dhspublic/ display?theme=13&content=3345&print=true.

6. Halchin, L. Elaine (2004) "Location of Federal Government Offices", Congressional Research Staff Report to Congress. July 14, 2004.

7. Department of Homeland Security (2004) "Performance and Accountability Report, Fiscal Year 2003. February 13, 2004.

8. Department of Homeland Security (2005) "Homeland Security Secretary Michael Chertoff Announces Six-Point Agenda for Department of Homeland Security". Retrieved July 24, 2005 from http://www.dhs.gov/dhspublic/display?theme=43&content=4598&print=true.

9. Department of Homeland Security (2005) "Department Six-point Agenda". Retrieved July 24, 2005 from http://www.dhs.gov/dhspublic/display?theme=10&content=4604&print=true.

10. Office of the Press Secretary (2002) "President to Propose Department of Homeland Security". June 6, 2002.

Chapter 11: Information Analysis

1. Best, Richard A., Jr. (2003) "Homeland Security: Intelligence Support", Congressional Research Staff Report for Congress. May 14, 2003.

2. EndNotes.Com (2003) "Homeland Security: Introduction". Retrieved April 11, 2005 from http://www.endnotes.com/homeland-scurity/39554/print.

3. Bush, George W. (2002) "The Department of Homeland Security". June 2002.

4. emForum.Org (2005) "New Homeland Security Operations Center Opens". Retrieved April 11, 2005 from http://www.emforum.org/news/04070801.htm.

5. Department of Homeland Security (2005) "Fact Sheet: Homeland Security Operations Center (HSOC)". Retrieved April 11, 2005 from http://www.dhs.gov/dhspublic/display?theme=30&content=3813&print=true.

6. Department of Homeland Security (2005) "Homeland Security Advisory System". Retrieved April 11, 2005 from http://www.dhs.gov/dhspublic/display?theme=29&content=3927&print=true.

7. Department of Homeland Security (2005) "Homeland Security Advisory System—Guidance for Federal Departments and Agencies". Retrieved April 11, 2005 from http://www.dhs.gov/dhspublic/display?theme=43&content=3928&print=true.

8. The White House (2002) "Homeland Security Presidential Directive—3". March 12, 2002. Retrieved April 11, 2005 from http://www.whitehouse.gov/news/release/2002/03/print/20023012-5.html.

9. Mrowka, Marcus (2003) "Threat Level Raises Concern", *The Fairfield Mirror*. February 20, 2003.

10. Zitner, Aaron (2003) "Ridge revises advice: Buy duct tape, but wait for signal", *The Detroit News*. February 15, 2003.

11. Best, Richard A., Jr. (2003) "Homeland Security: Intelligence Support", Congressional Research Staff Report for Congress. May 14, 2003.

12. Ibid

Chapter 12: US Secret Service

1. United States Secret Service (2005) "Protection". Retrieved June 24, 2005 from http://www.ustreas.gov/usss/protection.shtml.

2. United States Secret Service (2005) "Investigative Mission". Retrieved June 24, 2005 from http://www.ustreas.gov/usss/investigations.shtml.

3. United States Secret Service (2005) "Counterfeit Division". Retrieved June 24, 2005 from http://www.ustreas.gov/usss/counterfeit.shtml.

4. United States Secret Service (2005) "Financial Crimes Division". Retrieved June 24, 2005 from http://www.ustreas.gov/usss/financial_crimes.shtml.

5. United States Secret Service (2005) "Forensic Services Division". Retrieved June 24, 2005 from http://www.ustreas.gov/usss/forensics.shtml.

6. United States Secret Service (2005) "Frequently Asked Questions". Retrieved June 24, 2005 from http://www.ustreas.gov/usss/faq.shtml.

7. Bush, George W. (2002) "National Strategy for Homeland Security". July 2002.

Chapter 13: Critical Infrastructure Protection

1. Bush, George W. (2003) "The National Strategy for The Physical Protection of Critical Infrastructures and Key Assets". February 2003.

2. Bush, George W. (2002) "The Department of Homeland Security". June 2002.

3. Department of Homeland Security (2004) "Press Release: DHS Launches Protected Critical Infrastructure Information Program to Enhance Homeland Security, Facilitate Information Sharing". February 18, 2004.

4. Department of Homeland Security (2005) "Protected Critical Infrastructure Information (PCII) Program: Program Overview." Retrieved April 12, 2005 from http://www.dhs.gov/dhspublic/display?theme=92&content=3763&print=true.

5. Bush, George W. (2003) "The National Strategy to Secure Cyberspace". February 2003.

6. Department of Homeland Security (2003) "Press Release: Ridge Creates New Division to Combat Cyber Threats". June 6, 2003.

7. Bush, George W. (2002) "National Strategy for Homeland Security". July 2002.

Chapter 14: Border and Transportation Security

1. Department of Homeland Security (2005) "Security Our Borders". Retrieved April 20, 2005 from http://www.dhs.gov/dhspublic/display?theme=50&content=875&print=true.

2. Department of Homeland Security (2005) "Department Subcomponents and Agencies". Retrieved April 21, 2005 from http://www.dhs.gov/dhspublic/display?theme=13&content=4082&print=true.

3. Department of Homeland Security (2005) "Securing Our Borders". Retrieved April 20, 2005 from http://www.dhs.gov/dhspublic/display?theme=50&content=875&print=true.

4. Transportation Security Administration (2005) "Aviation and Transportation Security Act (ATSA), Public Law 107-71". Retrieved April 21, 2005 from htgtp://www.tsa/gov/public/display?theme=38&content=0900051980003581&print=yes.

5. Department of Homeland Security Office of the Inspector General (2005) "Review of the Transportation Security Administration's Role in the Use and Dissemination of Airline Passenger Data (Redacted). March 2005.

6. United States Congress (2001) "Public Law 107-71, Aviation and Transportation Security Act". November 19, 2001.

7. U.S. Customs and Border Patrol (2005) "Welcome to U.S. Customs and Border Protection". Retrieved April 21, 2005 from http://www.cbp.gov/xp/cgov/PrintMe.xml?xml=$/content/about/mission/cbp.ctt&location...

8. Department of Homeland Security (2005) "Immigration and Customs Enforcement (ICE) Fact Sheet. Retrieved April 20, 2005 from http://www.customs.gov/xp/cgov/PrintMe.xml?xml=$/content/enforcement/amo/newsroom.

9. Department of Homeland Security (2005) "Securing Our Borders". Retrieved April 20, 2005 from http://www.dhs.gov/dhspublic/display?theme=50&content=875&print=true.

10. Department of Homeland Security (2005) "Immigration and Customs Enforcement (ICE) Fact Sheet. Retrieved April 20, 2005 from http://www.customs.gov/xp/cgov/PrintMe.xml?xml=$/content/enforcement/amo/newsroom.

11. U.S. Immigration and Customs Enforcement (2005) "Office of Investigations". Retrieved April 22, 2005 from http://www.ice.gov/graphics/investigations/index.htm.

12. Department of Homeland Security (2005) "Immigration and Customs Enforcement (ICE) Fact Sheet. Retrieved April 20, 2005 from http://www.customs.gov/xp/cgov/PrintMe.xml?xml=$/content/enforcement/amo/newsroom.

13. U.S. Immigration and Customs Enforcement (2005) "Detention and Removal Operations (DRO)". Retrieved April 22, 2005 from http://www.ice.gov/graphics/dro/index.htm.

14. Department of Homeland Security (2005) "Immigration and Customs Enforcement (ICE) Fact Sheet. Retrieved April 20, 2005 from http://www.customs.gov/xp/cgov/PrintMe.xml?xml=$/content/enforcement/amo/newsroom.

15. U.S. Immigration and Customs Enforcement (2005) "Federal Air Marshal Service". Retrieved April 22, 2005 from http://www.ice.gov/graphics/fams/index.htm.

16. Department of Homeland Security (2005) "Immigration and Customs Enforcement (ICE) Fact Sheet. Retrieved April 20, 2005 from http://www.customs.gov/xp/cgov/PrintMe.xml?xml=$/content/enforcement/amo/newsroom.

17. U.S. Immigration and Customs Enforcement (2005) "FPS Historical Background". Retrieved April 22, 2005 from http://www.ice.gov/graphics/fps/org_hb.htm.

18. U.S. Immigration and Customs Enforcement (2005) "Federal Protective Service". Retrieved April 22, 2005 from http://www.ice.gov/graphics/fps/index.htm.

19. Department of Homeland Security (2005) "Immigration and Customs Enforcement (ICE) Fact Sheet. Retrieved April 20, 2005 from http://www.customs.gov/xp/cgov/PrintMe.xml?xml=$/content/enforcement/amo/newsroom.

20. U.S. Immigration and Customs Enforcement (2005) "Office of Intelligence". Retrieved April 22, 2005 from http://www.ice.gov/graphics/about/organization.

21. Bush, George W. (2002) "The Department of Homeland Security." June 2002.

22. Ibid

Chapter 15: The U.S. Coast Guard

1. Bush, George W. (2002) "National Strategy for Homeland Security". July 2002.

2. The U.S. Coast Guard (2005) "U.S. Coast Guard Overview Briefing". Retrieved November 30, 2004 from http://www.uscg.mil/news/Cg101/CG101.html.

3. Bush, George W. (2002) "National Strategy for Homeland Security". July 2002.

Chapter 16: Planning Scenarios

1. Fickes, MichaeL (2005) "High-Tech Vision", *Government Security*. April 1, 2005.

2. The Homeland Security Council (2004) "Planning Scenarios Executive Summaries". July 2004.

Chapter 17: Emergency Preparedness

1. The United States Congress (2002) Public Law 107-296, "The Homeland Security Act". November 25, 2002.

2. Bush, George W. (2002) "The Department of Homeland Security. June 2002.

3. Federal Emergency Management Agency (2005) "About FEMA. FEMA History". Retrieved April 23, 2005 from http://www.fema.gov/about/history.shtm.

4. The United States Congress (2002) Public Law 107-296, "The Homeland Security Act". November 25, 2002.

5. Sylves, Richard T. (1998) "The Political Policy Basis of Emergency Management", Emergency Management Institute. pp 42-44. July 1998.

6. Waugh, William L. (2000) "Public Administration and Emergency Management", Emergency Management Institute. pp 3-27..3-29. March, 2000.

7. Sylves, Richard T. (1998) "The Political Policy Basis of Emergency Management", Emergency Management Institute. pp 112-114. July 1998.

8. Sylves, Richard T. (1998) "The Political Policy Basis of Emergency Management", Emergency Management Institute. pp 114-115. July 1998.

9. Sylves, Richard T. (1998) "The Political Policy Basis of Emergency Management", Emergency Management Institute. pp 116-120. July 1998.

10. Federal Emergency Management Agency (2005) "The Disaster Process and Disaster Aid Programs". Retrieved June 6, 2005 from http://www.fema.gov/library/dproc.shtm.

11. Bush, George W. (2002) "National Strategy for Homeland Security". July 2002.

Chapter 18: DHS Organization

1. Emergency Management, Clackama County (2005) "Emergency Management: Recovery". Retrieved April 26, 2005 from http://www.co.clackamas.or.us/emergency/recovery.htm.

2. The White House (2004) Executive Order 13354, "National Counterterrorism Center". August 27, 2004. Retrieved April 26, 2005 from http://www.fas.org/irp/offdocs/eo/eo-13354.htm.

3. Department of Justice (2003) "Fact Sheet: Terrorist Screening Center". September 16, 2003. Retrieved April 26, 2005 from http://www.iwar.org.uk/pipermail/infocon/2003-September/000593.html.

4. Department of Homeland Security (2004) "National Response Plan". December 2004.

5. Ibid

Chapter 19: First Responders

1. Department of Homeland Security (2005) "About First Responders". Retrieved April 28, 2005 from http://www.dhs.gov/dhspublic/display?theme=63&content=237&print=true.

2. Government Accountability Office (2005) "Homeland Security, Management of First Responder Grant Programs Has Improved, but Challenges Remain". February 2005.

3. Bush, George W. (2002) "National Strategy for Homeland Security". July 2002.

4. Department of Homeland Security Office for Domestic Preparedness (2004) "Homeland Security Exercise and Evaluation Program, Volume 1: Overview and Doctrine." May 2004.

5. Government Accountability Office (2005) "Homeland Security, Management of First Responder Grant Programs Has Improved, but Challenges Remain". February 2005.

6. Department of Homeland Security Office for Domestic Preparedness (2004) "Homeland Security Exercise and Evaluation Program, Volume 1: Overview and Doctrine." May 2004.

7. Government Accountability Office (2005) "Homeland Security, Management of First Responder Grant Programs Has Improved, but Challenges Remain". February 2005.

8. Department of Homeland Security Office for Domestic Preparedness (2004) "Homeland Security Exercise and Evaluation Program, Volume 1: Overview and Doctrine." May 2004.

9. Department of Homeland Security Office of Domestic Preparedness (2005) "Equipment Funded". Retrieved April 30, 2005 from http://www.ojp.usdoj.gov/

odp/grants_equipment.htm.

10. Department of Homeland Security Press Office (2004) "DHS Equipment Standards". February 26, 2004.

11. Department of Homeland Security Office for Domestic Preparedness (2004) "Homeland Security Exercise and Evaluation Program, Volume 1: Overview and Doctrine." May 2004.

12. Department of Homeland Security Office for Domestic Preparedness (2005) "Exercises". Retrieved April 30, 2005 from http://www.ojp.usdoj.gov/odp/exercises.htm.

13. Department of Homeland Security (2005) "About First Responders". Retrieved April 28, 2005 from http://www.dhs.gov/dhspublic/display?theme=63&content=237&print=true.

14. Bush, George W. (2002) "National Strategy for Homeland Security". July 2002.

Chapter 20: Exercise Programs

1. Department of Homeland Security Office for Domestic Preparedness (2004) "Homeland Security Exercise and Evaluation Program, Volume 1: Overview and Doctrine." May 2004.

Chapter 21: Homeland Defense

1. Bowman, Steve (2003) "Homeland Security: The Department of Defense's Role", Congressional Research Staff Report for Congress. May 14, 2003.

2. National Defense University (2002) "Homeland Security: The Civil-Military Dimensions", a report based on a Symposium at the National Defense University, Washington, D.C., September 19-20, 2002.

3. Bowman, Steve (2003) "Homeland Security: The Department of Defense's Role", Congressional Research Staff Report for Congress. May 14, 2003.

4. National Defense University (2002) "Homeland Security: The Civil-Military Dimensions", a report based on a Symposium at the National Defense University, Washington, D.C., September 19-20, 2002.

5. McHale, Paul (2004) "Statement Before the 108th Congress Subcommittee on Terrorism, Unconventional Threats and Capabilities". March 4, 2004.

6. Bowman, Steve (2003) "Homeland Security: The Department of Defense's Role", Congressional Research Staff Report for Congress. May 14, 2003.

7. McHale, Paul (2004) "Statement Before the 108th Congress Subcommittee on Terrorism, Unconventional Threats and Capabilities". March 4, 2004.

8. Bowman, Steve (2003) "Homeland Security: The Department of Defense's Role", Congressional Research Staff Report for Congress. May 14, 2003.

9. McHale, Paul (2004) "Statement Before the 108th Congress Subcommittee on Terrorism, Unconventional Threats and Capabilities". March 4, 2004.

10. The White House (2003) "Fact Sheet: Strengthening Intelligence to Better Protect America." Retrieved May 3, 2005 from http://www.whitehouse.gov/news/releases/2003/01/print/20030128.html.

11. McHale, Paul (2004) "Statement Before the 108th Congress Subcommittee on Terrorism, Unconventional Threats and Capabilities". March 4, 2004.

12. Bowman, Steve (2003) "Homeland Security: The Department of Defense's Role", Congressional Research Staff Report for Congress. May 14, 2003.

13. Doyle, Charles (2000) "The Posse Comitatus Act & Related Matters: The Use of the Military to Execute Civilian Law", Congressional Research Staff Report for Congress. June 1, 2000.

14. National Defense University (2002) "Homeland Security: The Civil-Military Dimensions", a report based on a Symposium at the National Defense University, Washington, D.C., September 19-20, 2002.

15. Bowman, Steve (2003) "Homeland Security: The Department of Defense's Role", Congressional Research Staff Report for Congress. May 14, 2003.

16. National Defense University (2002) "Homeland Security: The Civil-Military Dimensions", a report based on a Symposium at the National Defense University, Washington, D.C., September 19-20, 2002.

17. McHale, Paul (2004) "Statement Before the 108th Congress Subcommittee on Terrorism, Unconventional Threats and Capabilities". March 4, 2004.

18. National Defense University (2002) "Homeland Security: The Civil-Military Dimensions", a report based on a Symposium at the National Defense University, Washington, D.C., September 19-20, 2002.

19. McHale, Paul (2004) "Statement Before the 108th Congress Subcommittee on Terrorism, Unconventional Threats and Capabilities". March 4, 2004.

20. Bowman, Steve (2003) "Homeland Security: The Department of Defense's Role", Congressional Research Staff Report for Congress. May 14, 2003.

21. McHale, Paul (2004) "Statement Before the 108th Congress Subcommittee on Terrorism, Unconventional Threats and Capabilities". March 4, 2004.

Chapter 22: Legislating Homeland Security

1. Bush, George W. (2002) "National Strategy for Homeland Security". July 2002.

2. Doyle, Charles (2002) "The USA PATRIOT Act: A Sketch", Congressional Research Staff Report for Congress. April 15, 2002.

3. Vayda, John P. (2005) "Legislative and Regulatory Responses to Terrorism in the United States of America". Retrieved May 4, 2005 from http://www.nb-ny.com/paper_jpv2.html.

4. Thompson, Kristin (2002) "Legislative Response to Potential Bioterrorist Threat", Monterey Institute of International Studies. Retrieved May 4, 2005 from http://cns.miis.edu/pubs/week/020708.htm.

5. Greenberg, Taurig (2002) "Legislative Update: Enhanced Border Security and Visa Entry Reform Act of 2002", *GT Business Immigration Observer*. June 2002. Retrieved May 4, 2005 from http://www.gtlaw.com/practices/immigration/newsletter/archives/006/item07.htm.

6. Kirk, Robert S. (2001) "Selected Aviation Security Legislation in the Aftermath of the September 11 Attack", Congressional Research Staff Report for Congress. December 14, 2001.

7. Frittelli, John F. (2003) "Port and Maritime Security: Background Issues for Congress", Congressional Research Staff Report for Congress. December 5, 2003.

8. American Legislative Exchange Council (2005) "50-State Summary of Homeland Security Legislation". Retrieved May 4, 2005 from http://www.alec.org/viewpage.cfm?pgname=4.292.

9. Bush, George W. (2002) "National Strategy for Homeland Security". July 2002.

Chapter 23: Science & Technology

1. McQueary, Charles E., Undersecretary for Science and Technology (2004) "Meeting the Challenge of Protecting the Homeland", *TechComm National Journal of Technology Commercialization*. February-March, 2004.

2. Bush, George W. (2002) "The Department of Homeland Security". June 2002.

3. 107th Congress (2002) "H.R. 5005 To establish the Department of Homeland Security, and for other purposes". June 24, 2002.

4. The National Academies (2002) "Homeland Security: NAS Report, New Department Focus of Congressional Activity". June 25, 2002. Retrieved May 6, 2005 from http://www.agriculturalsecurity.homestead.com/files/Downloads/Resources_Links/HOMELAND.html.

5. American Geological Institute (2002) "Update on Homeland Security Issues", Government Affairs Program. November 25, 2002. Retrieved May 6, 2005 from http://www.agiweb.org/gap/legis107/homeland.html.

6. 107th Congress (2002) "H.R. 5005 To establish the Department of Homeland Security, and for other purposes". June 24, 2002.

7. Department of Homeland Security Science and Technology Directorate (2004) "Developing Technology". Retrieved October 4, 2004 from http://www.dhs.gov/dhspublic/display?theme=53&content=3521&print=true.

8. Department of Homeland Security Science and Technology Directorate (2004) "Mission Brief". November 2004.

9. Department of Homeland Security (2005) "About the Directorate—Science & Technology". Retrieved May 18, 2005 from http://www.dhs.gov/dhspublic/interapp/editorial/editorial_0530.xml.

10. Department of Homeland Security Science and Technology Directorate (2004) "Mission Brief". November 2004.

11. McQueary, Charles E., Undersecretary for Science and Technology (2004) "Meeting the Challenge of Protecting the Homeland", *TechComm National Journal of Technology Commercialization*. February-March, 2004.

12. Fickes, Michael (2005) "High-Tech Vision", *Government Security*. April 1, 2005. Retrieved May 19, 2005 from http://govtsecruity.com/mag/hightech_vision/.

13. Department of Homeland Security Science and Technology Directorate (2004) "Mission Brief". November 2004.

14. Fickes, Michael (2005) "High-Tech Vision", *Government Security*. April 1, 2005. Retrieved May 19, 2005 from http://govtsecruity.com/mag/hightech_vision/.

15. Department of Homeland Security Science and Technology Directorate (2004) "Mission Brief". November 2004.

16. Department of Homeland Security (2005) "Supporting the DHS Mission". Retrieved May 19, 2005 from http://www.dhs.gov/dhspublic/display?theme=27&content=47&print=true.

17. Department of Homeland Security (2005) "Homeland Security Centers of Excellence". Retrieved May 6, 2005 from http://www.dhs.gov/dhspublic/display?theme=27&content=3856.

18. Department of Homeland Security Science and Technology Directorate (2004) "Mission Brief". No-

vember 2004.

19. Louisiana Office of Homeland Security and Emergency Preparedness (2004) "U.S. Department of Homeland Security Launches Office of Interoperability & Compatibility". Retrieved May 18, 2005 from http://www.loep.state.la.us/newsrelated/dhs_LauchesOfficeInteroperability.htm.

20. Department of Homeland Security (2005) "About SAFECOM". Retrieved May 18, 2005 from http://www.safecomprogram.gov/SAFECOM/about/default.htm.

21. Department of Homeland Security (2005) "Biowatch Fact Sheet: Early Detection, Early Response." Retrieved May 6, 2005 from http://www.milnet.com/wh/DoHS/BioWatchFactSheetFINAL.pdf.

22. Department of Homeland Security (2005) "DHS Science and Technology Countermeasures Testbed, New York Project Office." Retrieved May 18, 2005 from http://www.eml.doe.gov/Test_Eval/.

23. Department of Homeland Security Science and Technology Directorate (2004) "Mission Brief". November 2004.

24. Department of Homeland Security (2005) "Cutting Edge Technology to Protect America". Retrieved May 18, 2005 from http://www.dhs.gov/dhspublic/theme_home5.jsp.

25. Department of Homeland Security (2005) "Science & Technology Directorate Overview Briefing". November 2004.

26. Department of Homeland Security (2005) "Homeland Security Science and Technology Advisory Committee Charter". Retrieved May 19, 2005 from http://www.dhs.gov/dhspulbic/display?=theme53&content=3403&print=true.

27. Department of Homeland Security (2005) "Fact Sheet: Homeland Security Establishes the First Government "Think Tank" Homeland Security Institute". Retrieved May 19, 2005 from http://www.dhs.gov/dhspublic/display?theme=43&content=3507&print=true.

28. Bush, George W. (2002) "National Strategy for Homeland Security". July 2002.

Chapter 24: America's New Normalcy

1. Advisory Panel to Assess Domestic Response Capabilities for Terrorism Involving Weapons of Mass Destruction (2003) "V. Forging America's New Normalcy: Securing Our Homeland, Preserving Our Liberty". December 15, 2003.

2. Bush, George W. (2002) "National Strategy for Homeland Security". July 2002.

Appendix E: Intel Community

1. Intelligence.Gov (2005) "United States Intelligence Community". Retrieved July 3, 2005 from http://www.intelligence.gov/.

State Contacts

#	State	Contact/Title	Phone	Address
1.	AK	BG Craig Campbell Adjutant General	1st: 907.428.6003	Alaska Division of Homeland Security and Emergency Management P.O. Box 5750 Fort Richardson, AK 99505-5750 http://www.gov.state.ak.us/omb/Homeland1.pdf
2.	AL	James M. Walker, Jr., Homeland Security Director	1st: 334.956.7250 Fax: 334.223.1120	Alabama Department of Homeland Security P.O. Box 304115 Montgomery, AL 36130-4115 http://www.dhs.alabama.gov/
3.	AR	Wayne Ruthven Director	1st: 501.730.9750 Fax: 501.730.9754	Arkansas Department of Emergency Management P. O. Box 758 Conway, AR 72033-0758 http://www.adem.state.ar.us/
4.	AZ	Frank Navarette Homeland Security Director	1st: 602.542.4331	Arizona Office of Homeland Security 1700 W Washington Phoenix, AZ 85007 http://www.homelandsecurity.az.gov/
5.	CA	Rick Martinez Chief Deputy Director, Office of Homeland Security	1st: 916.324.8908	Governor's Office of Emergency Services 3650 Schriever Avenue Mather, CA 95655 http://www.oes.ca.gov/Operational/OESHome.nsf/1? OpenForm
6.	CO	Pamela Sillars Acting Deputy Director	1st: 303.273.1770 Fax: 303.273.1688	Office of Preparedness, Security, and Fire Safety 15055 South Golden Road, Room C-13 Golden, CO 80401-3971 http://www.ops.state.co.us/
7.	CT	Vincent DeRosa Deputy Commissioner, Div. of Protect. Svcs.	1st: 203.805.6600	Department of Public Safety Division of Homeland Security 55 West Main Street Waterbury CT 06702 (203)805-6600 http://www.state.ct.us/dps/PS/index.htm
8.	DC	Margaret N. Kellems Deputy Mayor for Public Safety and Justice	1st: 202.727.1000	DC Emergency Management Agency 2000 14th Street NW, 8th Floor Washington, DC 20009 (202) 727-6161 http://www.dcema.dc.gov/dcema/site/default.asp
9.	DE	Philip Cabaud Homeland Security Director	1st: 302.744.4101	Department of Safety and Homeland Security Delaware Emergency Management Agency 165 Brick Store Landing Road Smyrna, DE 19977 http://www.delawarepublicsafety.com/
10.	FL	Guy M. Tunnell Commissioner	1st: 850.410.7233	Florida Department of Law Enforcement 2331 Phillips Road Tallahassee, FL 32308 http://www.fdle.state.fl.us/osi/DomesticSecurity/

#	State	Contact/Title	Phone	Address
11.	GA	Bill Hitchens Director of Homeland Security	1st: 404.635.7030 Fax: 404.635.7031	Georgia Office of Homeland Security Post Office Box 1456 Atlanta, Georgia 30371-2303 http://www.gahomelandsecurity.com/
12.	GU	Frank Blas Homeland Security Director	1st: 671.475.9600 2nd: 671.475.9602	Guam Homeland Security Office of Civil Defense 221-B Chalan Palasyo Agana Heights, Guam 96910 http://www.guamhs.org/main/
13.	HI	BG Robert Lee Adjutant General	1st: 808.733.4301 2nd: 808.733.4542 Fax: 808.733.4287	State of Hawaii Department of Defense Office of the Adjutant General 3949 Diamond Head Road Honolulu, HI 96816-4495 http://www.dod.state.hi.us/index.html
14.	IA	Ellen Gordon Administrator, Emergency Management	1st: 515.281.3231	Iowa Homeland Security and Emergency Management Division Hoover State Office Building, 1305 E. Walnut, Level A Des Moines, IA 50319 http://www.iowahomelandsecurity.org/
15.	ID	MG Jack Kane Adjutant General	1st: 208.422.5242 Fax: 208.422.6179	Bureau of Homeland Security 4040 Guard Street, Building 600 Boise, ID 83705-5004 http://www.bhs.idaho.gov/
16.	IL	Carl Hawkinson Deputy Chief of Staff for Public Safety and Homeland Security Advisor	1st: 217.782.2700 2nd: 217.782.7860	Illinois Emergency Management Agency 110 East Adams Street Springfield, Illinois 62701 http://www.state.il.us/iema/index.htm/
17.	IN	Eric Dietz Director, Indiana Counter-Terrorism and Security Council	1st: 317.323.8303	Indiana Government Center South 302 West Washington Street Indianapolis, IN 46204 http://www.in.gov/c-tasc
18.	KS	MG Gene Krase Administrator for Emergency Management	1st: 785.274.1121 2nd: 785.274.1109	Kansas Emergency Management 2800 SW Topeka Blvd. – Topeka KS 66611-1287 http://www.accesskansas.org/kdem/
19.	KY	Ray Nelson Executive Director, Office for Security Coordination, KY Homeland Security	1st: 502.607.1257 Fax: 502.607.1468	Kentucky Office of Homeland Security 200 Mero Street Frankfort, KY 40601 http://homelandsecurity.ky.gov/
20.	LA	MG Bennett C. Landreneau Adjutant General and Director of the Louisiana Office of Emergency Preparedness	1st: 225.925.7500 Fax: 225.925.7501	Louisiana Office of Homeland Security & Emergency Preparedness 7667 Independence Blvd. Baton Rouge, LA 70806 http://www.loep.state.la.us/homeland

#	State	Contact/Title	Phone	Address
21.	MA	Edward A. Flynn Secretary, Executive Office of Public Safety	1st: 617.727.7775	Secretary of Public Safety One Ashburton Place, Suite 2133 Boston, MA 02108 http://www.mass.gov/portal/index.jsp
22.	MD	Dennis Schrader Homeland Security Director	1st: 410.974.3901	Governor's Office of Homeland Security 100 State Circle Annapolis, MD 21401-1925 http://www.mema.state.md.us
23.	ME	MG John Libby Adjutant General Homeland Security	1st: 207.626.4440 2nd: 207.626.4429 Fax: 207.626.4430	The Adjutant General And Commissioner Camp Keyes Augusta, Maine 04333-0033 http://www.state.me.us/mema/homeland/index.htm
24.	MI	COL Tadarial Sturdivant Director, Michigan State Police	1st: 517.336.6198 Fax: 517.333.4987	Michigan State Police Headquarters 714 S. Harrison Road East Lansing, Michigan 48823 http://www.michigan.gov/msp
25.	MN	Rich Stanek Commissioner of Public Safety and Homeland Secu- rity Director	1st: 651.296.6642 Fax: 651.297.5728	Homeland Security and Emergency Management 444 Cedar Street, Suite 223 St. Paul, Minnesota 55101-6223 http://www.hsem.state.mn.us/
26.	MO	Michael Chapman, Director Missouri Office of Homeland Security	1st: 573.522.3007 Fax: 573.522.6109	Missouri Office of Homeland Security PO Box 749 Jefferson City, MO 65102 http://www.homelandsecurity.state.mo.us daniet@mail.oa.state.mo.us
27.	MS	Robert Latham Executive Director Mississippi Emergency Man- agement Agency	1st: 601.960.9999	Mississippi Office of Homeland Security P.O. Box 958 Jackson, MS 39205 http://www.homelandsecurity.ms.gov/index.html
28.	MT	Jim Greene Administrator, Disaster and Emergency Services	1st: 406.841.3911	Disaster and Emergency Services P.O. Box 4789 - 1900 Williams Street Helena, MT 59604-4789 http://www.discoveringmontana.com/css/default.asp
29.	NC	Sec. Bryan Beatty Secretary, Dept of Crime Control and Public Safety	1st: 919.733.2126 Fax: 919.715.8477	Department of Crime Control and Public Safety 4701 Mail Service Center Raleigh, NC 27699-4701 http://www.nccrimecontrol.org/
30.	ND	Doug Friez Homeland Security Coordi- nator/Emergency Mgmt Director	1st: 701.328.8100 Fax: 701.328.8181	Department of Emergency Management PO Box 5511 Bismarck, ND 58506 http://www.state.nd.us/dem

#	State	Contact/Title	Phone	Address
31.	NE	Lt. Gov. Rick Sheehy Lieutenant Governor	1st: 402.471.2256 Fax: 402.471.6031	Nebraska Emergency Management Agency (NEMA) 1300 Military Road Lincoln, NE 68508-1090 http://www.nebema.org/index_html rick.sheehy@notes.state.ne.us
32.	NH	J. William Degnan Acting Director	1st: 603.271.3294 Fax: 603.271.1091	New Hampshire Department of Safety James H. Hayes Safety Building 33 Hazen Drive Concord, NH 03305 http://webster.state.nh.us/safety/index.html
33.	NJ	Sidney Caspersen Director, Office of Counter- terrorism	1st: 609.341.3434 Fax: 609.341.2958	New Jersey Office of Counter-Terrorism 25 Market Street P.O. Box 091 Trenton, NJ 08625-0091 http://www.state.nj.us/lps/oct/
34.	NM	General Annette Sobel Homeland Security Director	1st: 505.476.0267 2nd: 505.476.9635 Fax: 505.476.0270	New Mexico Office of Homeland Security P.O. Box Drawer 2387 Santa Fe, New Mexico 87504-2387 www.governor.state.nm.us/homelandsecurity/
35.	NV	Giles Vanderhoof Homeland Security Director	1st: 775.687.7320	Nevada Homeland Security 2525 South Carson Street Carson City, NV 89701 http://homelandsecurity.nv.gov/index_home.htm
36.	NY	James McMahon Director	1st: 212.867.7060 Fax: 212.867.1725	State Emergency Management Office 1220 Washington Avenue Suite 101, Building 22 Albany, NY 12226-2251 http://www.nysemo.state.ny.us/
37.	OH	Kenneth Morckel Director of Public Safety	1st: 614.466.4344	Ohio Department of Public Safety Charles D. Shipley Building 1970 West Broad Street P.O. Box 182081 Columbus, Ohio 43218-2081 http://www.homelandsecurity.ohio.gov/hls.asp
38.	OK	Bob Ricks Secretary of Safety and Security	1st: 405.425.2001 Fax: 405.425.2324	Oklahoma Office of Homeland Security P.O. BOX 11415 Oklahoma City, OK 73136 http://www.homelandsecurity.ok.gov/ coffice@dps.state.ok.us
39.	OR	Ronald C. Ruecker Superintendent of Oregon State Police	1st: 503.378.3725 Fax: 503.378.8282	Oregon Office of Homeland Security PO Box 14370 3225 State Street Salem, Oregon 97309 http://www.oregon.gov/OOHS/index.shtml
40.	PA	Jonathan A. Duecker Director, Pennsylvania Of- fice of Homeland Security	1st: 717.651.2715 Fax: 717.651.2040	Pennsylvania Office of Homeland Security 40 Citation Lane P.O. Box 5349 Lancaster, PA 17606-5349 http://www.homelandsecurity.state.pa.us/

#	State	Contact/Title	Phone	Address
41.	PR	Annabelle Rodriguez Attorney General	1st: 787.723.7924	Attorney General Department of Justice Commonwealth of Puerto Rico P.O. Box 902192 San Juan, PR 00902 http://www.justicia.gobierno.pr/
42.	RI	MG Reginald Centracchio Adjutant General	1st: 401.275.4102 Fax: 401.275.4338	Rhode Island Emergency Management Agency 645 New London Ave Cranston, RI 02920-3003 http://www.riema.ri.gov/ reginald.centracchio@ri.ngb.army.mil
43.	SC	Robert Stewart Chief, SC Law Enforcement Division	1st: 803.737.9000	South Carolina Law Enforcement Division 4400 Broad River Road Columbia, SC 29210 http://www.sled.state.sc.us/default.htm
44.	SD	John A. Berheim Director, Division of Emer- gency Management	1st: 1.866.homeland Fax: 605.773.6115	S.D. Department of Public Safety Office of Homeland Security 118 W. Capitol Ave. Pierre, SD 57501 http://www.state.sd.us/homeland/
45.	TN	MG (Ret.) Jerry Humble	1st: 615.532.7825	Tennessee Office of Homeland Security Wm. R. Snodgrass TN Tower, 25th Floor Nashville, TN 37243 http://www.state.tn.us/homelandsecurity/
46.	TX	Jay Kimbrough Deputy Attorney General for Criminal Justice	1st: 512.936.1882	Texas Department of Public Safety Division of Emergency Management P.O. Box 4087 Austin, Texas 78773-0001 http://www.demwmd.com/index.k2?did=551305
47.	UT	Scott Behunin Division Director, Compre- hensive Emergency Man- agement	1st: 801.538.3400 Fax: 801.538.3770	Division of Emergency Services & Homeland Security Rm. 1110, State Office Bldg. Salt Lake City, UT 84114 http://www.cem.utah.gov/
48.	VA	George Foresman Assistant to the Governor for Commonwealth Prepared- ness	1st: 804.225.3826	Office of Commonwealth Preparedness 202 N. 9th Street, 5th Floor Richmond, VA 23219 http://www.commonwealthpreparedness.virginia.gov/
49.	VT	Kerry Sleeper Commissioner, VT State Police	1st: 802.244.8727	Vermont Homeland Security 103 South Main Street Waterbury, VT 05671-2101 http://www.dps.state.vt.us/homeland/home_main.html
50.	WA	Timothy J. Lowenberg Major General The Adjutant General	1st: 253.512.7298 2nd: 800.258.5990	Washington Military Department Emergency Management Division Building 20, M/S: TA-20 Camp Murray, WA 98430-5122 http://emd.wa.gov/ Joe.Huden@MIL.wa.gov

#	State	Contact/Title	Phone	Address
51.	WI	General Al Wikening Homeland Security Advisor	1st: 608.242.3210	Department of Military Affairs 2400 Wright Street Madison, WI 53704 http://homelandsecurity.wi.gov/
52.	WV	Joe Martin Secretary, Dept. of Military Affairs and Public Safety	1st: 304.558.5380 Fax: 304.344.4538	West Virginia Division of Homeland Security and Emergency Management 1900 Kanawha Blvd. E. Bld. 1 Rm. EB-80 Charleston WV 25305 http://www.wvs.state.wv.us/wvoes/
53.	WY	Joe Moore Director, Wyoming Office of Homeland Security	1st: 307.777.4663	Wyoming Office of Homeland Security 122 West 25th St. Herschler Bldg, 1st Floor East Cheyenne, Wyoming 82002 http://wyohomelandsecurity.state.wy.us/

Intel Community

Definition

The Intelligence Community (IC) is a federation of executive branch agencies and organizations that work separately and together to conduct intelligence activities necessary for the conduct of foreign relations and the protection of the national security of the United States. These activities include:

- Collection of information needed by the President, the National Security Council, the Secretaries of State and Defense, and other Executive Branch officials for the performance of their duties and responsibilities;

- Production and dissemination of intelligence;

- Collection of information concerning, and the conduct of activities to protect against, intelligence activities directed against the US, international terrorist and international narcotics activities, and other hostile activities directed against the US by foreign powers, organizations, persons, and their agents;

- Special activities;

- Administrative and support activities within the US and abroad necessary for the performance of authorized activities; and

- Such other intelligence activities as the President may direct from time to time.

Members

1. Air Force Intelligence	6. Department of Energy	11. Marine Corps Intelligence
2. Army Intelligence	7. Department of Homeland Security	12. National Geospatial-Intelligence Agency
3. Central Intelligence Agency	8. Department of State	13. National Reconnaissance Office
4. Coast Guard Intelligence	9. Department of the Treasury	14. National Security Agency
5. Defense Intelligence Agency	10. Federal Bureau of Investigation	15. Navy Intelligence

An IC member is a federal government agency, service, bureau, or other organization within the executive branch that plays a role in the business of national intelligence. The Intelligence Community comprises many such organizations.

1. Army, Navy, Air Force, and Marine Corps Intelligence Organizations – each collects and processes intelligence relevant to their particular Service needs.

2. Central Intelligence Agency (CIA) - provides accurate, comprehensive, and timely foreign intelligence on national security topics to national policy and decision makers.

3. Coast Guard Intelligence – deals with information related to US maritime borders and Homeland Security.

4. Defense Intelligence Agency (DIA) - provides timely and objective military intelligence to warfighters, policymakers, and force planners.

5. Department of Energy – performs analyses of foreign nuclear weapons, nuclear non-proliferation, and energy security-related intelligence issues in support of US national security policies, programs, and objectives.

6. Department of Homeland Security (DHS) - prevents terrorist attacks within the United States, reduces America's vulnerability to terrorism, and minimizes the damage and recovers from attacks that do occur.

7. Department of State – deals with information affecting US foreign policy.

8. Department of Treasury – collects and processes information that may affect US fiscal and monetary policy.

9. Federal Bureau of Investigation – deals with counterespionage and data about international criminal cases.

10. National Geospatial-Intelligence Agency (NGA) – provides timely, relevant, and accurate geospatial intelligence in support of national security.

11. National Reconnaissance Office (NRO) - coordinates collection and analysis of information from airplane and satellite reconnaissance by the military services and the CIA.

12. National Security Agency (NSA) - collects and processes foreign signals intelligence information for our Nation's leaders and warfighters, and protects critical US information security systems from compromise.

All the responsibilities of the CIA, DIA, NSA, NRO, and NGA are concerned with intelligence. Therefore each of these organizations in its entirety is considered to be a member of the Intelligence Community.

The other organizations are concerned primarily with missions and business other than intelligence, but do have intelligence responsibilities. In these cases, only the part of the organization with the intelligence responsibility is considered to be a part of the Community. In the case of the US Navy, for instance, only their Office of Naval Intelligence is an IC member. The rest of the Navy supports the DoD in missions other than intelligence.

Intelligence Oversight

The Intelligence Community is subject to external oversight from the Executive and Legislative branches.

Within the Executive, the IC works closely with the National Security Council (NSC).Other Executive organizations involved in oversight include the following:

- The President's Foreign Intelligence Advisory Board (PFIAB): The PFIAB is an entity within the Executive Office of the President formed "to assess the quality, quantity, and adequacy" of intelligence collection, analysis, counterintelligence, and other activities of the IC. The PFIAB reports directly to the President, and provides recommendations for actions to improve and enhance the performance of intelligence efforts. It also examines issues raised by the President or the Director of National Intelligence and can make recommendations directly to the DNI. Membership of the PFIAB consists of not more that 16 persons appointed by the President.

- The President's Intelligence Oversight Board (IOB): Once a separate organization under the President, the IOB was made a standing committee of the PFIAB in 1993. The IOB is composed of four members of the PFIAB appointed by the Chairman of the PFIAB. The IOB conducts independent oversight investigations as required and reviews the oversight practices and procedures of the inspectors general and general counsels of intelligence agencies.

- The Office of Management and Budget (OMB): OMB is part of the Executive Office of the President. It reviews intelligence budgets in light of presidential policies and priorities, clears proposed testimony, and approves draft intelligence legislation for submission to Congress.

Within the Congress, principal oversight responsibility rests with the two intelligence committees. By law, the President must ensure that these two committees are kept "fully and currently" informed of the activities of the Intelligence Community, including any "significant anticipated intelligence activities." Notice is also required to be provided to both committees of all covert action programs approved by the President as well as all "significant intelligence failures."

- The Senate Select Committee on Intelligence (SSCI): The membership of the SSCI has ranged from 13 to 17, with the majority party in Congress having one more member than the minority. Members of the SSCI serve 8-year terms. In addition to its role in annually authorizing appropriations for intelligence activities, the SSCI carries out oversight investigations and inquiries as required. It also handles presidential nominations referred to the Senate for the positions of DNI, Principle Deputy DNI, Director of the Central Intelligence Agency, and Inspector General of CIA, and reviews treaties referred to the Senate for ratification as necessary to determine the ability of the Intelligence Community to verify the provisions of the treaty under consideration.

- House Permanent Select Committee on Intelligence (HPSCI): The membership of the HPSCI is currently set at 19 members and is proportional to the partisan makeup of the entire House of Representatives. Members may be appointed for terms up to eight years. Like its Senate counterpart, the HPSCI conducts oversight investigations and inquiries in addition to processing the annual authorization of appropriations for intelligence.

Other Committees: In addition to the intelligence committees, other congressional committees occasionally become   involved in oversight matters by virtue of their overlapping jurisdictions and responsibilities. The armed services committees of each House, for example, exercise concurrent jurisdiction over DoD intelligence activities; and the judiciary committees in each House exercise concurrent jurisdiction over FBI intelligence activities.

Conclusion

Through these interactions, the IC keeps policy and decision makers well informed of intelligence related to national security issues, and Congress maintains oversight of intelligence activities.[1]

474